My Weakness
for
His Strength

My Weakness
for
His Strength

MICHAEL WELLS

Abiding Life Press

© 2011 by Michael Wells
Published by Abiding Life Press
A division of Abiding Life Ministries International
P.O. Box 620998, Littleton, CO 80162

Printed in the United States of America
ISBN: 978-0-9819546-2-2

Translations used for Bible quotations are most often
New American Standard Bible
The Holy Bible, New International Version
The Amplified Bible
The Message: The Bible in Contemporary Language by Eugene H. Peterson

Cover designed by Bob Fuller of Fuller Creative.

To the God who does much with little,
more with less,
and everything with nothing.

Contents

Contents | 🍇

Introduction

In the pages that follow, you will not find what is considered to be a "typical" devotional book. Devotional books generally are small, expository teachings concerning the Bible. The origins of this book are quite the contrary, not taking the systematic approach through the Bible, although the solutions discovered in the Person of Christ were witnessed to by the Bible. Each article was not written as an exposition on the Bible but an exposition on man and how specific problems that Christians deal with were addressed as the author labored with many hurting Christians in a counseling setting. Each session was a bit of an adventure as neither I nor the one I was discipling had predetermined what form the solution would take. However, I did know this: That form would be Christ-centered.

This is Volume I of a series. The title was specifically chosen from the secret that the Apostle Paul discovered, which is that power is perfected in man's weakness, not in man's strength. There is something about the flesh of man that desires to give to God and receive in turn. The paradigm in this book recognizes that God gives, period, over, and over, and over again, as an extreme example of His love, so that man has nothing in which to boast. If I could say I had done great things because I had a great inner strength, I would have something in which to boast. However, the fact is that what He has done in my life and in the lives of others has come out of our acknowledgment of weakness. To that end, we thank God, who has maintained us, for what He creates, He maintains. You will read in these pages the many God-given solutions to man, despite man's lack of worthiness.

DAY 1
Abide Is The Hardest Word

Abide in Me, and I in you. As the branch cannot bear fruit of itself unless it abides in the vine, so neither can you unless you abide in Me.

— JOHN 15:4

Having spoken through hundreds of interpreters in nearly that many languages, I consistently find that the hardest word in the Bible to translate is *abiding*. Many languages use the word *remaining*, and yet that does not quite cover this important word, for Jesus did not use an analogy of the vine, saying that He was like a vine; He said that He was the Vine. Every vine preaches and teaches Jesus. Abiding is the culmination of His work and is everything, for in abiding we receive the Everything, Jesus. Is it not amazing that the whole work of Jesus is revealed in this one word? It would also make sense that the enemy would work to obscure the word. Abiding: holding me in Him, His life in me, cleansing, revealing what I am, kept safe from so much disease, a moment-by-moment existence, eternal life. Abiding, abiding, abiding. Wonderful!

DAY 2
Add a One to All Your Zeros

Jesus said to him, "I am the Way and the Truth and the Life. No one comes to the Father except through Me."
— JOHN 14:6

While I was in India speaking at a school, one of the dorm parents asked to talk to me. He turned out to be a great blessing to me as he sat sharing about so many things. He had been a Brahman, one of the elite of Hinduism, worshipped as a god. He had always been taught that there were many ways to God, and yet he began to wonder, "Do I have the right way?" It was this questioning and the Holy Spirit that had brought him to Jesus. Once he confessed his faith, he was banned from going to his house, and after sixteen years, his father died without reconciliation. He is now tolerated and allowed to visit his house, so long as he does not stay. He really does not care, for he has found Jesus. The most interesting point he made was about writing on a chalkboard his qualifications for being a Christian. Under talent he put zero. Under ability he put zero. Under intelligence: zero. Under people skills he put zero. In every category, he put a zero. He looked on the board and all he had written was a line of zeros. Then a man said to him, "Let me show you something. All you have are zeros, six to be exact. Now we will add one to all the zeros, the only ONE that matters. We will add Jesus to all your zeros." The man then put a one at the front of all the zeros and said, "See? When I added the ONE to the front, where Jesus belongs, your zeros have now become one million. Add Jesus to your zeros and your weaknesses become your strength."

DAY 3
A Christian Cannot Sin

No one who is born of God practices sin, because His seed abides in him; and he cannot sin, because he is born of God.

— I JOHN 3:9

I really enjoy I John as the great book of abiding. If we are in Him, we will see exactly Jesus flowing from us. If we are not in Him, we will fail. We will have times when we are not abiding, and in those times He is greater than our sin. As we abide, His anointing is teaching us; we actually will not need a teacher (I John 2:27). I cannot say that I have ever surprised an abiding Christian with a truth he did not know.

Those that are born of God cannot sin! Do you sin? Does this mean that you are not born of God? No! Let me explain, for this passage has tripped up more than one believer. As a Christian you cannot sin; that is a fact. You do not believe me. Well, let me explain it this way. I say to the five-year-old boy, "You cannot drive a truck." Is my statement true? Yes! He cannot drive a truck. Later, the boy gets in the truck, inserts the key, turns the ignition, and moves the truck forward until it runs into a tree. At that point are you ready to admit that the boy can drive? No! Even though he has been turning the wheel, starting the engine, and accelerating the truck, we all agree that those actions alone do not constitute driving. He is not going to get his driver's license any time soon. In the same way the Christian cannot sin. Oh, he may get in the seat and display the right actions, but he cannot go anywhere with it. Nothing is done properly, and we will not give him a license verifying that he is a sinner.

A woman told me that she was thinking of having an affair, of becoming an adulteress. I exclaimed, "You cannot!" "Who will stop me?" she wanted to know. I explained that I was not going to stop her, but the seed of life in her, Jesus, would never let her become an adulteress. "You may go through the actions, but you will not be able to get your license as an adulteress. You will never be comfortable doing that." Although she did initially proceed down that road, she turned back. Her outer life could not maintain its stance against the Christ that dwelt within her.

Struggle reveals that a believer cannot sin. It really stinks to have one's heart condemn him. One day the believer wakes up and says that it is just not worth it, and then he finds that Jesus is greater than the heart. Beautiful.

DAY 4
A Monumental Task: Bring Every Thought Captive to Christ

We are destroying speculations and every lofty thing raised up against the knowledge of God, and we are taking every thought captive to the obedience of Christ, and we are

ready to punish all disobedience, whenever your
obedience is complete.
— II CORINTHIANS 10:5 & 6

Some time ago, I gave myself a challenge to spend one week not thinking about myself. It sounds easy, does it not? Of course, psychologically speaking, this is denial and a very poor practice, but we are all still waiting for the demonstration of the truth of that theory! Well, the first day of withdrawal was the hardest. The battle for the mind was incredible! The obsessive mind of a hardened self-absorption addict became much clearer. It was an amazing experience. I would find myself constantly thinking of what I could tell someone who disagreed with me. I would stop that thought and next would come a flood of thoughts about people who had offended me. I went from having thoughts of grandeur to thoughts of self-hatred. I would block the progress of those and next would come self-righteousness, followed by unrighteousness. Everything that hinted of Mike was captured and brought to Jesus. Then there were fears concerning my children, worries about finances, and bewilderment over the future that, again, were captured and brought to Jesus. Afterward came all of the legitimate concerns. What about the schedule for the Amazon? What am I going to do with the government committee in Fiji? What about the German translation of my book? Again, everything brought to Jesus. It was work, but I did not merely take the thoughts captive, I took them to Jesus as captive thoughts, and when I came to Him, I asked a simple question: "Now, would You please tell me something about You?" He always did. In the course of a week I became lighter, and lighter, and lighter; I felt so free! I was surprised that everything that had filled my mind in the past really did not matter. All I had was the moment, and if in the moment He was teaching me about Himself, this moment was glorious. I discovered just how much the flesh—preferring to be under the rule of something other than Jesus—hates to come as a captive to Him. Also, the whole adventure was measurably easier any time I was serving others and ministering. It was a great week, a tremendous week, the value of which I would not exchange for anything.

DAY 5
A Special Experience

And the Word became flesh, and dwelt among us, and we saw His glory, glory as of the only begotten from the Father, full of grace and truth.

— JOHN 1:14

On a particular night a pastor gave me complete freedom to speak, and I will always remember it. The topic I chose was an attribute of God I appreciate so much: faithfulness. We have failed, but He is faithful and does not keep lists of wrongs, is not provoked, and is steadfast when we are faithless. The congregation was receptive, and

I believe that God revealed a new aspect of who He is to many. The pastor took the stage and began to pray and weep. As one the group prayed for God to reveal that He is a loving Father. All month I had been practicing allowing my soul to feed on His wisdom, His will, and His peace that are in me. I must admit that my soul was very full. When we began to sing "Hold me now and let your love surround me," I was expecting just that, but love did not merely surround me! My soul was so full of His love that it began to flow out of me to others. I wanted to run and hug everyone, to pray for the sick, and to pray for those in distress, though not me, but Him in me. The overflow of my soul was of Him, and I could see that His love in me wanted to take the form of flesh and blood to minister in a concrete way. I was not just preaching about love but demonstrating it! I could see how the Word became flesh; the soul of Jesus was so completely full of God that a human body could not hold it all, so it spilled out to others. "And the Word became flesh and dwelt among us." Jesus can manifest Himself through us, and we receive the awareness that there is nothing that faith in Him cannot do, nothing that Jesus cannot do. I see that I cannot schedule God, but as my soul is fed, I also see how I could pray for healing and another would receive it, for the Spirit is scheduling me. Christ is in us! Christ knows who needs what, and He can move through us to heal or help. On this day I watched God move from head to heart. We are vehicles for the living Word to take form. We are not Jesus, or God, or special, but we have been crucified with Christ, and it is no longer we who live but Christ that lives in us (as in Galatians 2:20).

DAY 6
Abiding-Life People

But thanks be to God, who always leads us in His triumph in Christ, and manifests through us the sweet aroma of the knowledge of Him in every place.

— II CORINTHIANS 2:14

In the Rocky Mountains we have what is called the "high country," my favorite place. As I ascend in the hot summer, I can experience what appears to be a perpetual springtime. Beautiful! In late summer I find the berry bushes and the wild strawberries. They have not been tampered with and therefore are very small in appearance, but grand in flavor. They are not like the huge grocery-store berries that are big but have no flavor. These are small and powerful, and they are hard to get to because of the bushes and thorns. Attempting to eat them means I will be scratched. Is it worth it? It is to me. Many fruits are bigger, but not tastier. When I eat one of these berries, the small seeds have a tendency to stick in my mouth. I spit them out in the hope that there will be new growth.

In many places I have seen the message of abiding in Christ initially spit out, only to grow years later. The seed of abiding is so resilient. Abiding-life people are like the berries at high altitude: small with a fragrant aroma and the fruit so pungent. Let the years speak against the minutes; we are the lesser people in this great time, the abiding people, the berries of high altitude, the fragrant aroma of the world.

DAY 7
Affairs

No temptation has overtaken you but such as is common to man; and God is faithful, who will not allow you to be tempted beyond what you are able, but with the temptation will provide the way of escape also, so that you will be able to endure it.

— I CORINTHIANS 10:13

Many believers I meet are struggling with the fantasy of what an extramarital affair would provide. They have not bought into the truth that all of us fall out with God before we fall out with one another. What happens next is the placement of legitimate emotions in an illegitimate place. Often I am asked the question, "Is it possible to fall in love with more than one person?" Of course it is, and I like to add, "That is why I stopped dating once I got married!" Romantic love is an emotion, the expression of which is not limited to one event. In one way, emotion is under our control; in another, it is not. For example, a car pulls out in front of us, our child runs in front of a car, or we hear of the death of a friend. During events such as these, emotions are not under our control but are functioning as they were intended, with stimuli producing legitimate emotions in legitimate situations. However, the possibility exists of putting legitimate emotions in an illegitimate situation, and either way the emotions feel the same. Remembering a hurtful event from the past—such as the death of a loved one, a breakup, or some harsh rejection—brings emotions not tied to a present event, but to something in the past; legitimate emotions are falsely weighing in to disrupt today's situation. The danger is that emotions can outweigh fact, making them feel legitimate for the present situation. This same thing can happen to men and women who have not set boundaries for themselves and talk flirtatiously to the opposite sex, milk acceptance, and leave covert messages that they are available; some even continue to date others after marriage. They place legitimate emotions that should be reserved for their mate in an illegitimate place. Since the emotions are real, they begin to believe that the place they are expressing them is valid. This is deception. I have watched firsthand as men and women have trashed out their whole families while believing God has finally sent them the perfect partner. It is distressing to watch the new, illegitimate couple clinging to one another in the eager attempt to prove to every observer that each of them has made the perfect decision regarding the perfect person, and that they have never been happier. Legitimate emotions went off to a place they should never have gone. The believer finding himself in this deception will not, by his own strength, get out. He should begin by asking our Lord to go with him every time he is with this other person, to open his eyes, and to break the emotional hold that, though real, is not right. He must determine in the Lord never to allow emotions to stray to a wrong place again to cause the trouble.

DAY 8
All Things Are Rubbish?

*More than that, I count all things to be loss in view
of the surpassing value of knowing Christ Jesus my Lord,
for whom I have suffered the loss of all things,
and count them but rubbish so that I may gain Christ,
and may be found in Him.*

— PHILIPPIANS 3:8

What a statement! "I count them but rubbish." I wonder if you believe that. What is it that brought you to Christ? What has been the event that took you deeper? Was it a rebellious child, an unbelieving mate, a handicap, financial difficulties, a failed marriage, or an unfulfilled dream? What was it? Did it take you to Jesus, or are you stuck on self? Have you been able to count it as rubbish? Sometimes when someone is telling me about a problem, I say very sternly, "Rubbish, all rubbish!" The event that brought a person to a deeper walk with Christ is not as important as the walk. The lesser gives way to the greater. Some are just stuck at their disappointment because of not having admitted that the whole thing is rubbish. Yes, divorce is a tragedy and a failure on someone's part, but we do not let such a shortcoming define us. The Lord defines our lives, and if He is for us then who can be against us? We simply let Him define us. Paul's comment came out of deep losses, and yet when he could see the comparative worth of knowing Jesus, those things became as rubbish.

DAY 9
Alleys That Become Avenues

What, then, shall we say in response to this? If God is for us, who can be against us?

— ROMANS 8:31

Often we are frustrated by the hindrances that are posed by other believers. Many are enjoying their walks in the flesh and spread their pettiness around to others. Once a police officer, an unbeliever who investigated the occult, asked me an interesting question. "Why is it that Satanists we have investigated belong to churches?" I asked if he knew what they did within the church. He said that was an even greater mystery, for most merely disagreed and caused division. The disagreements, he went on to say, were over minute issues such as the color of the pews, worship times, how to stripe a parking lot, or the size of coffee cups. Little did he know that this would be the most effective place for a Satanist to work, because believers, in turn, who have not found their identity in Christ will often have their identity centered around the same types of issues and will dig in to be proven right, for to admit that they are wrong about coffee cups or stripes is tantamount to admitting to being worthless failures.

If our goal is church growth, full pews, a comfortable budget, and harmony, then difficult believers are a hindrance. However, if our goal is the release of the life described on the mount in Matthew 5, then these very people are the avenue. We cannot desire to be spiritual giants while refusing the very experiences that could make us grow toward that end. How do we know that the Life within can love an enemy prior to our having one? How do we know that we are enabled to pray for those who persecute before we are persecuted? How do we know that the extra mile can be offered until it is required? The believers that appear to be hindrances actually pave the avenue for discovering, revealing, and releasing the Life of Jesus that is within, the Life that has overcome every hindrance to the spiritual man. I love our freedom and the way God works! I love Jesus, for if God is for us, who can be against us?

DAY 10
And Those Others

and others experienced mockings and scourgings yes, also chains and imprisonment. They were stoned, they were sawn in two, they were tempted, they were put to death with the sword; they went about in sheepskins, in goatskins, being destitute, afflicted, ill-treated ({men} of whom the world was not worthy), wandering in deserts and mountains and caves and holes in the ground. And all these, having gained approval through their faith, did not receive what was

promised, because God had provided something better for us,
so that apart from us they should not be made perfect.
— HEBREWS 11:36-40

Are you one of the "others" who has trusted God for a restored relationship, the health of a child, a godly home, the salvation of a relative, or just the simple stirring of God within that brings assurance? If you have trusted and not given into despair, then you are one of the "others" who give something to God that no angel in heaven can give Him, and that is faith. The "others" may walk in darkness, seeing nothing their whole lives, and yet stand fast, believing in a God they cannot see. Can you imagine how pleased He is? You are pulled on all sides to give up, and yet you have chosen to believe without seeing! You have stood fast in the midst of the reversals! The world is not worthy of you, and to it you simply do not belong! Your place is above, seated with the Father and judging angels! If you have believed and not received, count yourself blessed.

DAY 11
Anger and Addiction

Cease from anger, and forsake wrath; do not fret,
{it leads} only to evildoing.
— PSALM 37:8

Over the years I have noticed a strong correlation between anger and addiction. Addicted people appear to be angry about their past, their present, their loss of control, the relationships in their lives, and life in general. I have also noticed that many addicted people are very soft and sensitive people, and that would make the events that surround them more painful. It would appear that as life spirals out of control, they get angry, do not know what to do with the anger, and deaden it with a sedative, be it pornography, drugs, alcohol, food, overwork, slander, fantasy, obsessive thinking, reading, and the list goes on to include anything that gets their minds off the situation, quiets the nervousness within, and eases the awareness that life is not going well and they cannot fix it. I remember the story of the drunk Irishman who, being asked why he was drunk, responded, "It is the quickest way out of Ireland that I know!" However, addiction has its downside. First, by not facing the situation straight on, but avoiding it by using a sedative, the addict remains emotionally thwarted, a perpetual adolescent. Second, creativity is stifled. A recent survey revealed that depressed people are 70% more realistic about what is happening. The non-depressed, in optimism, are ignorant of how bad things really are. The point is, when a situation comes, the depressed are the first to see it. If they refuse the sedative, they will be the first with a solution because of creativity! Third, addiction leads to condemnation, which leads to self-hatred, which leads to more addictive behavior and more condemnation in an endless cycle. Fourth, there is the deception that addictive people have lost their free will. Fifth, addiction makes problems multiply. There is the out-of-control situation, then the addiction, and finally the results of addiction.

One problem can easily become three or four, and all of this is the consequence of anger that needs to be addressed.

Anger, mentioned 266 times in the Bible, is the fall of many and the cause of untold suffering and impulsive destructive behaviors. The person free from anger is a giant. Proverbs 16:32, "He who is slow to anger is better than the mighty, and he who rules his spirit, than he who captures a city." One controlled by anger will need to be rescued over and over again from addiction. Proverbs 19:19, "A man of great anger shall bear the penalty, for if you rescue {him,} you will only have to do it again." Ecclesiastes 5:17, "Throughout his life {he} also eats in darkness with great vexation, sickness and anger." The bottom line is something every addict knows, that "the anger of man does not achieve the righteousness of God" (James 1:20). So, what do we do with anger? Ephesians 4:26, "BE ANGRY, AND {YET} DO NOT SIN; do not let the sun go down on your anger." Also, Ephesians 4:31, "Let all bitterness and wrath and anger and clamor and slander be put away from you, along with all malice." Easier said than done until we consider the alternative.

How easy is it to be angry? What is the cost of anger? First, we need to get a God! We must be done with acting as though we have no God, with the tiredness and anger that accompany playing God. If we have a God, we must let Him be God. It helps to define clearly what are His responsibilities and what are ours. It is His responsibility to cause all things to work together for good, provide daily, keep us from temptation, and comfort His own. Second, when a situation comes from the past or present, simply say amen and yield to Him! In saying amen, we are not saying that nothing matters. What we are saying is that we are giving our situation to God and refusing to carry it any longer. Third, stop trusting the addiction. We cannot play any more mind games that allow us to be in a place where we mysteriously "fall." Fourth, we need to confess that our "chooser" is not broken. Fifth, when the draw to the addiction comes, we call on the Lord for deliverance. "Jesus, fill in me the need I hope this addiction will meet!" Sixth, be honest. If we like the addiction, we need to tell Him. If we do not plan on leaving it, tell Him. If we love it more than Him, tell Him. And then tell Him it is His. Watch what He will do. He is not dead, of that we can be certain!

DAY 12
Are They Really Hearing Jesus?

*Now we have received, not the spirit of the world,
but the Spirit who is from God, so that we may know the
things freely given to us by God, which things we also speak,
not in words taught by human wisdom, but in those
taught by the Spirit, combining spiritual thoughts
with spiritual words.*

— I CORINTHIANS 2:12, 13

Over the years I have had similar experiences to yours of people walking up to me to tell me that they had a word from Jesus for me. These words have been as varied as the people. Some have told me I was out of God's will to be traveling to minister and needed to return home immediately. Others have told me that the Lord was telling me to go out. Go out or come in, which is it? All purport to be speaking on God's behalf, so how to know the difference? There is no doubt that genuine words from Jesus can come through the conduit of another believer, but His word will not be an attempt to create something in us, but to witness to what is already there. God is a very intimate God and normally does not tell our secrets to another; He is far too confidential for that. Therefore, someone's telling me I have a "hidden sin" or a "dark heart" is not received. When a word does come that could be construed to be negative, it will—if it is truly from the Lord—lift the spirit, for with the word will come the power and the truth to set me free.

Another problem with some so-called "words of the Lord" is the carnal one's use of them as a method of manipulation, invoking the Lord's name and our love for Him to move us in his direction. Saying, "The Lord said . . ." really means, "Keep your distance, and no rebuttals allowed." A sure sign that this is happening is that the one speaking refuses to be questioned. The carnal person will want his to be the last word. Probably the most pertinent question when determining if something is from God or is a judgment of man is simply, "Why did Jesus not tell me Himself?" Normally when a child goes to a sibling to represent the parent, something is not right. If the parent wants to tell a child something, he simply tells him; he does not send another child to speak for him. If God wants to tell us something, and we know His sheep hear His voice, why would He send someone else? There are examples of His doing that in the Old Testament, and the people knew exactly what the prophet was talking about; it was not something vague or something that they could not see was wrong. This brings us to one other point: the carnal makes things vague to protect himself. It reminds me of the Asian fortuneteller standing on the corner and saying to each person passing by, "You seem happy, but something is wrong deep inside!" On any given day, that would apply to at least half of the people. God has no need to be vague, and neither are His words calculated to please the flesh. "You are going to have an expanded ministry!" "You are going to have all your riches returned to you!" "You are going to have healing!" It is all so appealing to the flesh. I would rather hear, "You are in Him, and so being in Him, He will bring the revelation of Christ in you, the hope of glory!" Carnal men want to give a word that is spectacular. Always question the motive behind what is being said. The "word" should bring neither condemnation nor exaltation; its object should be to move you toward Jesus. I have received tremendous encouragement from the words of believers that were not from them but from Him. Do not let the fact that there are phony words given deter when a blessing is to be had. Simply judge what is being said.

DAY 13
Are You a Castaway?

How then shall the Scriptures be fulfilled, that it
must happen this way?

— MATTHEW 26:54

There are many passages concerning the exemplary lifestyle of the believer. "If you wish to enter into life, keep the commandments: You shall not commit murder; you shall not commit adultery; you shall not steal; you shall not bear false witness; honor your father and mother; you shall love your neighbor as yourself . . . sell your possessions and give to the poor." "But when the young man heard this statement, he went away grieved; for he was one who owned much property." The young man would have been even more disturbed had he hung around to hear a little more of Jesus' teaching, for he would have discovered that his statement that he had kept the commandments was a bit premature. "For if you think it in your heart, you have done it!" In the end, who is guiltless? Can anyone stand the examination? This leads us to wonder: Did Jesus come in order to exclude men? It would appear so. However, He clearly teaches that He does not want to exclude but to include, yet His teaching does exclude, and often Paul's does, as well. What is going on? Something simple! When man sees that his own behavior and work have excluded him, he can cast himself on Christ and His forgiving love that includes. Yes, something must be cast away, and it must be man's efforts, so that he can throw himself on Him.

Things have to happen a certain way. One Scripture must be read in light of all others and never taken alone.

God is multifaceted; if He is putting a believer out on one count, it is only so He can bring him in on another. This is the love of God! We must lose our righteousness daily to be able to accept the Lord's. We must admit what we are not and then, like Abraham, move out of works and into faith for our justification.

DAY 14
Are You In or Out With the Legalists?

Seeing that His divine power has granted to us everything pertaining to life and godliness, through the true knowledge of Him who called us by His own glory and excellence.

— II PETER 1:3

It is interesting to watch the legalists drawing a person in but never really letting him in. He is manipulated to join, manipulated while working to remain, and yet never quite led to believe he is acceptable. If he complains, he is accused of being in rebellion and bringing dishonor to the Lord. He is finally put out, for the task of a legalist is to continue to make laws until he finds one that a person cannot keep. The rejected person is left depleted, spiritually abused, confused, lost, and wondering if he even has a faith. Such is the case for many who suffer under very legalistic pastors. Exclusiveness is encouraged in legalistic churches where there is the need of something to work for other than the revelation of Jesus within the believer. Pastors in such circles need to be needed. I am reminded of the opposite of this as demonstrated in Sundar Singh, who refused to pray for people and made them stand and pray themselves. Why? He was adamant about the point that there is one mediator between God and man: Jesus Christ. Nearly every time I meet a person who has come into some kind of personal relationship with Jesus, he says that he has been persecuted in some way by a legalistic pastor. One couple wept telling about how they met Jesus but are not allowed to partake of communion so long as they do not agree that the only person who can administer communion is the pastor and that the pastor is God's voice. They questioned where that was in the Bible, and that put them in even worse standing with the pastor. As believers we can be happy that Jesus is alive and ultimately is our Pastor!

DAY 15
Are You Qualified?

*He came to His hometown and began teaching them
in their synagogue, so that they were astonished, and said,*

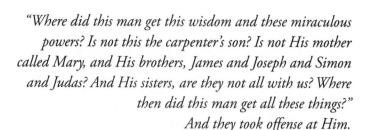

"Where did this man get this wisdom and these miraculous powers? Is not this the carpenter's son? Is not His mother called Mary, and His brothers, James and Joseph and Simon and Judas? And His sisters, are they not all with us? Where then did this man get all these things?"
And they took offense at Him.

— MATTHEW 13:54-57

Often people are questioned as to where they are from so that who they are and what they are about can be discounted. In the same way, people look for a source for God so He can be discounted; they have a vested interest in His existing only in the imaginings of man.

The topic of qualifications has come up more than once in my life, normally in one of two forms. Either someone is attempting to position himself above me in spiritual competition or he wants to discount what I say. The competition is obviously counterproductive, for once a person feigns spiritual authority over another, he proves that he has none. When qualifications are used to discount the teaching, question after question is asked until that end is achieved in the person's mind. The funny thing is that the majority of Bible schools and seminaries could be sued for false advertising, for only Jesus Himself can create in a person what their brochures claim can be provided through education. Also, there is the problem of wisdom. It is so disheartening for one who has spent so much time in school and trusts in his knowledge when an abiding brother or sister without such systematic instruction says something that thrills the heart. This causes jealousy and resentment among the educated ones who rely on the training of their flesh. We are given everything pertaining to life and godliness in Christ Jesus the day we believe in Him; there is no more qualifying to be done. In fact, when any Christian starts requiring me to meet some criteria, I know I am with a carnal man and will leave.

DAY 16
Are You Walking In Darkness?

Who is among you that fears the LORD, that obeys the voice of His servant, that walks in darkness and has no light? Let him trust in the name of the LORD and rely on his God. Behold, all you who kindle a fire, who encircle yourselves with firebrands, walk in the light of your fire and among the brands you have set ablaze. This you will have from My hand; and you will lie down in torment.

— ISAIAH 50:10, 11

Often I have described faith as a room we must all enter one day. Upon entering, God turns off the lights, removes the emotions of His presence, allows thoughts to run wild, and permits the enemy to whisper, "If . . . if only you had not sinned, if only you had married someone else, if you had just made better decisions, God would be with you, you would not be in this darkness, and you would have wonderful feelings." In this room believers struggle to understand what is happening; confusion is magnified if faith has never been rightly explained, for it is in just such a place that faith is developed as the assurance of things hoped for, the conviction of things not seen in our lives. In that darkroom we believers cannot see the Lord, yet we can do something that no angel in heaven that sees Him and believes can do. When we cannot see Him in this room and yet believe, we become very pleasing, for it is said that without faith we cannot please God. It is counterproductive to try to make our own light or attempt to stir up feelings, create an experience, or give in to depression, which is nothing more than anger without the excitement. Like the woman in labor who must not fight against pangs but let the baby come, we need not fight the darkroom but rest there and wait. He is coming! The greatness of faith is proven by how long we can wait.

"BEHOLD, HE IS COMING WITH THE CLOUDS, and every eye will see Him, even those who pierced Him; and all the tribes of the earth will mourn over Him. Even so. Amen."— Revelation 1:7

DAY 17
Aspen Groves

*And the {seed} in the good soil, these are the ones who
have heard the word in an honest and good heart, and hold
it fast, and bear fruit with perseverance.*

— LUKE 8:15

I love to walk in the aspen grove, said to be the largest living organism. The aspen does not have seeds but sends up shoots from its roots. One tree, then, can spawn a thousand; a whole forest is often attached to one tree! Amazing! So it is with Jesus, the firstborn of a new race of man. He does not drop seeds here and there, for every true tree must come from the root of the True Tree; we must all be attached to Him. In the aspen grove some trees are great, some weak, some dead, and some, apparently, doing nothing. Yet every one of them is attached to the same root; they all have the same potential. It is a mystery why some grow and some fail, some become large and some stay spindly. It is a surprise that the greatest trees fall in the worst winter storms, their bark becoming the food that will sustain the deer. They become great only to become food for something else. Well, amen! Are you willing to be an aspen that is attached, becomes great, and one day is food to nourish others?

DAY 18
Attraction Versus Respect

For all that is in the world, the lust of the flesh and the lust of the eyes and the boastful pride of life, is not from the Father, but is from the world.

— I JOHN 2:16

There is a difference between attraction and respect. When we hold true godly respect for another, it sends us in praise and gratitude to Jesus, in Whom we can experience more of whatever attributes we have been seeing and enjoying in the other person. In the context of respect, we think only of how we can encourage the other person on in the Lord, and we leave his or her heart with God. Attraction wants to experience some of that heart for one's self, and it is a pity that we currently see this often in congregations. The men or women are listening to a female or male speaker and thinking what a great experience it would be if married to that "wonderful" person. That is attraction, not respect. To look at someone and say, "If I were younger and unattached, there would be no question about pursuing that person," is attraction. What does that statement have to do with respect? Respect is gender neutral and, generally, attraction is gender specific and can grow so far as lust. So what is the point in understanding the difference between the two? Primarily this: How do we confess if we do not know what to confess? If we must admit that we have been dabbling in attraction, the solution is easy: Confess it and move into respect. The lack of distinction between attraction and respect has led to much spiritual abuse. Believers are listening too much to men and not to God; they are following too many men and not Jesus. Respect will never lead us into the type of situation where attraction allows us to go; respect keeps us following Jesus. Perhaps this can help us understand why some in the Church get sidetracked.

DAY 19
Back to the Hub

And the peace of God, which transcends all understanding, will guard your hearts and minds in Christ Jesus.

— PHILIPPIANS 4:7

A brother in Christ told me of his experience ten years ago when he woke up after a stroke to find himself paralyzed on one side. He described his frustration, anger, and bewilderment at his condition. Next, he related the end results of his stroke: a deeper love of God, a keener awareness of His grace and power, and a renewed life of worship. He concluded by exclaiming, "I wish everyone could know the Lord this way!" I observed his countenance and thought how if I could guarantee everyone who attended a weekend seminar what this man had, I could charge a $10,000 registration fee and pack the place. However, if I had to announce that the registration fee to bring people back to the center was not $10,000, but a stroke, I am quite sure that registration would drop off drastically.

The registration fee back to the center is different in tone and severity for every person, but might include something like the loss of a loved one, dealing with a rebellious child, exhaustion from raising small children, illness, job insecurities, or myriad other circumstances that make us realize we need God alone in His rightful place back in the hub. In Him alone we find our rest, and no emphasis, doctrine, or experience we previously looked to for producing abundant life can tempt us back to trust it. When others beckon us out by a new Jesus-plus emphasis, we think, *Enjoy your detour; I am not leaving the center.* We learn that nothing is bad that follows Him or arises from our relationship with Him, but anything that goes ahead of Him, purportedly supporting Him, is to be avoided and feared. We become voices for the center. I often ask myself the question, "Michael, what do your friends know you for? What emphasis stands out?" It prompts good reflection, for I want to be known for promoting life in Christ with nothing that must be passed through before getting to Him.

DAY 20
Basic Religion

For everyone born of God has overcome the world. Who is it that overcomes the world? Only he who believes Jesus is the Son of God.

— I JOHN 5:4, 5

Religion at its most basic point is man's attempt to be like God through mind, will, or emotion. This first appeared in the Garden, where religion took the place of relationship. Man does not like his own condition and aspires to ascend and be as a god; God does not like man's condition, either, and so He intentionally descended to become a victorious man who lived as God would on earth, and though worry, doubt, fear, anxiety, sin, the enemy, and depression would come calling as temptations, He rejected and overcame them all. He now gives us this life of a victorious God/Man that we, too, might live a life that is free. Jesus is the ultimate definition and fulfillment of religion, for He was the man who was, in fact, God, able to take away all superstition, all that is inconsequential, and all irrelevant arguments, leaving us with true, full, and abundant life. The kingdom of God within us brings its own set of invisible laws that, when observed, bring happiness. The enemy would have us believe that we are unhappy until we give in to sin, and yet sin brings misery. True happiness comes when submitting to the laws within and is possible only through receiving His life. The kingdom of God does, in fact, equal life.

DAY 21
Be Convinced in Your Own Mind

One man regards one day above another, another regards every day alike. Let each man be fully convinced in his own mind.

— ROMANS 14:5

Whatever you are doing and whatever you believe, be convinced in your own mind that it is right. There are many beliefs that I hold because fact and faith have met at a point called truth; I am convinced of such beliefs and will not budge from them. I do not make any of them a test of fellowship except for those that center directly in Jesus. He was the Word that became flesh, it was the Father working through Him, and He did take my sin and my old self to the cross, thereby conquering sin, Satan, the world, death, captivity, and hell; and He ascended to the Father, where He remains alive today. There are many more things surrounding Him of which I am convinced. The important thing for a believer is that he be convinced in his own mind. This is precisely why I will not make decisions for people but rather stand beside them as they make the choices, some of which are very difficult. Once, because I said nothing against an abused woman seeking a divorce (in reality, she never ended the marriage; he did through years of abuse), I was accused of promoting divorce. First, I have given much of my life to the hope that God would work through my words as I advised couples in order to prevent divorce, but it is true that I did not tell the woman to get a divorce or not to get one. Am I the one that will stand before God for her actions? Do I know all of the issues? Do I presume to understand all the workings of God in a life? Though God said to stone the adulteresses, He had His man, Hosea, marry one! Believers need to hear God and be convinced in their own minds. I want them still to be convinced in their own minds five years from now. If God has spoken to them, who am I to tell them that they cannot hear His voice? "But you, why do you judge your brother? Or you again, why do you regard your brother with contempt? For we shall all stand before the judgment seat of God. So then each one of us shall give account of himself to God" (Romans 14:10, 12). On another occasion I was asked why I did not work harder to stop a divorce. I just looked at the person and said, "I am not for divorce. However, neither am I for child abuse, drugs in the home, verbal abuse, causing little ones to stumble, thievery, lying, or adultery. In this situation, how did you come to the conclusion that out of all the variety of sins the husband was bringing into the family, the primary consideration was that the woman was guilty of divorce?" I suppose that we pick out one sin, the one failure that we have not had, label it as being the most important, and camp there in order to lay claim to self-righteousness. I am not favorable toward any failure; however, a true cross-section of the Church proves that these things occur. One man actually had the hide to tell me this: "If my wife really believes what you are telling her—that she can wait on God to see how He uses this present situation in her life—then she should not mind if I move my girlfriend into our basement apartment. I will sleep three nights a week with my wife and four with my girlfriend until I decide which one I want to be with." I nearly went off beam at his using the wonder of God's "causing all things for good" as an excuse to sin! I gave him an earful, but later, when she said she was divorcing, I kept silent. I only asked that she be convinced in her own mind.

Whatever you do, be convinced in your own mind that you have heard Him and are moving with Him. He is the issue. If you listen to others you will only be confused. "Brother, you are disregarding the Scriptures!" Well, may that never be! It is just that I put them in a different order when looking at them. I first go to the Scriptures that deal with cause and then consider consequence. Divorce is a consequence of a cause. If the man were not drunk and beating his family, would the suggestion of divorce ever come up? You who hate divorce, are you willing to commit to ceasing your condemnation of the one who sees that as the only way out and to taking time to disciple the man, taking responsibility for his actions? I did not think so; you are just comfortable judging an easy target. On the other hand, I have witnessed God do wonderful things in those prepared by Him to have humble and broken hearts. Those, no matter how bad marriage got, never were convinced in their own minds to leave, and that conviction bore a different fruit. I am just happy that it is not my place to pretend to sort things out; I leave that to God.

DAY 22
Bearing Fruit

*Abide in Me, and I in you. As the branch cannot bear
fruit of itself, unless it abides in the vine, so neither {can}
you, unless you abide in Me. I am the vine, you are the
branches; he who abides in Me, and I in him, he bears
much fruit; for apart from Me you can do nothing . . . By
this is My Father glorified, that you bear much fruit, and
{so} prove to be My disciples.*

— JOHN 15:4-5, 8

The believer can choose between two pairs of eyeglasses
through which to read the Bible. The first pair will
transpose and distort everything into a list of what the
believer must do to be acceptable to God. The second pair,
clear and accurate, reveals to the believer all that God has
done. During my devotional time in the early years of my
Christian walk, I wore the first pair of glasses exclusively.
Passages on the topic of fruit-bearing always discouraged
me. After all, I needed to bear fruit, for if I did not, I
would be cut off. I needed to bear fruit to prove that I was
a Christian, and this fruit had to involve effort, frustration,
and rejection.

What changed? I switched glasses and began to see
things as they really are in proper order. All the numbers
we use—phone, social security, bank account—have to
be used in the order in which they were given. Mix up

any group of numbers and render them no longer useful for calling home, collecting a check, or making a deposit. There is an order to be respected. When we look at the list of things a believer is to do, we must make special effort to keep them in God's order, for in that way we will find fruit-making a very pleasurable experience.

The beginning in God's order is abiding! How do we abide? He has put us in Him, He holds us in Him, and it is His life flowing though us. The emphasis is not on us but on Him, for He has done it all. Only believe it, confess it, and acknowledge it. Once our focus is on Him, His life flows, we bear fruit—the end result of the proper order—and the Father is glorified. It is His doing. If we will agree with Jesus that we are abiding, fruit will come and He will be glorified. He gets the glory and is the glory because He does the work.

DAY 23
Being Built

Being confident of this, that he who began a good work in you will carry it on to completion until the day of Christ Jesus.

— PHILIPPIANS 1:6

I have worked in the building trade, and one of the most annoying things that can happen to a builder is to have the homeowner continually telling him how to do his job. I overheard a friend say to a questioning believer, "Do you really think God is waiting for you to come around and give Him some advice, because He is fresh out of ideas?" I laughed, thinking of all the advice that I have given God concerning the completion of the work He started in me. My personal issue is not what God needs to do to complete what He has begun, but what has He given me to do in the interim? What must I do? Jesus answered and said to them, "This is the work of God, that you believe in Him whom He has sent" (John 6:29). Many respond, "I cannot just wait." I like hearing those words, "I cannot"; they confirm the foundational reason that we came to Christ. "I cannot" is only a statement of defeat if not followed by "He can!" Not only that, He can finish the work without our direction.

DAY 24
Being Nosy

Consider the ravens, for they neither sow nor reap; and they have no storeroom nor barn; and {yet} God feeds them; how much more valuable you are than the birds!

— LUKE 12:24

I had to laugh one day when a brother questioned an elderly prophet of God: "How are you supported?" The old man responded, "Why are you asking? Did God tell you to give me something? If He told you to give me something, even if I am covered in gold and jewels, you had better give it. If He told you not to give me something, and I am in the ditch, naked and starving, do not give. So what did He tell you to do?" At that the man went silent and looked at the ground. The old prophet said, "So you were just being nosy," and walked off. I have often been asked the same question: "How are you supported?" It should be obvious. Without tricks, gimmicks, endless mailings and appeals, or manipulation to attract them, I am supported by those who have heard from the Lord and responded accordingly. I often answer the question by saying, "I am a bit embarrassed. I have a friend to whom I tell my needs, he has a father that is very rich and has many contacts he can connect with, and the money is sent to me." I can see the look in the questioner's eyes as he goes from wondering how I could be surviving in such a small ministry to thinking how lucky Mike is to have such a friend. "My Friend," I continue, "is Jesus. His Father's children are my supporters." Many just cannot believe that God provides. Often a couple engaged to be married will tell me they are calling off their wedding because of finances. My response is always the same: "Did God tell you to get married? If He told you to and you do not, you will have worse problems than unemployment!" The lesser gives way to the greater. If God tells a believer to do something, he should do it and not shame himself by being unbelieving, for with the call will come the provision.

DAY 25
Belonging to Jesus

Whether Paul or Apollos or Cephas or the world or life or death or things present or things to come; all things belong to you, and you belong to Christ; and Christ belongs to God.
— I CORINTHIANS 3:22, 23

Do you know that you belong to Jesus? Of course you do! You do not belong to man, to an organization, or to an institution. You belong to Jesus; you are His, and He belongs to you. There is so much comfort in that fact. Do you know, also, that there was enough dynamite in one thing that Jesus said to blow to pieces any institution? "Man was not made for the Sabbath but the Sabbath for man!" In short, we are not commanded to prop up the kingdom of man, period! Many will work on the good heart of a believer to get him to serve in the building of their kingdom. We do not work for man's kingdom, for we are not made for man; we are made for God. In Buenos Aires, Argentina, at the end of the walking boulevard named Florida Street, there is a large, beautiful tree with branches so big that sticks are placed vertically under the limbs to support them so they do not break off. The immense weight of each limb is unbelievable, but one little stick keeps it supported. So many in the Kingdom of God are little sticks kept busy supporting the dead weight of the kingdoms of man. We must refuse this role and not be concerned with man's extending his image. We are created for the ONE, for Jesus, and Him we do not support; He is the ONE who supports us. "For My yoke is easy, and My load is light" (Matthew 11:30).

DAY 26
Bitterness

*See to it that no one comes short of the grace of God; that
no root of bitterness springing up causes trouble,
and by it many be defiled.*
— HEBREWS 12:15

On occasion I will talk to a brother (or sister) contemplating divorce, and I will immediately explain to him how he is presently feeling. Often his response will be, "How did you know exactly how I was feeling?" "Quite simply," I tell him, "I just described the characteristics of a bitter person." His mate's behavior is not dictating how he feels, although he believes it is. Bitterness is the true dictator, a most divisive and destructive force to which many believers have succumbed. "Let all bitterness and wrath and anger and clamor and slander be put away from you, along with all malice. And be kind to one another, tenderhearted, forgiving each other, just as God in Christ also has forgiven you" (Ephesians 4:31, 32).

What are some of the common signs of bitterness in a relationship? The bitter person is responsible for them, remember, for it is not the actions of others that cause bitterness, but rather a hard heart and ears attuned to the enemy's accusing voice that give bitterness the soil it needs to grow. There is a difference between being offended and being bitter. We do not find Jesus, the one Man in all of humanity who was offended the most, ever bitter. Blame must rest squarely on the shoulders of the person who is bitter. Bitterness is an attitude that grows until its roots are entangled throughout the person's mind, will, and emotions. Any attempt to remove this poisonous plant will be met with resistance through desire, intellectual arguments, and the sense of hopelessness. Bitterness can even be considered an addiction, for there is a soothing inner calm in those who have become accustomed to it; though everything outside them is out of control, they can at least direct their bitterness and make others pay for the perceived wrongs they have done. The majority of believers under emotional stress will either have an outer expression or an inner explosion (which normally converts to depression), and with the passing of time all is forgotten. However, the bitter have done neither of these, and anger and resentment have accumulated to the point of the persons' accepting a lifestyle, a path allowing for the luxury of avoiding personal responsibility for the remainder of life. A child is bitter toward the parent, and the more the child fails in life, the more anger he exhibits toward the parent. This is living in a distorted reality, a neurosis. When events begin to pressure the bitter people into accepting blame, they immediately recall all of the wrongs that have been done to them, once again avoiding life. An interesting thing about bitter Christians is that they often maintain their bitterness under the guise of being extremely spiritual, "so spiritual" that God has called them to suffer by being cut off from others, and yet the proof of carnality is that everyone who has disappointed them is covertly punished for the perceived failure.

DAY 27
The Bitterness Trap

. . . promising them freedom while they themselves are slaves of corruption; for by what a man is overcome, by this he is enslaved.

— II PETER 2:19

When circumstances in life get the best of them, sometimes people passively respond by taking blame, rolling over, playing dead, and accepting all responsibility. There is no fear of change, for each morning brings comfort in the knowledge that whatever happens throughout the day, they are to blame. Similarly, but conversely, bitterness can become a compulsion; it assures a person that no matter what problem has arisen, someone else is to blame. Yes, bitterness develops the type of dependence seen with cigarette smoking, a habit which when started can be enjoyed when a person desires, whether after dinner, at a party, or during leisure times. Soon enough there develops an interesting phenomenon wherein instead of exercising free will, the smoker heeds the domineering call of the cigarette and goes whenever it calls. At this point there is addiction. A person specially created to listen to the glorious Father above listens instead to a cigarette below. The creature is a slave to a new master. When the misery of this revelation sets in, the smoker begins to make a series of vows and smokes hundreds or even thousands of what become known as "the last cigarette." Soon frustration, anger, and even depression develop.

At first bitterness is used as an excuse, but with the passing of time bitterness uses us. The fact most evident, yet rarely discerned by the bitter, is that whoever they are bitter toward has become their god. While in the wilderness, Jesus heard Satan make the request to "fall down and worship" him. The word "worship" involves the giving of attention; Jesus replied that only God would have His attention. Most of us have been hurt by others, but making them our gods by continuing to give them our attention is a greater tragedy. Do we want to worship those who offend, abuse, beguile, use, and neglect us? Jesus gives commands not to make us more acceptable to God but to ensure our happiness. Forgiving makes any person happy! When we forgive, we rule! When we do not forgive and become bitter, others rule us. The command to love is not for the good of others but for our own good. What a deception the enemy imparts, that to obey will hinder our happiness. A paramedic once made the observation that he had never had an emergency call from a Bible study, yet he had received many calls from bars and parties. The commands make us happy and do us great good.

DAY 28
Bitterness Bondage

It was for freedom that Christ set us free; therefore keep standing firm and do not be subject again to a yoke of slavery.

— GALATIANS 5:1

Bitterness is oppression from the enemy, who has invested many hours whispering about the supposed misery caused by others. The most predominant trait of the bitter is that he considers himself a victim, having had to suffer and go it alone without help, support, or respect. He is isolated, forced to a place of self-sufficiency. No one even cares, and he is angry. This attitude of bitterness can begin with a dislike, distrust, or even hatred of one's mate, but soon turns into hatred of the opposite sex. Women are viewed as complaining, impossible to please, picky, manipulative, non-submissive, rebellious, and domineering; they only care about seeing a paycheck, they lack respect, and a man never knows what he is coming home to. To a bitter wife, men are seen as proud, insensitive, arrogant, passive know-it-alls who only care about themselves, sex, and having their egos continually stroked; they are slow to fulfill their responsibilities and cannot do things right. Soon both spouses decide that they can live without sex, communication, approval, or the support of their mates. I have talked with couples that had mutually decided through bitterness to withdraw sexually from one another for periods of more than ten years. These attitudes will often be communicated to the children of the couple through various overt or covert messages, leaving many today fearful of the opposite sex.

It takes a surprisingly short amount of time for bitterness to become a person's comfort zone. It is actually easy to withdraw and put the mate under the magnifying glass, waiting for the next word or action that will prove the negative assessment of the relationship and the hopeless state of the mate. I have been amazed at how frustrated a bitter believer becomes at the suggestion that his mate may not be as bad as he believes. He hates to hear such a thing! As I draw attention to the bitter one's inability to love in spite of offenses, the conversation is immediately turned away from his failure back to the inexcusable behavior of the other. I can only ascertain that this type of person has every intention of remaining bitter.

DAY 29
Blood That Possesses Its Own Life

So Jesus said to them, "Truly, truly, I say to you, unless you eat the flesh of the Son of Man and drink His blood, you have no life in yourselves. He who eats My flesh and drinks My blood has eternal life, and I will raise him up on the last day. For My flesh is true food, and My blood is true drink. He who eats My flesh and drinks My blood abides in Me, and I in him."

— JOHN 6:53-56

I was thinking how the heart must pump the blood to the lungs in order for the blood to carry oxygen throughout the body and keep it alive. The life is in the blood, and that life is oxygen. Giving someone mouth-to-mouth resuscitation is restoring his life. It makes sense that God breathed life into man and man became a living soul. The breath of God, coming from outside man, is the life. In fact, all of creation is receiving life from God moment by moment. He is all around us. What if we had blood that had its own oxygen and did not need an outside source? Then we could live without breathing! In a spiritual sense this is exactly what we have, the blood of Jesus that possesses life in itself, not requiring an outside source of life like our blood does. The blood of Christ will allow our spirit and soul to go on living when the body is destroyed and the world as a source is gone.

DAY 30
Boring!

> *For we do not preach ourselves but Christ Jesus as Lord,*
> *and ourselves as your bondservants for Jesus' sake. For*
> *God, who said, "Light shall shine out of darkness," is the*
> *One who has shone in our hearts to give the Light of the*
> *knowledge of the glory of God in the face of Christ.*
> — II CORINTHIANS 4:5, 6

I had a life-changing revelation when I was talking to a man who had suffered abuse as a child that ended in his spending nearly the next forty years in counseling. He would tell the counselors about a beating, show the scar, they would talk to his invisible father in a chair, and so on. I listened to this man, wondering what Jesus would say. I am often just as surprised as those I am discipling at what the Lord gives me, and this time when it came I leaned forward, put my hands on his knees and said, "Listen very carefully, for Jesus has told me what to say. It is only one word, but if you receive it, it will change the course of your life. If you do not listen, well, amen." The man leaned toward me and listened intently as I spoke the word, "Booooooring!" He just stared at me, but again I said, "Booooooring! Your story is boring; I am bored to death with it; I cannot stand to hear any more of it. Why have you not gotten a life? It is a terrible shame that you were beaten as a child; it is bad that it ruined the first twelve years of your life. However, it has become a tragedy because you have allowed it to steal another forty years. How long can you go on talking about the first twelve years of your life? It is boring; you are boring!" I explained that I was sick of myself, too; I was bored with Mike. I am exhausted from thinking about myself, who did what, said what, reacted, rebuked, hated, or liked me. Self-life is all so boring. Jesus is not boring. I had challenged myself to go one hour without thinking about myself. It took months, but I finally did it. Then I did it for one day and finally one week, the best week of my life; it added much to rather than detracting from my life, and I had a great time. I challenged him that I, too, would be bored and depressed if all I did was think about him. Again, the advice was to get a life, get Christ's life. As I was talking, his wife interrupted and said to him, "Go look in a mirror! You will be surprised with what you see." He did and discovered that he was smiling. He acted shocked and said, "Why would I be smiling?" The answer was simple, "For the first time in over forty years your eyes are on Jesus." There is nothing His nearness will not cure. To be happy one must give himself to something greater than himself. The thing far greater than man is God.

DAY 31
Branches on Branches?

I am the vine, you are the branches; he who abides in Me,
and I in him, he bears much fruit; for apart
from Me you can do nothing.

— JOHN 15:5

The heart of the believer is where God's divine umbilical cord stops. Through that cord His life flows to the heart and then is pumped throughout the whole being. The eyes of the Christian become His, seeing what He sees; the ears hear things not spoken. The hands, feet, and strength, all are His. The heart of the believer is the place where the branch attaches to the Vine and receives His life. A branch properly attached to the Vine will find the full life of the Vine, and with it, the ability to accomplish what a branch by itself could not, such as bear fruit. Our collective goal as believers is to see every member so recognizing his attachment to the Vine that the supernatural flows out of him. However, we live in a world of kingdom builders, branches whose goal is having other branches attached to them, not to the Vine. They do not want the connected branches to succeed, to have their own ministry and calling, or, heaven forbid, to bear more fruit than they do, for they want the branches to be credited to them as their own fruit. Many "founders" of ministries view those around them as their possessions fastened to them, so they are not free with the people or able to hold them with an open hand. If one poor branch has the revelation of being attached to the Vine and begins to bear fruit and begin another ministry, he will always be remembered by the "grand branch" as an indebted traitor and taker. My advice to every leader is to let the people under him go, for it is only right that God attach them to Himself instead of to any person. Exodus 7:16, "And you will say to him, 'The LORD, the God of the Hebrews, sent me to you, saying, "Let My people go, that they may serve Me in the wilderness." But behold, you have not listened until now.'"

If you are a branch attached to a branch, you must also let go. If you do not, when the branch fails you will find yourself falling. Attach yourself to the Vine and do all things as unto the Lord, having as your life source always the Lord Himself. Do not let a leader keep you in bondage with the promise of what he does for you; he did not call you or choose you, God did. Your allegiance is first to God. Do not be a branch on a branch.

DAY 32
Bullies

And they rose up and cast Him out of the city, and led Him to the brow of the hill on which their city had been built, in order to throw Him down the cliff.

— LUKE 4:29

I suppose that at one time or another all of us have had to deal with a bully. What makes people bullies is their ability to set themselves above us and intimidate. Physical bullies use brute strength to create the fear of being hurt and in that way control us. Intellectual bullies point out our stupidity and inferiority. Materialistic bullies make successful acquisition of possessions the focus. Religious bullies draw attention to their righteousness, making it quite clear they are grateful for not being miserable sinners and failures like the rest of us. Verbal bullies delight in their ability to speak quickly and leave us speechless in our inadequacy. The political bully understands all the intricacies of the whole world and wonders at the absurdity of our opinions. Finally, outward-appearance bullies exalt themselves because of beauty or dress, insinuating that we are ugly and must therefore take our lower place in the caste system.

When discussing a bully, we must understand two points. First, any power that he has over us we have yielded to him in the sense that we, like him, falsely believe that the greatness of a person rests in strength, beauty, intellect, material possessions, self-righteousness, or a quick mind. The proof is in statements like this: "I feel like a wimp because I got scared and did not stand up to the bully." Who said we were wimps for not standing up to someone walking in the flesh? I know who says so! The bully and those of us being intimidated, and I believe both are wrong. We must not let the bullies define what weakness is. If we do, we will find ourselves with false definitions. The spiritual man is to set the standard; he is judged by no one but judges all things. I Corinthians 2:15, "But he who is spiritual appraises all things, yet he himself is appraised by no man." The spiritual man refuses to measure up to the standard set by the carnal or to play the bullies' games that set themselves above to lord it over others. Rather, the spiritual man places himself below all others, creating a contrast between him and all bullies that puts incredible judgment on them. The spiritual operate from a definition of man that necessitates loving and serving, not standing up to a bully. To the intellectual we can say, "We are not wise in our own eyes." To the materialistic bully, we say, "We live as the sparrow and lilies." To the verbal bully, "We bless," and to the religious bully, we can assert, "We trust not in our works, but in Christ's." By deferring to the bully, rather than scraping and clamoring to reach his self-proclaimed level, we conquer and overcome. We must not be intimidated by a bully, for in so doing we fall into his false concepts of life.

DAY 33
Buried Alive

Have this attitude in yourselves which was also in Christ Jesus, who, although He existed in the form of God, did not regard equality with God a thing to be grasped, but emptied Himself, taking the form of a bond-servant, and being made in the likeness of men. And being found in appearance as a man, He humbled Himself by becoming obedient to the point of death, even death on a cross.

— PHILIPPIANS 2:5-8

Man needed redemption not only from sin but also from himself. In order to accomplish that, God had to become a man, be victorious over all that vexes mankind, return to heaven, and from there dispense His victorious life to all who would ask. We have to wonder what it was like for Him who created the entire universe to wake up in the morning and discover Himself in the body of a baby. Imagine waking up and finding yourself in a coffin six feet under the ground. Would you panic, beat the sides of the coffin, yell, scream, and plead for deliverance? The body in which He found Himself was indeed a coffin, for in it He would die, but when God yielded Himself to living as a man, He humbled Himself.

DAY 34
Buy a Sword!

And He said to them, "But now, let him who has a purse take it along, likewise also a bag, and let him who has no sword sell his robe and buy one."
— LUKE 22:36

What a thing for the Prince of Peace to say! Why buy a sword? Earlier He had said that when He was with the disciples, they had need of nothing. But now they are in need of everything! What would it take to replace Jesus? When He was with them, they needed nothing, but since He was leaving, they would need everything, even swords. Peter tried to use the sword and was rebuked because Jesus was still with them. They never did need the purse, the bag, or the sword, for Jesus returned from the dead and they were able to live freely in the fact that He was with them. In my own personal life, how could I replace Jesus if He were to leave me? I move in and out of countries freely with the plane tickets that I need and so much provision, every bit of which is given by Him. How would I replace Him? If Jesus leaves a Christian organization, what will it take to replace Him? How many meetings? How many fund drives? How many employees? One friend, upon being told that a church had experienced a visitation of the Lord, responded, "If He visited you, you might want to ask what made Him leave in the first place!"

DAY 35
Can a Christian Be Demon Possessed? No!

So if the Son sets you free, you will be free indeed.
— JOHN 8:36

1. There is never a hint in Scripture that the solution to a believer's problem is demon possession. The Epistles deal with a variety of practical problems from self-righteousness to unrighteousness, and nowhere is the casting out or denouncing of demons given as a solution.

2. For the unbeliever the condition of internal demon possession is dealt with by casting out the demon. For the believer, the external works of the enemy (temptation and false doctrine) are to be resisted and stood against.

3. The Greek word for demonization (daimonizomai) is translated "to be possessed by a demon." In context, it is translated as one who has a demon dwelling in him. The word is only used in the Gospels. Those who believe in the possibility of demon possession of Christians often make the distinction between possession in the spirit of man, possession in the soul (mind, will, emotions), and possession of the body. However, Jesus makes it clear that casting out the demons is analogous to casting out the inhabitants of a house (Matthew 12: 28, 29, 43-45). I Corinthians 6:19 states that the body is the temple of the Holy Spirit, and Paul there speaks of the body, not the soul or spirit, for the body encompasses all. How, then, can it be said that the demon could be in the body of the believer but not in the spirit? The body is the Lord's. John tells us that "greater is He who is in you than he who is in the world" (I John 4:4). A demon cannot enter a believer and take over, for it is God's house the demon would be attempting to enter. Remember when the High Priest went with fear and trembling into the Holy of Holies? Are we to believe a demon can enter the Holy of Holies established in the believer?

4. There are many passages that declare that Christ's victory over Satan is so complete that Satan cannot come back and take (possess) the believer (John 17:15; I John 5:18; II Thessalonians 3:3).

5. The concept of worship, by its very nature, involves the giving of attention to the respected being. Many believers devote precious time focusing on the work of Satan, hence, in some type of convoluted manner, worshipping him. So much time is spent binding, rebuking, and casting out demons that could have been spent worshipping Jesus. People that constantly focus (worship) on the demonic have an oppressed look, which they take as a proof of the great battle they are in, though the battle has already been won by the only One worthy of the fight. They have the countenance they have earned from not setting their minds on the things above.

6. "If only you had seen what I have seen!" This appeal to experience falls flat. Traveling as I do, I have seen things that I would not even pen. Though I saw them, neither Scripture nor the Holy Spirit testify to their likelihood; they merit only the trash bin. It must be recognized that Satan is a liar through and through.

7. There is the problem of categorizing as demons the deeds of the flesh listed in Galatians 5. The flesh cannot be cast out but only denied by taking up the cross. I asked a question of a pastor who was casting demons out of believers: "You claim to be casting out by name attributes that Scripture identifies as the deeds of the flesh. That cannot be done. In six months what are you going to tell that eighteen-year-old boy when his hormones are surging and he is once again lusting? Will you tell him the demon of lust returned?" His answer surprised me: "No, then we will tell him to abide!" Obviously my next question was: "If abiding works,

then why would it not work in the beginning?" If the desire is to confuse and oppress, tell a believer who is struggling in mind, will, or emotions that his problem is a demon.

8. Finally, I remember when this teaching of demons plaguing the Church was introduced in the early seventies. Where are those same proponents today? If demons were the real problem with defeated Christians, then why are the same men not loudly proclaiming the message throughout the Church today? The world is getting worse. Have those men cast out all of the demons? No, the men are still around but have moved on to "new" spectacular methods, programs, and causes. Yet the old banner continues to be picked up by others.

DAY 36
Cast Your Burdens Upon the Lord

Cast your cares on the Lord and He will sustain you; He will never let the righteous fall.
— PSALM 55:22

Often we find ourselves carrying too heavy a burden. Instead of casting it on the Lord, there is a temptation to bring a temporary relief by casting it on another person, who also cannot carry the load; in fact, it can wipe him out.

There is absolutely nothing that the person can do to help us except for one thing: turn our eyes back to the Lord. Other believers are a great asset and blessing to us when they assist us in self-examining by ultimately turning our eyes to Jesus. I believe it is important to examine our ways and then turn to the Lord. Any issue, topic, or situation that surfaces can immediately be stopped from spreading destruction through the body of Christ by laying the burden on the Lord. He can carry it, and we can receive an immediate lift in our spirits.

DAY 37
Cease Striving

Cease {striving} and know that I am God; I will be exalted among the nations, I will be exalted in the earth.
— PSALM 46:10

Jesus carries so little only because we refuse to give other stuff to Him. The passage above from Psalms is clear on the directive that we cease striving, or literally "get our hands off." Why do we keep our hands on? There is only one reason, unbelief. We believe we will do a better job than will He. Pride trusts in the very slightest bit of self-strength. Humility has laid aside all strength, embraces weakness, and surrenders to God.

There is another side to trusting self. Not only are we filled with worry over all that we need to do, we never move into the supernatural to experience what He can do. The secret is that when we place our anxiety upon Him, not only does He carry it, but also He picks us up and carries us to new places. Often I meet someone from my past who does not understand how I could ever have gotten a book published, been invited to speak, or received listeners. They know me and enjoy pointing out my shortcomings. What they point to is that in which I glory: weakness! In weakness I gave my worries, and in weakness Jesus imparted His strength. "For indeed He was crucified because of weakness, yet He lives because of the power of God. For we also are weak in Him, yet we will live with Him because of the power of God directed toward you," II Corinthians 13:4.

Give everything to Him. Begin with the words in your mouth, "Jesus, I cast every anxiety on You. I take my hands off, and I know and trust that I have a God." In this way you become free. Let Him take you to places only His strength can. I have never yet seen a sparrow planting seeds or burdened as to the outcome of a crop. The bird is free from the seed-planting business. "Therefore, do not fear; you are of more value than many sparrows," Matthew 10:31.

DAY 38
Chicks!

O Jerusalem, Jerusalem, who kills the prophets and stones those who are sent to her! How often I wanted to gather your children together, the way a hen gathers her chicks under her wings, and you were unwilling.

— MATTHEW 23:37

An interesting thing about eggs is that not every hatchling is equally successful. One chick will come out first, a second starts out painfully slowly, one can only get his head out, and some never come out. Yet all are given birth by, and loved by, the mother. I have noticed the same thing to be true in Christians. Some come in glory, some struggle, some never come, and some just die. I am saying this only to acknowledge my ignorance; I neither have answers nor believe faith calls for answers. I have engaged in discipleship all these years and have found believers I could place in all of the above categories, for I know there are those who love Jesus and just do not get very far. The legalists would call them lost. Yes, they will straightforwardly call them lost until they find in their own families those who are "lost." Any who have ever had a suicide or an early death among their loved ones know what I am talking about. I have personally known people who committed suicide. I will not say that most of them were unbelievers. To me, they were believers who just could not get any more than their heads out of the shell; for a variety of reasons they just never could rise above their circumstances, lying emotions, or the voice of the enemy. Yet I believe that I will see them in heaven. Others may have a different opinion. Remember, I am not saying that

I understand; I am only making observations. Anyone who has risen above difficult things in his own life should ask why; what was it that enabled him to do so? I do not believe he will rightfully credit anything other than the grace of God. Well, amen. I believe that all the chicks were given birth by and loved by the Father.

DAY 39
Choose Today!

I call heaven and earth to witness against you today, that I have set before you life and death, the blessing and the curse. So choose life in order that you may live, you and your descendants.

— DEUTERONOMY 30:19

What must I do that God will not do for me? I must choose. It is amazing that we believers want discipleship, communication, understanding, counseling, church, youth groups, reason, manipulation, protection, and Jesus to do for a person what only choice can do. It took years for me to come to the place where I could believe it, but now time has rendered its verdict and the argument is settled: Not even wisdom can override choice; people must choose. The problem is that people return to the place they never really left, and too often they have never chosen. We can tell when the alcoholic has really chosen, for choice is not made in the bar but before he gets there, and he stops going. Similarly, we can tell when the struggling homosexual has chosen. His choice is not made at the meeting places but before, and he does not go to them. It is easy to spot one who has moved out of making judgments, for he does not back out in the middle of the conversation but refuses ever to enter in. Choice is something no one can make for someone else! As the Bible says, we are free. We have a new lineage, the Bible says. We are not slaves to sin, the Bible directs. However, one must choose to live in the light of these truths or they will never become real to him. I believe less and less in the "Christian struggle." Sin does not reign over us to make us struggle. The struggle is not with sin but with choice. In our pride we still believe that sin is holding something for us, and we refuse to choose truth. This creates a vacuum, and a lie fills the void. There are many idols/coping mechanisms that we are carrying in our bags to cover up our responsibility to make choice. We use the ugly past, hurtful events, and rude statements to justify the hidden fact that we are refusing to choose. Not making a choice will keep us immature. At an early age we decide either to face life head on and mature or find a sedative to get us through. Obvious sedatives are drugs, alcohol, and sex, but there are many others that are even more insidious for their comparatively covert nature, such as withdrawal, blame giving, depression, sports, titles, competitiveness, and even computers; I have heard more than one wife complain that her husband appears to be addicted to video games. When the pressure is on, any of those things might be picked up to keep the mind off the problems, but by doing so the person remains in bondage. Therein lies the problem that when any such sedative is finally laid aside, the person engaged in it discovers he is at the same emotional age as when he picked it up. Many times a woman has discovered that once her alcoholic husband sobered up, he went around acting as though he were thirteen. She begins to wonder if it were not better to have him passed out in a chair. In short, we are given the directive to "put aside childish things," and this will take choice.

DAY 40
The Will of God Is That Man Can Choose

Your kingdom come. Your will be done,
on earth as it is in heaven.
— MATTHEW 6:10

As I think through choice, it seems that one key deception is that choice is not resident in the human realm but is held by God. Many ministries make a covert claim that their information holds the key to making a person choose. The brochures of seminaries claim that they are in the process of "producing men and women of God!" Just how does a book, a professor, or a building produce a man or woman of God? If the very best information is not chosen and followed—and we all know some students will follow and some will not—then what good is it? For the students who do choose to follow, was it the school that made them choose? Is it right for the institution to focus on the one who chose and use him as an example of the power of its teaching? A lesser truth gives way to a greater one, so was it the information or the will that was the change factor? I used to do this myself! I would only tell the victory stories that came out of my counseling, and the subtle message was, "See what power there is in this teaching?" Claims are made for methods, teachings, ministries, and institutions that even Jesus Himself would not make, for Jesus never indicated that He could make a choice for the people.

We are all partly responsible for the continuation of the deception; we cannot just blame the institutions. We want to hear that a program can do for our mate or child what only their choice can do. We seek out and pay these institutions to lie to us! Notice those same confident experts who promise to turn a situation around never offer a money-back guarantee. Why? I have watched the human-behavior experts in court, under oath. All of a sudden what used to be an absolute becomes a vague mumbling with a resounding, "I cannot help someone who does not want it!" True, but this was not said initially when clients were being drawn in. We must realize that if God Himself cannot make a person choose, then what about us? We will never be able to make someone choose. Herein lies a warning about how some will allow us to believe that we are in charge of their choices. This is a trap, for they will continue to choose what they want and covertly manipulate us into taking responsibility for it! We will find ourselves working all the harder, pleading, watching, and attempting to control their behavior, all the while having enabled them to become free from their responsibility.

DAY 41
Choice or Default

I call heaven and earth to witness against you today, that I have set before you life and death, the blessing and the curse. So choose life in order that you may live you and your descendants.

— DEUTERONOMY 30:19

Two addicts receive the same information, and subsequently one stops substance abuse and the other does not. Why is that? Is it not choice? There is a deception involving the belief by those who need to make a choice that they cannot do so, that it is impossible in certain areas of life to choose a different way. Many simply believe that they are stuck with their obsessions, addictions, anger, self-righteousness, and all the other deeds of the flesh. They are like the person standing in the snow outside of his house, holding the key to the locked door and screaming, "Would someone please let me in?" How can the believer be stuck and locked out of victory when he is the only one holding the key? Let me illustrate. One man said to me, "I am addicted to pornography!" At that I responded, "I imagine your family is sick of watching porno with you!" He replied, "Oh, no! I never look at it around them!" My question is simple: How can he be addicted if he can choose when and where he watches the porno? How can a drug addict not be able to choose against taking drugs when he chooses to purchase them and chooses to do them out of sight? We hate to be confronted with this truth, but we are doing exactly what we want to do and choose to do! We are not unable to choose; we simply do not want to choose the right thing. We are in unbelief and are constantly choosing. We have to pick between the words of Jesus and the voice of the flesh. When we CHOOSE the flesh, it is an inescapable fact that we have chosen bondage and have chosen on the side that resists the spirit. We are where we are today because of personal choice.

Some will argue, "It was not my choice to be molested, to have an alcoholic parent, to be emotionally and verbally abused, to be abandoned, to be unloved, and more." All quite true, and at first a person may well react out of instinct. However, with maturity he chooses through his lifestyle what his reaction toward earlier events will be. After getting the proper information, some choose not to see God working, thereby opting to remain victims and blame others, to make those around them miserable, to make others pay, to live in self-hatred, and to try to undo the past by duplicating it. Two people with a common, horrific event in their lives may, years later, have developed into very different people, with one being sweet and the other bitter. Why? We want to avoid the obvious and give excuses, but the fact is that one believed that choice was greater than the past, and the other did not.

DAY 42
Choice Between Life and Death

With good will render service, as to the Lord, and not to men, knowing that whatever good thing each one does this he will receive back from the Lord, whether slave or free.
— EPHESIANS 6:7, 8

We have been looking at problems encountered with our ability to choose, and one involves the feeling that apart from Him we can do something. It is true that outside of Christ man still has the power of choice; however, a man wanting to be the god of his life will only choose the things that strengthen the flesh; he will eat from the tree of Good and Evil, choosing self-righteousness or unrighteousness, the only choices made by any man except for those living in and abiding in Christ. Many in the "power of positive thinking" crowd teach that man can choose whatever he wants, including his destiny, that it is completely up to him what he becomes. The crux of this type of teaching does not include any reliance on Christ, so it simply cannot be true. A person can choose, but all choices will strengthen the flesh, causing a great outbreak of the flesh later. The Pharisees chose some incredible disciplines, and their flesh was so strengthened that they killed Jesus. In the same way a person can choose unrighteousness, which will cause an outbreak of self-righteousness later. I have heard former addicts speak with absolute contempt of drug addicts that they know. The unbeliever is a slave of sin. Just like any other slave, in his mind he can despise following the master, but he must choose to follow or suffer the consequences. My point is that even being a slave does not negate the fact that one still must choose.

DAY 43
Choice That Promotes Life

Jesus said to him, "I am the way, and the truth, and the life; no one comes to the Father but through Me."
— JOHN 14:6

Finally, the truth is that in Christ I can choose no longer to sin! In Him I am free! A new birth happens once, but conversions, or changes in thinking, occur throughout one's life. One day I stopped thinking that Jesus was a man in history and began to think that He was a man that was alive today. It was a conversion in my thinking, one of many to come. The first choice we make is the choice to believe in Jesus as the Sacrifice for our sin, a choice preceded by our own failure and sin. The second choice will come by the same means, failure and sin; we must choose Him as our Way, our Truth, and our Life. Years and sometimes decades exist between the first and the second choice. For many of us, these are the lost years, the wilderness years, or the dark nights of the soul. During these years two dynamics meet daily in a clash, leaving few unscathed; on the one hand is the strong desire to "pay back" Jesus for all that He did and has done; we feel this is primarily accomplished by "acting" like Jesus. This is, of course, exactly what it is, an act! Initially believers are convinced that we have retained some strength, hold some solution, and possess something at our disposal that will make us act like Jesus. There will likely be something hidden, a secret, so most of us really do not want Jesus invading every area of life, not when we can continue to believe in our way, our truth, and our life and discreetly to trust our idols, sedatives, victimization, bitterness, anger, and passivity to resolve life's daily issues and enable us to imitate Jesus. When things go well, we are confident and full of pride and glory. When things fall apart, we blame ourselves or others, leading to depression, frustration, and the wish for life to pass. The time between the two choices is a very mean time, for man was not created to imitate Jesus, but to be a vessel for the living Jesus. As believers approach the second choice—The Choice— we are confounded by all of the other choices that are presented to us in the form of advice. If only there were more Scripture memory, quiet times, prolonged studies, witnessing, or stronger resolve, then we believers would be like Jesus. The tension of trusting self (a self that prefers its reign to the reign of Jesus in our life) for the provision to act like Jesus is absurd and will eventually cause the believer to begin to break in pieces. In the power of a self that has at its disposal all the old methods of performing and coping, we try to displace self. Think of the absurdity of self's removing self; that actually keeps self actively alive! Man becomes a house divided and begins to fall apart.

The dichotomy of wanting to act like Jesus in the flesh and at the same time to have flesh despising the potential rule of Jesus creates a tremendous amount of guilt, which is said to be the undertaker's best friend. However, guilt in the hand of God produces some wonderful results. We believers become weary of being and feeling guilty, and it is in this state that the enemy takes opportunity to whisper to us, in a voice that sounds like ours, "I cannot change. I cannot choose a better way. I am stuck!" Imagine hearing such a thing when we hold the key of choice in our very hand. At this time, the fullness of time, we believers are ready for another conversion in the form of recognizing that it is not about imitating Jesus but participating in His Life, being attached to the Vine, and having exactly Jesus flowing through us. As the Holy Spirit brings the revelation, we do not hesitate or argue but embrace the fact. We are abiding, Christ is in us, and apart from Him believers can do nothing. Jesus is now accepted as life, and The Choice is made.

DAY 44
Choice as a Lifestyle

Then Jesus again spoke to them, saying, "I am the Light of the world; he who follows Me will not walk in the darkness, but will have the Light of life."

— JOHN 8:12

After The Choice, the door is open to making hundreds of choices, each of which will have to do with the progressive conversion of seeing Jesus as the Way, the Truth, and the Life in a particular situation. Each conversion (change in thinking) is uniquely situated in the order in which a believer needs to have it. The revelation that Jesus is living in a person comes more from what the person refuses to do than what he does do! The believer chooses to refuse bitterness, anger, justification, debate, hatred, self-righteousness, and competition, and instead follows the will of God. However, he knows that no matter how quickly or wholeheartedly the choice is made, it is really not his doing, but that of the Jesus that indwells him. The choice is not to ask Jesus for help to act like Him, but to ask Jesus to act through him. It is not the surrender of the will in passivity but the activation of the will through choosing Jesus. The choosing Christian never says, "Jesus, help me say the right thing. Jesus, help me love. Jesus, help me be pleasing to God. Jesus, help me be more like You." No, the choosing Christian says, "Jesus, be my words, my love, my acceptance, and my life," and allows the peace of God to rule in his heart. Any variation in peace causes him to back up, listen, and invite Jesus to be his Way, his Truth, and his Life. The choosing Christian discovers he can do things he never thought possible, things that in self were not attainable. The abiding/choosing Christian can say no to the lust of the eyes, the lust of the flesh, and the boastful pride of life; he can say no to appetites because he is dead to sin and, in Christ Jesus, no longer a slave to it. Christ in him living through him as though it were he becomes a reality. The chooser is as active as the chooser was in Jesus, Who daily chose "not My will but Thine." He chose not to follow anything but God's will to the point of death! An active chooser picks not to be like Jesus but for the will of the Father to live out of him through Jesus.

Practically speaking, those we love the most will hurt us the most. I do not believe the abandonment from the crowd was as vexing to Jesus as the abandonment from those into whom He had poured His life. How could He be so positive as to say, "You will sit on twelve thrones"? Jesus made a choice to be yielded in His heart and embrace "not My will but Thine," and the Father's words came. So the believer is offended by one he loves; something rude is said, there is an explosion, past events are brought into the present, and the wound is deep. However, the believer has had a conversion and accepts that Jesus is his Way, Truth, and Life. Choosing anything other than "Your will, not mine" will result in feeling lost, lied to, and the stench of death the flesh brings with it. The abiding/choosing believer just will not sacrifice the peace of the Way, the Truth, and the Life. Therefore, in the situation, he pauses, invites Jesus to be his life, his words, his love, and his wisdom. He hears His voice, "a kind word turns away wrath." Jesus would only do through him what is best for him; love can do nothing else.

DAY 45
Concrete For Rebar

I can do all things through Him who strengthens me.
— PHILIPPIANS 4:13

Did you know there is no strength in concrete? The strength is in the steel the concrete encapsulates. A building that is only concrete will quickly crumble, and a building that is only steel will move and bend. The concrete is not the strength but holds the real strength, the steel, in place. The same is true of the body's skeleton being held in place by the muscles and skin. Likewise, Jesus in me is my steel; His will is the steel and my will is the concrete. When I choose, the concrete is poured and it sets, after which the steel will not move. His love in me is the steel, but I must set it in place by my will. I choose Jesus in the situation. I hear His words and I set the concrete in place by an action of my will. The believer, upon being offended, yielding, and hearing His voice, now sets the whole thing by taking one step forward and hugging the person, saying, "I love you." It was Jesus in him loving, but the Christian set the whole thing in motion by a choice. Next, the believer feels the concrete set, the strength of the steel is revealed, and the believer actually experiences supernatural love. Wonderful! It does no good to withdraw and wait to get stronger; these are faith decisions resolved in a believer who learns that Jesus is the Way, the Truth, and the Life. Choice is merely setting the concrete around the steel that is in him.

Does this mean that Jesus needs me? Yes! Many are repulsed by the thought of Jesus in need, but He showed us that He lived His whole life in need. God created the world and gave dominion to man. In so doing He is bound to work through man. Jesus had to become a man; it was the plan from the beginning, the lamb slain from the foundation of the world (Revelation 13:8). He needs those—the concrete—that will choose Him to be expressed through them.

DAY 46
Christ's Gain

In bringing many sons to glory, it was fitting that God, for whom and through whom everything exists, should make the author of their salvation perfect through suffering.
— HEBREWS 2:10

On a recent international trip I was sitting on the front pew waiting to preach. During the song service I looked on the wall at a picture of Mary holding Jesus. God becoming a man! I have always thought of the great loss Jesus experienced in having to leave heaven to become a man. I had never before thought there was gain for Him, but there are two areas of gain that I see. First, though I know little about Him, I know He is the lover of my soul. God created man like a fine automobile, but a car cannot drive on its own. I have seen in the bottom of a ferryboat a tangled and beaten-up heap of cars after a storm at sea. Those lost cars had no drivers. Jesus stepped in to become the driver in man and to make the creation perform perfectly. He comes to dwell in each of us, to drive, so to speak.

Second, when spirit dwells in flesh, the spirit will either be perfected or destroyed. In heaven, without hindrances, spirit never really sees its limitations. This is partially the problem that Satan had, thinking he was equal to God. Putting spirit in flesh is redeeming for the spirit as the short course in revealing weakness. Once spirit has lived in flesh and found that it is conquered by flesh (spirit is willing but the flesh is weak), spirit enters into humility. Clinging to and empowered by God, spirit perceives something it never would have if not presented with that new level of need: a deeper experience of the glory of God as He meets the need. Spirit as it lives and is being perfected in flesh reveals the glory of God. Having descended and ascended, does Jesus see the Father differently? If so, is it gain? Jesus was made perfect through suffering. What does this mean for me? Jesus put Himself in a place of great need, but God did more than meet the need. So maybe God the Father will never seem the same for Jesus. Has the Father gotten even more wondrous and beautiful to Jesus? Maybe for the first time in my life, I am happy that I began as a man. Having God help me in my weakness gives me a view and experience of God that no angel will ever have. We are spirits trapped in flesh; in our weakness He becomes our strength.

DAY 47
Christian Fatalism

He is before all things, and in Him all things hold together. He is also head of the body, the church; and He is the beginning, the firstborn from the dead, so that He Himself will come to have first place in everything.

— COLOSSIANS 1:17, 18

I was once in Burma to teach when my father and I had the opportunity to visit the world's largest stupa, the Buddhist temple that looks much like the cap on a Russian building and is representative of the large bubble that the Buddhists say makes up life. As the bubble stands alone, the weather attacks it and causes misery. For the Buddhist, to exist is pain and suffering, which is why nirvana is the ultimate goal of Buddhism, the reaching of a point of no longer existing and no more associated pain. Unfortunately, the Church is filled with a similar type of fatalism, for many believe that life in Christ will be miserable, nothing will work out, and the only relief that comes will be sometime in the future when they enter heaven. Is the Christian life merely a bubble with nothing within? Will we not have relief until we cease to exist in this body? May it never be! There is a special something within the Christian bubble, and all suffering has the purpose of releasing what is within, which is the life of Christ. Suffering releases love, joy, peace, patience, kindness, goodness, faithfulness, gentleness, and self-control. We need not be fatalists. We suffer the realities of being on planet earth, but we really live because of them! We must not let the enemy turn us into Christian fatalists.

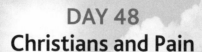

DAY 48
Christians and Pain

*Our present sufferings are not worth comparing with the
glory that will be revealed in us.*
— ROMANS 8:18

The question often arises, "Are Christians supposed
to suffer, to experience difficult times, and generally to
find themselves unhappy?" Pain and suffering are realities
common to all of mankind. The believer and unbeliever
alike suffer outwardly from nature, the physical body, or
from others, but a believer does not have to experience
destructive inward suffering such as that which plagues
those who do not know Christ. Christians have suffered
calamities common to everyone in the world but not
necessarily reacted in a like manner, whether with
depression, anger, frustration, or discouragement. Life
seems to deal its blows without partiality, and yet response
is varied, depending on the inner attitude of the sufferers.
It has been said that what becomes of us in the long
run depends upon what life finds in us! Suffering leaves
some bitter and others sweet! In the mountains it is not
uncommon to see a half-dead aspen tree. The sun that
shines on all of the branches brings increased life to some
and quickened decay to the others, depending on what
is inside the branch. Like the sun, suffering leaves some
persons withered and weak while others, because of the

life within, are stronger and more prepared for any amount of suffering.

I remember discipling two women, each one suffering at the hand of an unfaithful husband who sought to justify his behavior by picking his wife apart. One woman became absolutely radiant through her suffering, for she found Christ to be her ally and her all; the other became bitter and, to be honest, quite ugly as her inward stress disfigured her. Two women undergoing the same event displayed different reactions. One possessed an inner life that had met rejection and overcome with love; the other had not drawn from the source of her inner life and had been overcome by the rejection. As a believer, I cannot always determine what happens to me, but I can direct how it will affect me. If I am driven to reliance on the Lord, then the event will make me happy and more useful, bringing me to a fuller life. Events of life can either make me common or spiritually alive. I need never deal with pain on a human level; I bring God into my pain, for He can take what appears to be senseless suffering and turn it into a fountain of spiritual life. Suffering can have its roots in evil, but the issue is not really the basis from which it came but where it is permitted to take me. Placing God in the center of pain allows Him to guide me to deeper life. The cross is the perfect example of God-guided pain, where great suffering became life, not only to Christ, but also to millions.

DAY 49
Christians Do Not Need To Make Excuses

What good will it be for a man if he gains the whole world, yet forfeits his soul?

— MATTHEW 16:26

On a train in Europe I was sitting next to a couple of unbelievers and slowly beginning to talk about Jesus. They paused for some time before shooting me their pet trick question, "What do you think of holy wars? I do not see how we can call a war holy! It seems hypocritical!" I did not give a defense, though I knew he was talking about the Christians. Instead I began to talk about the Muslims, those most associated with holy wars, since they believe that their kingdom expands through the acquisition of lands. Once they have held territory, if they are ever forced to leave, they will have a holy war to repossess the place. Next are the Hindus, who, though forbidden to kill an animal, are allowed by their holy book to kill humans to expand their kingdom. These, too, are considered holy wars. The Buddhists also allow for the killing of people to protect or extend their kingdom. Finally, there are the Catholics, who through their holy wars were able to extend their kingdom and possessions. Holy wars as we know them are entirely an attempt to extend earthly kingdoms. All of this brings us to Jesus. He never had a holy war. His was not a visible kingdom made of land, possessions, and image.

His kingdom is invisible; nevertheless, to make gains in this kingdom requires a war. One fellow had been listening intently and asked, "What do you mean?" "Christ would rather gain a man's heart than take the man's home. He would rather see the light of God replace the darkness in man. There is no comparison." "Interesting! May I write to you and discuss this further?"

DAY 50
Claiming Your Heart

Take care, brethren, that there not be in any one of you an evil, unbelieving heart tha falls away from the living God.

— HEBREWS 3:12

Problems are common to mankind. Jesus Himself, having the body of a man, living in a man's world, and relating to others, makes an obvious statement, "In the world you have trouble." Yes, problems do exist. However, we must remain mindful that problems can never become our primary focus.

In Matthew 17:1-9, the writer relates to us that Jesus took with Him to the high mountain Peter, James, and John. When Moses and Elijah appeared, Peter exclaimed,

"I will build three tabernacles!" Of course it made sense to Peter to build one for each of the three, for Moses represented the law, Elijah the prophets, and Jesus grace and the new covenant. Peter made the mistake of equating the three. Immediately a cloud overshadowed them and the voice proclaimed, "This is My beloved Son, with whom I am well pleased; hear Him!" The disciples fell on their faces, Jesus touched them, the cloud departed, and only Jesus remained.

The highest part of a man's being is his heart, made only for one to occupy, that one being Jesus! If Moses and Elijah were not allowed to tabernacle on an equal plane on the mountain with Jesus, then should He have to share space in our hearts with our failures, our past, our mates, our children, other church members, sickness, or our financial situation? Many suffer from a crowded mountaintop; too many things occupy the place that only Christ is to possess. He is, in fact, King of the mountain, and once we give anything equal standing with Christ, no matter how good it appears or how great was its value in the past, a cloud will immediately overshadow our spirits. We will sense defeat, anger, frustration, and fear. The enemy will whisper that in order to get rid of the cloud, we must focus on all those things that bring the cloud; they must be resolved. However, the Holy Spirit whispers the opposite: Forget what brought the cloud, focus anew on Christ, and light and life will return. Not until we fall to our faces, yielding to the voice proclaiming, "This is my Son," will the cloud and our spirits lift.

DAY 51
The Blunter Side of Life

But the Lord answered and said to her, "Martha, Martha, you are worried and bothered about so many things."

— LUKE 10:41

Imagine a piece of steel five feet long, twelve inches wide, and two inches thick. You are told that you cannot rest until you have driven the object completely into the ground. Your work would be cut out for you; in fact, I doubt the job could be accomplished in one day, and you would become full of frustration, depression, fear, and anger. However, if one end of the steel were tapered sharply, like that of a pencil's tip, the task would be much simpler.

The average believer experiences much fear because his life is not focused on one thing but has become blunt with diverse points of interest, activity, and concentration: marriage, children, sin, others, vocation, and failure all get equal billing with Christ. Only when Christ alone becomes the soul's focus will the believer's life become sharpened and easily able to cut through the daily problems of life. Depression and anger come only when something other than Him is placed on the mountaintop of the heart.

Would you be a happy believer? Then remember there is nothing that the presence of Jesus will not cure. With this in mind your life will have focus and the edge to drive through any hindrance.

DAY 52
Comfortable With His Will?

And when you are praying, do not use meaningless repetition, as the Gentiles do, for they suppose that they will be heard for their many words. Therefore do not be like them; for your Father knows what you need, before you ask Him. Pray, then, in this way: Our Father who art in heaven, Hallowed be Thy name. Thy kingdom come. Thy will be done, On earth as it is in heaven. Give us this day our daily bread. And forgive us our debts, as we also have forgiven our debtors. And do not lead us into temptation, but deliver us from evil. For Thine is the kingdom, and the power, and the glory, forever. Amen.

— MATTHEW 6:7-13

The simple question occurs to us from time to time: If God knows what I need before I ask, and His will is going to be accomplished, then why should I even pray? Well, let us look at the facts. God is very comfortable with His will; it is a perfectly beautiful thing to every child of His. However, the more I focus on things of this earth and not the things of God, the more uncomfortable with His will I become and the more I must attempt to play God, for though I have God, I am living as though I do not. As I look at Him from a self-imposed distance, I become increasingly leery of His plans. What He is doing makes very little sense. In the end, I will come up with all sorts of anxiety-laden proposals for my life.

The secret is that prayer is not primarily for changing the will of God but to make us comfortable with His will! As we acknowledge His nearness to us, His love, voice, and care will be experienced. Remember, it is unbelief to think we ever have to move into the presence of God, for we constantly live in His presence. However, we sometimes act like children confined to a very small room, and though the Father is near, we stand aloof, facing the corner with our backs to Him. As we experience the character of God in prayer, we can shout, "Thy will be done!" We see there could be nothing better than His will! We want it, we pray for it, we want it for others, and we are comfortable.

DAY 53
Communicating Feelings

Search me, O God, and know my heart; test me and know my anxious thoughts. See if there is any offensive way in me, and lead me in the way everlasting.

— PSALM 139: 23, 24

Very few couples ever learn to communicate on the important level of how they feel. Most people live out of feelings, which should be communicated even if they are not based on fact. However, when beginning to describe how they feel, people often get bombarded with facts from their spouses intended to discredit what was said. It is interesting to watch the confrontation of a carnal person. First, he tries denial: "I did not do it!" Second, there is the rationalization of his/her behavior: "I had to do it." Then comes the accusation: "You made me do it," or, "You have done the same thing yourself." None of this makes for great conversation that goes anywhere. The spiritual man does none of the above when confronted, neither immediately accepting (unless conviction from God previously existed) nor immediately rejecting the claims, but laying his heart before God and letting God probe. If what was said is true, then there is repentance.

Let others tell you how they feel. You may be hearing only false feelings, but a spiritual response from you will help reveal this. Get in the other person's shoes and understand the feelings and why they might be occurring, without responding in a manner calculated to defend your self. This will help both of you move past those feelings to the Truth, Christ.

DAY 54
Complete in Him

But we preach Christ crucified, to Jews a stumbling block, and to Gentiles foolishness.
— I CORINTHIANS 1:23

I rejoice to begin each sermon with this statement, "I have nothing that you need." It is true! Anyone who has Christ is in need of nothing that I have. Paul says in Colossians 1:28, "And we proclaim Him, admonishing every man and teaching every man with all wisdom, that we may present every man complete in Christ." Any person in Christ is complete; if so, then what will I add to that completeness? I might spend some time expounding on what completeness in Him means, but I have nothing to give by way of an addition. The believer is complete.

In advertising I was taught that a hook is necessary in order to make a product appealing, cause it to stand out from others, and even make it an object of lust. Unfortunately, Christianity has become a product with apparently hundreds of brands that compete with one another. Careful listening reveals the hook adopted by proponents of each brand. Some travel around the world placing their feet on the soil they are to pray for, some know Greek, some boast in having received a one-time fix or an incredible experience, and some have even had an exchange. All of the hooks may sound good and have their own certain appeal, but the hooks are also exalted above the person of Christ. Many of these things will be revealed in someone's completeness in Christ, but they do not make that believer special or more complete. I call it pyramid preaching when someone purports to stand above the crowd to proclaim his Jesus-plus addition, looking down on the lowly masses of believers, encouraging them to become like him, and all the while emphasizing his superiority and their inferiority in the faith. Pyramid preachers exhaust me.

The day you accepted Christ you moved to the top of the pyramid, and no one has something that you need, for you have everything in Him. True faith spends more time advertising Christ than it does the spectacular that comes from Christ. Rejoice in faith, Believer, for you are complete in Christ.

DAY 55
Condemnation Reveals the Heart

There is therefore now no condemnation for those who are in Christ Jesus.

— ROMANS 8:1

Often when I am speaking I want to make a point by asking everyone in the audience that has experienced condemnation as a Christian to raise their hands. Everyone who raises his hand has, at one time or another, been like the Galatians, who had cast Christ aside and put their trust in something else. "You have been severed from Christ, you who are seeking to be justified by law; you have fallen from grace," Galatians 5:4. When we have trusted in something other than Christ and have failed, we felt condemned because we believed that our standing in God was based on our behavior. The sense of condemnation is a revelation of where our hearts look to find peace, either in Jesus or in our own effort. Obedience is a separate topic from acceptance. If acceptance were based on our obedience, then what would Christ really mean to us? As it is, with our acceptance secured in Him, He means everything to us. If we want to be free from condemnation, we must not determine to do better but rather confess our disbelief in the Son, turn from it, and acknowledge His work.

DAY 56
Contrast Changes People

And if any place will not welcome you or listen to you,
shake the dust off your feet when you leave,
as a testimony against them.
— MARK 6:11

As a believer you must understand that it is contrast, not conflict, which changes people. If someone will not be quiet and let others talk, do not bring it to his attention; simply be quiet yourself and let him talk. Contrast will be the loudest protest. There are some topics that you simply cannot discuss with certain people. Those topics are easy to spot, for when you make an observation, halfway through the sentence, before you have completed the thought, they will be disagreeing with you. Do you have to discuss those topics? If not, simply change topics, continue loving, and move on. The contrast is that you did not get upset over those things.

Over the years, through several hundred hours of lecturing, I have developed something of a thick skin. I have been accused of things I was not doing or teaching, of things I was doing, and of things I could not see I was doing. However, experience has proven that the best approach is to keep my eyes off the accusations and on the Father, to maintain moment-by-moment abiding. In that context, with His light shining on my problems, His might is there to set me free, and He is the One I want to please.

DAY 57
Crying

Those who sow in tears shall reap with joyful shouting.
— PSALM 126:5

Whatever Jesus did or said had eternal significance. Often I like to go through the gospels and only read the red-lettered words of Jesus; I love to hear His teaching. I thought recently that I should ponder the very first thing that He ever uttered while living as a Man on earth. Actually, it was not a word, but a sound, a cry. The first thing that came out of the mouth of Jesus was a cry. What is the message in God Himself crying, what does the cry of a baby solicit from us, and what have our own tears taught us?

The cry of a baby demands examination of the situation by the parents and their provision of what is needed. A cry is a proclamation of helplessness, dependence, trust, and need, the recognition that "I cannot." If Jesus would acknowledge His existence in such a way, then should we not also? When we cry, we are heard by the same Father in heaven who heard Him.

There is simply too much stress that comes from not crying. Several years ago a chemical was discovered in the brain of anxiety-ridden people. For years chemists have attempted to neutralize the chemical in hopes of bringing relief to the suffering. To date no medication has proven effective. However, if the tears of the afflicted are analyzed, one will find the anxiety-causing chemical being released. Tears acknowledge the true condition within that we cannot always see or express. We were not created to be God but to need God. Trying to fulfill a job description for which we are not created causes anxiety. Tears are proof that we have begun to give up on playing God. It is pride that keeps us from crying out and therefore keeps us in misery.

If we humans run to the sound of a cry and act on behalf of a distressed person, how much more will the Lord respond to the cries of His children? Just as parents do not always pander to a child's every cry, the Lord does not always intervene immediately to relieve our sources of misery; but as we acknowledge, "Apart from You I can do nothing," look for the Great "I CAN" to eventually move in. Both our waiting and His moving build faith.

DAY 58
Daily Decisions

He again fixes a certain day, "Today," saying through
David after so long a time just as has been said before,
"TODAY, IF YOU HEAR HIS VOICE, DO NOT
HARDEN YOUR HEARTS."
— HEBREWS 4:7

I believe a common misconception concerning decision-making is that it is for the future, when decisions are just for today. God is the God of today, and therefore, decisions must be made in the light of our relationship with Him today. If a decision can be made presently that locks up the future, how is that living in faith, which is the assurance of things hoped for and the conviction of things not seen? Let me give an example. A young woman prayed and asked God to lead her in a decision concerning marriage. Everyone, myself included, believed that she was free to become engaged to a certain young man, and so she did. Several months later, when she called her fiancé at the university, she learned from his roommate that he was off visiting his fiancée in another country. She called the number the roommate gave her and discovered that her beau was breaking off his engagement to her in favor of marrying another. In conclusion, she stated, "I will never know what the will of God is; I believed it was His will for me to wed this man." Was she right in getting engaged? Had she heard the Lord? Did she make a mistake? I think not. The enemy would have us believe that a decision made today must affect all eternity; that simply is not true. Walking in faith means making decisions not based on outcome but founded in the principle of the Lord's leading and what He is teaching today. I believe she made the right decision on the day she agreed to marry the fellow. Later, because of that decision and the subsequent breakup, God has done some wonderful things in her life. She drew near to God in her pain, discovered a comfort in Him that she had never known before, and was now moving again in faith. Only God knows the future, so a decision made today may not affect the future like we thought it would, but that does not lead to the assumption that we were erroneous in hearing the Lord when the decision was made. It was a steppingstone to the future. The important thing is hearing Him today.

"Today, if you hear His voice, do not harden your heart." If I walk in the valley of the shadow of death TODAY, He is with me. However, if I want to ponder walking in the shadow of death tomorrow, He is not with me. If I move into the future, I will move alone. He is the God of today.

DAY 59
Death!

For the Lord Himself will descend from heaven with a shout, with the voice of {the} archangel, and with the trumpet of God; and the dead in Christ shall rise first.
— I THESSALONIANS 4:16

I find it interesting that when humanism competes with any religion, it self-proclaims its superiority. It cannot compete with Jesus, who was, to say the least, unique and not of the world; He brought us the wisdom of heaven and teaching not heard in any religion. He is higher than all the man-inspired philosophies, systems, compassion, or love. The humanists are working hard to make Christianity out to be a hate religion. We know that true hate is to see a man being destroyed and to say nothing. If only for this reason, the humanists prove themselves to be full of hate, which does not exclude them from being wickedly wise. Since the believer has the hope of heaven, death on earth is not paramount in our thinking. It is here that the humanists believe they have found the chink in our armor. They are all about life on earth and want to appear to be very compassionate. They constantly cry, "See the suffering children, see how many have died from disease, see how easy it would be to alleviate suffering, and see how we have the answer?" The humanist has made death out to be the worst thing possible; it reveals his heart, for to him it will be the worst thing possible. However, we are not to be deceived into his way of thinking. Death is not the worst thing that can happen to a person, whose life on this earth was never meant to last forever. Christians are a unique group that does not fear death. Yet more and more believers are sacrificing integrity and effort to support the cause of doing anything and everything to see life on earth continue. Matthew 10:28, "And do not fear those who kill the body, but are unable to kill the soul; but rather fear Him who is able to destroy both soul and body in hell."

DAY 60
Did God Create Pride?

Do you not know? Have you not heard? The Everlasting God, the LORD, the Creator of the ends of the earth does not become weary or tired. His understanding is inscrutable.

— ISAIAH 40:28

God has several names, which allows us to form a better understanding of Him who made us. "Creator" is one of those names. Art reveals something about the artist, and creation reveals something about the Creator. To God, the creation is an extension of His character, not an "it," an object to be used or something without life. No person can set boundaries for what the Creator creates, for anyone who attempts to do so has been created himself; any boundaries are self-imposed by the Creator, but they are absolute. Some of the boundaries of creation include these: He will show regard, respect, and love for the work of His hands rather than treat it with indifference; He will remove chaos; He will take responsibility for what is made. This is ultimate humility.

"And God created man in His own image, in the image of God He created him; male and female He created them" (Genesis 1:27). "Then the LORD God said, 'Behold, the man has become like one of Us, knowing good and evil'" (Genesis 3:22). Everything else is created by God but is not like God. However, the Creator creates man in His own image. Being like God affords us the ultimate choice of either walking in humility or pride. Humility voluntarily chooses to esteem God and all things created. Pride chooses to treat God and His creation as enemies, with no regard, respect, or caring; pride would invite in confusion and take no responsibility.

Pride does not emanate from the Heavenly Father, so where did it come from? Since God in humility has chosen to treat creation as a living thing, and in His image we are given choice, pride originates in the choice. Humility relates to creation, but pride is indifferent to all things and treats them as though they are dead! Pride makes God out to be dead, man to be dead, truth to be dead, and hope to be dead. It even murdered the most alive Man that ever walked on the earth! Is it any wonder that we are commanded to pray, "Deliver us from evil"? God in humility creates, and pride, by its very nature, destroys. We see, then, why pride can so easily take created beauty, treat it indifferently, and cause the result: an unnatural thing called sin. Many refuse to hear it, but AIDS came about this very way. AIDS is not created by God; it is the result of pride! AIDS does not have its root in the Creator; the fingerprint of pride is all over it. AIDS and every other sin enters the world through pride, and all the created world then bears the weight of it, moaning as it looks for its redemption.

DAY 61
Did God Create Satan? Sin?

There was a man in the land of Uz whose name was Job;
and that man was blameless, upright, fearing God,
and turning away from evil.

— JOB 1:1

It is helpful to understand that pride comes before sin. Pride misuses the natural, as mentioned above, and sin is the result. Pride would dominate with no regard for that which it controls. This is where Satan reveals himself to be pure, unadulterated, unrefined pride. God did not create Satan; He created a heavenly being that chose pride, and this resulted in something called Satan. He is like the locust that devours without ever looking back and then moves on to the next living thing. The enemy has no regard for human life or things created above in the heavens or below on the earth. He destroys and takes no responsibility for it. Satan sought to totally destroy Job, and for what? For nothing! For his pride alone does Satan destroy! If Satan is destroying your family, know this: it is for nothing!

Sin is not a created thing but something that comes as a result. Created things are formed from nothing and exist as though they always were. Sin is the result of two created things being misused. For example, men and women have a natural sex desire; that is not sin. But then pride comes bringing chaos with no consideration, and the two natural desires interact in an unnatural act—sex without marriage—and sin occurs. Sin is therefore a result of pride.

The mule—the outcome of the mating of a horse and a donkey that cannot reproduce itself—can be an example of something that is not a created being but is a result. Because the mule is a result being, to be rid of it we would have to attack that from which it springs, its source; all mules would naturally disappear if every horse or donkey were killed. Sin is a result of two natural things doing the unnatural. Sin is the result of the inner and outer life of man saying no in pride to the Creator. Sin is a parasite on the back of creation, the unnatural living on the natural. This is why God did not attack the result (sin), but allowed the inner life (Adam life) to be killed on the cross with Christ, and thus sin's source (Adam Life) was destroyed. The new inner life we receive, Christ's life, never agrees with the unnatural and brings the outer life under its subjection. Every person who becomes a believer brings a deathblow to sin and death. "For the flesh sets its desire against the Spirit, and the Spirit against the flesh; for these are in opposition to one another, so that you may not do the things that you please" (Galatians 5:17).

DAY 62
Discipline Versus Punishment

*Furthermore, we had earthly fathers to discipline us, and
we respected them; shall we not much rather be subject to
the Father of spirits, and live?*

— HEBREWS 12:9

Church discipline has often baffled me, for it seems to be much more church punishment than discipline. A man was trapped in sin, but he repented; a year later when he told the church leadership of his experience, they disciplined him. He had moved past the sin, yet they punished him and stripped him of his position. I think that his experience may be common, because many seem to have no understanding of the purpose of church discipline, for which I will offer an explanation. We fall out with God before we fall out with one another or fall into sin. Sin is the cobweb, but the falling out is the spider. We need not go for the cobweb when we can go for the spider. If brothers or sisters have fallen out with God, they will begin to walk in the flesh and infect the whole body. We must discipline them. We need not punish them, since sin and punishment are one and the same; the moment they started sinning, they started punishing themselves. What they need is the discipline of falling back in with God, of spending time with Him, of listening to Him, and of being loved by Him. Pull them aside and discipline them by seeing that they spend time with Him and urging them away from all that would distract from Jesus. Steer them away from leadership, giving them time to listen to the good Shepherd; let them be disciplined while falling back to Jesus. Once this is done, all is complete. No longer bring up the failure; whatever it was is not as critical as the fact that they were deceived into falling away from the abiding presence of Jesus. There will be the odd time when we discover that the persons never really wanted Jesus and they do not want Him now. They do not need to be put out of the fellowship, for God has already done that. Just agree with what He has done and wait. If they fall back into Jesus, they will then be welcome.

DAY 63
Division of Soul and Spirit

For the word of God is living and active. Sharper than any double-edged sword, it penetrates even to dividing soul and spirit, joints and marrow; it judges the thoughts and attitudes of the heart.

— HEBREWS 4:12

Many are in the process of having soul and spirit divided. Life is to be found within the spirit, yet many interpret quality of life in the spirit by what is happening in the soul. The day Christ entered the believer's life, He brought along a treasure chest full of all that is needed for successful living. The chest holds acceptance, love, assurance, security, commitment, and daily help. This chest, however, lies in the spirit, though the immature believer continues to look outside of the spirit for fulfillment. He turns to the soul for completion through the intellect (if only he can understand how he acts), through a strong will (if he can only change what he hates and acquire righteousness), or through changing emotions (if only he could feel loved, accepted, and valued). He looks to the body for satisfaction in attractiveness. Fulfillment is believed to come through the accolades of others: children, mates, friends, family, parents, and co-workers. Titles and vocations promise to fill the emptiness.

If you were God, what would you do to divide soul and spirit to force the believer to look deeper and discover all the riches of Christ that dwell within the spirit? That would be important, for if the believer could discover that true life is within, then nothing outside him would be able to destroy him. It does not mean that the believer would live the life of the unaffected (as a Hindu), but it does mean that the believer would be able to sing hymns in prison. First, would you not make all knowledge fail and emotions sink and lose their attractiveness? Second, would you not allow the will of man to fail him as it loses control in some area of life? Finally, if you were God, would you not cause both the world and all those in whom the believer trusts to fail to meet his deepest needs?

This is the dark wedge, the sword that God drives between soul and spirit. "The word of God is living and active, and sharper than a two-edged sword, able to divide soul and spirit." The "Word of God," naturally, refers to Jesus. He personally does the work of dividing, and when the separation is occurring, many believers despair and consider this experience to be the most difficult of all; they become frantic, worried, confused, angry, and bitter as they clamor for the return of happiness in the flesh.

However, we should be encouraged that it is through this very experience that we grow to become men and women of faith. The whole process is called the baptism of fire, whereby the leaven of the past is totally stopped. [This is in reference to the means of preserving wine from becoming vinegar in biblical times. Once the wine had reached its peak fermentation, the entire container was lowered into a fire, killing any leaven that would continue the fermentation process.] We learn that nothing outside the spirit can ultimately destroy us. We discover our freedom from all that used to hold us hostage. We learn how sufficient He is to supply our every need. And when the process is completed and we enter into ultimate productivity and true humility, we may possess nothing outside of the spirit, but neither does anything possess or hinder us. We now understand the great emptiness that resulted from seeking life outside the spirit. Those lesser things we trusted have dried up. Future confrontations by external adverse circumstances will not stifle and hinder the release of life. We have walked the path intended for those who would experience the very deepest work of the Lord. We cannot emphasize enough to others the importance of completing the course and learning about life in the spirit. We are free, we have found the life within, we live out of the treasure chest, and we are thankful.

DAY 64
Do Carnal People Want Truth?

*In whose case the god of this world has blinded the minds
of the unbelieving so that they might not see the light of the
gospel of the glory of Christ, who is the image of God.*

— II CORINTHIANS 4:4

*For a child will be born to us, a son will be given to us;
and the government will rest on His shoulders; and His
name will be called Wonderful Counselor, Mighty God,
Eternal Father, Prince of Peace.*

— ISAIAH 9:6

When Christ enters a heart, a person's eyes are opened
to see things clearly as they are. The illusion of the world is
revealed—its inconsistencies and lies—and this knowledge
is then used to turn him to the pursuit of the invisible
kingdom, the kingdom of the Son of God. He is discerning
and verbalizing things he never before could have and
enjoying revelation that is so freeing. There is a problem,
though, in that it is only natural for him to believe that
others would like to have what he now possesses that makes
a new worldview seem so obvious.

For instance, it is estimated that across the United States
50,000 new laws are passed every year. In twenty years that
is one million new laws. Each law could be construed as
a means to take away a public right. At a minimum the
government has determined that a million rights that we
had twenty years ago may no longer be rights. In fact, the

government does not seem to believe that we have rights that cannot be eroded, while at the same time an attempt is made to stir women into thinking that abortion is a right, a ridiculous assertion. However, it is quite clear that not all unbelievers would like to listen to this type of logic, and it is a mistake to believe that carnal man wants truth (neither did the believer when he was carnal). It is only as we love the TRUTH that true things become appealing and compelling. Therefore, our job is not to dissuade men concerning their inconsistencies and illogical thinking, but to persuade people of the TRUTH. Many Christians have gotten involved in politics because they saw things clearly and assumed that constituents wanted to hear true things. They were disappointed to the extent that carnal, fallen man does not want to hear true things no matter how intellectual or refined the thought might be.

DAY 65
Do - Do

Did you receive the Spirit by observing the law, or by believing what you heard? Are you so foolish? After beginning with the Spirit, are you now trying to attain your goal by human effort?

— GALATIANS 3:2, 3

We know that the warnings in the book of Hebrews, chapters 3 and 4, center in the refusal of the believers to enter into the rest of God. Like the Galatians, they were trusting in their ability and had laid aside the work of Christ.

Our carnal side is accustomed to working in order to be pleasing rather than working because we are pleasing. Working to be pleasing feels natural, for we are conditioned from birth that our efforts will gain the desired rewards from others. The tree of the knowledge of good and evil encourages this distorted perception of living by teaching that doing evil will produce rejection and doing good will supposedly produce righteousness and acceptance. When we approach Scripture with this false theology, all we see are the do's, those things that we need to accomplish. The problem is that man has never been able to do enough to gain God's acceptance; that is the very reason that we need Christ. The belief that doing can replace faith will make us so discouraged that we will be forced to return to Him by way of the doing of the Son. Hence, we experience the goodness of God, which leads us to a deeper understanding of Christ and a submission to the work of the Savior within.

Here is an interesting Scripture in the Old Testament that describes what happens when man will not rest in the work of God.

"'This is the resting place, let the weary rest'; and
'This is the place of repose'—but they would not listen.
So then, the word of the LORD to them will become:
Do and do, do and do, rule on rule, rule on rule;
a little here, a little there—so that they will go and fall
backward, be injured and snared and captured."
(Isaiah 28:12, 13)

Either we rest or God will wear us out with the do's!

DAY 66
Do The Strong Have Something That You Do Not?

. . . to another faith by the same Spirit, and to another gifts of healing by the one Spirit.

— I CORINTHIANS 12:9

I said something to a pastor that gave me great joy. "Do you realize, Brother, that none of the great preachers have anything that we do not?" It delighted me to know that this man had everything that other "great" men had; he was just as good a preacher, just as gifted from the Spirit, and he had a great faith. What he did not have is something, sadly, possessed by many of the greats; he did not have appealing flesh. He was preaching from the cockpit of an old airplane that had been assembled onstage for effect, and he was performing miracles desirable to the flesh. He was not an overly attractive man; it was obvious that in the flesh he did not have everything the "great" men do, but he was not striving to be great in any sense.

I love the Spirit, and, in a sense, I love the flesh, for both are the great equalizers. In the Spirit we all have the same gifts and there are no "great" men. In the flesh, the "great" men are not any better than the "poor no-hopers" to whom they are ministering. It is great!

DAY 67
Do We Need To Confess EVERY Sin?

If we confess our sins, He is faithful and just and will forgive us our sins and purify us from all unrighteousness.

— I JOHN 1:9

In the Old Testament times, a sacrifice was made available that would cover any unknown sin. God provided for the fact that man sinned unknowingly. God is absolute, and sin is sin. It is interesting that those who dogmatically say we must confess every sin have only confessed every sin of which they are aware, not every sin. The Apostle John was a holy man who stayed next to Jesus, was the first at the tomb, was loved by our Lord, and is referred to as the apostle of love. Yet in Revelation, in the presence of Jesus, he falls down in fear as a dead man. Ultimately, trying to confess every sin is impossible. Not everything that is true is truth; a teaching may come from Scripture and be true but not truth. How do we tell the difference between the two? Teaching that lands at our feet and tells us what we must do is not truth. Teaching that ends at the feet of Jesus and explains what He does for us is truth. Jesus is the way, the truth, and the life; few doctrines are truth. We have all witnessed how easy it is for people to become obsessed with confession and, in so doing, to neglect a focus on Christ. We have a sacrifice that is for unknown sin, Jesus. There is no hindrance between the believer and God.

How, then, does a sin come to mind to be confessed? As I said before, we have only confessed according to our perception. Often I counsel people and see in their lives sin with which God is not yet dealing; if I were to bring up that sin that God has not yet brought up, I introduce it without power as mere judgment on my part. When God reveals sin to a person, the revelation comes with the power to be free. Confession is then a delight. God pursues His purposes with a measureless I.Q. we can think of as well over 999 trillion. His conviction will come in an orderly manner, for He knows when, where, and in what order to work. God will convict as needed, and the believer will confess and experience the freedom that was always his in Him. In the meantime, he has a sacrifice for every sin.

DAY 68
Does God Have a Sex Drive?

For the eyes of the LORD move to and fro throughout the earth that He may strongly support those whose heart is completely His.

— II CHRONICLES 16:9

Does God have a sex drive? Maybe a better question would be, "Why does God give man a sex drive?" There are few things within man as dangerous as the sex drive, which has been the cause of untold misery and suffering. Why, then, knowing the misuse that would come about, did God give man such a desire? Man is made in the image of God, and therefore, understanding God can come from looking at man, just as looking to God can bring understanding about man. As we look at man the legitimate question can be asked, "Does God have a sex drive?" The answer is an astounding, "Yes!" However, we must define the sex drive properly. Its purpose is actually the pursuit of intimacy. This is why those addicted to sex will never find satisfaction, for they are attempting to fulfill the craving for intimacy through the repetition of a physical act. Sex without intimacy is nothing more than feeding the flesh a junk-food snack, which brings only a very temporary physical satisfaction. The question, then, becomes, "Does God have an intimacy drive?" Yes!

I was joking with some of the young men in a Bible school and telling them I knew that as they entered the lecture hall, their eyes were moving to and fro in the hope of making eye contact with one of the young women. If that happened, they would get encouraged and next begin to pass by the girl on a frequent basis in anticipation that perhaps the fleeting glance was something more. If that effort were rewarded, they would have the confidence to talk to the girl, ask her out, and begin to woo her. One day they would be quite excited if the young woman told them that she had chosen them! It is the drive for intimacy that causes all such behavior.

Now multiply the sex drive times one hundred, call it the drive for intimacy, and you will begin to get a picture of the drive for intimacy that exists within the love of God.

His eyes search to and fro for the one who will meet His glance. If our eyes meet His, he begins to woo us, and one day we choose Him! God's drive for intimacy is so great, and yet it is constrained by our choice. He does not practice spiritual rape. We must choose Him, desire Him, and respond to His advances. How often we hear how man thinks that God does not love us! That is foolishness!

Through God's drive for intimacy, He wants to conceive something in our spirit, not our mind, will, or emotions. "Joseph, son of David, do not be afraid to take Mary as your wife; for the Child who has been conceived in her is of the Holy Spirit" (Matthew 1:20). We stand enthralled at a virgin birth where Christ was formed in Mary. However, He has been birthed in us, also. A conception, in the love of God, has taken place in every child of God. When the sex drive is defined properly as the drive for intimacy, we understand both God's heart and man's need for intimacy. Satan does not have a creative bone in his body; he must watch to see what God is doing and then tempt us with something that is off. We see this clearly when Moses was with the magicians that could only attempt to duplicate what God did first. Therefore, when God creates the drive for intimacy, Satan sees the opportunity for perverting it and offers man the possibilities for physical activity with the exclusion of intimacy. The problem with a lone physical act's not bringing the desired expression of intimacy yields a drive for sex that is quite animalistic and unsatisfactory. There is no need to discuss where it goes from there. Sex as expressed in the world is simply off!

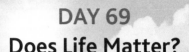

DAY 69
Does Life Matter?

Whether, then, you eat or drink or whatever you do,
do all to the glory of God.
— I CORINTHIANS 10:31

I often hear sermons wherein the listeners are admonished to live for the future. The argument is that all we possess, anything we have ever done, or any illness that has overcome us will not matter in heaven. In fact, the worries, hurts, and disappointments of today are not even to be considered in light of the great someday when we will be in heaven and all of God's promises are revealed. All that will matter in heaven are the things of heaven. However, the goal in life when this emphasis is embraced becomes "hanging in there," just toughing it out until heaven. Consequently, this emphasis leaves some of us believing that the daily components of life simply do not matter. The contention that life is misery was continually told to one struggling fellow; he was assured that if he would just hang in there until heaven, relief would then come. Finally, he made what would seem to be a quite logical leap as expressed in his suicide note. In light of how he perceived that teaching, he simply decided to bypass the struggle and misery of daily living and go directly to bliss.

Some emphasize knowledge as the end goal of the earthly, daily experiences of life. That is, every situation in life is to teach us something. If we are faithful to learn, we go to heaven having become experts at living on the earth. However, the understanding of how to live on earth would not appear to be of great practical value in heaven, and who among us maintains that learning the hard way from our experiences is appealing? Do we relish a continuing education course that instills firsthand knowledge from such hardships as watching a loved one die, observing a child on drugs, hearing the news of an unfaithful mate, or losing a job? Just how will all of this knowledge help in heaven? If life is to teach, many believe they have already learned enough. Is life just an endurance test?

Others have declared that the purpose of life is doing. "It matters not what you believe; what do you do?" When things get tough, they assert, the tough get going. The adversities in life are meant to separate the sheep from the goats, the successful from the failures, and the weak from the strong. Every event in life is a challenge, but they maintain that man can get the job done. They will keep every command and despise those who do not. The interesting thing is that their definitions of success are always contrived to reflect the scope of their own abilities, and the problem is that if life presents one adversity that cannot be mastered, then what was the purpose of overcoming the previous thousand? I have consistently found that it only takes three questions to discover what any particular doer cannot do. I have seen many half-built bridges around the world; construction was going so well until some one thing hindered, but that one thing was the most important thing. Is the purpose of life's circumstances to see how much we can overcome?

I listened to an old man in Ukraine as he related his prison experience of twenty years, followed by another seven for refusing to renounce Christ. He told of miracle after miracle that took place during his incarceration. My spirit leapt within me, for I was so encouraged with hope by the testimony. I could not bring myself to say that all of his suffering was bad, for he had been led to participation in Life in new and wondrous ways. "And as for you, you meant evil against me, {but} God meant it for good in order to bring about this present result, to preserve many people alive" (Genesis 50:20). When it is revealed that "all things" work together for the good of those who love Him, we come to understand that nothing is meaningless. A flat tire, the rebellious child, empty pockets, a lost inheritance, or the death of a loved one all move me toward Life. Paul understood. "Bless those who persecute you; bless and curse not" (Romans 12:14). When God, in His love, mercy, and grace, decides to move me near, the problems line up one behind the other. They step forward one at a time until I give up and turn to Him. Once in His lap, I so enjoy myself that I look back at the problems and thank God for them.

We believers do not have to fear that when lying on our deathbeds we will have to say, "Life was meaningless." We did not know which car to buy, so we prayed. We did not know what to do for the child, so we prayed. We were suffering with ill health, and we prayed. We were rejected by family, so we prayed. None of the mundane or miserable circumstances of life were meaningless to us when they propelled us into the Father's presence.

DAY 70
Does Self Add To The Meaning of Life?

Nobody should seek his own good, but the good of others.
— I CORINTHIANS 10:24

There appears to be one common denominator in the multitude of approaches to understanding life, and that is self-life. "What is the benefit in life for me? Can suffering be justified for me? Can my marriage breakup, the loss of my job, my unwed pregnant daughter, my illness, or the rejection of others somehow be advantageous to me? Will knowledge help me? How will all my efforts profit me? If not now, will there be a good return for me in heaven? Will I find out then that I was really being blessed by all of those mishaps?"

Recently I was listening to a pastor in Africa relate how the marriage ministry had depleted the thrust of the church. Those participating had decided they were not to minister to others until every minute detail of their marriages was worked out. It seems the husbands could not justify evangelizing, ministering to the poor, or helping the sick as long as there was a dissatisfied wife at home. The pastor's conclusion was that the whole bunch had become too selfish; they wanted perfect comfort before they ministered to the world's discomfort. I agreed.

One fellow took care of his ailing parent only to ensure the security of his inheritance. A lady called nearly everyone in a small town to describe her husband's onset of cancer, and then proceeded to explain to each one how much she would be suffering! A man divorced his wife for a younger woman and then wanted to know how he was supposed to maintain his preferred lifestyle with the financial burden of a divorce settlement. It is often hard to discern if parents want the child to walk with God for the child's benefit or their own identity. Self is no stranger to desiring a throne, crown, and scepter and using others as its footstool.

Each day the first person we touch, clothe, see in the mirror, feel comfort or physical pain from, feed, and emotionally sense is our self. Is it any wonder that the enemy would choose to make self a stumbling block? Each day starts with us; why not continue from that point and make self the obsession? More often than not, the point stressed in teaching heard on radio or television is self, whether it is being blessed or cursed. The frustrating thing is that there is no happiness derived from self-absorption.

DAY 71
Self Is A Hindrance To God?

For by the grace given me I say to every one of you: Do not think of yourself more highly than you ought, but rather think of yourself with sober judgment, in accordance with the measure of faith God has given you.

— ROMANS 12:3

Stop for a minute and take a good look at the self of man. Man hates himself as just man! Self in Adam and Eve was attracted to the tree offering Godlikeness with its lists of what to do and not do. It was not life but bondage. True Life was a few feet away in a completely different tree; no serpent was tempting Adam and Eve to eat of that tree. Man left the Garden still hoping to fulfill the dream of being God; however, he has failed miserably. I have yet to see a monkey or a dog dressed in human clothing that looks anything short of inane. Similarly, man is man, and every attempt to cover himself with something more Godlike just leaves man looking stupid. Man may try to appear more tolerable by covering himself with knowledge, possessions, or power, and he might even surround himself with worshippers. Man can even use his own self-hatred by comforting himself with the feelings of humility, hopelessness, humanity, and victimization. From running inconsistent campaigns for the highest offices to committing suicide, man's actions prove that he has utterly failed at playing God.

We have become a society of selfish Christians—and I am not excluding myself—wrapping our lives around ourselves and bedeviled by how every action of others or ours affects our self-lives. We cannot tell the truth because someone may not like us, but we do not like ourselves when we lie. We desire others to meet our needs, yet when similar requirements are placed on us, we run, for to meet others' needs might necessitate neglecting our own. We change the teaching of Christ to fit ourselves and only end up changing ourselves into something that is not a good fit.

Now the good news: Nothing is naturally against the believer. There is not a single thing that goes wrong in our lives. There is nothing pitted against us. Life is not a meaningless, senseless string of disturbing occurrences. Life is not an endless exam administered by a demanding principal. Life is not an endurance test. Life is not accumulating as much knowledge as possible. Life is not staring at our spouses with heart-shaped eyeballs. Life is not being perfect parents, employees, or pastors. Life is meaningless and boring when it wraps itself around ourselves, draws our attention to ourselves, and leaves us wondering at our condition. Why? True life is Jesus and Life obsessed not on us but on the Father in Heaven.

All things are tools in God's hand, employed by Him in His ministry to us and in revealing His glory. John 12:28, "'Father, glorify Thy name.' There came therefore a voice out of heaven: 'I have both glorified it, and will glorify it again.'" Events and happenings are not the elements of life; rather, they are the elements that drive us to Life (Jesus). Nothing is bad if it drives us to Life. This awareness does not come through understanding but by revelation. Anything and everything that moves us near Life is good.

DAY 72
Removal Of Self-Centeredness Leads To Life

But {women} shall be preserved through the
bearing of children.

— I TIMOTHY 2:15

Preserved literally means saved, and saved, as used in the New Testament, refers to being delivered from the self and its manifestations. The greatest hindrance to being delivered from the events that present themselves today is self and its propensity toward obsessing on what will never help it . . . which is itself. A mother has a unique experience in that she might be the most self-centered person in the world, but then in an instant when the doctor lays a baby in her arms, her self-centeredness gives way to focus on another through caring for the baby. Life and death for the baby is determined by the degree to which the mother moves away from being self-centered. I have asked many in ministry, and all seem to agree that women respond first to the Gospel. Why? If they are mothers, then self, the only hindrance to Christ, has been dealt a severe blow in childbirth. With self-life knocked from the paramount position, the women can more easily draw near to Jesus, finding Life and deliverance.

"But {women} shall be preserved through the bearing of children." The understanding to be derived is not that women who cannot or have not had children cannot be saved from self-centeredness. I personally have never given birth to a child, and yet I have every intention of being saved! The analogy is twofold. The birth of a child removes self-centeredness, and this birth happened in pain. The believer has a new birth, a new life that has dealt a fatal deathblow to self; because of this death he can have Life. This birth came through pain. Is the woman's pain in childbirth bad? Yes, but I cannot believe it is not worth it after observing the countenance of my wife as she held each of our newborns. Is the pain of events, disappointments, and relationships really bad when they lead to Life? No, nothing with such a result is ultimately bad. Children of God are faith people and the only people on the face of the planet that can say that.

DAY 73
Reversals That Lead To Life

Just as it is written, "For Your sake we are being put to death all day long; we were considered as sheep to be slaughtered." But in all these things we overwhelmingly conquer through Him who loved us.

— ROMANS 8:36, 37

The kiwi plant of New Zealand must have a frost in order to bud and bear fruit and a later frost to force sugar into the fruit. When the weather does not thus cooperate, farmers will stress the plants to the point of death with a chemical in order to induce flowering and sugaring. It is the winter with its near-death experience that allows the kiwi to bear good fruit.

Believers will not bear fruit without near-death experiences of their own; the proof of resurrection power will always be the marks of death. Winter under God's supervision is not a bad thing, though that is the season in which the enemy will take advantage and seize his greatest opportunity; his activity, we should remember, is always overseen by God. Surely it is for the sake of pride that Satan continues to operate under terms wherein God turns what was meant for evil into good.

There was a fisherman whose fish were always fresh. In fact, he sold his fish alive, while the others found it impossible to keep their fish alive after taking them from the lake. It was discovered that his secret was to keep a catfish, a natural predator of the other fish, in the bottom of the tank to make the fish alert and active with their eyes on the enemy.

The enemy is the one who keeps us active and alert, for though he may place marks of death on us, in Christ we are always alive.

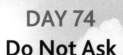

DAY 74
Do Not Ask

*Who knows whether He will {not} turn and relent, and
leave a blessing behind Him.*

— JOEL 2:14

*For who among men knows the {thoughts} of a man
except the spirit of the man which is in him? Even so the
{thoughts} of God no one knows except the Spirit of God.*

— I CORINTHIANS 2:11

I have often thought that theology is a course of study
for the unbelieving believer, a man with an I.Q. of 150
attempting to understand a God with an immeasurably
infinite I.Q. In the West we have developed an unhealthy
fascination with questioning and understanding God.
Unbelief can be measured in direct proportion to the
number of our questions. Where did God come from? Is
every action predestined? Why does God allow suffering?
What kind of a God lets people be abused? Why does
God not stop evil? If God knows all, why did He create
Satan? Why would God create men, give them the ability
to choose evil, and then send them to hell for so choosing?
Is God passively active or just passive in the affairs of man?

Of course, I could ask the unbelieving believer equally
pertinent questions that also cannot be answered. Why
did you not die as a child? Why did your parents stay
married when others have not? Why did God spare you

in the snowstorm when there were so many other driving fatalities? Why did you not get cancer after smoking for twenty years? Why have you been able to make a house payment all these years? With two parents who were alcoholic, why did you not become one? Why has your life been so good?

Faith consumes itself not with questions but with a person, and that person is Jesus. Simply put, we are asking too many questions that would never be issues were we in His presence. All fear of the future would leave my young children's faces when they were in my lap. Climb into His lap and rest in faith. We know very little of what God is doing or will do. We only know that what He is doing will work together for the good. If the above questions were important, they would have been emphasized in the New Testament. They were not; therefore, if they become the emphases, the real intent and purpose of life and faith will elude us, and in the end we will be depleted, still asking questions. I appreciated my father at my mother's funeral. He refused to verbalize any questions, choosing rather to state what he believed: "God is working it all out for good." Amen!

DAY 75
Do Not Muzzle the Ox

Do not muzzle an ox while it is treading out the grain.
— DEUTERONOMY 25:4

We are commanded not to muzzle the ox, a passage applied to the fact that a workman is worthy of his hire. However, in talking with many believers, I believe that it also can apply to our spiritual lives in a different way. In many of the countries that I visit, the people are working seven days a week. In Asia they are only now thinking of reducing to six-day workweeks. In the West, the cost of living has gotten to the point that both husband and wife must work, often only passing by one another sometime during the day. These situations have spiritually muzzled believers. We are not given the time of refreshing before the Lord that we need. We are not allowed to eat of the Lord. It is not right. Every believer needs to take time away. If Jesus took time apart, then we, His disciples, surely need it. Time apart with the Lord is not a luxury but a necessity.

One summer I finished my travels with a total of five days off from January to July; only a day here and there between trips did I have in which to prepare for the next trip. In the end I could not hold a cup of coffee without shaking. I took two weeks in the mountains to do nothing but pray. The tremors stopped, I was energized, and I was fresh in the Lord. I am seeing this as something every believer needs, not just half an hour in the morning but a few days away from others. I know that thought may be shocking to those who cannot imagine doing anything without their mates. However, everyone's place is in the hub of life with the Lord alone; it would be good for them to remember that wives or husbands first and foremost belong to the Lord. Concentrated time with Him will change everything. Everyone needs time to step back and watch what falls apart; those things were of man, and everything that stays is of His making. Believers would find that they can continue working if they are not muzzled.

DAY 76
Do We Not Have To Choose?

By myself I can do nothing. I judge only as I hear, and my judgment is just, for I seek not to please myself but Him who sent me.

— JOHN 5:30

We make the statements, "All Jesus ever did, He never did. The Man who did everything did nothing. We are to let Jesus work through us as God worked through Jesus." These statements prompt the question, "Do we not have to choose?" So often we hear about choosing correctly, about those Christians who refuse to do so, and about the issues of choosing and free will. However, the point is not choosing but what we choose. Of course we must choose; we choose to get up, go to work, eat, and so on. Again, the issue is what we are choosing. Once we establish the real point, we will come to a "Y" in the road. Go right and we will make the choices God wants us to make. Go left and we will be on the wrong road, where the emphasis is on choosing those things considered to be good: choose to pray, read the Bible, witness, stop the deeds of the flesh, and love an enemy. However, this is not the choice God wants us making. If we think the decision that we need to make is to lay down our sin, we are on the wrong track and can be sidetracked for years. It is easy to spot someone on the wrong road; he will say something like, "I should pray more, give more, do more witnessing, love more, be a better mate." This reveals a person that has made a wrong choice. So what is it God does want us to choose? First, choose to lose our kingdom, our glory, our pride, our righteousness, and our strength. This is the opposite of choosing to do better; it is admitting that we cannot do better. Second, we will be ready to choose to accept His righteousness, kingdom, glory, and strength. The third choice is to allow His life to flow through us, and we will then be living in dependence on the Son as He was with the Father. These three choices will produce and accomplish everything that was desired on the left road, but without the self-effort that leads to self-righteousness and the false sense that we are living "the good Christian life."

DAY 77
Doubt and Faith

I call heaven and earth to witness against you today, that
I have set before you life and death, the blessing and the
curse. So choose life in order that you may live,
you and your descendants.

— DEUTERONOMY 30:19

Choice is an interesting thing, for nearly all of creation is under compulsion. The caterpillar must become the butterfly; the acorn must become the oak tree. Only man can choose what he will be. Choice must have options; it is nonexistent unless there is more than one alternative. "Would you like a cup of coffee, a cup of coffee, or a cup of coffee?" "Well, thanks, I will have the coffee!" One cannot choose heaven if there is no hell, a blessing if no curse, a single life if not a married one, or a walk in the spirit if there is no flesh.

This brings me to my point. How can we choose faith if there is no doubt? Many are distraught when they see doubt creeping into their lives. However, doubt must appear if there is to be an opportunity for a faith choice. Doubt is the signal that faith is the other option. We need not be undone over doubt; we can push it aside without hesitation and move past it on the way to a faith choice.

DAY 78
Dressing Up The Deeds Of The Flesh

Pride goes before destruction, a haughty spirit before a fall.

— PROVERBS 16:18

In certain countries there has been an emphasis made by foreign preachers that God wants us wealthy. These "teachers" say that they can demonstrate their faith by how many material possessions they have. This has been a very vexing message for the local pastors to deal with, because many people are poor and have a tendency to see poverty as a curse. A cow zipped up in a horse suit is still a cow. Likewise, it is amazing how deeds of the flesh can be worked around until they are actually presented as spiritual virtue. Someone may say with pride and boldness, "I told him he offended me!" That person just admitted complete spiritual defeat. Another admits spiritual defeat when he says, "I believed God, claimed a jet airplane, and God gave it to me." We are to be seeking the things above. One fellow even said, "I cannot look at pornography too long because it is vexing to my spirit." He can look at it for a while, but he is too spiritual for a prolonged look? It is one thing to avoid thinking about our flesh, but quite another to actually make it out to be something spiritual; that reveals the heart of a true Pharisee.

DAY 79
East Meets West!

Let no man deceive himself. If any man among you thinks that he is wise in this age, he must become foolish, so that he may become wise. For the wisdom of this world is foolishness before God. For it is written, "He is the one who catches the wise in their craftiness"; and again, "The Lord knows the reasonings of the wise, that they are useless."

— I CORINTHIANS 3:18-20

Those in India say it, and it is an obvious truth: If you go east long enough you will find yourself west, and likewise, if you go west long enough you will find yourself east. Maybe those in the West have yet to travel far enough east, and those in the East have not traveled far enough west. Eastern Religion, in the absence of fact, draws pictures. There never was a boy with an elephant head, and drawing it does not make it so. Please, travel a bit further to the West. On the other hand, no one in the East would question the existence of God, and when I say that Jesus spoke to me, no one questions it, for God must be alive. However, in the West, many have yet to believe that there is evidence of a God, and to say one has heard Him is to border on insanity. Those in the West need to travel a little more to the East. In the East miracles are an accepted part of life, and yet they have opened the door to the false and the deceiving. In the West, those without an inner awareness that Jesus is actually alive and active IN them seek miracles

OUTSIDE them as proof that He exists. Move east a little and discover the greatest miracle: Christ can dwell within a believer. In the West it is believed that the flower must be dissected in order for man to understand it, and yet that destroys the beauty. In the East the flower must simply be smelled. In the West a bridge made out of water is unthinkable; in the East many have walked on ice across a great river. In Christ, East meets West; the facts of the earth and the faith of heaven blend perfectly without conflict. In Him everything created on the earth and in the heavens merges without contradiction. This place many believe is impossible to find, the place where East meets West, is not a place but the person of Jesus!

DAY 80
Embrace a Movement and Let Go Of Jesus!

I am weary of bearing them. So when you spread out your hands in prayer, I will hide My eyes from you; yes, even though you multiply prayers, I will not listen.

— ISAIAH 1:14, 15

We have been bombarded in America by methods for accomplishing so many things: evangelism, childrearing,

Bible study, Scripture memory, church growth, building expansion, giving, and counseling. There are myriad specialized ministries addressing how to reach the businessman, the doctor, the neighbor, the moms, the dads, the internationals, and more. It is astounding and reminds me of the story of the Indian visiting the Christian bookstore in London. He had never before seen so many books in one place! The owner, upon observing his awe, took him from category to category, showing him all of the books written about the aforementioned methods. At that, the Indian said, "When I see so many books I am left with only one question: Do Christians not know how to do anything?" We must, in my opinion, walk the way Jesus walked with God. He did not have a manual but simply (though it does not initially seem simple for those of us living in this world) kept His focus on the Father. He maintained that relationship and never appeared to be at a loss for what to do in any given situation. If it were true for Him, could it not be true for those of us who have believed in Him, for those of us for whom He prayed, "that they may be one as We are One"? Try to prepare for an upcoming situation and watch as it takes an unexpected, unprepared for twist. Spend the day with an abiding awareness of Christ and have His wisdom no matter what happens. The day spent working on methods to fix a problem is not a day focused on Him. A believer can do one or the other. Embracing the method means that of necessity He has been let go! The cost of a how-to seminar is way beyond the registration fee paid, for it will cost a believer both peace and readiness.

DAY 81
Equality!

*I am the vine, you are the branches; he who abides in Me,
and I in him, he bears much fruit; for apart from Me you
can do nothing.*

— JOHN 15:5

Within the heart of man is the inherent desire for the recognition that there is equality between all men. It should be admitted that class struggle exists only in attitude. Refusal to accept others' definitions of superior and subordinate classifications means that the distinctions dissolve as I view my fellow man. Class struggle is defined as one group's having less material gain than the next, and many have been persuaded to work to get out of their economic situation and rise to that of the so-called upper class. If we were to redefine "upper class" as those who were the happiest, most moral, and largest contributors to society, it would be discovered that many who are materially categorized as upper class are actually lower-class people. Laying all worldly designations aside, there are actually only two noteworthy groups to represent, the carnal animalistic group and the spiritual, who have Christ within and expressed outwardly.

Abiding is the great equalizer between believers. Abide in Christ and all that He is and has is received, just as the branch receives the full life of the vine. Do not abide and immediately experience being in the flesh. It matters not if the flesh is educated, rich, respected, admired, or refined; it is still flesh, falling so short of the spirit. The world has so many criteria by which it appraises man, so many levels of divisions. Yet we Christians have but one: Is a person abiding in Christ or not? Is a person expressing life in the spirit or carnality? To make sub-classes out of the carnal or the spiritual is ignorance rooted in pride and self-glory. No one is better than an abiding believer, who at that moment is an earthen vessel with a perfect life, the life of Christ, flowing through him. Does it get any better than that?

DAY 82
Experience

Even if I have truly erred, my error lodges with me.
— JOB 19:4

Our people must also learn to engage in good deeds to meet pressing needs, so that they will not be unfruitful.
— TITUS 3:14

A friend may show you a shortcut that saves several hours of walking, and you may prove your friend correct once you take his suggestion and walk the new way. If at a later time this same friend tells you that the path is destroyed and you are to go another way, should not your history with the friend dictate that you listen and follow through with his altered advice? Learning from his experience would help you not experience the wrong path yourself.

Experience is way overrated! Look at what experiencing is teaching our society! It is teaching that immorality can kill, set the wrong course for a young life, and set in motion addictions that can be fought for years. Experiencing is showing couples the damage done to marriages through bitterness, self-centeredness, and unfaithfulness.

Jesus did not need to experience every dull thing; He learned by a more excellent way, the way of faith. He became a man, lived as a man, and experienced living by every word that proceeded from His Father. Experience is good, but the experience we need is from listening to God, our Father. What Jesus teaches in Matthew 5 - 7 is not just a revelation from heaven that facts of earth do not confirm. All of life proves what He taught, for His teaching is written into creation itself. Therefore, we do not need more experience in going the opposite way, not only breaking the commands of the teaching but breaking ourselves against them. There is nothing new to be learned through experience; all guiding principles have been learned and written down in Scripture, in the visible and invisible world, and within man.

DAY 83
Events That Control Us

So let us know, let us press on to know the LORD. His going forth is as certain as the dawn; and He will come to us like the rain, like the spring rain watering the earth.

— HOSEA 6:3

One day I talked to two different women who had suffered abuse. One had gotten on and was free; the other was still controlled by the past. Just so, many people suffer the same types of abuse and yet have different responses. Some, it seems, barely have a hiccup, while others are driven to a mental institution. The event cannot be the determining factor; rather, it is the significance placed on the event not only by the victims, of their own volition, but by society at large. Many are told that their particular hurt will involve years of pain and mourning before recovery. After highly publicized shootings at a high school, a mother of one of the students was told by a psychologist, "You can now expect your daughter to get into drugs, alcohol, and rebellion because of her trauma." The mother wisely suspended her daughter's sessions with this "therapist." Significance was attached to the event to the extent of presuming the young woman's descent into negative behavior.

You have had hurts in your life such as rejection, disappointments, and failures. What significance do you attach to them? Legalists attach great significance to them, for their ministry is to keep people down. If you believe that a particular failure will determine the course of the rest of your life, we can be certain that major significance has been assigned to it. Is that in line with the significance that God attaches to it? Some believe that there can only be a good marriage where neither spouse has ever been raped or had an affair. At this point rape, for instance, is not just a one-time event, but is actually the stealing of a lifetime of happiness. Many will say, "But it is a fact! I was violated, cheated, and abused." I am not saying there is not a temporarily huge struggle, but a momentary event is not to steal happiness forevermore. God will not change the fact, but He will change its significance. Invite Him into the event by asking to see Him at work in the midst of it. You will see, as many have, "God causes all things to work together for good!" The fact is still there, but it gives way to a greater fact: that God is "I AM." Many have come to discover Christ as life through mistakes, sin, failures, broken relationships, death, abuse, rejection, lost dreams, unemployment, dysfunctional marriage, and more. As long as we live from the Tree of Good and Evil, deciding for ourselves which of our life's occurrences were good or bad, we will be divided. Live from the Tree of Life, and see Him in everything,

DAY 84
Evolution

*If you love Me, you will obey what I command. And I
will ask the Father, and He will give you another counselor
to be with you forever – the Spirit of truth.*

— JOHN 14:15,16

Some argue that man is evolving into a more sophisticated, superior creature. If so, why the necessity for all of those door locks? Why is the security business thriving with projected increased growth? When a solution to society's ills is put forth, I always like to ask the question, "If we follow your system of reform and enlightened thinking, will we all need fewer keys in the future?" Once again time has rendered its verdict: We need more locks now and will need more in the future. I saw a man holding a sign on which was written, "Visualize world peace." I asked if he would answer a question for me, and he agreed to do so. I asked, "How many times have you been married?" "Three," was his response. I pointed out that if visualizing peace was not working in his personal life, it might be presumptuous to think that it would work globally.

It would appear that man is not evolving but revolving around and around what continues not to be the Way! Jesus is the Way! Following Him changes the world, the individual, and others. Following Him is Life indeed!

DAY 85
Facts!

Then you will know the truth, and the truth will set you free.
— JOHN 8:32

All of us have participated in acts of unrighteousness, immorality, impurity, and more. We have participated in acts of self-righteousness, judgment, pride, and unbelief, both before conversion and after. These are things that come to haunt us, and not only does our own past behavior vex us, but also the behavior of those around us. What are we to do with these cold, hard facts?

The first step is to understand that not all true things are truth. I used this illustration in a meeting at a Chinese church: "I am not that impressed with the hospitality of the Chinese. I stayed with the Chinese pastor and he never offered me coffee although he knew I liked coffee, needed it, and wanted it. It is true!" Then I continued, "However, when I first got to the pastor's home, I told him, 'You do not need to offer me coffee; I brought my own!'" Now the truth was revealed. You can see that not all things that are true are truth. For a true thing to be truth, it must end at the feet of Jesus, Who is the way, the truth, and the life. It is possible for something that is true to lead you either to truth or away from it. Facts just lie there lifelessly, doing nothing, having no power except attraction. Some facts get our attention, and what gets our attention, gets us. Once we know the facts about our behavior and the behavior of others, what do we do with the information? Facts are history, and history is to be denied. (Luke 9:23, "And He was saying to them all, 'If anyone wishes to come after Me, he must deny himself, and take up his cross daily and follow Me.'") "Brethren, I do not regard myself as having laid hold of {it} yet; but one thing {I do}: forgetting what {lies} behind and reaching forward to what {lies} ahead" (Philippians 3:13).

Often the enemy uses facts to add to and augment his position. He will use true things, but he never uses them to lead a person to truth. He'll use them as additions that detract from the truth (Jesus). God is "I AM," the God of no additions. He simply is "I AM," without even true things and facts detracting from who He is. We are a people without additions. We have Jesus and do not need additional experience, more knowledge, another degree, or the spectacular; we have Jesus, the complete truth, and we need nothing else. In Him we are complete! The facts of past behavior, everything before this moment, are additional and encumbering. "Therefore, since we have so great a cloud of witnesses surrounding us, let us also lay aside every encumbrance, and the sin which so easily entangles us, and let us run with endurance the race that is set before us" (Hebrews 12:1). What do we do with facts, not only the facts of our own failures—past, present, and future—but also those of others around us? Once they have been removed by the blood of Christ, we refuse to wear them.

DAY 86
Facts Revisited

Trust in the Lord with all your heart and lean not on your own understanding.

— PROVERBS 3:5

Now I must go one step further in discussing facts. God permits what He could prevent. "And this we shall do, if God permits" (Hebrews 6:3). We quickly and easily praise God for all that He prevents. Any of us could have died in a car accident by now had He not prevented it. He has prevented and protected us from so much. We thank Him. However, there is something that takes much more faith: Can we thank Him for what He has permitted? How often we have heard people say, "How could a loving God allow such a tragedy to happen?" Maybe we have said it ourselves. If God were to pull us aside and ask the following question, how would we answer? "I AM is going to permit a failure in your life, your child's life, or in the life of your mate. Will you praise Me still? I will use the failure, not fight it; will you praise Me still?" What if we were asked this question the day before our or our family's failure in the past, present, or future? What would we say? I am not saying that God causes evil, but it is permitted. Can we praise Him for what is permitted? Can we see Him at work in it, or do we only see ourselves? The fact is that God hates sin, but there is another fact: He uses it. "And the Law came in that the transgression might increase; but where sin increased, grace abounded all the more" (Romans 5:20). What if God said, "I will allow your child to fail. I will use it. May I have his purity, the perfect life you wanted for him, and the life free of struggle you desired? I will permit and use the loss of those things to bring the child to Me"? He allows what He could prevent. Can we agree with His allowing? Can we let Him allow? Do we live to and for the facts, wanting to prevent all that brings people to Christ? Do we want to prevent facts? Are we angry about the facts? This does not just apply to our families. He has permitted so much in world events, past and present. Can we praise Him, the I AM, for what He in His wisdom permitted? Praising Him for what is permitted is the first step.

We also need peace with the facts of our failures and the failures of others. We need peace in the unexpected turn of events. Where do we find peace? The same place that I AM found it. Remember, after looking at the facts, the LORD said, "I will blot out man whom I have created from the face of the land, from man to animals to creeping things and to birds of the sky; for I am sorry that I have made them" (Genesis 6:7). God saw the facts and needed peace! Again, where did He find it? Jesus! "Surely our griefs He Himself bore, and our sorrows He carried; yet we ourselves esteemed Him stricken, smitten of God, and afflicted. But He was pierced through for our transgressions, He was crushed for our iniquities; the chastening for our well-being {fell} upon Him, and by His scourging we are healed" (Isaiah 53:4, 5). What grief? The grief that God had for making us! What sorrow? The sorrow that God had after making us! Jesus carried it all and in Him, God had peace.

Where will we find peace with the facts of our behavior and the behavior of others, past, present, and future? In Jesus! He is our Peace. Ephesians 2:14, "For He Himself is our peace, who made both {groups into} one, and broke down the barrier of the dividing wall."

What is as big as an elephant but weighs nothing? The elephant's shadow. Facts weigh nothing in the light of Jesus! I do not care about the facts! I have peace! I have Jesus! I am ready to press on in the great I AM!

DAY 87
Faith

Then He touched their eyes, saying, "It shall be done to you according to your faith."
— MATTHEW 9:29

Many hope to become rich through an inheritance or the lottery. There is another way to become rich: slowly, quietly, wisely, gradually, and faithfully. This way is much better, for it can be repeated over and over again. Similarly, there are two ways to enter into faith. One is through an explosion such as the Apostle Paul's. The other way is much more difficult but will reap the same results.

Many are waiting for God to perform some miracle before they believe. It is often taught that unbelief is a weakness, and yet we are not told what to do to be strengthened. Unbelief does not have its roots in weakness but in worldliness, self-righteousness, and pride.

Chapter 11 in the Book of Hebrews puts faith people into two categories. The first category belongs to those who because of their faith experienced great miracles. I have known believers who have had the Lord awaken them in the middle of the night and heal a broken bone, those who have actually seen the Lord, and one family who had a child raised from the dead. Their faith did not create the miracles but allowed them to receive them.

Hebrews 11:2, For by it the men of old gained approval.

11:5, By faith Enoch was taken up so that he should not see death.

11:7, By faith Noah, being warned {by God} about things not yet seen, in reverence prepared an ark for the salvation of his household, by which he condemned the world, and became an heir of the righteousness which is according to faith.

11:11, By faith even Sarah herself received ability to conceive, even beyond the proper time of life, since she considered Him faithful who had promised.

11:29, By faith they passed through the Red Sea as though {they were passing} through dry land . . .

11:30, By faith the walls of Jericho fell down, after they had been encircled for seven days.

11:32, And what more shall I say? For time will fail me if I tell of Gideon, Barak, Samson, Jephthah, of David and Samuel and the prophets,

11:33, who by faith conquered kingdoms, performed {acts of} righteousness, obtained promises, shut the mouths of lions,

11:34, quenched the power of fire, escaped the edge of the sword, from weakness were made strong, became mighty in war, put foreign armies to flight.

11:35, Women received {back} their dead by resurrection; and others were tortured, not accepting their release, in order that they might obtain a better resurrection.

DAY 88
Faith and The Others

And others experienced mockings and scourgings, yes, also chains and imprisonment. They were stoned, they were sawn in two, they were tempted, they were put to death with the sword; they went about in sheepskins, in goatskins, being destitute, afflicted, ill-treated ({men} of whom the world was not worthy), wandering in deserts and mountains and caves and holes in the ground. And all these, having gained approval through their faith, did not receive what was promised, because God had provided something better for us, so that apart from us they would not be made perfect.

— HEBREWS 11:36

We now move to the second category of believers, those who believe and receive nothing. They are called the "others." Are you one of the "others" who has trusted God for a restored relationship, the health of a child, a godly home, the salvation of a relative, or just the simple stirring of God within that brings assurance? If you have trusted and not given into despair, then you are one of the "others." The "others" give something to God that no angel in heaven can give Him, and that is faith. The "others" walk in darkness, seeing nothing their whole lives, and yet stand fast, believing in a God they cannot see. Can you imagine how pleased He is? You are pulled on all sides to give up, and yet you have chosen to believe without seeing! You have stood fast in the midst of the reversal! The world is not worthy of you! You simply do not belong! Your place is above, seated with the Father judging angels! If you have believed and not received, count yourself blest.

DAY 89
Faith Versus Works in Discipleship

*However, when the Son of Man comes,
will He find faith on the earth?*
— LUKE 18:8

Two ways problems can be approached are from a position of works—as in, "What must I do to improve the situation?"—or from a place of faith: "What must I believe and what must the Lord do to resolve the predicament?" A works position is based on unbelief, and the cause of misery is believed to be a wrong choice, lack of natural love, another person, finances, or a myriad of other natural events. The search for a solution lends itself to thoughts of, "What should I do?" or "What should I do if others are making me miserable?" The person attacking problems from a position of works has not yet come to believe that the nearness of Jesus will cure all of his ills, so he labors with the notion that Jesus will not help his particular circumstance. Since Jesus is not perceived to be the answer, he has moved into unbelief, and it is unbelief that will always ask him to do something.

Often I hear, "I just do not love my wife." Of course, this statement really means, "I find my mate unlovable, and she must change before she can be lovable to me." However, it is my experience that once there exists an attitude of, "I do not love you," no amount of change on the part of the mate or hours of personal discipleship will affect that attitude. "Trouble lies not in the trouble but in the heart's attitude toward the trouble." The works person would always rather examine the problem over and over again and skirt the issue of any wrong attitude of his own toward the trouble. Analyzing the problem allows the focus to be on someone or something else; examining the attitude puts the focus squarely on him.

I am not saying that the problem is not significant, but on a scale of one to ten, the problem may be a one to God and a ten in our attitude toward it. The problem and the attitude are two separate issues; the works person wants to make them one to keep attitude and personal responsibility from ever being addressed, while in truth, attitude is the greater issue. During a person's first discipleship session, I will explore his mindset in detail before addressing the problems. Once his way of thinking has been exposed, the problems become a lesser issue. In subsequent weeks if the person continues to rehash the problems, I know that our first discussion never really sank in. It is only as a person places his confidence in another, in Jesus, that he will move into the problem, through the problem, and out on the other side.

DAY 90
Falling Into Evil

But from the tree of the knowledge of good and evil you shall not eat, for in the day that you eat from it you shall surely die.

— GENESIS 2:17

Many are surprised when they fall; they were doing so well, they just did not see it coming. There was nothing evil in their lives; in accordance with deliverance teaching, everything evil had been "dealt" with in their lives. How did they fall? Instead of looking for the place where evil began, they should go back and look at the place of good, where they decided that their flesh had improved so much that they did not think about abiding when they entered their house, went on vacation, arrived at work, or taught the Bible study.

What "good-looking" flesh was it with which they had gotten involved? Was it living to people instead of loving them, people pleasing, manipulating, reworking the portfolio, counting the savings, or lusting for the latest from the material world? Were they agreeing to pacify others while staying silent to avoid conflict? Did they avoid telling the truth? Once the gate to the flesh corral is open, not only do the dark horses go out, but those of every stripe. Those who begin to walk in the "good" deeds of the flesh will soon find themselves in evil deeds.

Each day resolve not simply to turn away from evil, but to turn away from the "good" arising from what can be done in the natural, to avoid all strength in the power of the self-life, and to turn to Jesus.

DAY 91
Fasting

You have made known to me the path of life: you will fill me with joy in your presence with eternal pleasures at your right hand.

— PSALM 16:11

The Spirit drove Jesus to the wilderness, which, along with fasting, would prepare Him for the coming temptations. In the wilderness He was cut off from all outside support with only the Father on whom to lean. The soul—like a baby, with a need for mother's milk and constant feeding—can be fed from the outer life and world by choosing facts and emotional stirrings. However, being fed by the world is similar to giving water to a baby when it wants and needs milk. The baby will become fussy and testy. In the wilderness and in fasting, the soul has only one place it can feed, the Father! The soul (mind, will, and emotions) discovers the Father is the food that satisfies and chooses the wisdom of God over knowledge and His presence over feelings. "My soul is full," says the Psalmist. When full, no one can tempt a person with more food. When the soul is full of God, the world just cannot tempt with its offerings. Jesus said, "No," to stones becoming bread. He was full without bread. He said, "No," to kingdoms and the spectacular. He had what He needed and did not choose excess. He is holding all things with an open hand. Jesus stands at the door and invites us to eat with Him, to have our souls satisfied.

I have experienced a bit of giving myself to prayer and fasting and want to do more in the future. I love having a full soul, never once wanting food, lacking curiosity about my surroundings, not giving even a casual glance to shops, and not needing anything. It is like Thanksgiving dinner when I finally say, "No, thanks! I cannot hold anything else." No man can call another to a fast in the wilderness; the Spirit must drive him there! I would encourage prayer that He do just that, so we believers can get away from all the external supports, even if it is just one day sometime this year. He will fill our soul.

DAY 92
Fathers Who Lead

Furthermore, we had earthly fathers to discipline us, and we respected them; shall we not much rather be subject to the Father of spirits, and live?

— HEBREWS 12:9

Throughout history we can identify some who were born into the position of leadership and others who were chosen to lead. However, the Bible indicates that in the family, every man is commanded to lead. The world, by contrast, has taught that the family is ruled by the wishes of the majority. All types of media have subtly spread the impression that children should be consulted before making decisions and that the wife need only submit to the husband if he is in mutual submission to her. Accepting these diluted definitions of leadership has produced a generation of Christian fathers who are what might commonly be called passive dads. The father is not to rule through consensus; he does not take the counsel of children. Rather, he seeks God for guidance, which he will find in every situation. Leadership inherently involves followers, who will always have high expectations of a leader, and rightfully so. When we submit to a leader we desire that he be better than us, for our identity becomes intertwined in his. If we submit to a righteous man, then our self-esteem goes up, we feel good about being his servant, and we even see the glory of being subjected to him. We admire and appreciate him as well as desiring his direction, with the hope that he might lead us to the place where he is, for obviously he knows the way and is respected for it. When he asks of us things that we do not understand, we obey, trusting that somehow it will benefit us. Therefore, the two most frustrating things to a follower about a leader are when he cannot be respected and when he will not lead.

DAY 93
Fear

Who is there to harm you if you prove zealous for what is good? But even if you should suffer for the sake of righteousness, you are blessed. And do not fear their intimidation, and do not be troubled, but sanctify Christ as Lord in your hearts.

—I PETER 3:13-15

We are not suited for fear, which began for mankind in the garden when Adam and Eve fell away from the presence of God. Before that, they had been filled with confidence and assurance of the future, since they possessed a God. Man was not created to be independent, and in that sense, fear is the result of not staying dependent on every word that proceeds from the mouth of God. Fear is the friend of sin, Satan, and the world, for it makes us buy insurance, new cars, and investments; constantly focus on money; refuse a risk; and stay at a job we hate. We were created for trust and calm, so fear in our mind, will, and emotions creates sickness in our bodies.

We must become free from fearing anything less than God, and that is simpler than it sounds. We allowed fear in when we were taught it, and now we must invite it out. Fear is not dealt with through endless examination; we can refuse it. Look at fear and ask why we would allow it in our lives. We need to recognize we have a God and then change our minds about letting fear dwell in us. Some East Indians have an interesting way of physiologically dealing with thoughts they seem stuck with but do not wish to entertain: They bat their eyes! They say they cannot continue with a thought while batting their eyes. A change of activities might also help the mind get unstuck from the bad-habit rut of reviewing fearful thought patterns. Invite the fear out verbally, and then go to a mirror, examine the face's worry lines, and begin to laugh. Remember that fear is the result of being self-centered, not God centered, and it has been called the measure of the distance between man and God.

DAY 94
Feeling Guilty

There is therefore now no condemnation
for those who are in Christ Jesus.
— ROMANS 8:1

Jesus is the Way written into every fiber of our being and consciousness. When we invite our own way into our being, we come apart, so sin and punishment are one and the same. Guilt, then, comes not solely for what we have done but to keep us from doing it again. Guilt is not the result of our actions; coming apart is the result of our actions. Guilt's primary purpose is for the future avoidance of repeating bad choices. This is an important distinction to make, because guilt is not dealt with by mentally going back into the past, but by making a change of direction now; at that, guilt not only goes away but also has a positive effect on our lives. Once the change in direction has occurred, any reappearance of the sense of guilt over an issue is false guilt.

One man I knew, then a great-great-grandparent, had slaves in the home as a youngster; when he would come home from school, he would find his favorite slave, an elderly man, and make him give him rides on his back, up and down the road. Once the boy became a man, the day came when guilt visited him. Vexed by his selfishness, his way, he realized he had never thought about whether the old man was tired or not after having worked all day, and as a boy he had made the man continue to labor. He was guilty of his selfishness. He could not go back to that time as a child, but he could change direction that day, which he did, and from then on he chose always to help anyone who had been a slave. Guilt had played its part, done its job, and was no longer needed, having produced a positive outcome. After the change in direction, if guilt did return, it would be false guilt sent by the enemy for waylaying condemnation. Guilt that leads to a change in direction is true guilt. Guilt that leads to condemnation is false guilt.

DAY 95
Feeling Overwhelmed

Woe to you, scribes and Pharisees, hypocrites, because you travel about on sea and land to make one proselyte; and when he becomes one, you make him twice as much a son of hell as yourselves.

— MATTHEW 23:15

If one were to take all of the lists of the emphases from every group or denomination and stack them on his desk, he could make a complete collection of all things that presumably urgently need to be done by the Christian. All of the books on prayer, spiritual warfare, marriage, family, authority, church, witnessing, forgiveness, abuse, counseling, spiritual experiences, and intellectual pursuits could be stacked up; he could just keep adding, placing on top whatever all the groups say that believers really need to know and do. One might want to start in the city next to mine, where there are over two hundred international ministries, each distinctive and each with its own special emphases. Next, if the person is strong enough, brave enough, and has the will power, he can dive in and start doing all of the above. How long would it take him to be exhausted? See how high Jesus set the bar? He did it for a reason: to exhaust us and push us to something much more simple, abiding. Simple abiding; I love it so much. I do not need the list of what Jesus did; I have exactly Jesus dwelling in me. Simply acknowledge that in Him we abide. Throw away the stacks, sit back, and let Him show us what He will do through us today. We will not be able to compete, and others will try to condemn us when they see our freedom, but the Lord's works, true works, will put them to shame. Rest in Jesus just for the joy of it. No one can keep all of those lists but Him, and even Jesus did not keep them all at once! We will keep what we need to keep in His order as He keeps it through us. It is not passivity, for we must show up; that is the one thing we must do. We can put our hand on our hearts first thing in the morning and say, "Jesus, You are welcome here. Come and live what needs to be lived this day." Enjoy the blessed rest.

DAY 96
Feeling Unstable?

. . . a double-minded man, unstable in all his ways.

— JAMES 1:8

It is said that if you want the fruit, dig without damaging the root; if you do not want the fruit, lay an ax to the root. In short, deal with the real issue. If a believer lacks peace, he should go to the root. Jesus has given the promise that we will have perfect peace if our minds are on Him. That means there can be only one reason for the lack of peace. Truth is not only preached, it is demonstrated. That is the preface.

So many today are unstable at home, work, and within. Road rage does not happen on the road; today people are so mad when they get in their cars that all it takes is a little inconvenience to reveal the buried anger. Dad is explosive, Mom is short-tempered, the kids are impulsive and rebellious, and all are unstable. Could it be that people are unstable not because of a poor childhood, abuse, prejudice, pain, hurt, or anxiety? Could it be that people are unstable because they are double-minded? "Let God be found true, though every man [be found] a liar" (Romans 3:4). Double-minded is to want for one's self and, at the same time, to want for another. A father wants the new woman, the new car, and every minute of time for himself; yet he wants to be a loving, giving, caring father. If he gives in to the father and husband side of himself, the enemy is whispering how much he will lose. If he gives in to self, the enemy makes sure he cannot stand the image of being a bad father. What to do with this kind of double-mindedness? He does not know what to do, so he gets angry.

If you are unstable, ask God to show you where you are double-minded. What are you doing that you should not be? What should you be doing that you are not? Where is the battle between self and the cross?

DAY 97
Finding The Way

Jesus answered, "I am the way and the truth and the life."
— JOHN 14:6

It is urgent today that mankind find a way to live. So far what usually is discovered is how not to live. Many continue to seek for the method, the understanding, or the system that will guide them. In Africa a traveler finds many places where there are no trails through the jungle, so he must hire a guide. The local name of the guide when translated into English is The Way. The way is a person! In the jungle and chaos of life, the Way is not knowledge but a Person.

It is told in India of a young girl trying to put together a jigsaw puzzle of the world, but she could not. Upon turning the pieces over she discovered a different puzzle much easier to put together: a picture of Jesus. Once Jesus was the focus, even the pieces of the world came together. He is the Way that is needed to make our world simple. Pray with me that God would allow us to proclaim the Way with all of the force, power, and conviction that He possesses.

DAY 98
Flesh Is Flesh

That which is born of the flesh is flesh, and that which is born of the Spirit is spirit.
— JOHN 3:6

You have flesh! The flesh, simply defined, is the body, mind, will, and emotions of man under the control of something other than Jesus. Believers and unbelievers alike have flesh. Walking in the flesh is the opposite of abiding in Christ. Have you seriously considered that your flesh will never improve? It is an important point. How can we expect the flesh to be anything other than flesh? Flesh is flesh and can do nothing that is of the Spirit. We have seen bad flesh and are often on a continual quest to find good flesh in ourselves, our mates, our church family, and our children.

Once I was visiting with a couple about the husband's affair. The wife, legitimately, was quite hurt. But the longer she talked, the more something illegitimate came to the forefront: flesh! This woman wanted her husband to guarantee that his flesh would never again do such a thing. How can he do that? He cannot, for that type of bad flesh does that kind of thing. The flesh's determining to do better will change nothing, for flesh does not control flesh. It is futile to find out what the flesh can do but worthwhile to discover and admit what it cannot do. Good flesh cannot lead a godly life. I wanted the husband to recognize that he is weak and that repeating the same mistake was completely possible. Then I wanted him to move into Christ and discover that His power is manifested in the man's weakness. Flesh is completely subjugated when a believer is abiding. On the other hand, the wife wanted his flesh to determine to live spiritually. She did not understand what I was saying, which was understandable. She thought I was giving him an excuse. I was not. I just wanted to get to the spider and stop sweeping cobwebs. She had found something good in her own flesh—that she had never had an affair—and was clinging tenaciously to the hope that good flesh could help her husband. "Because the mind set on the flesh is hostile toward God" (Romans 8:7). Why do we always attempt to find good in our flesh? The best of flesh is the worst of it, for it keeps us from humbly seeking Christ. She got the point and released her husband to abide in Christ rather than promising to make bad flesh act nicely.

Finding something good in the flesh is so vexing, consuming, and defeating. Why do we defend ourselves?

Because we are holding on to the belief that there is something good in our flesh! Why can others control us by leaving us out? Because there is something good in our flesh that deserves better treatment! Why do we react and not respond to those around us? There is something good in our flesh that must be respected! Agree with God and admit that there is nothing good in your flesh, and then agree with others. When told you are proud, say, "Yes, and you have not see the worst of my flesh!" When told that you are stupid, worthless, inferior, and angry, simply agree! Agree that in your flesh dwells no good thing.

DAY 99
Flesh Is Hostile

The mind set on the flesh is hostile toward God, for it does not subject itself to the law of God, for it is not even able to do so, and those who are in the flesh cannot please God.
— ROMANS 8:7, 8

The attempt to find something good in the flesh causes a distortion in personality and a multitude of emotional dysfunctions. Today there appears to be an expanding problem with pornography due to Internet access. Believers have worse problems than unbelievers when it comes to this pursuit. One unbeliever said it this way, "Why would I look at pornography? If I wanted to have an affair, I would just have one! I do not see the attraction of a pictorial depiction over a person." He was being honest. He did not have obsessions in his mind because he acted out in the flesh. The believer is always more obsessive than the unbeliever, because the believer has tried to find something good in his flesh. He sets a standard to keep so that he will have every appearance of being "good." He will only look and not handle, taste, or touch in order to believe he has found something good in his flesh. He can even congratulate himself, saying, "At least I have never been with another woman physically." However, standards (i.e., the law) never keep the flesh good. The man looks, has a sinking feeling, knows that he should not, feels condemned, falls into self-hatred, and in the end is constantly thinking about staying away from pornography. Thinking about not looking is now the standard for finding some good in the flesh. The interesting thing about it is that in thinking about staying away from it, it is now actually the focus of life, much more so than for the unbeliever that did not set a standard to begin with! The standard to keep the flesh good actually made it bad, since the flesh is flesh and hostile toward God!

We either walk in the Spirit (attached to the Vine, acknowledging the flow of the life of the Vine through us) or we walk in the flesh. Simply put, there is nothing good to find in the flesh, and that is why it is so important to acknowledge that we are abiding in Him. Flesh will not improve. Only when Christ—Who lived in flesh and overcame it—is flowing through us will we experience power over the flesh. At that point victory is a natural thing, not contrived, not achieved by the effort toward improving, but through the fact of subduing.

The question may arise, "Mike, you say that we are holy, righteous, and acceptable because the life in us—His life— is all these things. You say the old nature and old man are crucified, and yet you say that in the flesh there is no good thing and it will never improve. Are you not saying that the old man is still alive?" No, I am not saying the old man is alive. My identity is in Christ, not in the flesh that I will one day lay aside. I have a new life and a new man that is holy. However, this inner life is in a body with mind, will, and emotions. When Christ is my focus, Christ's life flows from my spirit through mind, will, emotions, and body, and they are used as intended by His life/my new life. When I close the door to Christ's life, the body, mind, will, and emotions run wildly into the good or bad expressions of my condition called flesh. Why does God leave such a way of living possible for the believer? Quite simply, it is in order to keep us focused on Him. We get miserable in our flesh, and that misery will always drive us back to moment-by-moment abiding in Him. In our flesh dwells no good thing, but in Him dwells everything.

DAY 100
Flesh Is The Opposite Of Faith

*Now faith is the assurance of {things} hoped for, the
conviction of things not seen.*

— HEBREWS 11:1

Flesh and faith are opposites. In the flesh, we will have
no hope; we will despair of our situation and believe that
all things justify that. Faith has hope in all things. The man
of faith has hope for the marriage; the woman of faith is
filled with expectation for what God can do. Flesh will only
believe what is seen; faith believes what has been given but
cannot be seen in the individual's life.

The fruit of the Spirit is also the opposite of flesh, which
may attempt to imitate fruit of the Spirit in the power of
self. It is hard to grasp, but a fleshly person is one who
attempts to have love, joy, peace, patience, kindness,
goodness, faithfulness, gentleness, and self-control in the
power of self. The fruit of the Spirit must come naturally
and must be genuine. See how plastic the Hare Krishna
folks, the Jehovah Witnesses, the Mormons, Humanists,
and all other cults look when trying to manifest the fruit of
the Spirit? Flesh is attempting to look good, but it is flesh
nonetheless, and it has Christians working for what has
already been given. This work, the opposite of faith, keeps
us from experiencing what is only given by faith. To have

failed, and then to punish ourselves in order to have God see us, and to plead with Him for restoration, is working in unbelief for what we have already freely been given. The work is keeping us so busy that we do not have time to stop and recognize that we were never cut off. It can sound so good to work for the things of God, to attempt to take hold of them in our power, but remember, the best of the flesh is the worst of it. Flesh is the opposite of faith.

DAY 101
Following the Image Myth

And Jesus said to them, "Follow Me, and I will make you become fishers of men."
— MARK 1:17

I refuse to give names, but I have talked with many who have walked with some very well known men in the Christian faith. One person privately told me the leader of a certain great movement was a jerk; in fact, his own staff was afraid to confront him, for he would proudly hand them their heads on a platter. Neither the man nor his reputation is our concern; I just want to make the point that none of those we idolize fit the life of Christ as described in Matthew 5, 6, and 7. I was actually told that one leader had such repulsive manners that he was kept from the public and sheltered by his inner circle, who circulated stories of his greatness and thus created an image of him for "the good" of others who followed his teaching. In the end, ten generations removed from the founder, disciples were still attempting to emulate the behavior of someone who did not even exist. Can you imagine their frustration? How often we find ourselves following the image some man has projected of what following Jesus is to look like. I say that we are to cast all images aside, not elevate any man, and just follow Jesus. In so doing, we will never be disappointed.

DAY 102
Forcing Miracles!

Now it came about on one of {those} days, that He and His disciples got into a boat, and He said to them, "Let us go over to the other side of the lake." And they launched out. But as they were sailing along He fell asleep; and a fierce gale of wind descended upon the lake, and they {began} to be swamped and to be in danger. And they came to Him and woke Him up, saying, "Master, Master, we are perishing!" And being aroused, He rebuked the wind and the surging waves, and they stopped, and it became calm. And He said to them, "Where is your faith?"

— LUKE 8:22-25

Jesus is asleep, the storm comes, the disciples are frightened, and they call on Him. Should we not always call on Him in a storm? They do, and they are rebuked with, "Where is your faith?" Why? They only did that in which so many today glory, which is forcing Jesus into performing a miracle. Some have made whole ministries out of forcing Jesus to do things and being applauded for their great faith. Yet, when the disciples force deliverance, they are rebuked for having little faith. Again we ask why. Jesus had permitted the storm for their perfection. The process was interrupted by unbelief, and Jesus stopped the storm. He did a miracle at their bidding, but it was not a positive. They should have crawled next to Him and gone to sleep, resting through the storm that would not have touched them either way. The storm's effect on them was not the issue. What the storm could perfect in them or expose in them was the issue. Again, in today's Christianity, calling on Jesus and forcing a miracle is often viewed as proof of spirituality, when just the opposite is true. For example, one has a rebellious child. The parent has pleaded and reasoned; he has acknowledged that he is in a storm. Now a choice must be made between panic and calling on Jesus to stop the situation or going to lie down next to Him and resting. Believer, when the next storm comes, and it will come, what will you do?

DAY 103
Forgiveness and Confession

Be on your guard! If your brother sins, rebuke him; and if
he repents, forgive him. And if he sins against you seven times
a day, and returns to you seven times, saying,
"I repent," forgive him.

— LUKE 17:3, 4

A break in a relationship generally has the following sequence. First, there is an offense within the relationship; next, a break in the relationship; hopefully, repentance by the offender; forgiveness by the offended party; and, in the end, restoration. In the passage above Jesus is not sanctioning what is currently passed off as wisdom, and that is going to those who have offended and telling them that they are forgiven, when they have never asked for forgiveness. Jesus is clearly speaking of one who "returns to you seven times, saying, 'I repent'"; it is that one who receives forgiveness. It cheapens forgiveness to give it when people are not asking for it; it actually cheapens relationships. Now, what are we to do when someone has offended us and yet refuses to show that he is sorry or in need of forgiveness? First, we make sure that God has worked a basic principle in us, that of accepting the truth that we are to be offended until we cannot be offended. If others can offend us, then self is still actively seeking its own good and others can control us. Do any of us have a legitimate right to be offended? Next, we do not have the Scriptural right to be offering forgiveness where there is no repentance, so what is there to do? Do we walk in unforgiveness? No, for that is when we bless those who curse us. By blessing those who curse us, we will be able to keep the offenders from living rent-free in our head. Of course, when someone does repent, we must forgive.

DAY 104
Freedom

Not that I speak from want; for I have learned to be content in whatever circumstances I am.

— PHILIPPIANS 4:11

There are two ways a person is controlled by alcohol; one is the constant thought of getting it; the other is the nagging thought of staying away from it. Either way, alcohol is the focus. This is also true when it comes to material possessions. Many attempt to prove their value through the fancy type of car they drive, while others want to hide what God has graciously given them so they will not be thought of poorly by other believers who own less. In either case, life is lived unto man. I remember visiting a pastor who had been imprisoned many years for his faith. During the incarceration he lost his family, inheritance, and friends. One would think that with such an experience he would have been radiating humility. However, the opposite was true; he was full of pride, almost demanding worship because of the suffering he had undergone. My brother and I made a quick exit from his church. Freedom will not make us any more or less spiritual than imprisonment. Spirituality comes from a simple recognition that we have nothing. In the midst of any situation, we walk with an empty bag, having nothing but what the Lord gives us in the moment. If we walk in humility, we can walk in wealth or in poverty and still find ourselves growing, full of hope and love, and being springs of living water at which others may drink.

DAY 105
Freedom in Christianity

It was for freedom that Christ set us free . . .
— GALATIANS 5:1

Christianity is the only religion that uses the term freedom. It is not surprising, in that much of religion ultimately offers its adherents nothing but a whirl around emptiness, with all teaching leading to nothing divine, a doctrine without power, and a system that will not work in the world and must be practiced in relative seclusion. If not for manipulation, intimidation, brainwashing, control, fear, guilt, and bondage, maintaining a religious system would be impossible. Jesus is not a religion; with Him we have a relationship, and relationships are most enjoyed when those involved want to be with one another. I remember a fellow telling his wife, who could not decide if she wanted to leave or not, "When I come home from work at night and see your car there, and know that you are waiting for me, I must know you are there because you want to be there." This man had given his wife freedom to leave. He did not want a relationship based on duty, guilt, compulsion, or responsibility, but on love. Love is freedom. The believer is free to walk with Christ or not; Christ does not enjoy man's attempts to walk with Him when he really does not want to be with Him. Who would?

If you do not desire to walk with Jesus, it is only because you do not know Him or have drifted away to the point that familiarity with Him is a thing of the past. For His character is such that you should be doing everything possible to be with Him. Jesus is secure in Himself and knows what fellowship with Him brings; you, therefore, are free to partake of His riches or free to walk in the dry desert bereft of His presence. I love freedom!

DAY 106
Freedom From Religion Is Freedom From the Kingdoms of Man!

And Jesus seeing their faith said to the paralytic, "My son, your sins are forgiven." But there were some of the scribes sitting there and reasoning in their hearts, "Why does this man speak that way? He is blaspheming; who can forgive sins but God alone?" And immediately Jesus, aware in His spirit that they were reasoning that way within themselves, said to them, "Why are you reasoning about these things in your hearts? Which is easier, to say to the paralytic, 'Your sins are forgiven'; or to say, 'Arise, and take up your pallet and walk'?"

— MARK 2:5-9

Men are kingdom builders, and kingdoms need subjects. We are raised to be subjects when told such things as, "You do not have to respect the President but you must respect the office of the President." This may be translated to mean, "Whatever you do, you are not to come out from under our kingdom! What would a kingdom be without subjects?" Kingdom builders must offer something, for if they cannot, the subjects might go elsewhere. Now, kingdom builders never give anything of substance. All things of substance are hoarded for themselves. They merely give something with the appearance of substance in order to keep the subjects interested and loyal.

Religion is a kingdom with leaders who must keep devotees in subjection. Out of necessity they must give something that cannot be attained elsewhere. Remember, it will only be the appearance of getting something; the followers never really get anything except more bondage. Every man everywhere knows he has sinned and fallen short. Deep within is a fear of the consequences. The Scribes and Pharisees were offering forgiveness, restoration, and freedom. The catch was that adherents had to jump through all of their hoops, and no matter how many were jumped through, they were always able to produce one more. The vast majority of people, wanting what was promised, continued to be in subjection. The kingdom went on until Jesus appeared on the scene, and in one little sentence He destroyed it all. He brought "whosoever will" out from under subjection. The sentence referred to is this: "My son, your sins are forgiven!" Jesus did not say, "will be," or "keep trying," or "check with me next week," "complete your memory work," or "take a little more time in prayer." No, "Your sins are forgiven!" No hoops, no bondage, and no need for dependence on the kingdom of man! No more religion! Religion was destroyed at its basic foundation. Man is to be in bondage to no religion. Jesus has forgiven him and has given what others promised in exchange for devotion and servitude. Man is free! We belong to no kingdom but His.

DAY 107
Freedom in Relationships

Whatever you do, do your work heartily, as for the Lord rather than for men, knowing that from the Lord you will receive the reward of the inheritance. It is the Lord Christ whom you serve.

— COLOSSIANS 3:23, 24

Many have yet to know the freedom that Christ gives every believer. Many are still in bondage to others. I have mentioned this often, but it bears repeating. When another person's words and behavior can change our words and behavior, we cannot be Spirit-controlled, but we are other-controlled. A significant element of freedom is the abandonment of the control of others, for nothing brings as much internal conflict as being controlled by the behavior of others. Several Chinese Christians imprisoned for their faith were fed very little, had sparse quarters, and had been locked up unjustly. Yet the thing that vexed them the most was the attitude of the guards and their selfish cellmates! They were in bondage to others, a much worse state than bondage to circumstance, quality of living, or will. Christians suffer from bondage to the behavior of others, when we must learn the joy that comes from being free! When the Chinese group learned to love the guards and cellmates, expecting nothing in return, they experienced true freedom behind their bars.

Why do the actions of others affect us so? Why do our mate's attitude, teenager's mood swings, boss's jab, parent's control, neighbor's selfishness, and elected official's peccadilloes bother us so? What is the root? The source is our pride that places us on a throne, connives to have us be worshipped, builds us a reputation, exalts us above others, finds our identity in surroundings and possessions, wants us unique among the herd, brings us to believe in our superiority, and leaves us in bondage to all those who would not support its lofty goal of giving us ascendancy. However, Jesus came as a servant, not in pride, and His servanthood kept Him free. When pride rules, we are slaves to all that would hinder its success. When servanthood rules, we are free to love, forgive, turn the other cheek, and bless those who curse, for who could hinder such goals? Our desire must be freedom from pride and, therefore, freedom from the behavior of others.

DAY 108
Purchasing Freedom From Others

Do nothing from selfishness or empty conceit, but with humility of mind regard one another as more important than yourselves.

— PHILIPPIANS 2:3

As in every other aspect of the Christian walk, we want the spiritual work God will accomplish in us, but we do not want the experiences that bring it. I cannot say I blame the believer that avoids the experiences that gain his freedom. I am grateful that since I was first aware of Him,

He has answered my prayer: "Father, all that You wanted to accomplish in man through Your sending Jesus, accomplish in me. When I complain, please do not hear me. When I fail, let it be covered in the blood of Jesus." I have not wanted the experiences that accompany learning to be free from others, but He has been faithful to bring them anyway, and I thank Him.

We purchase freedom from others with the currency of pride. Let me illustrate. A woman had a very critical, judgmental, and unloving husband. His attitude and behavior when arriving home dictated hers. Why? Pride. She felt she deserved to be treated better, for she was set apart for Christ. The treatment that Jesus received from others was not good enough for her; she deserved nicer. She was in bondage and needed to purchase freedom. Since the currency would be pride, she was instructed, "Each time your husband comes home upset and angry, you are to go sit in his lap and give him a kiss." She could see that freedom would be a costly purchase. However, she paid up, and today she is free.

A husband with an unfaithful wife finds himself in court. The judge awards the home, most of the income, and child custody (with the exception of one weekend a month) to the wife. She is angry (attempting to justify her affair) and uses every opportunity to gain advantage over the husband. She refuses to drop off the children, tell him of school events, or make him aware of medical concerns. She tells the children, "I must protect you from your father." He is working sixty hours a week to provide, attempting to be an active parent, and wanting his children to grow in the Lord. He is also a slave to his wife's behavior. The solution for him is to buy his freedom with pride. Love the judge, the wife, and the circumstances; make the support payments, allow the abuse, and be free. Look deeply into the face of the one who is bringing the discomfort and ask the question, "Do I want that countenance?"

There is an employee whose promotion came because of his ability to point out the flaws in others. This week you are under his microscope, and you have come under bondage. Buy your freedom with pride. Go to him and ask, "Can I do something extra to help you? I know you must be under stress." You will be amazed at the freedom that comes.

Freedom is not cheap, and yet it is purchased with a commodity that you should never have possessed, pride. Since it is a currency that does not belong to you, feel free to spend all of it! In the end you will have a wonderful portfolio of freedom.

DAY 109
Generational Curses

Therefore if any man is in Christ, {he is} a new creature; the old things passed away; behold, new things have come.

— II CORINTHIANS 5:17

He predestined us to adoption as sons through Jesus Christ to Himself, according to the kind intention of His will.

— EPHESIANS 1:5

Often I hear of those purported to have generational curses. The cause of their present-day calamity is ascribed to the curse received by an ancestor, whether it came from God, idol worship, or a witchdoctor; it does not seem to matter. Whole meetings are dedicated to breaking the curse. Where is this in the Bible? Oh, yes, there is one passage alluded to in the Old Testament. Deuteronomy 5:9, "You shall not worship them or serve them; for I, the LORD your God, am a jealous God, visiting the iniquity of the fathers on the children, and on the third and the fourth {generations} of those who hate Me." Adoption in the Old and New Testaments is much different than today's concept of adoption, wherein there is an acknowledgement of both birth and adoptive parents. Adoption in the Bible is understood as a new birth, and the adoptee is taken out of one family and placed into the genealogy of the new family. Hence, when we become children of God by adoption once we are born again, spiritually speaking, the genealogical curse, if such did exist, would be broken. Another problem with the false teaching of a genealogical curse for a born-again believer is that it is oppressive and irrational, because everyone could trace his lineage back to someone who had not loved God, and again, we have a new root, Jesus the Vine. This brings up a several points. First, in the New Testament, with all of the idol worship that the Romans had introduced to the believers, there is not one occasion in the Epistles where a solution offered to a problem was the breaking of a curse. Second, if it is God Who has cursed someone, do we really think that a man could break it? Third, as mentioned above, once born again, a person is in a different lineage, the lineage of Jesus, with God as the Father. Is He cursed? No, He is blessed,

Jesus is blessed, and we are blessed because we are in Him. There is no curse over us. The only curse, so to speak, is that of unbelief, which allows the elect to be deceived into such notions as white magic to lift curses.

Many have met these arguments with cries of, "if only you had seen what I have seen!" I have seen it. If we are to question our thoughts to examine the source, should we not on occasion also question our emotions, our experiences, and what we see? Our deceiver is a liar from the beginning. Anyway, why is it easier to believe that nearly everyone is influenced by curses when it would make much more sense, seeing that Christ is infinitely more powerful, to believe that if a person has some Christian ancestors he would have a special dispensation? And for those who appeal to Deuteronomy? Look at what happens later in the book, where God is explaining consequences He would remember " . . . to the tenth generation" (Deuteronomy 23:2), and then He parenthetically notes what He does with those who curse His children. Deuteronomy 23:5, "However, the LORD your God would not listen to Balaam but turned the curse into a blessing for you, because the LORD your God loves you."

DAY 110
Get Off Of The Throne!

> *Do not lay hands upon anyone {too} hastily and thus*
> *share {responsibility for} the sins of others;*
> *keep yourself free from sin.*

— I TIMOTHY 5:22

Society has worked overtime to relieve humanity from personal responsibility. However, when we are not personally responsible, we hold others accountable for our behavior. Conversely, there are always blame-takers, those who are willing to take responsibility for others' actions. I often find parents who take complete responsibility for their adult children's behavior, husbands and wives who confess to wrongdoing after being let down by their mates, neighbors who believe they could have prevented a divorce or suicide, and believers who think that with effort they could have prevented the failure of another.

Paul makes it clear that it is error to take responsibility hastily, for we can unconsciously share in another's sin by jumping in to help someone. People-pleasers want to help by rushing in to prop someone up, to make him feel better, to give him position that God is not giving, and, consequently, to participate in the sin of another. When the believer so identifies with others that he takes responsibility for their actions, he presumptuously seats himself on the throne of God without the power of God. To play God without His outlook and resources is a frustrating role, for a man judges what he thinks he needs to do and has nothing with which to do it. No believer can play the Holy Spirit, for it is His job to convict of sin and, with the conviction, bring power to overcome.

Anxiety will naturally increase for the believer caught up in responsibility. The only solution is to rest in God and step off of His throne. The believer can easily relinquish responsibility for others if he remembers that if he cannot change one hair of his own head from black to white, and so he has no chance of changing others, except through prayer. Prayer of this type is soothing, for it releases the believer from responsibility and gives all of the burdens to God. Prayer makes God not a partner, not a participant, but the One now solely responsible, and a Christian can return to living the life of a sparrow.

We must not let the carnal fill our backpacks with bricks of obligations to which we must attend as they encourage us to act, when we can do the hardest work a Christian can do, which is to trust God for the changes needed in everyone, even in ourselves.

DAY 111
Give Me

And may the Lord direct your hearts into the love of God and into the steadfastness of Christ.
— II THESSALONIANS 3:5

I suppose that nearly everyone has a private box, drawer, or filing cabinet where precious mementos from the past are kept. As I was cleaning out my own drawer of this type, I could not help but notice a conspicuous absence of anything from my grandfather. He was the man who was the greatest influence in my life, and yet he had given me no pocketknife, screwdriver, coin, hand-me-down, gun, or anything! He went to the discount department store every Christmas and bought me underwear; on birthdays it was socks; all other holidays I was invited to his farm for a meal. The underwear and socks have long since worn out. Perhaps it would have been nice to have a little something from someone so loved, but I know that what attracted me to him and to other family members was never what they gave, but who they were. I just plain enjoyed their presence. I relished the family gatherings on the front porch of the farm, always followed by some type of work project like cutting wood or building fences or barns. The fellowship always made the work a delight. What my grandfather gave in fellowship and love had me driving to see him every chance I got. Though at times that was no small sacrifice, I never, ever thought about it in that manner. It was worth the trip just for the fellowship, not for any material gain.

What did Jesus really give the disciples? Not possessions, power, or prestige! He gave them Himself, His fellowship, with no contracts, business deals, or services. They had the opportunity to walk with God, to walk with life itself. I believe that we grow in the revelation of His fellowship day by day, and little by little the business aspect of why we stick with Christ gives way to the appreciation of fellowship, until we recognize that were we to die today, life would have been worth it just for the wealth of fellowship with

Jesus. We have walked with God, and that is more than enough. The promise of heaven appeals to us because of the precious One we know will be there. We would choose His fellowship even without the promise of heaven! We need no other keepsakes to tuck away in our spiritual drawers, boxes, or filing cabinets. We are happy in fellowship with Jesus!

Sometimes I wonder about appeals made for coming to Christ. "He has a wonderful plan for your life" (the plan is in this brochure). "He will take away all your problems" (problems are the issue). "He will heal you" (look what I can swap you for healing). "He will change your marriage" (the service to be performed is obvious). "He will keep you from stumbling" (the barter system can work in your favor). "He will keep you from hell" (sounds expensive, what will that cost?). "The devil will no longer bother you" (did not think I could get rid of him). It sometimes seems that there is always a hook to make people come to God, and the hook is promoted as the real reason for coming. All things are given to us in the context of our fellowship with Him; therefore, our fellowship should be the issue, not what He is going to give. Fellowship is not a contract, an agreement between two parties for compensation from service rendered; that is called "going to work." Fellowship is free! Fellowship does not entail any discussion toward agreement on what each participant will bring to the table; it is not the doing of business, it is the exchange of something much more important than money, the exchange between valuable persons. Any work accomplished within the context of fellowship is beside the point.

DAY 112
Give Me Jesus! Please!

Sir, we wish to see Jesus.
— JOHN 12:21

I want Jesus! I want to see Jesus! In me, around me, in all things created, in everything good and bad, I want to see Jesus. I keep getting in trouble for saying it, and I do not understand why. I am more excited about Jesus than anything else. I will tell you a secret, something rarely heard, "He is not dead!" Jesus is alive. I am more excited about this living Jesus, raised from the dead, than I am the Bible, church, material gain, health, relationships, or all else that, when compared to Him, is considered rubbish. He must come first, or nothing else will have significance, meaning, or life.

Jesus is alive, but where do we look for Him? Amazingly, the very Jesus we read about today does not live on or in a page. He lives in us, if indeed we have recognized Him as Lord. There is no need for us to read the Bible to have something put into us, when its purpose is to reveal and witness to what is already in us, Jesus. We may or may not want to hear or read the words, but we know we want the Living Word, the life that the page is proclaiming and pointing to.

God is very excited about Jesus. He does not want you to be like Jesus; He wants an exact expression of Jesus flowing out of you. God does not intend for you to spout out the things of God; He wants you pouring forth the very articulation of God, Jesus Christ. It is your birthright! Is it possible? Is it believable? It is truth! The Man who did everything did nothing, and you could do greater things, not know greater things but do greater things (loving an enemy, forgiving, being a leaven, and having a peace that passes understanding). It will not happen without Jesus exactly presenting His Life through you. Do not substitute anything for Him; that will end in disaster. Good is the enemy of the best. Do you believe it? Just keep wishing to see Jesus! With Him comes everything that you have looked for in vain outside of Him. I am tired of teaching, tired of knowing, exhausted with putting into others, and weary of hoping for change. I want to know Christ in me. I want you to know Christ in you. I wish to see Jesus!

DAY 113
Give Me More Of The Word

And He gave some {as} apostles, and some {as} prophets, and some {as} evangelists, and some {as} pastors and teachers, for the equipping of the saints for the work of service, to the building up of the body of Christ.
— EPHESIANS 4:11, 12

During the course of my life if God would permit me to understand and live John 15, I would exit earth quite happily, for I have devoted my life to this one Man and what He describes in this one chapter. I preach it from what I think is every angle, and then He shows me another. If in these times we could see that Jesus dwells in us, what a difference it would make, but that great truth must come through revelation. I am aware that words will not do it. Jesus must do it. In preaching John 15, I discover that I am forced to experience it when Jesus comes for my words. Well, amen. What confuses me are the many who do not understand this passage, or even Jesus for that matter; they clamor: "Could you quote more Scripture in the course of your lectures?" My response, "Do you understand the Scriptures that I have quoted? Are they practiced in your home, job, and life?" Most are honest enough to say, "No, I am not experiencing John 15, but it would make me feel better if you used more Scripture." Amazing! I could go speak at a seminar and just read the Bible; I wonder if that would be enough Scripture! How many would come to hear me read? However, I believe God has given gifts to men that will allow them to be instruments of revelation. I cannot think of anything but John 15, and if one has gotten it, I will be moving on to someone who does not have it.

Church life would immediately be transformed if we understood the basics of the Christian life; few have camped at them long enough to get them. Those without the foundational truths begin to build, only to see the building crumble or go up in smoke as hay, wood, and stubble. The Bible is a witness to Jesus; it is not the information book, the magic book, or the book to change us. We are not to go to it for anything other than a witness to Him. It will not create His presence, but it will tell us that He lives in us. We do not need volumes; we need a few simple little passages to bring the revelation of Jesus.

DAY 114
Give Us a Government

"Give us a king to judge us." And Samuel
prayed to the LORD.

— I SAMUEL 8:6

I must admit that one of my greatest struggles has been to see God in government. As I ministered in so many countries, I could not help but see the abuse of government when carnal man takes control. I have often been asked how I can believe in a God who permits suffering. My response is consistent: "How can you believe in man, who causes the suffering?" The amazing thing is that we the people have yielded to these carnal men the authority over us. In man's carnality he cannot even settle an argument with a neighbor. He believes himself to be right and cries, "Give us a king to judge us!" Well, we have all gotten our kings, our judges, and we got more than we reckoned for. Justice has a price, freedom! In the end every man would have been better off to give the neighbor whatever he had taken, to forego the king and judge, and to trust God to fix the whole thing. We can see that governments come into existence because of man's lust of the eyes, lust of the flesh, and boastful pride of life. It was man's carnality that put a king in charge; now the king counts on man's carnality in order for him to stay in power. The carnal liberal and the carnal conservative both want to impose their wishes on the other. The carnal king (government) listens so intently because, after all, he is needed. All the while this friction is used to keep the king in power, and while in power, what does he do? He placates both sides while oppressing, stealing, appropriating, and financing every deed of the flesh. "Give us a king!" What a mistake. The founding fathers of the United States saw it and tried to stop it. Their solution was a government under God. The carnal are like mushrooms, hidden until the fullness of time when a simple afternoon storm reveals that they surround us. Kings do not want God to stand in the way of their greed. Therefore, God is pushed out in favor of injustice upon injustice and more injustice. And the wars! The cement that holds kingdoms together is a mixture of the blood of so many sons. Enough! My point is that the flesh of man cannot change, and neither can the nature of a government. Zipping a pig up in a horse suit makes him no less of a pig. The fact is that Jesus is coming, so what do we expect governments to look like before He comes? Does the Bible teach that all nations will forsake Him, except the United States will stand fast with Him? No! The flesh is flesh and hostile to God; all governments are an outgrowth of flesh. What, then, are we to do? We are aliens and sojourners; the affairs of government are not our affairs. In the meantime, we pray for those in authority, for with the position they sought will come judgment.

DAY 115
Giving All

*Love the lord your God with all your heart and with all
your soul and with all your strength.*

— MARK 12:30

Many make the mistake of wanting to understand exactly what is entailed in their commitment to give all to God before they take the step. They must realize that giving our all cannot be understood before it is revealed over the years we live with the Lord. We will not know what giving all means until we die; all that Jesus personally means to us is not revealed in one day, but rather over the course of a lifetime. A good analogy is marriage. In the wedding ceremony we pledge to give all, but we will not know exactly what all is involved in that until the day that we die. In giving all to God, the important thing is that we do it once with our mouth; though we may feel nothing or experience no change, He will reveal in stages what we have done with those words.

DAY 116
"Go and Tell No One"

God, after He spoke long ago to the fathers in the prophets in many portions and in many ways, in these last days has spoken to us in His Son, whom He appointed heir of all things, through whom also He made the world.

— HEBREWS 1:1, 2

Have you ever noticed that often after Jesus performed a miracle, He did not want the beneficiary to tell anyone? Why? He simply did not want to attract a following among those that are merely drawn by miracles. He was interested in those that would be attracted to God. Today there are many who want to appeal to the crowds by miracles, such as the miracle of the one-time fix. Jesus is still looking for those that will come to Him in faith and love Him, not for a miracle but because of who He is. It should be noted that when God gave dominion over the earth to man, in many ways He tied His own hands. He must now work through man. In the Old Testament, "God spoke long ago through the Fathers and the Prophets." Today, He is speaking "in Son." We must in these times hear the Son and not seek after the miracles.

DAY 117
Go Slowly, Do Not Get Depressed, Take Your Time

You have shortened the days of his youth.

— PSALM 89:45

I was talking to a fellow who was discouraged that at age 22 he had not seen that Jesus was his life. I laughed. "Brother, if you could know all that you need to know before entering heaven at age 22, God would not have set the length of man's life at seventy years! Relax." God has created this world for a purpose, and it functions under His permission. There are things that can only be learned here. We are in the process of losing all in order that we might gain everything in Him. In one study the average age of coming to see that Christ was actually in a person was said to be between 55 and 70. We simply cannot receive it all at once! We are not intended to get it all at once! We are in a process!

DAY 118
Goals

But the goal of our instruction is love from a pure heart and a good conscience and a sincere faith.

— I TIMOTHY 1:5

I have often thought how odd it is that at a relatively young age we are expected to discover something to do for the rest of our lives. I can remember being asked, "What are you going to do with your life?" Life has a diminishing quantity, and being responsible for doing something wisely with it can be overwhelming. In some countries the decision is not nearly so vexing, where caste and economy determine what one will "do with his life." Nevertheless, everyone must determine how to spend his time on earth.

Imagine the goal of life as being the hub of a wheel, with life's activities being the spokes that support it. The hub should always be faith in God. We exist to grow in faith, a goal worthy of our lives. We can look at every situation as to how it affects faith and belief. Giving our life to faith is satisfying, because faith is fulfilling and nourishing. In order for life to have a purpose, it must be given to something greater than itself. Faith gives life a purpose.

Dissatisfaction arises when something that should be a spoke, a support for the goal of life, moves in to replace the hub. At this point one will always feel depleted. For instance, having children builds faith, just as not having children builds faith. Raising a child in today's world will keep one constantly trusting in Jesus; not having a child, when man is created to procreate, will also keep one's eyes focused on Jesus. In these two cases, the spoke leading to the center is different, but what it leads to, faith, is constant. However, when a child that one has, or the child one wishes he had, becomes the goal of life, faith is not built and life loses its meaning. The same is true of having or not having marriage, health, money, vocation, ministry, or security. Though spokes differ widely, life can be enjoyed as long as faith in the Lord is the goal and life's pursuits teach and lead to faith. Look around and view all of the spokes, but the hub in which one stands is not visible. Relax in what is not seen: our God. Faith is the hub, and we have a God.

DAY 119
God is Creative in the Weak

No one puts new wine into old wineskins; otherwise the wine will burst the skins, and the wine is lost and the skins as well; but one puts new wine into fresh wineskins.

— MARK 2:22

God can only do something creative through a weak, unknowing person. Familiarity with a job encourages doing it the same way and not, in humility, seeking Him for His way. For example, a person with thirty years of successful experience with missions, teaching, or church building will not, generally speaking, seek the Father for how He wants things done today or in a new place. It will be done the same way without thought, and the person will find himself in a rut. The problem with many churches is that they either stay in a rut or go examine other people's ruts instead of going to the Lord and discovering whether there is something new that He would do. I meet many people fearful to take up the call of God. They do not know how to preach, they do not know how to lead, and they do not know enough about the topic. But here is a secret: water cannot be put in a full cup; new wine cannot be put in an old wineskin. The fearful person is the perfect one in whom God can be creative. If he believes he cannot do something, he can admit it and let the Lord do something new. This message of Christ in man is old, and yet with each generation God would make it fresh. In weakness, allow Him to do just that, make it fresh.

DAY 120
God Is Love

Beloved, let us love one another, for love is from God; and everyone who loves is born of God and knows God. The one who does not love does not know God, for God is love. By this the love of God was manifested in us, that God has sent His only begotten Son into the world so that we might live through Him.

— I JOHN 4:7-9

God is love. We are not told that God is understanding and reason, for these two do not bring lasting change at the core of man's being. We are not told that God is willpower or emotion, for these also leave man unchanged. No, God is love. This simple statement affects every area of life. I have seen bumper stickers, protest posters, and music stating, "All we need is love." That is true, but if God is love then we are just as correct to say, "All we need is God." It is impossible to bring love into any situation—marriage, world affairs, politics, or relationships—without bringing in God, its source. So often in personal discipling I am made aware of the hatred couples have for one another, man has for himself and others, and families have for its members. It is easy to talk of understanding, false concepts of others, and learning to walk a mile in others' shoes; however, as I speak of those things I see the strong resolve on the faces of the offended to continue hating. Therefore, God must always be brought into the equation. Where there is no Jehovah there is no love, period!

I remember getting in on a political discussion with atheistic friends from another country and now living in the U.S. In the middle of the discussion I said that I wanted to tell a story, and I told one about Jesus. When I finished I noticed that their collective countenance had changed; the looks of frustration from concentrating on the inconsistencies of government gave way to peace and contentment, yet they were not believers. If we are created by Him and held together by Him, then the very mention of His name will bring a lift to our being. Doctors tell us that the human body runs best on love and that it cannot flourish in hatred. God is the love that body, soul, and spirit all desperately need. The next time you are in conflict, simply bring God into the discussion and watch the hostilities diminish. Do not bring teaching about God or pet theologies, but bring the living Christ into the equation and watch Him do what understanding cannot.

DAY 121
God's Children

And do not be conformed to this world, but be transformed by the renewing of your mind, so that you may prove what the will of God is, that which is good and acceptable and perfect.

— ROMANS 12:2

Do you really believe that the Lord's return and the end of this world will be prompted by the doings of politicians or polls? By the opinion of an entertainer who a short time ago was a waiter? Does the late-breaking news really mean anything? Why am I, as some accuse, being so negative? As a child of God a man is of greater importance than anyone in the world; his opinions count more, he is more unique, and he has more value. Do not forget it. We are to live above the world, not allowing it to tell us who our enemies are, whom we are to serve, who is important, or to whom we are to listen. At the heart of the world's system are ticks attaching themselves to living things, God's people, and trying to suck life out of us by continually telling believers we are in some way defective. The world's system needs people and yet despises them. The "great and mighty" need the weakest to maintain their position, and actually, since they can never rise above the thing they need, they are really quite weak. It would be nice if ticks only took what they needed and left, but they never do. They always lay more eggs, and so the world continues to perpetuate itself.

The pull of the world is unbelievable. Jesus could have extended His kingdom through government and worldly cooperation, but He fled from those at every point, so what business would we have courting what He avoided? Jesus steered clear of the world, so how could we consider ourselves strong enough to stand in its strongholds without compromise? I am privileged to meet with the most famous, special, and chosen people in the world every day, those who have been called out of the world, the believers. We are not of this world. Is that not good news? The standard of the world does not apply to us, and we are blest and happy to know one another. This kingdom is passing and will give way to His; in this we can rejoice. Be not conformed! We are in but not of the world. The Holy Spirit whispers, "God so loved the world that He gave His only Son." This we must remember as we approach the world from which He, and He alone, redeemed us.

DAY 122
Got a Word?

Peace I leave with you; My peace I give to you . . .
— JOHN 14:27

Sadhu Sundar Singh had one word that kept him at the feet of Jesus, something that every Hindu seeks, in vain, to find. It is the Hindu word for peace. In Jesus he had found peace. When questioned about his faith by the Hindus, he would often say, "Peace, peace, where else could I go for peace but Jesus?" An old man God worked through to bring Christ to the remote area of Eastern Nepal had a different word. His word was revelation. Jesus had brought him revelation, knowledge of the heart instead of the head, something that could only be found in Christ. Upon being beaten and left for dead for preaching, he would not surrender his calling to do so or acknowledge any but Jesus. His reason: "Where else would I go for revelation?" I was traveling with one of my Indian teachers, told him of the two men, and asked what significant word he held dear. Without hesitation he said, "Because! Because He went down, I have gone up. Because He died, I live. Because He experienced hell, I will experience heaven. Simply because. The word because is keeping me near." So what is your word? What is the word that keeps you at the feet of Christ? My word is welcome. I remember being in His presence, and there was so much going through my mind; I was thankful, I had been forgiven, and I appreciated all that He had done through me. Before I could say a word, He spoke that word to me: "Welcome." I did not have to say a word; I was welcome! Everything was okay! Then He said it a second time, "Welcome," but the meaning was different. He was welcoming me into His presence, into participation with His Son, and into the revelation of His Son. Again, I was welcome! It is a little word that means so much to me. He is happy to say, "Welcome," to me. "Welcome" keeps me at His feet. When I asked Betty, she had one word, with. He is always here with us to the end of the age, and He will never leave nor forsake us. Because

He is with us we have everything. There are many words that believers have sent me. What is your special word?

DAY 123
Grace

Though He scoffs at the scoffers, yet He gives grace to the afflicted.

— PROVERBS 3:34

There is much written about grace today. Not that my two cents amounts to much, but I wanted to give my definition of grace. It need not be preached, but it has been proven through the experience of many believers.

Grace: At my point of need, God is everything to me that I thought He was not!

Moses had spent forty years being trained to be everything that accompanied being a young man of the royal family; he was equipped to be a god, a Pharaoh. He spent another forty years in the wilderness discovering what he was not. Finally, he was prepared to lead, having realized that he was a "not." God told him what to go do, and Moses accurately responded, "I am not able." God's response was, "What is that to Me? I AM!"

God is to me all that I am not. First I must acknowledge that I am a "not." Next, He tells me what He is, which includes everything to me of which I might have need that I am not! I am not a good father, a good husband, a good Christian, or a good witness! This is my point of need. Grace comes and meets me at my point of need! I did not think He could be those things to me. However, as I recognize abiding, He is to me all that I thought that He was not. There is a life in me, His life, that is a good father, husband, and witness, and He is everything to me that I am not.

Look at what you are not. Do not determine to work harder, but call on the grace of God. At your point of need, He is everything to you that you thought He was not.

DAY 124
Grieve Not the Holy Spirit!

Do not grieve the Holy Spirit of God, by whom you were sealed for the day of redemption. Let all bitterness and wrath and anger and clamor and slander be put away from you, along with all malice. Be kind to one another, tender-hearted, forgiving each other, just as God in Christ also has forgiven you.

— EPHESIANS 4:30-32

Why are we not to grieve the Holy Spirit? Many have taken this passage to mean that they can push the Holy Spirit to the place where He will either leave or God will severely punish them. However, we must first look at why the Holy Spirit is given. Acts 9:31, "So the church throughout all Judea and Galilee and Samaria enjoyed peace, being built up; and going on in the fear of the Lord and in the comfort of the Holy Spirit, it continued to increase." The Comforter is technically a Helper. John 14:16, "And I will ask the Father, and He will give you another Helper, that He may be with you forever," and John 14:26, "But the Helper, the Holy Spirit, whom the Father will send in My name, He will teach you all things, and bring to your remembrance all that I said to you." So, then, how does the believer grieve the Holy Spirit? Simply by refusing His help.

Often I have had the unpleasant experience of "helping" someone learn the computer. I must admit that most of the time it has been a grievous experience, for, out of necessity, the person learning must be at the keyboard, the control center. The problem is that he is always asking questions, and then before I can suggest the answer, he starts moving the mouse all around, madly clicking here and there and already creating a problem much worse than if he had done nothing. He wants help but does not want help, and I am grieved. I am the helper there to make his life easier, but to the extent that he refuses to listen, his life will be less than productive and he will know nothing. I was there for his good, not my own, and if he does not listen, I am grieved for him but have not cut him off. The same is true for our children. As parents we are helpers. However, if our young ones refuse to listen and go their own way, we are grieved for their sake. The Holy Spirit only tells us the things that will make us happy; if we follow, the Holy Spirit is not grieved. It is a difficult concept, but sin no longer hurts Jesus; He already died for the sin of all men. We are not to sin because sin hurts us, and when we are hurt, the Helper is grieved. Therefore, to be happy and not grieve the Helper, do the following, "Let all bitterness and wrath and anger and clamor and slander be put away from you, along with all malice. Be kind to one another, tenderhearted, forgiving each other, just as God in Christ also has forgiven you."

DAY 125
Hatching Others' Eggs

And they said, "Believe in the Lord Jesus, and you shall be saved, you and your household."

— ACTS 16:31

It is rightly said that God does not have any grandchildren! Christianity is not hereditary, but at times we might wish it were so. God's desire is to have a unique relationship with each of us; the one He has with me is not the one He wants with you. My wife and I have three children; I deal with each one differently in the context of three unique relationships. It would be odd to have the same type of relationship with all of them; it would not work. What goes on between God and each believer must be his own. A problem arises when we are convinced to so regard other believers' relationships with the Lord that we coddle and nurture the truth that they have learned, when, in fact, God wants to birth something unique in us. There is a wonderful book, Hudson Taylor's Spiritual Secrets; I believe everything that he said in the book. However, the book never changed me or had much effect at all. Why? I think there is a clue in the title. It is called Hudson Taylor's Spiritual Secrets and not Michael Wells' Spiritual Secrets. Hudson Taylor's secrets are not mine; I have my own spiritual secrets, just as the Lord will show you what He views as important in your life. I will give you a hint: The areas of your life in which He is working have something to do with the exact place you are at today, exact in job, family, and internal struggles. It is important that you hatch the egg that is yours and stop thinking you are to hatch other people's eggs.

DAY 126
Holy Spirit

But when He, the Spirit of truth, comes, He will guide you into all the truth; for He will not speak on His own initiative, but whatever He hears, He will speak; and He will disclose to you what is to come. He will glorify Me, for He will take of Mine and will disclose it to you.

— JOHN 16:13, 14

A model of man is often shown using three concentric circles representing body, soul, and the spirit, which is the innermost circle. Without any one of the three, man would not exist; the three elements must exist together in a constant intimate exchange. Man is made in the image of God, so we can apply the model to God. The innermost circle could represent the Father, the Source of the Source. The middle circle would stand for the expression of the Source, or thought and word. Hence, Jesus said He viewed the Father as the greater, because He is the Source of the thought and word; and yet, it is also true that neither operates alone, and thought and word are equal to the source. Jesus is the Word and the Father is the Source of the Word. The Word and Source are One. The activity of the Source and Word would be the Holy Spirit, for the Holy Spirit (Activity) is birthed from Source (Father) and Expressed Thought (Son). The intimacy between the Father (Source) and the Son (Expression of the Source) reveals the third part of the Trinity, the Person of the Holy Spirit. This is why Jesus said that man could slander the Father or the Son, but it was blasphemy to speak ill of the Person of the Holy Spirit, the best that can be produced from the intimacy between the Father and Son.

We think of a spirit in terms of angels and demons, yet in the language of the Bible, spirits also bring with them atmospheres. When visiting a house that has a spirit of conflict, it makes sense to enter into conflict. When visiting a house with a spirit of joy, it is easy to be happy. Joseph Stalin carried with himself an atmosphere of fear and murder. The Holy Spirit is not found in heaven, sitting on a throne to be worshipped. Rather, the Spirit that emanates from the Father and Son is a Holy Spirit, a Person with an atmosphere whose presence and power is so great that for those under His influence, being Holy makes sense and becomes possible. The Holy Spirit, when He comes, invades the world, pushes the world away, and brings a heavenly contrast. When a person finds himself in the presence of the Holy Spirit, that one's life is immediately contrasted with the atmosphere of holiness.

A woman had been married five times and was currently having an affair. She also had moved her son's homosexual boyfriend into her home and encouraged their relationship. One day when driving home, she stopped to ponder the mountains, and the Holy Spirit with His Atmosphere fell on her. At that moment she could see the evil in her life and was so ashamed that she was completely undone; her lifestyle no longer made sense, and she sought change. The Holy Spirit brings contrast. We can see why David said, "Take not Thy Holy Spirit from me." When the Holy Spirit's Atmosphere, exuding from the presence of the Father and Son, encompassed him, he found power to live in holiness, power to seek wisdom for God's people, assurance that his kingdom must be God's kingdom, and loss of worry, doubt, and fear. Jesus said to the disciples in John 14 that this same Holy Spirit had walked with them, but it would come into them. The atmosphere created in the intimacy of God, the best of His love, would now dwell in them.

It is not ludicrous for us to believe that Thought/Word could become a flesh-and-bones person in Jesus. The people came to see the Word, and the Word was dressed in swaddling clothes. The people's attention was not consumed with the clothing but with the Word that had become flesh. Why would it surprise us that an atmosphere of holiness would describe the Person called the Comforter? This Holy Spirit—with His Atmosphere that brings the presence of God to men, gives men power, renders irrelevant worry, doubt, and fear, and makes change natural—came clothed in tongues of fire. The clothes are not to be worshipped, but the awe-inspiring fact is that coming from the intimacy of the Father and Son, a Spirit has come that makes the life of the Father and Son possible and sensible. We can see why the people were praying "in the Spirit," why so much can be done "in the Spirit." The proof of the Spirit cannot be condensed to miracles, gifts, or fruit, all of which can be duplicated by the enemy. Two proofs that the Spirit has come in a person are that Jesus will be lifted up and men will be drawn to Him, and there will be a conviction of anything that is against Christ. These are things that the enemy never copies. We are to be filled with the Spirit, filled with His atmosphere that comes from the Father and Son. We see why the terms Spirit of Christ, the Spirit of the Father, and Holy Spirit can be used interchangeably.

DAY 127
He Blesses and We Bless

And God is able to make all grace abound to you, so that in all things at all times, having all that you need, you will abound in every good work.

— II CORINTHIANS 9:8

Many times we meet people we consider to be a curse or, at least, far from a blessing. I have noticed believers that are self-centered takers who have made comfort their goal in life, and their inactivity is a general drain on the body of Christ. Yet I have noticed that God has provided for them in the midst of their immaturity, supplying jobs, house payments, help in the midst of a variety of crises, and myriad other blessings. Why is that? I suppose it happens for the same reason that He has blessed us so many times when we were out of tune. The observation has left me wondering at the grace of our God; in fact, it has left me glorifying my God. The point is that if God can bless when His children are out of tune, then should we not do the same? His grace is an example of the grace that exists within us by His indwelling Life. We have no excuse not to bless those that curse us, because whatever we believe is an offense, we must understand that the offense caused to the Father is incalculably greater, and still He blesses. His sun shines on the good and the evil. His grace is more than our example, for it is our life. His grace toward others in the midst of their failures can encourage us, for in it we can see His response to us in our failures. Is it any wonder that we love Him?

DAY 128
He is Everywhere

And He is the radiance of His glory and the exact
representation of His nature, and upholds all things by the
word of His power. When He had made purification of sins,
He sat down at the right hand of the Majesty on high.
— HEBREWS 1:3

Often we forget that God is in everything. We do not view it as does the pantheist, but rather from the standpoint of creation. Since God holds all things together, all things can teach us something about Him. Years ago when my son was young, he and I were in the back yard trimming away new apple shoots. I stopped and explained that if we were quiet, opened our hearts to the Lord and listened, we could learn something about the Father through pruning the tree. Soon my son brought me a new green shoot and a dead, brittle shoot from the year before. I watched as he tied the green shoot in a knot and untied it; he then took the dead, brittle shoot and broke it in two. I asked what that taught him about the Lord, and he responded, "If I have Christ's life in me, what breaks the world will only bend me." I told him he had discovered a great truth that would carry him all through life if he would hide it in his heart. "Surely you desire truth in the inner parts; you teach me wisdom in the inmost place." –Psalm 51:6

When walking we can ask God to speak to us. Once when I was with my Indian teacher walking in the mountains, he stopped by a half-rotten gigantic log and asked what I saw. I noticed that this log, long after its death, was still leaving its mark; we still had to step over it. In the same way I said that I wanted to be a believer who after death still left his mark among family, friends, and even unbelievers. He pointed out a branch in the trunk; because of the extensive decay, I could see that the branch had been attached to the very center of the tree, enveloped and held in place by it. He pointed out that we are attached to the Vine's center, with Jesus holding us in place.

DAY 129
He Is The Glue

For by Him all things were created, {both} in the heavens and on earth, visible and invisible, whether thrones or dominions or rulers or authorities—all things have been created by Him and for Him. And He is before all things, and in Him all things hold together.

— COLOSSIANS 1:16, 17

I have often looked at world economies and wondered what was holding them together; they should not work. I look at governments and wonder at their existence. What is keeping them going? Families that are cold and dysfunctional; how do they keep running? Individual lives that are empty, hopeless, shallow echoes of the flesh; how do they manage to carry on? All things visible are held together by something presently invisible, Jesus. It is not true that man needs to be dependent on God. Why? Because he is dependent already, and whether or not that truth is acknowledged makes very little difference to the fact of the matter.

Jesus Christ is holding together the dictator, as well as those who persecute. He is holding together the criminal, the politician, the unethical businessman, and anyone else who would oppress. For many, such a realization would give cause to blame God. "Who could worship a God that holds together the wicked, self-centered, and abusive people?" But for me, the recognition has brought a great peace and rest. I know that if He holds them together, then He is ultimately in charge and can cause all things to work toward His end. The One who is the Glue is Love, and love will not harm me. I do not have to panic or invite in fear of the future as I look to the government. My life is not in the hands of the visible, but in the hands of the Glue that holds together my world, my family, my emotions, my will, and my deepest life. I can leave it to others to plot and plan how their own efforts can best control their visible world; they will try to find security in vocation, in assets, in family, and in others; my world is held together by the Divine Glue of love. Amazing! Amazing love! I have no worries!

Carnal man is blind; he builds but neglects to recognize the Glue that has His own mind, will, divine plan, and goal. Carnal man lives in pride and independence but has not succeeded in running and hiding from God, for Jesus is right there in the midst of all that has been created, a "Holy Spy" in all the secret places of man's heart and accomplishments. The Divine Glue will determine the end of all things, even of those who think they hold themselves together. When He mandates the end, He can simply remove Himself from the visible governmental powers, and they will be no more. When the Glue withdraws, all will crumble.

I believe that Christians can be quiet and let the years speak against the minutes, willing to wait as they watch God's plan revealed. We must have the faith to see Him as the invisible Glue in charge, in ultimate control, working all things to His end; and then we must rest and watch with joy the unfolding of the glorious days ahead. Our God is doing all things perfectly.

DAY 130
Jesus Is The Issue

Then Jesus said to him, "Go, Satan! For it is written, You shall worship the Lord Your God, and serve Him only."
— MATTHEW 4:10

But He said to them, "I have food to eat that you do not know about."
— JOHN 4:32

Jesus, during the wilderness experience, a time of being cut off from all outside sources of appetite, fed His Spirit with the things of God (peace, will, wisdom). He had no appetite for the things of the world, and so the temptations would have been foreign to Him, things He would have had to try to choke down with water, bit by bit. He just said, "No." We have all had times in our lives when sin held no attraction because God was our focus. When He is not our focus, we obsess on our own spiritual condition, which does nothing in terms of bringing about a remedy.

Can you take up the challenge to stop thinking about your own spiritual condition? It is more difficult than you think, but your spiritual condition is not the most important matter; Jesus is of ultimate importance. Your latest tragedy is not the concern; His spiritual position is the issue. Lay everything aside to read about Christ, think about Him, pray to Him, and ask Him to pray for you. Forget the earthly concerns and lose all appetite for sin, for in Him you will find everything you have looked for elsewhere in vain.

I do not live for what others consider to be the spectacular; what I consider impressive is being able to walk across the room and bless the enemy that has offended. But I will mention one thing that happened to me, and it can be taken or left! I do not intend to start a cleverly devised, fantastic ministry centered in an experience. Having said that, one night I awoke to a sound that I cannot describe, for there are no words with proper definitions to describe it. I heard it in that place of connection to God, in the spirit. The sound was sad, lovely, compassionate, and painful, but again, these words fall short of expressing what was revealed to me to be spiritual weeping in heaven. To enter into it was painful and yet releasing (if those words even make sense), as if I were entering into the pain of God. In ministry I will continue to emphasize that what He permits, He could prevent; that this world is not out of control; and that He created the world to accomplish in us His purposes: the loss of our pride, strength, righteousness, glory, and kingdoms. However, through this experience, which lasted off and on for several days, I was aware of the pain in heaven over the very things that exist on earth. Why do I share this occurrence? For the simple reason that we think too much of ourselves, our tragedies, our injustices, our losses, our sicknesses, and too little of Him and the weeping of heaven. I will never forget that sound. I can nearly close my eyes and hear it now! We, as believers, need to remember we are destined for heaven!

DAY 131
He Is Not Dead!

This is now the third time that Jesus was manifested to the disciples, after He was raised from the dead.
— JOHN 21:14

Often I talk about hearing Jesus. Indeed, every believer does hear Him and will discover that all of his clever little thoughts about Jesus were the voice of God all along. "My sheep hear My voice" is an absolute truth! We do hear Him. I enjoy being taught by God, and yet when I say that, I am sometimes looked upon as an alien. The fact is that He is not dead! He is alive, having come out of the grave, and He speaks to His people. We approach the Scriptures to find Him, to hear Him. We want the Bible to speak to us. We are not reading about His life like we would read about other teachers. We are not attempting to heed what was said by a teacher long dead and gone; Jesus is not dead! The Living Word will speak to us; we can approach Him personally. He is alive!

Stop and meditate on it if it seems doubtful that He is alive and will speak! Have you let Jesus speak to you? Have you heard from Him? There is no need merely to sing about Jesus or fancy Him in mind or emotions when He can be met and walked with. He is alive!

DAY 132
The Great Shepherd

THE LORD is my shepherd, I shall not want. He makes me lie down in green pastures; He leads me beside quiet waters. He restores my soul; He guides me in the paths of righteousness for His name's sake. Even though I walk through the valley of the shadow of death, I fear no evil;

for Thou art with me; Thy rod and Thy staff, they comfort me. Thou dost prepare a table before me in the presence of my enemies; Thou hast anointed my head with oil; My cup overflows. Surely goodness and lovingkindness will follow me all the days of my life, and I will dwell in the house of the LORD forever.

— PSALM 23:1-6

The Lord is my Shepherd, what a wonderful thing! He is not my general, employer, or warden, demanding that I walk lockstep behind Him; nor is He ever fearful that I might get out of line, make the wrong decision, or make a choice unpleasing to Him. As the Shepherd, He leads me.

As a young boy I sat one moonlit night on the back porch of the farm and listened to my grandfather complaining about the sheep, and why not? The night before, we had pulled into the driveway just in time for the headlights to catch a coyote jumping a fence while holding a young lamb by the throat and flung over its back. So this next night we had sat on the roof of the barn waiting for the coyotes to return. After many hours we had taken a break and gone to the house for a cup of coffee. In the short time it took us to return, several sheep had already been slaughtered, though there had not been one sound of alarm from them. Another time I watched with amazement as several of the sheep followed one another into the thick muck of the feedlot, sinking deeper with each step until they were completely stuck and crying out for help. It was so evident that sheep farming was an expensive, exasperating, and frustrating business. Grandpa had to do everything for them, and they were so stupid. I once said, "Grandpa, let's just get rid of all the sheep!" I actually thought that I would be commended for my insight, but immediately he responded, "Oh, no; I like them!" That simple statement revealed that he was a shepherd at heart. I loved that shepherd, for many times I found myself stuck, stupid, and following the crowd; yet though I was exasperating, frustrating, and expensive, I saw him exhibit the same heart toward me. Now if we multiply this simple illustration by one trillion, we will vaguely begin to see the heart of the Great Shepherd.

DAY 133
He Leads Me Through My Choosing

I am the good shepherd, and I know My own and My own know Me, even as the Father knows Me and I know the Father; and I lay down My life for the sheep.

— JOHN 10:14, 15

What are we like as sheep? Sheep naturally follow; they know the voice of the one who protects and provides. They can be led, unlike most animals that must be driven. They do not have the constitution for a fight; once on their backs, they just cry out. They have no apparent plan, and they like to spread out. A good shepherd does not fight the nature of the sheep but uses it; he understands the weaknesses of the sheep and fills the gap. Though the sheep may sleep when the wolves are about, the shepherd will not. The sheep have no clue about the cares and needs of tomorrow, but the shepherd does. The sheep have neither a plan nor a method of realizing it, but the shepherd does. In every way that the sheep are weak, the shepherd is strong.

How is all this of practical value to us today? I would like to apply it to decision-making, since most believers simply do not recognize their weakness in that area or, consequently, their need for the Shepherd as their strength. The Shepherd has been leading us in the natural events of life; that is His job. He is only asking us to be what we are by nature, and that includes how we do not know the future, exactly what we should be doing tomorrow, or the exact place He is leading us. If we did grasp all those things, we would not be walking by faith and could not possibly be pleasing to Him, for "without faith it is impossible to please Him" (Hebrews 11:6). But what do we naturally do? The answer is different for each person. I know what I naturally do: write, lecture, travel, disciple, and walk. No one has to tell me to do these things, for I have naturally grown into doing them since I became a believer. This is the sheep-life for me today. For you it may be taking care of the kids, cleaning the house, and uttering a few pleas to God in the scarce few quiet moments between the demands of being a mother and wife. It may be that you commute, work, commute, return to play taxi driver, put out a few fires in your relationships, and before bed find a few moments of time for the Scriptures. The important thing is whether or not you can believe that He has led you to that place. If you think you are responsible for the place you are in, then unbelief has an inroad and you will be wasting time thinking of the "what if's." I believe the times I was in school, a leatherworker, a construction worker, unemployed, a manager, a janitor, a Christmas-tree harvester, an auto mechanic, a teamster, a campus minister, a remodeler, a painter, or an international speaker, I was always being led! I have a Shepherd who leads me through the natural, and I will not believe anything else, for here is a secret! The sheep are led, they know not where, but confined in the vast pasture they get to pick the grass that is most appealing to them. He led me into marriage, yet I chose my wife. He led me to school, but I picked which school. He led me to move to Tennessee, New Mexico, Kansas, and Colorado through natural events, yet I chose to go to those places. He was leading, I was picking, and I always picked the perfect thing. Yes, He is leading through my choosing. Today He has led me into an international ministry, and I get to pick where I want to go. I cannot make a mistake, because I am in the pasture to which He led me. Do you see that the decision is always made in the context of the pasture within which He has placed you? He is leading you in a pasture; nothing in it can cause your undoing, so you are free to pick any of the things that you see (obviously we are not talking about the sin that may trespass through your pasture). This is a faith walk; if you are unbelieving, you dare not enter into this discussion. A small God makes for big decisions on your shoulders, while a big God makes for small decisions. Unbelief makes for labored decisions, while a big God speeds things up.

DAY 134
Thy Will Be Done

*In everything give thanks; for this is God's will
for you in Christ Jesus.*
— I THESSALONIANS 5:18

Can you believe it? You do not rule your believing; your believing rules you! Often your faith will be the mere size of a quarter, but you will find yourself in a situation the size of a plate. At first you will want to shrink the situation to fit what you can believe God for, but God's plan is to have you expand your faith. Your Shepherd has led you to the exact place you are at today, so today you can choose the grass in your meadow that looks best to you. I do not believe that I have ever made a mistake. That is not to say I have not sinned, erred, or failed. But I have never made a mistake in knowing the will of God. I simply acknowledge that He is leading, next I make a decision according to what looks good to me, and then I say, "Father, I want Your will, not mine. I choose such and such." Next, I act. God has been faithful to close doors to all that is not of His will.

"I know it could not be God's will for me to do that, because I want to do it, and it would be so much fun!" What a statement of unbelief that is. Who put the desire for something in you from the beginning? Are you really so smart as to have conjured up the desire all alone? Why do some people want to stay home and others travel? Why does it not bother me to go without food or to sleep on a dirt floor with no heat? It is because God put it in me. Why would some people abhor such a thing? God has not put it in them. I am glad that God put something different in Betty from what He put in me. She prefers home because God put it in her, and because she prefers home, I have a foundation from which to travel. It all works together, in faith!

DAY 135
Having an Explosion

He must increase, but I must decrease.
— JOHN 3:30

How does one take the smallest particle and make it smaller? By exploding it! The nucleus of the atom is a very small thing, and yet it can be made smaller through an explosion. There is a lesson here for all that would decrease that God might increase. The smallest bit of self-life will be made smaller only after God magnifies it through an explosion. "Oh, I was doing so well loving God and walking in holiness, and then you entered the room. I can walk perfectly well with Jesus until you enter the room. I do not really have any problems, and walking in the Spirit is natural, until you enter the room." Though we do not like being confronted with it, whenever a "you" in our life enters the room, our self-life explodes! We did not think that we had a self-life that ugly until it was inescapably revealed to us. We need not be discouraged or avoid the person or the situation, when we can see God and have a move in Him. He is only exploding self so that it might decrease in us. We can simply acknowledge to Him the flesh when we grasp our weak inability to love. We decrease that He might increase.

DAY 136
He Who Knew No Sin Became Sin

He made Him who knew no sin to be sin on our behalf,
so that we might become the righteousness of God in Him.
— II CORINTHIANS 5:21

Spiritual glue is holding all things together (Colossians 1; Ephesians 4; Acts 17). Jesus is the invisible nuclear glue that is holding all things together. He is the positive. Like opposing ends of magnets, God is naturally attracted to man, and man is very drawn toward God. Think, though, of trying to force together two positive sides of magnets; those repel one another, and it is very difficult to bring them near to one another. Man is fine as long as he views himself as the negative that he is when compared to all that is positive in Christ. However, through pride and believing himself sufficiently positive not to rely on God, man invites sin into his being, which causes the glue holding him together to be repelled by the sin. The glue withdraws, and the man is less and less a reflection of the image of God. If sin continues to be invited in, the man will, in time, no longer resemble the image of God; in fact, the sin makes him sick. God did allow for a fix for all of this. The sin could be taken out of a man and placed on an animal, though because an animal is not created in the image of God, sin so distorts it that it must be killed. The animal was a good representation of the loss caused by what man had done. For example, a dove represents freedom, song, and peace, all things that man lost through sin and the dove would lose by way of death. Sacrifice of a man was never required until the fullness of time when the sins of the whole world (past, present, and future) had reached their culmination. On the cross God broke the divine umbilical cord that ran from Himself to the Son and placed on the Son the sins of the whole world. That sin was so great that it drove the very life out of Him, at which point sin, Satan, the world, death, captivity, and hell encased Him. He sank to the depths of hell but, to the surprise of all, broke out! He conquered all that had encased His life, ripped open the gates of hell, preached, and even took captivity captive to disable the free exercise of its power. He then waited until God raised Him back into His slain body, in which awaited the sins of the whole world. This time He entered back into the body with the power of an indestructible life, met the sin, and conquered sin in the body! His Life was so powerful that it even transformed His earthly body. It is one thing to accept that He has done all that in His body, but the next step is for the believer to acknowledge the truth that Jesus can do it in his own body! He can, He will, and He has.

DAY 137
He Will Keep You

I am coming to you, Holy Father, protect them by the power of your name.

— JOHN 17:11

There are always times in a believer's life when present circumstances and the baggage of the past simply overwhelm him. It is as though all of hell's forces are unleashed upon him. Emotions are confused and the mind races to find a way out, although there seems to be none. At this point it is important that the believer NOT look to his own ability to be kept. He must remember that it is God who does the keeping; if it were up to him to keep himself, he would have been overcome long ago. Therefore, each night before he goes to sleep, he can lay the future before the Lord. "Lord, I cannot keep myself, all is confusing, all appears hopeless, and now YOU keep me." HE WILL KEEP THE BELIEVER! IT IS HIS JOB!

DAY 138
Healing

*Until now you have asked for nothing in My name; ask,
and you will receive, that your joy may be made full.*

— JOHN 16:24

Though death is something everyone will experience, it is written within man not to obsess on death lest he get nothing else done. He would not get in an automobile, join the army, take an airplane trip, or go skiing or hunting because of the thought that those activities could lead to death. Often the closest we come to confronting our own mortality is when we experience firsthand the terminal illness of a loved one. In this situation, what is the sick one to do? First, he recognizes that death is an enemy. Many believers submit to death rather than fight it. An elderly saint told me that he did not want to die yet and be with the Lord in heaven. "It has taken eighty-five years to learn what I have about Christ and the Christian life. I want to stick around and share it with as many young believers as I can." To that I say, "Amen!" Second, the ill person can discern if God has, indeed, told him that it is time to leave and go be with Him. These first two issues are crucial for him to deal with.

What are those of us who love the ill one to do? It should not come as a shock that anyone is dying, "inasmuch as it is appointed for men to die once" (Hebrews 9:27). Since we are all born to die, we must see that the process toward death and what the process accomplishes are actually more important issues than death itself. First, we are to pray with absolute confidence for the loved one's healing. I prayed for the healing of my grandmother, grandfather, and mother right up to the very moment that they passed away. Why? Praying for the sick is commanded, and if I pray in faith, even though the person is not healed, I enter into the category of the "others" of Hebrews 11:39: "Having gained approval through their faith, [they] did not receive what was promised." Frankly, though the physicians diagnose, God will have the last word. I will pray, and if I do not receive that for which I ask, I will continue to trust and love God.

Second, every event in life occurs to create faith, and we are not of those who rebel against faith. As a young parent I had to come to grips with my inability to be omnipresent for my children. I began to be full of fear of the park, of their walking to school, of the bullies, and of influences in homes that I could not control. One day, on my knees, I acknowledged, "Lord, these are Your children. Thank You that You watch over them and allow nothing to enter their lives that will not be used by You." My eyes and heart could rest. The loved one is the Lord's, but we forget! What is coming into the ill person's life has first passed through His hands and will be used for His purposes. What we see is part of a necessary process. At this point in my life there is absolutely not one single thing that has happened to me that I would change. All of it has been for my good. God shows no partiality, and everything that happens to the ill person is for his good. This awareness stirs faith. If the end of illness is death, then a loved one has gone to be with the Lord. I have a friend who loves hunting and was able to take a trip to Africa to hunt. When asked where my friend was, I would say with excitement, "He is hunting in Africa!" I said it with a lift in my voice, for I was happy for him. To say a loved one is with the Lord is not a depressing statement.

Third, we come to understand that we all need suffering. In the one who is ill, suffering is good preparation for the laying aside of the worn-out body that had heretofore encased the soul and spirit but is not suited for heaven. Suffering brings the greater acceptance of the temporal, for though much of life has consisted of the physical, the suffering person is ready to lay aside the body and leave the material world. At the same time, watching the suffering of a loved one prepares us to let go of him more willingly. I have known many who have lost a loved one instantly through something like an auto accident or suicide (there is also a process, which we have not discussed here, for those who undergo instant death), and those understandably need a more extended process of letting go after the fact of death. In the end, we see that God is, in fact, in all things. "Thou dost make Him to rule over the works of Thy hands; Thou hast put all things under His feet" (Psalm 8:6).

DAY 139
Heavy Loads

*Make it your ambition to lead a quiet life and attend to
your own business and work with your hands,
just as we commanded you.*
— I THESSALONIANS 4:11

"Do not let down and do not stop working; the time
is near!" "Are you doing all you can? People are dying,
so where is your vision for missions? Get up! Go around
the block preaching; there are those in your neighborhood
who need saving!" "How can you enjoy your sandwich in
the restaurant? Do you not know that sinners surround
you?" "You only have so much time; do not waste it on
anything but ministry!" Blah . . . blah . . . blah!

Usually we hear such things from someone who is in
"full-time ministry" with no other job commitments. In
the majority of the places to which I travel, those with
whom I minister have full-time jobs and consider all of
their activities to be an extension of ministry. "Ministry"
must be redefined; it is not constant talking! Saint Francis
said that we are to do everything possible to share the
message of Jesus Christ, and then if we absolutely have to,
say something! That is an overstatement, since the world
must see but also must hear. The beauty of our "religion"
is that we do not have to get out of the world, like the
Buddhist, in order for it to work. It works right where
we work! We do not have to move up a priestly ladder
climbing toward heavenly work and moving away from
earthly work. Our faith has its impact in the everyday tasks.
As we live in Him and He lives through us, life's activities
are filled with Him. I Corinthians 10:31, "Whether,
then, you eat or drink or whatever you do, do all to the

glory of God." Paul did not separate our work under the headings of "secular" and "religious"; he combined it with the use of one word, all. "Do all to the glory of God." Separation of the all that a believer does has led many to feel as though they are second-class believers, who then become dissatisfied with their vocations while looking for "the great Christian someday," a day when ministry will fulfill them. Considering the list of admonitions at the start of this article, how do any of them apply to the first thirty years of the Savior's life? He had a Kingdom to start, apostles to train, the whole of mankind to save, and yet for years He continued to work at a carpenter's bench! In Him we see that the life of heaven and the life of earth can become one in the daily tasks of humanity. I remember succumbing to the teaching that spirituality equals activity. I felt condemned if I were not witnessing to everyone I met, yet the effort was rarely fruitful. I then discovered rest and became motivated to live for the glory of God. I stopped pressing for salvation decisions and began looking for ways to love. Rarely a week goes by that I do not find myself witnessing, but now it is natural, not contrived of my own doing, and it is fruitful. I love Christianity, for there is nothing else like it; it is unique, absolute, and it is the way.

DAY 140
Holy Terror

Then the kings of the earth, the princes, the generals, the
rich, the mighty, and every slave and every free man hid in
caves and among the rocks of the mountains. They called to
the mountains and the rocks, "Fall on us and hide us from
the face of Him who sits on the throne and from the wrath
of the Lamb; for the great day of their
wrath has come, and who can stand?"

— REVELATION 6:15-17

There is a magnificent cathedral in Hamburg, Germany, called St. Michael's. What I like the most is that adorning the front of the church is the statue of the fallen angel Lucifer, so muscular, so full of anger, so frightening, and yet lying flat on the ground, wings broken, and a foot on his neck! Towering above him is Archangel Michael with his shining, peaceful countenance. He holds his enemy down with one foot and points a spear, which is the cross, at the head of Satan. The scene is awing to behold. It is more correct to portray one angel defeating another than to portray God fighting something that is created, but it got me thinking how we are so fearful of darkness, things that go thump in the night, and evil. Many movies and books have been developed to play on these fears. As children we would see "The Mummy" or "Werewolf" and not sleep for several nights. However, those things are not as frightful as God. To come in contact with darkness does not frighten the children of the light, but to come in contact with pure holiness and light is, on the fright scale, much worse.

We learned early on in life that contrast makes us uncomfortable. For instance, teenagers offer free cigarettes to their friends who do not want to smoke. What will the greatest contrast be like when man stands before a light so pure that it will seek out every bit of darkness? Each dark spot in man will be burning like a red-hot ember! We need a good movie to be made about real fear that comes from seeing holiness, from seeing God.

DAY 141
Hopeless

. . . having no hope and without God in the world.
— EPHESIANS 2:12

I was standing talking with one of the brothers in Odessa at the Black Sea when a very old, neatly dressed, small woman with a cane approached and began to speak. Though I did not understand her Ukrainian words, I understood her look, one that vexes me more than any other and is observable in many parts of the world. I have seen hunger, emotional hurt, desperation, panic, fear, and anger written all over people's faces, but this one look captures my attention, disturbs my spirit, and causes sleeplessness. The look is that of hopelessness, a blank stare seeming to convey a feeling akin to what would be experienced if a person were walking alone on a country road at night surrounded by fog, in a deep darkness like Pharaoh experienced, a darkness that could be felt! I reached in my pocket and gave her five dollars, nearly one month's retirement pension. Her face remained expressionless as the tears formed in her eyes. She grasped my hand and kissed it, then turned and walked away. I despise hopelessness, especially when I see it on the face of a believer. What is its primary cause? "Thou will keep him in perfect peace whose mind is set on Thee" (Isaiah 26:3). When a believer lacks hope and peace, the first question that is to be asked is, "What is your mindset?" There is no peace when the mind is set on oneself. When the mind is set on Jesus, its true dwelling place, we have peace and hope. His presence brings hope. But no one need take my word for it when he can so easily find out for himself.

DAY 142
How, Exactly, Do I Abide in Christ?

Then He said to them all: "If anyone would come after Me, he must deny himself and take up his cross daily and follow Me. For whoever wants to save his life will lose it, but whoever loses his life for Me will save it."

— LUKE 9:23, 24

Abiding in Christ is something that every believer has experienced, and yet it seems most difficult to maintain. I have been asked, "What do you struggle with?" Like all teachers I struggle with the thing I most often teach, abiding! All of my other failures originate from this one.

When Christ is my focus, nothing really bothers me, and when He is not, the smallest event can create a spiritual domino effect. So the question, "How, exactly, do I abide?" is a significant one.

Let me share a few insights. First, abiding is not something that we do but the awareness that we trust the Lord completely. Psalm 139:7, "Or where can I flee from Thy presence?" Second, abiding is not dependent on us but on Christ, so it is a faith issue. He is the One keeping us in the abiding relationship, the branches in the Vine. Third, if we do not know how to set our minds on things above, then we can at least discover what it is to set our minds on the flesh and refuse to do it! Examine Luke 9:23 to understand the flesh, and if we say no to every opportunity to set our minds on it, by default the mind must go to the spirit. Fourth, abiding is the beginning point of an abundant spiritual life; therefore, all powers meet at this point. When forces would move you from your position in Him, do not succumb to the voice that whispers, "It does not work; it is not for you. You are exactly where you were years ago!" Once I was in a boat that capsized, and I was pulled under the water. I did not immediately begin to think, *Well, I guess I will never have air again! Air sure does not last very long; it sure is not worth the effort of breathing!* No, no, no! All I thought about was getting back to where there was air. We are not to let failure move us away. Rather, we can get back, start breathing again, and let our focus rest in Christ.

DAY 143
The Crucified "I"

I have been crucified with Christ; and it is no longer I who live, but Christ lives in me; and the {life} which I now live in the flesh I live by faith in the Son of God, who loved me, and delivered Himself up for me.

— GALATIANS 2:20

What is the "I" that was crucified with Christ, and exactly how did that "I" get crucified? I am always making a feeble attempt to give definition to phrases that have for so long been used by believers that few stop to think about and grasp their meaning. Think of how the phrase, "How are you today?" got so overused that saying it today just means, "Hello." Rarely does someone care to hear a prolonged assessment of the state of another's health and disposition. The world and the enemy have plotted to overuse words to reduce their significance, words like *Jesus* or *love*. "I have been crucified with Christ" has been thrown around, quoted, and memorized to the point that its meaning and importance have been diminished. My motive in discussing what it could mean is that believers might increasingly understand it and incorporate it into their being. If the reader differs with my definitions and descriptions, I urge you to search for a definition that you can satisfactorily accept, that it might encourage you in your walk with Christ.

Imagine a team of physicians converging on a live man lying on an operating table; they were charged with the task of finding the "I" in the man. Would they be able to find it? No! It is because the "I" of Galatians 2:20 is not a material thing but an attitude; the "I" has wrapped itself, like the roots of a great tree, around every visible fiber of the man. Try to cut it out of the mind and next find it in the will; remove it from the will and discover it has grown back into the mind. "I" is the attitude of glory, pride, righteousness, and strength; in short, it is the attitude of wanting to be God. Being made in His image is not enough, for "I" wants to be worshipped and occupy the center of the universe that belongs to God. The body cooperates, for since it was made from the dust, it is not drawn to the spirit and therefore enjoys the indwelling "I" that allows the flesh to follow flesh.

A wet sponge placed on a dry one will become dry itself, because its water will flow to the other in transference. The day one believes on Jesus, God takes his body and nails it together with Christ on the cross, nailing, as it were, the two sponges together, the believer's dripping with proud "I" and Christ's empty "I" of humility. What happens next is transference; the believer loses all of his "I" attitude and life as it soaks into Him. When it is all over, the believer is nothing but a dry sponge, no anti-God attitudes and no life. The believer's "I" coming into Jesus to do battle for supremacy is no different than the other battles He had already won; He kills the believer's "I" attitude or life center. It may not be hard to imagine one sponge soaked with "I" being nailed to the One void of "I," but what of the billions of people, and all at one time? There was so much anti-God "I" in Jesus on the cross that the Father had to cut the umbilical cord. The great I AM, Jesus, the Word, had always been in unbroken fellowship with God, Who was Jesus' "I" attitude and life. The break killed His body. II Corinthians 5:21, "He made Him who knew no sin {to be} sin on our behalf, that we might become the righteousness of God in Him."

DAY 144
The Crucified Christ

But may it never be that I should boast, except in the cross of our Lord Jesus Christ, through which the world has been crucified to me, and I to the world.

— GALATIANS 6:14

When people saw Jesus they were seeing God, for He was attached, so to speak, by a divine umbilical cord to the Father, whose LIFE flowed through Him. Satan could not defeat God in heaven, so he thought he would try again with his next best chance, which was when God was no longer in heaven but on the earth. Wrong! It was the same God on earth in a body, and in that body God defeated sin, the world, and every aspect of the flesh. How? The "I" attitude of Jesus intertwined throughout His mind, will, emotion, and body was this: "Of My own self I can do nothing." To the world, He hung on the cross as a defeated man; in actuality, there hung the greatest conqueror the world would ever know.

Jesus' body went to the grave, but His LIFE departed and descended. Jesus had no choice but to descend when He died; that is what was happening to dead people. There were a couple of battles along the way, all easily won by the power of an indestructible life. Death encountered a new foe, LIFE, and death went running. Captivity was taken captive, and a Man tore open the very gates of hell and preached! All who believed in Jesus left with Him. In short, Hell was plundered. What a time! Next, God reconnected with Him to raise Him from the dead, and Jesus returned to His body in the tomb. His life was so powerful, having overcome sin; Satan; the world; the mind, will, emotions, and body of man; the "I" attitude; and Death, Captivity, and Hell, all by doing nothing of "Himself." When this powerful life reentered His body, His body was instantly transformed by the power of an indestructible life. His fleshly body could not decay; it was overcome by LIFE and was transformed. We men can only take our spirit along where our body allows us to go. His transformed body had to go wherever His spirit went. If He wanted to walk through a wall, His transformed body followed. Lest we forget, when He returned to His body, He was soaked with the "I" that proved the Love of God, an "I" attitude that trusted God and was holy, righteous, acceptable, and dependent.

Remember that every believer is the dry sponge attached to the soaked One that fills him. Formerly dead in trespasses and sins, believers are filled with a new "I" that soaks into their whole being and gets into every corner until thinking, will, emotions, and body all change. Believers may look the same but they are not; they are having a conversion, being filled with His Spirit, His "I" attitude, and His life. Again, like the great tree root, this divine "I" wraps itself around everything. The flesh of man does not like it, for in the past the flesh was allowed to follow flesh; now the flesh must fight to do so. However, it is fighting an "I" that has already overcome flesh and counterattacks from a place of victory. Believers are filled with THE SPIRIT and are raised up.

DAY 145
Crucified With Christ

What shall we say then? Are we to continue in sin that grace might increase? May it never be! How shall we who died to sin still live in it? Or do you not know that all of us who have been baptized into Christ Jesus have been baptized into His death? Therefore we have been buried with Him through baptism into death, in order that as Christ was raised from the dead through the glory of the Father, so we too might walk in newness of life. For if we have become united with {Him} in the likeness of His death, certainly we shall be also {in the likeness} of His resurrection, knowing this, that our old self was crucified with {Him} that our body of sin might be done away with, that we should no longer be slaves to sin; for he who has died is freed

from sin. Now if we have died with Christ, we believe that
we shall also live with Him, knowing that Christ, having
been raised from the dead, is never to die again; death no
longer is master over Him. For the death that He died, He
died to sin, once for all; but the life that He lives, He lives to
God. Even so consider yourselves to be dead to sin, but alive
to God in Christ Jesus. Therefore do not let sin reign in your
mortal body that you should obey its lusts.

— ROMANS 6:1-12

The believer could not handle being attached directly to the Father, but Jesus attaches him to Himself through an umbilical cord. Jesus is the transformer that makes the power coming to the believer safe; He is the mediator in heaven providing a constant flow so that the attached believer can always be soaked with His "I." In a very real sense, then, the believer is in heaven with Him, and conversely, when the believer is on earth, so is Christ. He will carry out His work through the believer while He is in heaven, much like the Father did through Him while He was on the earth. A believer has entered into the same kind of relationship that Jesus while on earth had with the Father. A believer has what Jesus had, an "I" that of its own self can do nothing, but he will do greater things, because when Christ was on the earth, He was working toward victory, but the Spirit that now dwells in a Christian works from victory. A believer will do so much by doing nothing! He must not have tunnel vision and see himself as either independent or a passive tool, either in control of every action or having no control over his actions. The spiritual place, called "abiding," is neither, best illustrated by the vine and branch. As a branch the believer is unique and independent but must use the freedom to choose to do nothing unless the Lord is doing it through him. The believer needs to see he is in control of his actions, and the action he needs to take is inviting Jesus to come and soak him and be his life in the present situation. In the end he will have an expression of Christ through him that is not he. Throughout the recorded life of Jesus we see Him proving that this spiritual place exists, and though few today might discover it, it does exist.

Those present at Pentecost were unique; they had believed in Jesus before all of His victories had been accomplished. They believed in Jesus but had yet to have their "I's" crucified and replaced with His. Therefore, after His resurrection, as these various groups of believers were gathered together, Jesus, in one climactic moment, did an instantaneous, mass removal of the carnal "I's" in these believers, replacing them with His divine "I." The people found themselves without their carnal "I's," attached to the Vine, with the flow of the all-powerful new "I," the Holy Spirit, in them. Each was given, along with the consistent fruit of the Spirit / "I," a unique expression of Jesus through them in the form of a spiritual gift. It is here that we first see the body of Christ. The Holy Spirit is exactly Jesus, just as Jesus was exactly God; to see Jesus was to see the Father. To see the true manifestation of the Holy Spirit will be to see the exact expressions of Jesus.

As a side note, Jesus was never weird! In the Hindu world, the gods are always weird, with oddities such as a man, monkey, or cow god. Jesus never portrayed God as something strange, abnormal, or out of place; He did not go off into any visions or dreams. He was not trying to be mysterious. He was not starting a cult and threatening people to stay with Him. He was not psychopathic but balanced and sane, addressing the real issues. Time with Him was worthwhile, He never misled, nor did He go on continual emotional rampages. The expression of His Spirit will be no different. The new "I," His Spirit, or His Life, was not given so the believer could have an emotional high point. It was not given as a sedative to block the world in which we live. It is not given to resurrect the old "I." Sometimes those who by temperament are Doers believe that the Holy Spirit came to make them prophets once they receive Christ. For them the "Holy Spirit" is power over others. The new "I" definitely is not given to exalt man, nor is it given to entertain. The Holy Spirit will give experiences manifesting the very life of Jesus, the life portrayed in Matthew 5, 6, and 7. The flesh is not interested in these, for with His filling, the believer will find himself being offended until he cannot be offended, forgiving, laying down his life, returning good for evil, walking across the room to kiss an enemy, and failing at everything he independently tries to do. Many genuinely do not want to be filled with His Spirit; they prefer a counterfeit spirit that promises to meet their perceived needs. Well, amen, we have all been there, but when we admitted where we were, we could leave the miserable place.

I personally believe there are still some, as in the days of the early Church, believing in Jesus but not yet knowing that the old "I" is crucified and replaced with the new "I." In this frustrating state the believer is trying to whip the old anti-Christ "I" into imitating Jesus. Why would I say that such believers exist today? I believe that I was one. I have always believed in the man Jesus, and I actually always believed that I was called to minister. Yet I never knew that my "I" was crucified, that "I" was buried and raised again. I never knew He could be my new "I," LIFE. Then one day He revealed it to me. He stopped being my Savior from sin and became my very life. It is so nice to be alone with Him and soaking up His "I"!

DAY 146
The Cross And The Flesh Pool

Who, although He existed in the form of God, did not regard equality with God a thing to be grasped, but emptied Himself, taking the form of a bond-servant, {and} being made in the likeness of men. And being found in appearance as a man, He humbled Himself by becoming obedient to the point of death, even death on a cross.

— PHILIPPIANS 2:6-8

Why would Jesus put His life in flesh? To answer that question we must ask another. Why did God put Jesus in flesh? The obvious reason is that He must dwell in the flesh, overcome it, and come back to dwell in our flesh as One who has already conquered. However, there is another reason. Being in the flesh would push Him to a moment-by-moment abiding in the Father. The flesh is permitted because it is used of God to push us to Him. Once we acknowledge that apart from Him we can do nothing, He then does everything. The flesh is only vexing if we do not want to be with Him and at the same time we do not want to walk in the flesh. They tell the story in Korea of an old man in the fish market. All the other vendors had big tanks, just like his, filled with fish, with this one exception: Their fish died as soon as they were put in the tank, and he sold his fish alive. Upon investigating, it was discovered that the old man had put in his tank the fish's predator. By alertly swimming to stay away from the predator, the fish stayed alive and fresh. The flesh is just that for us. Truth is not only preached but demonstrated. In the state of recognizing abiding (again, abiding is not worked for but recognized), the flesh is not bothersome. Being in the likeness of a man, he emptied Himself, fell under God's love, obeyed in everything, and there never was or has been a man on earth that had more joy.

I am happy that my flesh has driven me to God. When I empty myself, accept the death of the old "I" and let Him do everything, I feel like the happiest man on the earth. Ministry is pressure when a believer is bound in the power of a dead old "I" to create something that will please God. However, Jesus did not create ministry, He participated in it by letting God work the ministry through Him. I am not creating ministry; I am walking with Him, and of myself I can do nothing. Next, I stumble into a situation, and He is in me, ready to meet it. It is I, but not I! It is very easy to pray, "Jesus, like a Shepherd, lead me!" I have extended that attitude to my ministry. I do not have a big one-year, three-year, and five-year plan, but I do have a plan. Every morning I pray, "Jesus, like a Shepherd, lead me." Over the years, through the experience of trying to minister in the power of the flesh and at the same time attempting to tame the flesh, I have been broken. The Lord used my flesh to bring me to the place I am today, where I can say, "Apart from You I can do nothing," and, "Jesus, like a Shepherd, lead me." The failings from trusting my old dead "I" have caused me to rest and wait on the new "I" to act. If ever I lose this attitude, the flesh is there to make me miserable and, in so doing, drive me back to Him.

DAY 147
Humility: The Secret To A Deeper Life

Your attitude should be the same as that of Christ Jesus.
— PHILIPPIANS 2:5

We must remember that humility is not saying, "I am nothing," but rather, "I possess nothing." This attitude allows us daily to secure the experience of His life within us. However, if we stop and listen, how much boasting about what is possessed do we hear? There is boasting of the past in what we had, of the future in what we will have, and of that bright child, the brilliant career, or those flashy material goods that we now hold. "Jesus Who, being in very nature God, did not consider equality with God something to be grasped, but made Himself nothing, taking the very nature of a servant, being made in human likeness" (Philippians 2:6, 7). The dreaming about what we will someday possess or what we have already lost takes our attention away from the greatest thing that we possess now, in this moment, the presence of Christ, Himself, within! This is more than man in his wildest dreams, in and of himself, could ever attain.

DAY 148
"I Do Not Believe Because Of The Crusades!"

Brethren, I do not regard myself as having laid hold of it yet; but one thing I do: forgetting what lies behind and reaching forward to what lies ahead, I press on toward the goal for the prize of the upward call of God in Christ Jesus.

— PHILIPPIANS 3:13, 14

You may not hear it in the places you travel, but I have heard it so many times I actually find myself finishing people's sentences for them. They do not believe in Christianity because of the Crusades! If it is not the wars, the people may finish the sentence with what a pastor once did, the behavior of the television evangelists, or the tenets or actions of some associated with a certain denomination. They have ready examples of abuse by Christians, whether in the past or present, that exempt them from having to question their own lives and allow them to discount Jesus and every positive example of believers. Make a list and put in the left column those things Christians have done wrong and in the right column the contributions of believers. From talking on the phone to turning on the lights, from getting vaccinations to women's and children's rights, from everyday great inventions that have become commonplace to mass education, the world is indebted to the inspiration received by Christians. The unbelieving world stands on the backs of the believers, reaps the benefit of believers, and makes their complaint against the believers. I just cannot recall a plethora of scientific contributions of Hindus or atheists. The argument against Christ because of the behavior of a few is flawed, if not ridiculous. Horses have killed people, so will I never own a horse? Electricity has killed people; do I not want electricity in my house? Cars kill people; should I never own a car? Doctors have immoral procedures; will I never go to a doctor? People kill people; should I never listen to another person? The Crusades took place; I will refuse any contact with Christianity. It is absurd. The issue is not the Crusades; the issue is pride, which no argument will break, for by its very nature pride is blindness that only Jesus can break through. Before a word is spoken to a proud person, it is predetermined that it will not be received. The only reason for speaking to such a one about it is the revelation of his heart and a coming judgment.

DAY 149
"I Do Not Feel Him!"

In order that in Christ Jesus the blessing of Abraham might come to the Gentiles, so that we would receive the promise of the Spirit through faith.

— GALATIANS 3:14

If I as a believer do not feel the presence of Jesus and go looking for Him, what am I actually seeking? I already have Him, but I am actually seeking to have my unbelief confirmed. If I do get the feelings that I have found Him, I have now been deceived, for He is always there, always with me, so I have just had an experience that is contrary to Scripture. We could easily make a list of all that we are in Him and all that we have already received; that would help us discover that we are working in unbelief to get what we already have. It is important to remember that what we receive, we receive by faith. The opposite of faith is work, so if we are working for what can only be received by faith, we have canceled our faith and the experience of it. Work does the exact opposite of what we think it will. Nearness to the Lord is given by faith; work for it and we cancel His nearness, leaving us to work all the harder and still never have the experience. It is a tightening spiral. Stop and acknowledge Him. Enter into rest. Stop seeking for Him. We already have Him!

DAY 150
"I Have No Personal Relationship With Christ!"

The glory which You have given Me I have given to them, that they may be one, just as We are one; I in them and You in Me, that they may be perfected in unity, so that the world may know that You sent Me, and loved them, even as You have loved Me.

— JOHN 17:22, 23

God brought order out of chaos as His Spirit moved. He does the same for us, but we must follow the order. Therefore, we will look at the order of things before examining the statement in the title, which is an assertion I often hear.

1. God's goal is building our faith, the assurance of things hoped for and the conviction of things not seen—or felt—in our lives. When we are in what could be called faith-growing situations, then nothing is out of order in our lives. Rather, everything is in perfect order. We cannot have the things of God (love, awareness, and feeling) by effort. They come through the acknowledgement of faith (without feeling or even experience).

2. Some say to me, "Mike, you have a great ministry." I stop them and say, "This is not my ministry, but it is preparing me for the ministry." No one's job, family, circumstances, or feelings are their ministry; those things only prepare us for true ministry in His presence for eternity.

3. The purpose of life on earth is to form us into safe persons in heaven. Made in His image yet born separated from Him, we busy ourselves setting up our own kingdoms wherein we, of course, are kings and queens. To the degree that we can control our circumstances, we believe we are strong. To the degree that we cannot control, we feel weak. We are only as strong as our weakest link. Therefore, during our time on earth we must lose control of mind, will, emotions, body, others, and overall strength, until ultimately we see the wisdom in forfeiting our kingdoms for His great Kingdom. If we are losing control we need not panic, because everything is going according to plan.

4. Every question we have about God and His dealings with us must be tempered with the remembrance of who He is. God is love, and as such He bears with us, believes in us, hopes with us, and reflects every other characteristic of love described in I Corinthians 13.

5. What is a personal, deep relationship with Jesus? All of the above are involved in it: growing faith, ministry, and the loss of control. Perhaps we have allowed others to define what a deep, personal relationship is, and we thus believe ours is nonexistent because we have not experienced what they define that relationship to be. Not everything that is true is truth. A teaching may come from Scripture and be true but not truth. How do we tell the difference between the two? True teaching that lands at our feet and speaks of what we must do is not truth. True teaching that ends at the feet of Jesus and explains what He does for us is truth, for Jesus is the way, the truth, and the life. If what we are hearing does not

end at His feet, it is not truth. What does land at our feet is the issue of our being unbelieving toward having a deep, personal relationship with Jesus and continuing to maintain that there is something lacking that we must do or find. Perhaps we have not had visions or miracles, He has not awakened us in the middle of the night to heal us, or not everyone in our family is perfect. Still, according to God's definition—the one that counts—we already are in a deep, personal relationship in accordance with the above.

Any believer who has said, "I do not have a deep, personal relationship with Christ," went left instead of right when it came to the fork in the road of experiencing God. Experiencing God could not be more than what He has given us as individuals to experience; the roadblock is in thinking that there is something more than what God with an IQ infinitely over 999 trillion has already initiated toward us. We are pleasing and close to Him because the life of Christ in us is pleasing and close. There is nothing more to do. Feelings of loneliness, separation, and depression may be there, but they will not go away while we are focused on them. This may appear vague as to the issue presented, but the issue is not the issue. We have proven that when things are in order, this aspect of flesh does not overwhelm us, so in that is the answer. In the end, we can own what we feel, tell God how we feel, leave it at His feet, and move on. If on a scale of one to ten it is a ten for God, He will deal with it. If He does not deal with it, then we know it is not in His order of things.

Because of Christ, we are in and experiencing a deep personal relationship with Him.

DAY 151
"I Feel So Guilty"

*I will go away {and} return to My place until they
acknowledge their guilt and seek My face; in their affliction
they will earnestly seek Me.*

— HOSEA 5:15

I must admit where I am before I can leave where I am.
I must own something to disown it, possess to dispossess!
Many suffer from guilt. There are many genuinely afflicted
believers who need the revelation that Jesus takes away
guilt and forgives and that there is no obstacle between
them and Him. However, there are several reasons why
guilt feelings sometimes will not leave, and those are what
are addressed in this article. For one thing, for all of the
believers who lack understanding of God's willingness to
forgive, there are an equal number who only feel guilty
because of what the revelation of their sin has done to their
image; it is not genuine guilt. A fellow slandered a brother.
Later, he began to think that the brother was going to find
out. He then started repenting and repenting, praying and
praying that the brother would not hear about it. He was
so sorry that he had said anything at all. However, after
talking with him I discovered that he was not nearly so
concerned that someone got the wrong impression about
the disparaged brother as he was that others might get the
wrong impression of himself as a slanderer! The guilt was
merely based in self-image. Sometimes guilt is just a feeling

with no center, as if the enemy wants believers wallowing in insufficient joy. However, there are times when guilt is not relieved because there has not been true confession, which does not consist of going around telling everyone what terrible persons we are. True confession is to God for an offense against Him. I have heard people say, "Jesus, I confess that I made such a fool of myself." What does that have to do with Jesus? That is embarrassment, self, and flesh. If we were not living to men, how would we know that we made fools of ourselves? Proverbs 28:13 states, "He who conceals his transgressions will not prosper, but he who confesses and forsakes {them} will find compassion."

DAY 152
"I Hate My Church!"

For the gate is small, and the way is narrow that leads to life, and few are those who find it.

— MATTHEW 7:14

"I am the only one at my church with the revelation that Jesus is my life and is everything! Where can I go to find a good church?" This is a common question and a valid complaint, for there are churches that do not mention a word about Jesus, that operate entirely in the flesh and manipulate to build numbers of members and quantities of coffers. Those types of churches do exist, as we can read in Revelation. I will not, through guilt, manipulate someone to stay in such a place unless he has the peace of God to stay. He may be the only one there loving Jesus above all else, and much is said in Scripture about the principle of the few. There simply are not enough of them, and, after all, it does not take much leaven to raise the whole lump. Being a lone voice in the wilderness is sharing in His sufferings.

A woman prayed me into her church, and I mean that sincerely; she prayed me in. I do not think anyone could have stopped me from being there. It took ten years of prayer, but she never wavered. I was so encouraged when I heard another woman, from a different church, talking to her at the break, saying, "I would love to have the Abiding Life conference in our church, but the elders would never hear of it." My friend responded, "Oh, I believed the same thing, and look at what God is doing! It took ten years of prayer, but I did not give up. It may take you ten years, but do not give up! The Lord will open a door that no man can shut."

A believer is where he is for a reason. If someone does come to see he is in Christ, and Christ is in him, do not expect him to stay around for long. The few are rarely allowed to bunch up. This is what makes special gatherings, retreats, and conferences so precious to me; the fellowship with like-minded believers is so refreshing.

Remember, though, that the few do not have something that other believers do not possess. The few, by faith, have simply recognized and believed what they have freely been given by the Lord. The few are not better or exclusive; in fact, they are more acquainted with suffering.

DAY 153
I Take It Back!

When they were filled, He said to His disciples, "Gather
up the leftover fragments so that nothing will be lost."
So they gathered them up, and filled twelve baskets with
fragments from the five barley loaves which were left over by
those who had eaten.

— JOHN 6:12, 13

In this astounding story Jesus had fed 5,000 people,
and what was left over, He wanted . . . but for what? What
are twelve men and a teacher on the move going to do
with twelve baskets of barley bread? I imagine that they
found a few hungry people along the way. The miracle
had provided exactly enough food for all of the people, so
I wonder if some, like the boy that offered the five loaves
and two fish, had their own food with them. When the
bread that Jesus gave came, they simply ate their own food;
they did not feel the need for His bread. Therefore, He
took it back. Matthew 7:6, "Do not give what is holy to
dogs, and do not throw your pearls before swine, or they
will trample them under their feet, and turn and tear you
to pieces." Jesus then continues with the theme that He is
the bread of life; He let us know that He was the true bread
that came down out of heaven. In the same way that some
would rather have their bread than His, there are those that
would prefer to have what the world offers than what Jesus
offers. For such people the bread is withdrawn. Sometimes

I am talking to someone and am met with one argument after another. That person simply is not interested in Jesus, so I say, "I take it back; I take back everything!" He may believe that I am retracting my conviction over what I have said about Jesus, but it is not so! I am withdrawing the presentation of Jesus. A word not received is a wasted word, and there must be no waste. I pick up the message and wait to give it to others who hunger for the bread that comes from heaven. On our journey we will always find a few hungry people.

I remember being in India. As I left the airport, a band of men were attempting to grapple my luggage out of my hands. I made it clear that I would carry them myself. Since I would not relinquish the bags, they walked alongside me, each with a hand touching the bags, so that when I arrived at the car they all asked for a tip. Reluctantly, I gave them all one rupee apiece. They began to curse at me and demanded more. I responded, "So one rupee is not enough?" I then took back from each man his one rupee. They expectantly assumed I would be giving them something bigger. Instead, I simply got in the taxi and rode away with them following me, now shouting and wanting the one rupee back. However, I had taken back what they did not like and was not giving it again.

Jesus offers the bread of life; if someone does not want it, He will take it back and leave the person exactly as he was before he heard of Him.

DAY 154
I Will Not Stand in Persecution

. . . and perseverance, proven character; and proven character, hope; and hope does not disappoint, because the love of God has been poured out within our hearts through the Holy Spirit who was given to us. For while we were still helpless, at the right time Christ died for the ungodly.

— ROMANS 5:4-6

While reading a devotional on sacrifice, I noted that a question was posed that went something like this, "Are you willing to be poured out for others, to be a doormat?" The gist of the thought was that a believer must decide today that when those opportunities come, he will pour out his life. I think all such challenges should be met with the attitude of praying, "Lord, You know me. I would save my life at every opportunity. I have learned from Peter that it is easy in this moment to say, 'No, never,' and then when faced with the opportunity not to deny You, not to rise to the test. I am weak. But this I would ask: When the moment of pouring out comes, would You grant me the grace to turn to You, to recognize abiding, and thus let the life that has been poured out, the life of Jesus, be poured out again through me?" Some consider the Christian standard of behavior to be higher than any other, and they consequently suppose their job is to raise the bar even higher for other believers. If that must be so, then I quit now! I know myself, and in my flesh dwells no good thing. The standard that Jesus set is higher because He was the One keeping it, and the only hope I have is that He live it through me. If I abide in Him, He will pick the moment when I will be poured out, and it may not be a spectacular event. Often it can be some simple interaction with a relative or acquaintance, and I find myself immediately offended. I can let the stirred flesh be used of God as a warning that I am moving into self-love. If I say amen, admit my condition, and invite Him to flow through me, I can walk toward the person and love him or her. Afterward, I will have been poured out, and it will be a pleasant experience because it was actually His being poured out through me. I refuse to jump on the bandwagon and sing the lines of a chorus that say, "I will ever seek You, I will never forsake You, I will always love You, and I will be holy for You." It is better to learn from David's mistake when he said those things and then had an affair. I will not throw words at commitment. Sometime today I will completely walk in the flesh, and it is that awareness that makes me turn to Him the second I get up. I do not want to surround myself with people who say, "I am ready for the persecution. I will not deny the Lord. I will witness to the end." They will be the first to deny Him! I want to be with those who fear their ability to stand, who are nervous about witnessing, who are afraid to make judgments, who have not been to Bible school, who fear their own wisdom, and who do not see how they could be fit for ministry. They will stand, for He will make them stand!

DAY 155
"I want to see Jesus!" "Do you?"

Now faith is the assurance of things hoped for,
the conviction of things not seen.
For by it the men of old gained approval.
— HEBREWS 11:1, 2

One day in my prayers I made a request: "Jesus, I would like to see You!" His response was, "Would you?" The normal way to enter into Jesus is through the unseen, that is, through faith. If we enter another way, we enter through the abnormal, the seen. Many could complain to God, "If you did for my relative what you did for Paul (strike him blind, speak to him, heal him, and teach him in the wilderness), he would believe, also." However, is a knockout experience what we really want for our relatives? Is it what we want for ourselves? Once one has entered into Christ through the seen, he is no less in Christ, but he has not learned faith, which by very definition includes belief in what is not seen. He must then enter dark rooms of suffering and lack, just to add faith to his spiritual arsenal. This principle is seen over and over again in saints' lives that have experienced the spectacular. They had to learn faith through dark nights of the soul. In the end, is it wise to want a vision or to be caught up to heaven? Such things bring great suffering in order to take us to a place of faith. If entrance into Christ came through trusting, though nothing was seen, be content to stay in a place of faith, in a place of the unseen, and in a place of believing. "Blessed are they who did not see, and yet believed" (John 20:29).

DAY 156
Identify the Enemy

For our struggle is not against flesh and blood, but against the rulers, against the powers, against the world forces of this darkness, against the spiritual forces of wickedness in the heavenly places

— EPHESIANS 6:12.

We attended a bullfight in Spain, which, though it may not be the pinnacle of enjoyable experiences, is nonetheless an interesting one. Having grown up around a farm, the kill before butchering was never something I looked forward to. Some would argue that the death of the bull in a bullfight is as humane as the death in a slaughterhouse. I do know that in the bullring the beast has his moments of glory, and after watching six bulls defy the matadors, my admiration for bulls has gone way up. As a child I was never allowed to touch a bull. When feeding the cows and petting them, the temptation was always present to likewise pat the bull, but any movement I made toward that end was met with a strong rebuke from my grandfather. He had hauled several bulls over the years and seen men gored; he never trusted any bull. The toros in Spain enter the arena full of attitude, muscle-rippling strength, and catlike quickness in an impressive show. They look for anything that is moving and immediately charge with power that is awing to witness; they send every matador scrambling behind a thick wooden wall, and then they hammer the wall with their horns. I had never witnessed that in a bull, nor had I seen that kind of endurance. Nothing about a bullfight is fair; the only way to make it less fair would be to remove one of the bull's legs! However, because of the bull's strength and superiority, the fight would take hours were the bull not slowed down. Carrying a spear, a horseman rides in on a heavily padded and blindfolded horse, and the bull immediately rushes him. The first bull we saw actually knocked the horse over and was able to gore it, even as the rider, falling down, drove the spear deep into the bull's back. Next, four matadors begin to wear the bull down with a series of charges at pink capes. When the bull is sufficiently tiring, another matador will come holding two colorful skewers. He allows the bull to charge him straight on and then jumps sideways, driving the skewers into the back of the bull. This is repeated three times. Even at this point the stamina of the bull is incredible. The matador, with his large red cape, will now come out to work the bull until it finally has its strength bled out of it, at which time, with an air of satisfaction, the man draws a sword; the great beast bows its head to hurtle one more time toward the rag that has given it so much grief, and the matador drives the sword into its great heart. Some matadors are better at this than others, but ideally, the bull's demise is quick, and it drops, immediately dead. The whole exhibition takes around fifteen minutes.

As I watched, I could not help but think about our fight against the "rulers, powers, forces of darkness, and spiritual forces of wickedness." In Christ, the battle is won. On the cross He did not say, "To be continued!" He said, "It is finished." Like the bull, we in Christ have the superior strength. However, the bull makes one fatal mistake by thinking the cape, a simple piece of lifeless rag, is the enemy, the source of its torment and pain! I kept thinking to myself, *If only you would stop fighting the rag, stop looking down, look up at the head, and move eighteen inches to the right! The battle would be yours.* Even to its dying breath the bull was eyeing the rag, when it was the matador that was driving the sword deep into his heart. A physically superior creature is defeated because of a wrong focus. How often in our spiritual battles the enemy has our focus on something other than him; we never pay attention to his ugly head. So many times I have talked to couples ready to divorce over absolutely nothing but a rag; the enemy has continually poked at them, making them think that the rag is what is hurting them. It is not the rag! It is the one behind the rag. Move eighteen inches to the right, go for the head, and you will see the truth of it. Many times I will stop in the middle of a situation and just say, "The Lord rebuke you!" I know the issue is not the issue; there is someone behind the issue, and I want to go for the head. The believer has the superior strength, but that will do him no good if his focus is in the wrong place. So many just bow and let the enemy drive the sword deep into the heart. There will nearly always be the need for a twenty percent improvement in any relationship; that provides the rag. Why let the twenty percent steal the eighty percent of joy? On any given day, one should immediately be able to say three things that are right about his situation and about his or her spouse. We need God's grace to recognize the head.

DAY 157
Flesh And The Ministry

There is therefore now no condemnation
for those who are in Christ Jesus.
— ROMANS 8:1

If God is revealing a person's flesh, should he stop ministering? It is not as odd a question as one might think. I am often asked it by those who do ministry, for it is a question that the enemy loves to plant in the mind of a disciple of Christ. After Peter's denial, should Peter have just quit? I believe that God is dealing with us continually and bringing us into conformity with what we have always had in Jesus. Ministry remains constant while our growth—the increasing revelation of what as Christians we have always had and been—is in flux. In short, much of our insight during times of ministry comes from having already been where the people are to whom we are talking. I often look across my office and see in a person the very things that have been in me. Our experiences equip us to minister. Peter denied the Lord and yet ministered on the very topic later. He had been there. If being there disqualifies a believer, Peter would have been disqualified. Past experiences (even failures) equip us to minister in the present, and though we have grown through them and can then minister from what we gained from them, that will not rule out the possibility of a life full of like experiences. This may sound odd, but personal growth in private areas of life can be unrelated to the ministry occurring today, even though it is preparation for further ministry in the future. Many make a mistake when they see flesh in their lives and proceed to listen to the enemy as he whispers that they are not fit, they will bring dishonor to Jesus, and they are hypocrites. The enemy's goal is accomplished to the extent that the believer withdraws from ministry. What does such retreat really accomplish? Time is taken away because of a newly revealed area of the flesh, and an attempt is made to fix the issue. The believer's eyes are taken off of Jesus, he is no longer giving of himself to others, and he becomes absorbed with the problem, all of which are counterproductive. Also, does he really believe that this will be the FINAL issue in his life? Does he believe that this revelation of his flesh is the last one? When a believer thinks that he has dealt with all the flesh that will ever be revealed, he is deceived and only seeing flesh from his own definition. He must come to see that the continuous process of revelation of flesh and resulting renewed reliance upon Jesus is what keeps his teaching fresh. "There is nothing the nearness of Jesus will not cure." Even today His nearness may be fixing a problem in any or all of us!

DAY 158
If I Were God, I Would Kill Me!

For thus says the LORD, sing aloud with gladness for Jacob, and shout among the chiefs of the nations; proclaim, give praise, and say, O LORD, save Thy people, the remnant of Israel.

— JEREMIAH 31:7

"If I were God, I would kill me!" Have you ever felt that way about yourself? Have you ever wondered why God even puts up with you? The life of grace is so much higher than the life of legalism! The legalist could never even comprehend the difference; he is accustomed to moving smoothly between good flesh and bad. However, the least attitude that is anti-Christ in grace people will not go unchecked! Not only are there the daily struggles of either recognizing that we are abiding or not, there is the issue of our growth. As we grow in Him, we look back at last year, the year before that, and even the beginnings of our Christian life with a sigh and a moan. "How could I have been like that?" All of this leads to an inner whisper, "If I were God, I would not have put up with me."

Why has He put up with us? It is because of the remnant! What remnant? There were many people in Israel who disobeyed the Lord, but there was always one man who obeyed and who became the remnant. It was because of the remnant that all the people were not destroyed; the remnant permitted God to put up with all the rest of the rebellious people. The remnant—the one man for the many—delighted Him. Noah and Moses come to mind; they dwelt in and among the people but were not like the people. The people did not change them; they worked to change the people's hearts. Because of the remnant God continued to work with the people. Every believer is multi-faceted in that his soul comprises mind, will, and emotions and his body harbors desire, habits, protection, and reproduction. Over the years, even as believers, our minds were filled with chaos, our wills pointed toward self, our emotions bred hatred and jealousy, and the bodies expressed every kind of desire. Our soul and body participated in the lust of the eyes, the lust of the flesh, and boastful pride of life. Why did God not just wipe us out? Because of the remnant! There was something in us so great that it allowed God to overlook all of the failures and continue with us. The remnant in us is Jesus! He dwells in our spirit, He is pleasing to God in everything, and because of Him God will not withdraw from us. Our flesh will never affect Jesus, but Jesus will continue to have an influence on our flesh. We will grow and the outside influences that had control over us will lessen as He increases and we have the revelation of our new life in Him. The Remnant is in us!

DAY 159
Ignore Your Plan

But My people did not listen to My voice, and Israel did not obey Me. So I gave them over to the stubbornness of their heart, to walk in their own devices.

— PSALM 81:11, 12

Sometimes I start a discipleship session with a question, "So what is your plan?" People generally are not sitting around waiting for advice on what to do. Before they ever step through my office door, they have decided exactly what course they are going to follow and are merely seeking counsel that agrees with their decision. Many times I talk to a husband or wife who has already decided that the way to fix their marital problem is to split up. Others decide the best way to correct their situation is to run, and some others believe that if the people around them would change, the predicament would then resolve itself. Our plan is not His plan, and experience will confirm that assessment. Our plans are often devised out of frustration, anger, disappointment, and hopelessness; and since they are anti-Sermon-on-the-Mount/Life-on-the-Mount, they include no love, no Spirit, no Christ, no brokenness, no laying down of our lives. The solution is not to correct our plan to make it something we can more comfortably live with; that would still only be our plan in different clothing. As Corrie Ten Boom said, "Just because there is a mouse in the cookie jar, that does not make it a cookie." Often we are in a state of so much emotional disruption that we just cannot think "spiritually." We are too consumed with the morbid satisfaction that comes from contemplating how we will get even with someone or make him pay for something he did or said. So we must have a plan for destroying the plan that will destroy us. Here is just such a plan: When entertaining any scheme that is anti-Christ, simply pray before falling off to sleep each night, "Father, please do not give me over to the stubbornness of my heart; do not let me walk in my own devices." Pray even when we cannot yet really mean it. God hears even idle words. He will hear, and He will answer!

My Weakness for His Strength | 263

DAY 160
Immediate Results

For indeed He was crucified because of weakness, yet He lives because of the power of God. For we also are weak in Him, yet we will live with Him because of the power of God [directed] toward you. Test yourselves [to see] if you are in the faith; examine yourselves! Or do you not recognize this about yourselves, that Jesus Christ is in you —unless indeed you fail the test?

— II CORINTHIANS 13:4, 5

Often we allow our eyes to drift from Christ to our problems and circumstances through the immediate-results syndrome, which dictates our success wholly by what we are currently experiencing, either positively or negatively! This syndrome is actually a major obstacle to faith. Let me illustrate. Most will agree that the United States is losing its economic edge because Americans, unlike those with an Oriental or Asian mindset, are not so willing to invest in something that will not reap immediate benefits. We want wealth right away, while they are willing to invest year after year, receiving much less current tangible rewards but knowing in the future they will be repaid tenfold their original investment, and the wait will have been very worthwhile. Having seen the wisdom in investing and waiting, they are not discouraged by any occasional hiccup in the current financial situation. The wisdom of their policy is now creating repercussions in our own economy. As we apply the principle to our spiritual lives, wanting immediate results is a hindrance to faith; in fact, this mindset will actually nullify faith! The greatness of our faith is not to be judged by how much we have received, but rather by how long we can wait and receive nothing! Faith makes my Christian walk a joy; therefore, if I have voided faith through wanting immediate results, I have also to the same extent annihilated joy.

When believers do not have a long-term plan, they become susceptible to the ups and downs of daily life. Their energies get focused on resolving right away whatever is placed in front of them in order that they might feel comfortable and secure in the moment. Next they become controllers, pushing God out of the way and beginning to try to fix in their own strength and with a variety of plans and manipulations what they perceive to be the real problem. In other words, they simply begin to play God. To say the least, in this way the Christian life becomes a struggle, filled with discouragement, depression, anger, and doom, with minds and emotions flooded with questions, accusations, and feelings of hopelessness from the enemy. It is tough to play God! All of this because things are not going as they feel they ought to today.

Imagine sitting in a bathtub full of water when somebody dumps into the tub a bucket of ping-pong balls on which are written all of the problems, circumstances, failures, and people that are causing you trouble. Your job is to somehow keep every ball under water. The whole exercise would at first be frustrating and in the end quite exhausting. This pictures, of course, the believer who is trying in his own strength to control every area of his life.

DAY 161
Impossibility Versus Accomplishment

Are you so foolish? Having begun by the Spirit, are you now being perfected by the flesh? . . . Now that no one is justified by the Law before God is evident; for, "The righteous man shall live by faith."

— GALATIANS 3:3, 11

Many aspects of the believer's life have been made out to be nearly impossible to accomplish. We are given reams of material on how to be a good parent, partner, and child of God. There seems to be so much information that we must know. How can we take it all in? How can we always do the right thing? And those who present to us the much needed information seem so much more spiritual than we are; they have done the right things all along, and they even have degrees in how to be successful. However, Scripture does not indicate that being a brother or sister in Christ, a parent, or a mate is all that difficult. In fact, there is very little in Scripture concerning what to do, but much about basic attitudes to have. "And so, as those who have been chosen of God, holy and beloved, put on a heart of compassion, kindness, humility, gentleness and patience; bearing with one another, and forgiving each other, whoever has a complaint against any one; just as the Lord forgave you, so also should you" (Colossians 3:12, 13). The Christian life is as simple as loving our wives, respecting our husbands, forgiving our enemies, not provoking our children, obeying parents, and working as unto the Lord. This is our long-term plan. In keeping it day by day we will see ups and downs, reversals, and the inevitable Christian hiccups, but we should never, never allow those daily things to sidetrack us from our long-term plan, which will reap its own reward in the fullness of time.

Often in our quest for immediate relief we see in others (and they see in us) things to change to bring instant comfort. Therefore, we set out to covertly or overtly change those around us through more control and more role-playing of God. Let me point out that if God believed a change in another person's behavior were as important as we believe it to be, He would already have changed it! A change in the behavior of Job's friends would not have lessened his plight one bit. It was Job's trust in God and the long-term result of faith that kept him. The whole test was calculated to clean up Job, not to change others. Others actually played very little into the scenario. God's role was primary, Job's secondary, and others' somewhere far behind.

DAY 162
In The Mode Of Doing

That their hearts may be encouraged, having been knit together in love, and attaining to all the wealth that comes from the full assurance of understanding, resulting in a true knowledge of God's mystery, that is, Christ Himself, in whom are hidden all the treasures of wisdom and knowledge.

— COLOSSIANS 2:2 & 3

There is a story told of a man who gave seminars all over the world on what a Christian must do to be a success. The man died and went to heaven. The first day in heaven he decided to put on one of his seminars on doing. He scheduled a large room, and thousands came to hear him. While he was speaking he noticed that Jesus was seated on the front row taking one page of notes after another, and this puzzled the man. At the break the man ran to Jesus and asked why He, of all people, would be taking so many notes. Jesus replied, "You see, this is the first time I have heard any of this Myself!" Doing makes the Christian life far too difficult! It is not the doing that must come first but the believing. Doing emphasizes immediate results and will not see us through to the end. However, believing will see us through to the very end, as it did every person of faith in Scripture. God has given every believer in every conceivable situation absolute attitudes to be kept. If we maintain those we will see the fulfillment in God's fullness of time. Continue to love, to submit, and to train; we may not directly see the positive from our attitude, but remember, this is our long-term plan, and in the midst of the ups and downs our spirits will remain calm.

Now what has been said previously centers in this one simple Scripture. "But I am afraid, lest as the serpent deceived Eve by his craftiness, your minds should be led astray from the simplicity and purity of devotion to Christ"

(II Corinthians 11:3). Is the Christian life simple? Is the answer to living alone, living with others, raising children, not having children, and every other struggle simple? Yes, yes, and yes again! In order for the Christian life to be one of simplicity, we must first realize that God does not give answers to every situation, but rather reveals attitudes for every situation, and second, that if these attitudes are maintained, we will not be free from the day-by-day ups and downs, but we will see the fulfillment of the promises in God's fullness of time. All of this promotes faith! "Yet, with respect to the promise of God, he did not waver in unbelief but grew strong in faith, giving glory to God, and being fully assured that what God had promised, He was able also to perform" (Romans 4:20, 21).

DAY 163
In My Flesh Dwells No Good Thing! How About In Yours?

For I know that nothing good dwells in me, that is, in my flesh; for the willing is present in me, but the doing of the good {is} not.
— ROMANS 7:18

I sat listening to a couple discussing a topic that is much more prevalent today than it was just a few years ago: pornography on the Internet. The husband had been caught looking at it. "I cannot believe you would do that," said the wife.

I looked at her and said, "I would!"

She immediately responded, "How?"

"It is simple. In my flesh dwells no good thing! Are you telling me that in your flesh dwells a good thing?" It took me years to realize that I—that is, my flesh—am never going to get better. When I am not abiding, the flesh is the same it has always been: hostile to God. That is why we teach a moment-by-moment victory and ultimate improvement only through Christ in us. I could look at the Internet sites but I do not, and not because I am strong, but because I know men much stronger than I am who get in bondage to it. Since that is the case, what chance would my flesh have? I do not look because I am weak, not because I am strong.

Do you believe that in your flesh (body, mind, will, and emotions under the influence of anything other than Christ) there is something good? Every time we look at a person and say, "I would not do that," we are saying that we are stronger than Christ. We know that all Christ ever did, He never did, for it was the Father working through Him. He not only taught abiding but lived it. When we succeed, it is not because of great strength, but because we have recognized abiding in Christ, and His grace and strength are on and in us. When we judge, look out! All God has to do is lift His grace and abiding presence for us to discover that we are just as weak as anyone else.

Have you admitted you are weak and in your flesh dwells no good thing? You must admit where you are before you can leave where you are. You must own a weakness before you can lose it. If I want to give you a cup, I can only give it if I pick it up and own it first. It is not until you own your weakness that Christ will be able to be your strength. For instance, if you will own that in your flesh you hate another race, you can give that shortcoming to God, and He can become your strength. Once you do this, you will not be a compassionate person loving someone from another race; you will be a person able to dispense the pure love of God. Admit you cannot be a husband, own it, and let Christ's love flow through you for your wife. But if you will not own it, you can never disown it.

"Power is perfected in weakness!" Think of a teacher, pastor, or elder. Do you know five of his weaknesses? Three? Just one? If you do not know any of his weaknesses, this person is attempting to minister in the strength of the flesh. If power is perfected in weakness, why hide it? It is because we want to appear strong and build our own glory. However, He is the glory, and He will never give His glory to another. We are wrong to teach Christians to be strong and hide weakness. All of us are strong in Christ and weak in the flesh. In my flesh dwells no good thing.

DAY 164
Independent?

And God created man in His own image, in the image of God He created him.
— GENESIS 1:27

Mankind clamors for independence and yet at every conceivable turn proves he is the most dependent of all creatures. Every person, with the exception of the insane, is bound to someone in some way. Man must carve out of his human surroundings an identity. The craving for dependence is so great that once the identity is solidified, only reactions within the comfort zone are sought. There becomes a set action, a desired reaction, and all else is avoided. The activist is bound to the one against whom he protests; having accepted the identity of activist, he will find it very difficult to live in a problem-free environment. Therefore, when one cause is won, the activist's organization is not disbanded, but a search begins for someone else to oppose to provide the greatly needed reaction. The bitter person needs a person to hate, the robber needs someone from whom to steal, the teenager with green spiked hair wants an adult to shock, the bully seeks a fearful soul, the athlete desires a crowd, bigots search out different kinds of bigots to judge, the philosopher pinpoints someone to belittle, the guerrilla militia is obliged to locate a conspiracy in the government, political parties require opposing factions, and the movie star craves an audience. This assessment is confirmed with the disheartening sentiment, "If the opposition did not exist, neither would we." How true that their very existence is tied to the thing they despise. Their life is dependent upon that for which they have contempt. Not very deep!

We were created by God for His glory and purposes. It is to be in Him that we find who we are, and it is in the context of His body that we find our proper place of dependency on others. By nature we are dependent;

we will serve something. I choose to be a child of God; therefore I need God. I will act, and He will react. But unlike dealing with the world, this cycle will not leave me depleted or being a slave to others. Rather, I will be built up and be free. I am happy to be a Christian!

DAY 165
Intellectuals

The Word became flesh and made his dwelling among us. We have seen his glory, the glory of the One and only, who came from the Father, full of grace and truth.

— JOHN 1:14

Some are viewed as great intellectuals, but I have a problem with intellectuals. They sit around a coffee table, do not live life, theorize about it, and never see the outworking of it. I like farmers. They think about something, go make it, and if it does not work, they will not keep making it. To me this is true intellectualism; the work is concrete and can be tested. Intellectuals want others to test their theories while they sit. This is the one thing I appreciate about Hemingway; he tested his life theories and killed himself as the logical end of what he believed.

For all of our culture's listening to "intellectuals," the "experts," and the "open-minded," real-life experience has surely proven that they know not and what they expound does not work. Our society is dying by degrees while educated in ignorance and in what does not work.

God did not give a teaching in the form of a book from heaven for men on earth. A book was not good enough for God. The Word became flesh; the teaching was all fleshed out in Jesus and proven by His life. God did not talk from heaven like an intellectual; He came to earth to show us how life works. The Man who did everything did nothing, since He said it was the Father doing through Him, and He says that greater things we can do. He must mean greater than His nothing. Can we rise to the challenge?

DAY 166
Is He Always With Me?

And lo, I am with you always, even to the end of the age.
— MATTHEW 28:20

I often say that I am preaching my own funeral, and this article will be one such time! I am always confronted with my own unbelief and inability to get the first things right. There are so many passages that need believing before we go on asking for more and attempting to understand more. We obsess over our past. We remember the hurts. We are "dealing" with them. We are struggling. We wish for a different past. Millions are spent on various coping mechanisms for the aforementioned, but in all of it we are avoiding a fact of faith: "If any man be in Christ, he is a new creation." We do not believe we are new creations. We want the feeling of it, the absence of memory, and something special. We want the fact of it without faith! Again, all that a believer wants, he has already been given, for the Lord has given us EVERYTHING pertaining to life and godliness. However, if we work for what we have by faith, we lose it. God is with us always, and yet often a busy mother, missing her quiet time, believes He is not with her. Many have not read their Bibles, attended church lately, or perhaps have fallen into the bad deeds of the flesh—or worse yet, the good deeds—and these all believe that He has left them. Is He with us always? Where do we stand in these things? So many spectacular meetings take place to convince us in the flesh of what only faith can assure us, that He is always with us!

DAY 167
Is It Easy To Walk In The Flesh?

It has given me great joy to find some of your children walking in the truth, just as the Father commanded us.
— II JOHN: 4

I am thinking how there exists in the life of the believer a healthy tension that can be likened to holding on to the top end of a vertical steel rod and bending it toward the ground. The farther it bends, the more tension there is. A believer can walk a little in the flesh without the tension's being so great. However, a large measure of walking in the flesh yields great tension. How long could a person hold a steel rod bent clear to the ground? The longer it was held, the more stress and strain there would be, and what would be the gain from such endeavor? I have observed God's people doing some ridiculous things, and I commented that they would not be able to withstand the tension of continuing in them. I was told of a friend's departure from his mate to go after another, but I knew his heart for God, and so my response was, "He will not be able to do that!" Oh, yes, he may initially go for it, but I knew he would not be able to bend the bar that close to the ground and hold it. I was right! We must be sensitive to a place of tension, because the flesh simply is not worth it.

DAY 168
Is Your Chooser Broken?

. . . choose for yourself this day whom you will serve . . .
but as for me and my household, we will serve the Lord.
— JOSHUA 24:15

Many believers act as though their choosers are broken, mistakenly feeling that their wills have been given over to the nearly robot-like control of the enemy. Conversely, they believe the remedy would be to have their wills given over to a robot-like response of obedience to God! In anger they shout, "God does not help me! I told Him to take over and He has not. I am giving up on God!" Either way they are acknowledging erroneously that they cannot choose and must therefore be under another's authority. If they can choose to get out of bed, what to eat, what to wear, and whom to date; then they have the ability to choose to walk away from sin, bad habits, and all other things that simply do not suit believers. However, there is a beginning place, a first choice, which is accomplished by saying, "Father, I choose Your will. I am too weak to know it or to walk in it, but I trust You to lead me to it. Thank You!"

DAY 169
It Gets Crowded On The Throne

Come and see what God has done, how awesome
His works in man's behalf.
— PSALM 66:5

"The wind blows where it wishes and you hear the sound of it, but you do not know where it comes from and where it is going; so is everyone who is born of the Spirit" (John 3:8). Nicodemus, a teacher of Israel, did not understand what Jesus was saying, because, like so many of us, he was conditioned to think that the work of God is always done by man, as if God is so small that He needs the help of man. In essence, Nicodemus believed, "God takes care of those who take care of themselves," being accustomed to thinking that people came into the kingdom through effort, strain, teaching, watching their every move, endless conversation, right training, and persuasive argument. In his mind, men did not change so easily as through God's working out a conversion by something as natural as birth. Nicodemus, a teacher of Israel, had crowded God right off the throne and was not a relaxed man!

Today, it seems so many things are needed to bring about conversion: a new church building, a special service with music perfectly calculated to move the unbeliever, youth discussion groups, psychological counseling, and exegetical preaching. Yes, with all of these surely God will be manipulated to move and bring conversions; the pews will fill and children will no longer experiment with drugs. It is getting more and more crowded on the throne.

The conversion that He brings is not to a system but to spiritual truth; it places concepts in our being, not in our minds. His conversion is His work and comes only through the power of the Spirit. There is room for only One on the throne.

DAY 170
It Is Easier To Be Man Than To Be God!

He has made everything appropriate in its time. He has
also set eternity in their heart, yet so that man will not find
out the work which God has done from the beginning even
to the end. I know that there is nothing better for them than
to rejoice and to do good in one's lifetime; moreover, that
every man who eats and drinks sees good in all his labor—it
is the gift of God. I know that everything God does will
remain forever; there is nothing to add to it and there is
nothing to take from it, for God has so worked that men
should fear Him. That which is has been already, and that
which will be has already been, for
God seeks what has passed by.
— ECCLESIASTES 3:11-15

I remember as a child wanting in the worst way a little motor scooter. As soon as my boys were big enough, I made sure that they got one. Fathers delight in helping their sons and even sharing in the accomplishments of their sons. I have known more than one man who, not having a father himself, was driven to be the best father possible. In short, loving fathers busy themselves with attempts to make life easier for their sons than it was for them. Could it be that God is also this way? Could it be that the life God has for me is actually better than His? It boils down to this: Is it easier to be man than to be God? Look at the life of God. Man has never really paid for sin; God has been picking up that tab all along. His creation sins and He pays. The ultimate payment came when His only begotten Son died. God has taken all of the responsibility to cause things to work together for the good, to take what He has made and redeem it in every possible way. He is putting together a grand jigsaw puzzle. All of the pressure is on Him. Would you really like to be God? To experience for one day what it is like to be driven by pure love? Could you bear up under His sorrow? Would you have the wisdom to govern? I have concluded that my life as a son is much easier than my Father's. I think I simply need to enjoy my inheritance. I am going to rest and appreciate the benefit from all of His work.

DAY 171
It Is a Relationship

This is the day the Lord has made:
let us rejoice and be glad in it.
— PSALM 118:24

A friend was sharing a very painful experience from his past. His father had become ill and was in need of constant attention, so he went to his father's aid and daily took care of his every necessity until the day of the father's death. However, the son was vexed by the realization that the reason he was caring for the father was that he knew that as soon as the father died, he would receive the inheritance. He said that it would have killed his father to know the true motive behind his son's service. Serving the dying parent that raised, nurtured, prayed for, and worried about the child simply for a monetary reward was not the relationship the father desired, though I suspect that same story could be told over and over again.

Often we hear something like this: "You must persevere in Christianity for the reward. Yes, life is miserable, but keep heaven in mind. Keep attending the meetings, doing your devotions, and studying the Bible, for in the end you will receive the reward of heaven." However, there is no mention of a relationship. John 15 - 17 makes it quite clear that a relationship is available for us today. God desires fellowship with us today. Much is said in Scripture concerning today. "Today if you hear His voice" (Hebrews 4:7). What a pity if we serve with only the reward in mind, when the very fellowship of God is our reward now.

DAY 172
Jesus, Please Make Me a Bipolar Manic-Depressive!

Peace I leave with you; My peace I give to you; not as the world gives do I give to you. Do not let your heart be troubled, nor let it be fearful.
— JOHN 14:27

Of course, "bipolar manic-depressive" is misdiagnosed more often than it is correctly diagnosed. The problem with such labels is that they, then, receive the treatment, not the individual. Well, amen. At any rate, as the world sees it, a bipolar person is one whose emotions swing abnormally from a depressive low to a giddy high in a matter of moments. Normal emotions are to roll slowly in response to events within and without a person. For example, in coping with the death of a loved one, the emotions of loss, loneliness, and even anger can take many months to level out at a place called normal. I would not look at a woman who had just lost her husband of fifty years and ask, "Why do you not laugh?" If she did laugh it would be abnormal; she would be bipolar. However, many Christians are praying that God would, for all practical purposes, make them bipolar when they have experienced a negative event, a failure in their lives, a disappointment with another, or an offense; once they forgive they want their emotions immediately to go from the bottom to the top. That, to me, is completely unrealistic. Forgiveness can occur in a moment, but the emotions will take their time in coming back to a place of normalcy. Emotions must be given time to calm down after the fact without attempts to have them be a bipolar-type up and down in an instant. Believers can acknowledge God in a death, move in faith, put their eyes on Him, and rejoice for the departed loved one, but the deep feeling of loss will take time to subside and give way to the feeling of hope. God works slowly. We are not to be praying to be bipolar. Our spirit will soar, but emotions will take awhile.

DAY 173
Judging Spirituality, Perceived Versus Real

Therefore you are to be perfect, as your heavenly Father is perfect. Beware of practicing your righteousness before men to be noticed by them; otherwise you have no reward with your Father who is in heaven.

— MATTHEW 5:48 & 6:1

I know of a man who preached in a meeting where over 50,000 came to Christ. I heard of a woman who was one of the world's great social workers. As attested to by eyewitnesses, a fellow raised a woman from the dead. Also, I have been where another woman started over 700 churches. Having traveled for years, this is only the beginning of what I have seen and heard. There is no need belaboring the point. Many, many believers have participated in seeing God perform great miracles and accomplish incredible tasks. My question is this: Were they spiritual people? The obvious answer would be, "Of course," for too often believers judge the spectacular as being the earmarks of spirituality. But were they? Israel's greatness was never to be found in the people but in their God. God accomplishes what He wills, and man takes the credit for it and uses it to build himself an image. To be honest, I do not know if these men and women were spiritual in the least. I have been shocked to see "great men" explode when they did not get the seat they wanted on the airline, when a car pulled in front of them, or when a subordinate questioned them. What one is at his worst is the level of true spirituality that he has achieved. Men on the platform often say, "It is only Jesus, praise God," and then accept the praise of men. Actions speak loudly. One woman could not stand to be questioned. She would explode and leave those around her in a verbal pool of blood. Another preacher would get out of the car if anyone disagreed. Well, we all have our bad moments and the flesh never improves; it is hostile to God. My point is that none of us need to be fruit inspectors or more voices pointing out the hypocrisy of believers. That has all been done before. We must have a different way of judging spirituality than being brainwashed by the loudest, the spectacular, and the dominating. They have defined spirituality to describe themselves and their flesh. However, Jesus gives us the true definition of spirituality. If what He describes is part of a believer's life, that one is a far greater success than any televangelist ever seen. We are blessed when we are at the end of our ropes. With less dependence on our selves, there is more of God and His rule.

DAY 174
Junk

More than that, I count all things to be loss in view of the surpassing value of knowing Christ Jesus my Lord, for whom

I have suffered the loss of all things, and count them but rubbish in order that I may gain Christ.

— PHILIPPIANS 3:8

One day I noticed a little old man living by a river in a shack so absolutely full of old junk that there was barely any room left for him; therefore, it was understandable that he spent his days outside the house just sitting and protecting the place, though what he owned was utterly worthless. I thought about what a blessing a flood would be for this fellow. He would, for sure, see it as a great tragedy, but I think not, for in a flood he could escape, and yet his stuff would be lost, washed downstream. Life would begin anew, and hopefully he would see that the value of his life was greater than the sum of all the junk with which he had surrounded himself. Each week I see believers that have been caught in some type of "flood"; all that was held dear has been swept away, expectations have given way to a sad reality, and they are initially devastated. All they see is the death, but I see death as a prelude to life, the removal of unnecessary junk that hinders our focus on Christ. Remember, the proof that Jesus presented to the disciples of His resurrection was that He bore the marks of death. Without death there is no life. The wisest thing to do on the cross is rest, for struggle only prolongs the misery. Rest during, in, and after the flood. All that is rubbish is being washed away for one thing, to reveal His life. "Who shall separate us from the love of Christ? Shall tribulation, or distress, or persecution, or famine, or nakedness, or peril, or sword?" (Romans 8:35)

DAY 175
Justification

Because by the works of the Law no flesh will be justified in His sight. Being justified as a gift by His grace through the redemption which is in Christ Jesus. For we maintain that a man is justified by faith apart from works of the Law.

— ROMANS 3:20, 24, and 28

I have heard some wonderful arguments concerning justification of self. Any number of times I have sat listening to eloquent reasoning, and after the person has made his case, he or she asks something like, "Would you put up with that? Can you see how it makes me feel? No one deserves to be treated this way, and what about the children? Should they have to put up with it?"

Everyone has some form of self-justification, and often people make some very good and strong arguments that would, in fact, justify their actions if they were living under the law. Therein lies the downside. Judging and justifying indicates a willingness to have God judge and justify. Who is that heady? I do not want to be justified; I want to live under grace. I want Christ's life in me to take the initiative to love and to bless in my daily interactions. I want His grace toward me. I want life. Observe the one justifying himself; is there a lift in his spirit? Do you want to be like that person? Does he exude life? We are not suited for self-justification; it depletes us, empties us, and leaves us under the law. No, thanks!

DAY 176
The Job Of Conscience

Because that which is known about God is evident within them; for God made it evident to them. For since the creation of the world His invisible attributes, His eternal power and divine nature, have been clearly seen, being understood through what has been made, so that they are without excuse.

— ROMANS 1:19, 20

The conscience of man is a wonderful thing. It might be called the thumbprint of God on our very being. Created by Him, with every fiber of our being held together by Him, and living in a world created for man, we find that we cannot escape God. The whole of our being agrees that there is a God. Every man knows it is so whether he resides deep in the Amazon or in the highest places of modern learning. All know of Him. I have a recurring experience with unbelievers in that they begin our meeting stating that there is no God, man evolved, and Christianity is an archaic set of rules that keeps man from living normally due to bondage under Judeo-Christian principles. Yet by the end of our session, if Christ has broken through, they will often say that they always knew there was a God, and if they had not found an answer that day, they were considering suicide! Imagine! They had earlier stated they had no need of an absent deity! Jesus made an interesting statement to unbelievers: "The Kingdom of God is in you"! How could this be? The very laws of the Kingdom of God are written in man's very members! It could be no other way, for we are made in Him. God is good, and everything created in Him must ultimately be good. That is not to say that man has not fallen into sin, but it affirms that sin is not normal for man, for if it were normal, man would grow and improve under it. The very opposite is true. Man is made for the Kingdom; its laws suit us best. Our conscience includes all of the above and is always pulling us toward God like a magnet. We know deep within that we need Him and sin never really suits us. That is why when some of the most notorious criminals are captured, they breathe a sigh of relief, acknowledging that they could not stop what they were doing, though they despised it and hoped for the day that they could rest from their wrongdoing. They would rather be confined in prison and not allowed to sin than to continue on.

Conscience drives man to keep, in some measure, the laws of the Kingdom of God without command. To a degree man does act decently, help others, sense compassion for others, and even treat nature with a measure of respect, all without the command to do so! Before I was a Christian I sold an old pickup truck that I had restored to a fellow passing through town. The next day after he departed the engine blew up. He called me, and I arranged for another engine to be installed at my own expense. When my grandfather found out what I had done, the only comment I received from him was, "You did the right thing." It was the right thing, and somehow I knew it and felt good doing it. Conscience in any society is invaluable; how can we put a price on it or fully describe its practical worth? Poverty and unemployment reached an all-time high during the Great Depression, and yet crime did not increase. Why? The conscience of man was still widely operative in our society. A few years back a movie was produced in the U.S. on the life of Christ; in a slanderous attempt to discredit Christianity, it portrayed Jesus as having had an illicit affair with Mary Magdalene. Though never popular, the movie was distributed and consent granted for viewing throughout the United States. Some in India attempted to show the movie there but were arrested. Why? The conscience of the people decreed that it was wrong to put anyone's god in a bad light. Would you like to live in a culture without a conscience?

Laws are given to keep man from destroying his conscience and to keep society from self-destructing before the message of grace in Jesus Christ can be preached. However, the carnal side of man has no wisdom and attempts to destroy all laws that hinder the expression and satisfaction of the flesh (animal nature); when these laws are destroyed, the collective conscience is destroyed. The attempt can be made to selectively destroy the conscience, but it cannot be destroyed cafeteria-style; the conscience is either wholly kept or wholly damaged. Once it is buried, any attempt made to replace it with laws will end in failure and frustration. How many outer laws that possess no power over man's flesh are needed to replace the conscience: one hundred, one thousand, ten thousand, ten million? How many? So as laws increase so does wickedness, and a monster is born.

DAY 177
The Death of Conscience

For the mystery of lawlessness is already at work; only he who now restrains {will do so} until he is taken out of the way. Then that lawless one will be revealed whom the Lord will slay with the breath of His mouth and bring to an end by the appearance of His coming; {that is,} the one whose coming is in accord with the activity of Satan, with all power and signs and false wonders, and with all the deception of wickedness for those who perish, because they did not receive the love of the truth so as to be saved.

— II THESSALONIANS 2:7-10

An assault is being made today on the conscience of those of us living in the United States. It begins with presenting our fathers, grandfathers, and founding fathers as ignorant, foolish believers. Then we are told that family does not matter, only our happiness. Sexual purity is outdated. We are not responsible for our own actions; others (whoever they are) are making our lives miserable. The pain that comes from believing and living with that approach is countered by a greater appetite for a variety of drugs, all calculated to numb our animal existence. To have an abortion and experience no remorse or guilt, the conscience must die, but when it dies, it takes down with it our self-love, other-love, and the love of creation. For a man or woman to abandon the family for a younger live-in, the conscience must die, but so do self-protection, other-protection, and a whole generation of would-be caring parents. To rationalize lying, stealing, and murder, the conscience must die, and along with it the joy of truth, the satisfaction of daily labor, and the appreciation of life. Those who kill a specific area of conscience to allow for the expression of their particular fleshly desire will in the end reap destruction from the hand of another. The conscience of the youth is being snuffed out little by little through television, music, sex, drugs, and all else that promises the pleasure of animal desire. It has been said that the fruit of sin is either green or rotten, but never ripe. The promised satisfaction of the flesh is always just around the corner, but never there today. How can it be? For the flesh is like the fire that never says enough! It cannot be satisfied. The world wants to avoid guilt at all cost. Much has been said about the damaging effect of guilt. However, I pray I am never delivered into the hands of someone who can no longer sense guilt. This person will have no conscience.

Seeing that nature abhors a vacuum, once conscience is destroyed it is replaced by anger, which allows for the freedom needed to follow selfish animal existence. Those without a conscience are in a constant state of anger. Notice how animals can get immediately mad! This condition of living for the present fulfillment of the flesh is actually intellectualized and made to appear something other than the shallowness that it is. Encouraging the death of the conscience becomes politically correct, intelligent, open-minded, caring, even heads above the poor ignorant masses. Rights become all important, lest the right to live as an animal be taken away. When it rains on the farm, the feedlot becomes quite muddy. The sheep and pigs venture out and both become stuck in the muck. The sheep begin to cry for someone to come and rescue them, while the pigs quite comfortably simply roll in the mud. The sheep are like men with a conscience, because they know they are not at home in the mire; the pigs reveal their true character. It would be quite distasteful were a pig to lie to himself and others about his true condition, making the muck out to be something of a lofty experience.

I have witnessed people's stress that comes from not having a job, from looking for a place to live, from having severe medical problems, and from having marital difficulty, and none compare with the misery that comes from having a child without a conscience. However, this is an exciting time to live! Never before has the first chapter of Romans (the foolish philosophy of evolution and the depravity of living without a conscience) or Proverbs, Chapter 1 (describes perfectly the gang mentality), meant so much. We are witnessing both firsthand. I am excited and have taken heart; I do not feel undone or hopeless, nor am I wringing my hands, because I have a God! That is right, I have a God! Do we think He does not see all? He is not caught off guard! He has given some over to their wicked desires (Romans 1:24). Do I worry about the believers' children in the midst of the above? No! He is the Gardener. We as parents have planted the seed of His Kingdom, the most powerful of all seeds, able to split the largest rock. He will water, He will cause growth, and He will reap the fruit. I have a God! How else will you find out that your God, the only God, the living God, can protect your family, provide in crisis, work miracles in family members, displace the enemy, and put to shame all worldly wisdom if you are never in the need of protection, food, miracles, wisdom, and victory? In the coming years, be prepared to expand! As our God provides, our faith will expand, and as it expands, so do we. I want to find out just how big God is. As we stand fast in the midst of a world without conscience, the great revelation that we have a God, the only true God, will become an actuality.

DAY 178
Knowing God

For the Law was given through Moses; grace and truth
were realized through Jesus Christ.
— JOHN 1:17

Law is the Word of God written down. Jesus, on the other hand, is the Word become flesh. That is an important distinction, since the Law centers around a page and Word become flesh around a person. The Law is heard and to a certain extent open to each individual's interpretation, because each person has a different heart dictionary that limits by subjective definition each word read. For example, the word comfort has different connotations for each individual. To read, "the God of all comfort," will mean a little something different to each reader. John 1:18 tells us that no man has seen God at any time. This simple statement rules out all who make absolute claims to knowing what God is like or who philosophize about God. Man does not know God. Through the mind, body, and world man can gain a concept of what God is and spend endless hours examining and propagating the notion. The imagining may appear very lofty; however, the assessment is still made from a heart dictionary and is therefore faulty. Only Jesus can explain Him. We find out who God is from Jesus or we never find out. This is why Jesus said, "I am the way, and the truth, and the life; no one comes to the Father but through Me" (John 14:6). If we want to know the reality of God, not just an appraisal, we must come to God through Jesus. "He who has seen Me has seen the Father; how do you say, 'Show us the Father'?" (John 14:9) If a disciple has not seen God, it is simply because he has not seen Jesus. Ten thousand years of human history proves that God cannot be described with words, He can only be revealed through a person. Jesus made God known through His life! The doctrines of God will leave a man prostrate in fear. The character of God revealed in Jesus leaves man walking, leaping, and praising God. Jesus reveals what is at the very heart of God, His love. Jesus is God's love in action, or Jesus is God's grace, for grace is love in action. Jesus makes God approachable while theology makes man turn and run. Written words will never draw man to God; only His love in the person of Jesus, the Word become flesh, attracts us.

DAY 179
Land Crabs

Who knows, God may turn and relent . . .

— JONAH 3:9

I was once told that I had bad theology. My response was, "Of course." Theology is the knowledge of God, and I would imagine that my knowledge is lacking in several areas. All I know of God for certain is what I see in Jesus;

apart from Him I know very little, and what I claim to know is probably wrong. It is somewhat like the little boy who was asked by his grandmother, "What are you drawing?"

"I am drawing God," he responded.

"But no one knows what God looks like!" she exclaimed.

"They will when I finish," he declared.

Many proclaim with a similar confidence exactly what God is like. However, the longer we listen, the more we learn about the theologian and the less we actually learn about God. One brother asserted at a meeting, "I am not against theology; I have just, personally, had enough to last me until Jesus returns."

I have always found the land crab interesting. He looks for a shell to move into, protects it with his life, eventually will find he has outgrown it, and so casts it off in search of a more suitable shell in which to hide. He never destroys the old one that is no longer good enough for him. Theology is just like that shell. With our eyes on the Lord we will always outgrow that in which we formerly took comfort, security, and pride. We are not crabs, though, and I wonder if we should not destroy the old rather than leaving it for someone else to put on, knowing all along that in the end it will be too small of an explanation for God. I suppose, though, that we all grow incrementally more than by leaps and bounds.

The Jews had God all figured out. It was simple: All prostitutes were to be put to death. But . . . then He told Hosea to marry one. The scribes and Pharisees knew it all, being experts in theology: The adulterous were to be stoned. They brought one such woman to the Living Word and found they had gotten it all wrong! Jesus said, "Neither do I condemn you; go your way. From now on sin no more" (John 8:11). Theology seems to be something that we will always outgrow, but there are simple truths about God that we can always grow into. God is love! He is gracious! He shows mercy! And God is full of compassion! This type of shell is worthy of leaving behind for others and never destroying.

DAY 180
Lazy Personalities

Accept one another just as Christ accepted you, in order to bring praise to God.

— ROMANS 15:7

We often talk about the different unique selves of thinker, feeler, and doer. I have purposely said less and less about those over the years, because the mind of man can easily grasp the concepts, and by so doing, might avoid grasping the revelation of Christ in us. I do believe that our uniqueness is important to understand. Problems can arise when many want their personality type to be understood by others and so exert pressure on them to recognize it.

Some use personality as an excuse to be lazy. For example, it is true that thinkers are not naturally social people, being more task-driven. I must understand that and not expect them to go door-to-door handing out tracts. On the other hand, they must see some of their deficiencies and put effort into functioning somewhat in social settings. Someone lacking communication skills, emotional skills, or relationship skills should LEARN SOME and not put the weight on the rest of the family to learn to cope with him. He can learn to give a hug, to ask a personal question about someone, and to verbalize how he feels. He can say, "I love you!" to the ones around him. Feelers can learn to carry through on a task, to clean the house, to be at a meeting on time, and to show the same interest and attention to their family members that they give a stranger. Doers can slow down, ask if there might be anything others need or would like done, listen and not react, let others in on the plan, and soften the facts. You see, our personality type is not an excuse to be lazy in the areas in which we are not naturally adept. We may be driving the people nuts around us. To say, "That is how I am, so live with it," is stupid. Thinkers want hugs but will not give any. Feelers want someone who will listen, but they will not listen. Doers want others to follow, and yet they will not follow. We must go outside of ourselves, recognize our weaknesses, own them, and invite Christ to be our strength. He will allow us to hug, listen, and follow.

DAY 181
Lesser Versus Greater

For they exchanged the truth of God for a lie, and worshipped and served the creature rather than the Creator, who is blessed forever. Amen.

— ROMANS 1:25

In seminars I like to emphasize the denial of self and spend a good bit of time examining and understanding the self that is to be denied. Denial of self is important to ministry and to the lives of every believer. The way of self is not the Way! Daily there are families, lives, and churches being destroyed because of self. However, we have a saying that lesser truth must always give way to greater truth. The denial of self, exchanged life, and abiding are all truths, but not the greatest truth. Every believer must be careful not to worship a lesser truth but allow the lesser truth to bring him to the greatest truth. We can run the risk of worshiping and serving something created rather than the Creator.

I once read a list of what it means to live in self-denial. The problem was that self-denial was portrayed as the greater truth. The article emphasized that we must be forgotten, neglected, disregarded, bear every annoyance, be content with bad food, never refer to ourselves, look for correction and reproof, sound out every bit of rebellion in our hearts, and so on. True, but a lesser truth, for there was nothing in the article about Christ. As we fellowship with Him, all the above that needs to happen does happen.

I will not spend the day focused on self-denial. As I have mentioned before, there are two ways to be controlled by self. One is by making every attempt to satisfy it, and the other is through doing everything to avoid it. Either way, it is worshipped by having attention. God is always to be the focus, and to the surprise of many, there are elements of self with which today He is not concerned about dealing. We must make the greater truth our focus, and then we may be assured that all lesser truth will not be neglected.

DAY 182
Let the Dead Bury the Dead

But Jesus said to him, "Follow Me, and allow the dead to bury their own dead."
— MATTHEW 8:22

I do not know about you, but I have had it with the media. This is not the age of information but the age of misinformation. When asked what I thought of the President, my response was, "I do not know him." The inquirer proceeded to tell me exactly what he was like. I asked him how he knew all of that. "Well, it was on television!" Amazing! I have done the very same thing myself. Actually, I have been in different parts of the world when things were unstable or in an uproar; not once have I found it to be like the reports on television. I listened to a reporter who was purportedly asking questions. However, he was only making accusations and then writing his own commentary. The fellow being thus "interviewed" finally asked, "Who told you I ever said such a thing?" The reporter went quiet, because no one had ever said that; he had made it up. There is the constant promoting of an agenda in the media. Why is all the bad news shown on TV? The news is calculated to stir our flesh to fear, resentment, frustration, anxiety, bigotry, and divisions. Once the bad news is received and our focus is on it, we will surrender our peace to it. There is always something the world offers to stir pride, to encourage self-righteousness or unrighteousness, and to make us think the world and its "elite" must act to fix things. It is all piffle. We cannot believe any of it. I can go months without watching the news and find nothing that has changed the next time I see a broadcast. It would be interesting to look at what was reported as absolute truth last year and see where the facts lie today. This brings me to my point: Should I just keep my head in the sand and ignore the world and what is happening around me? Jesus said it best: "Let the dead bury their own dead!" The things of the world creating the mess belong to the world; let them report on it and stew over it. They are dead; let them bury their dead. Put it all aside and follow Christ; we are alive in a kingdom of truth. The scuba diver ventures into a domain wherein the things that bother the fish ultimately do not bother him, for his world exists above. What happens in the world, even if it is true, does not change our job description.

DAY 183
Let the Dominoes Fall

What then shall we say to these things?
If God {is} for us, who {is} against us?
— ROMANS 8:31

I have met several people who believe me to be quite mad, in denial, unrealistic, and constantly seeing things through rose-colored glasses. While my glasses may rather be blood-colored, it is true that I see things differently. Remember as a child setting up all those dominoes in rows? What great fun it was to finally push them over, knowing exactly where they would end. Imagine today standing in the middle of a gigantic row of dominoes on the left and right, stretching out of sight. The choice is to push with left hand or right, having no idea where the last domino will fall. Many stand paralyzed, restrained, resigned, pessimistic, and hopeless; they close their eyes and push if they must, certain that the last domino will fall at a place not desired. I do not see it that way. I can push either side and know where the dominos will fall. The last one will fall at the feet of the Lord. There is nothing to worry about; God is for us.

In my day-to-day life I often describe an event by saying, "CATS! I came up cats!" It means that I was turned upside down and dropped from a high place. The expected outcome was that I would break my neck. However, the Lord mysteriously turned me over so that I landed on my feet. Cats! Everything is "cats" for me. He uses my enemies, He permits what He could prevent, and He uses the evil and flesh of men to reveal that He dwells in me. Poverty reveals His provision, sickness breaks pride, and want releases faith. Loss of control reveals that He is in control. I could go on, but why? Everything is "cats"! I do not see situations; I see Him. I may allow a situation to steal my awareness of His presence, but in His presence there are no losing situations, and His presence is ours for eternity.

I met an old Welsh preacher, well into his 90's, full of life and wisdom. He was such a delight to be with. He was blind; it seems that as he was preparing for ministry, he discovered that he was going blind. I asked his daughter, "What was it like growing up with a blind father?"

"Well, it was not difficult! I never did, and never have, heard him complain!"

He then said to me, "I am grateful that I am blind. If I could see I might have ended up like David. God knew what I needed. This has been the best." He was not in denial. The dominoes had simply fallen, with the last one landing at the feet of Jesus.

DAY 184
Leverage

I will not speak much more with you, for the ruler of the world is coming, and he has nothing in Me.

— JOHN 14:30

Satan is coming, and he has nothing in the Son of God. Satan is constantly looking for a leverage point, something in our flesh—the lust of the eyes, the lust of the flesh, and the boastful pride of life—with which he can move us closer to his goal. Often in the mountains I find myself wanting to move one of the large rocks off the driveway. I have a pole and a rock, but without a leverage point, usually a large piece of timber positioned under the pole, that rock is going to stay put.

Where we hold our image the enemy will always find a place of leverage. In Jesus there was no such leverage point. We have nothing in which to boast except the Lord. If we have considered ourselves crucified and buried with Christ, there will be no leverage point from which the enemy or his disciples can move us.

After a conference a fellow came up to me to say, "I do not think you are very holy!"

I did not waste time, but replied, "Oh, in my flesh dwells no good thing. Just the other day I was cussing a fellow that pulled in front of me. Can you imagine? I can tell you more if you would like. I promise you, I am worse than you perceive me to be. I have no holiness, and that is why I need His so desperately." What did the fellow say? What could he say? There was no leverage point. If in pride I had defended myself, the man would have succeeded in moving me out of Christ. What do I have to defend, anyway? God gave me, along with every person, the death sentence.

When your mate accuses you of being stupid, what harm is there in admitting to it? Once you do, the leverage is gone. When the boss accuses you of causing all of the problems, admit that you are a problem. There will be no more leverage. The enemy has a thousand ways of getting you to protect yourself, the same self that was crucified. Tomorrow, at work, at home, on vacation, the ruler of this world is coming for you. He has nothing in you, for it is no longer you. It is Christ in you.

DAY 185
Life

If any of you lacks wisdom, he should ask God, who gives generously to all. But when he asks, he must believe and not doubt, because he who doubts is like a wave of the sea, blown and tossed by the wind.

— JAMES 1:5, 6

We need an absolute way to live, a working religion. Carnal man has fought to have every hindrance to the passing pleasure of sin removed, and the result is a people adrift. Safety in being tied to the dock through moral absolutes was no longer valued; now he is free to drift, tossed back and forth in confusion and chaos, eventually thrown from the boat, groping for a life vest in the form of a system that will give him the freedom to experience pleasure, self-centered living, lack of struggles, and happiness, while at the same time make life make sense.

Does such a system exist? It does not exist in the theory of evolution. Man is an animal and yet higher than animals, for it is said he evolved; but where did conscience come from? Should the strong succeed? Those who count themselves among the strong would say, "Yes," while, "No" would be the answer from those who know themselves to be weak. It is chaos! Such a system does not exist in government; it does not exist in religion. While I believe the opposite also to be true, religion needs government to exist, for the religious will continue to blame the government for their failures. If only government would be eliminated, then religion would succeed; and yet, where religious systems like Islam take the place of government, the carnal desires of man merely go underground. We can therefore conclude that outward systems that encourage the flesh will cause man to break down and outward systems that attempt to hinder the flesh of man also cause man to fall apart. Only one option is left, and that is an inward system that is an absolute that allows man to thrive. If sin were natural, man would bloom, not rot, under it. The only thing that is natural for man is the absolute of Christ, for He created and holds man together. Hence, He is the Way!

DAY 186
Life Is So Daily!

But thanks be to God, who always leads us in triumph in Christ, and manifests through us the sweet aroma of the knowledge of Him in every place.

— II CORINTHIANS 2:14

A fellow was in my office complaining about his wife's behavior. When he finished, I began to speak. "Have you done the basics? Are you loving her? Are you bringing every thought captive to Christ? Are you being offended until you cannot be offended?"

"I've tried all that!" was his response.

How can any of us say, "I have tried all of that"? Did we try breathing, did we try going to the bathroom, did we try getting dressed, and did we try stopping at red lights? After trying all of them, did we decide never to try them again? How stupid. Some things are not things that we try, but things that we consistently do. Abiding is not something that we try; it is something that we do every moment of every day. Abiding in Christ, realizing that we are in Him and He is our focus, is not a light switch that is turned on once and stays on. I remember seeing a bicycle hooked up to a generator so that when a person was pedaling he got light, but it quickly extinguished when the pedaling stopped. The person could not stop pedaling and say, "Well, I tried that, but it does not work," when the problem is that he himself stopped working. There are many things in our lives that are not one-time things but daily. I remember a young woman telling me that she did not like marriage. I pressed her to reveal why. In the end she responded, "I guess it is just so daily." Well, amen! Abiding is not only daily but, more appropriately, moment by moment.

DAY 187
Life Teaches Him

I call heaven and earth to witness against you today.
— DEUTERONOMY 4:26

As my son prepared for college, I gave him the following admonition. "At the university you will be approached with all manner of sins. I am not asking that you do not participate. I would hope that you would not, but I refuse to play the Holy Spirit hovering above you. However, if you ever find yourself in sin, ask yourself if there is a lift in your spirit. If not, stop what you are doing. All your life I have taught you about Christ, and now life itself will teach you."

It is true that if something is not Christian, it is not natural. We say the Bible speaks to us with authority because God created it. God also created life, and life speaks just as loudly as Scripture. In fact, I believe that life is the greatest tool for witnessing that we have. We believers possess the only "religion" that the world supports. God created our faith, life, and world. I often let an unbeliever prove Scripture through his own experience of misery.

For just a moment lay aside theological knowledge and let me ask what life has taught you in regard to feeding the flesh, being bitter, hating an enemy, looking within, refusing to love, excusing disrespect, and avoiding God. While participating in these behaviors has life given your spirit a lift? Are you nourished by such behavior, or are you depleted? Stop, question, and think about your direction. What is life telling you? What life is telling you is consistent with Scripture. When I do roofing, I am careful not to let the hammer hit my fingers, as has happened several times in the past. Life has punished me when my fingers were hit. Jesus says to love an enemy. In the past I have chosen slander. Life taught me that slander hurts me. We believers have been taught far more through life than by reading, and why not? God is the Author of life, and for life to run smoothly, it must run in Him. Stop hitting your thumb.

DAY 188
The Limitations Of An Education

They do not know, nor do they understand, for He has smeared over their eyes so that they cannot see and their hearts so that they cannot comprehend.

— ISAIAH 44:18

Many parents have put much into the lives, character, and training of their children, only to be disappointed. Disappointed in what? In the inability of the training and education to produce what only revelation can. They had believed in the illusion called education at the expense of something higher in which to place their trust. They had exalted it and attributed to it characteristics that it does not have. When it comes to our life in Christ, we do not need a better education; we need revelation.

Jesus reveals to us the limitation of an education. The end result of hand picking twelve men to train and educate for three-and-a-half years was the lone teacher hanging on a cross with none of the disciples in sight. Yet, after revelation, those same men who denied Him were ready to die for Him. Peter denied the Lord not before a court of law, but in front of a sliver of a girl. This was the outcome of his education. After revelation he stood before crowds to proclaim Jesus. Only the Holy Spirit brings revelation.

If you want revelation for your child, you must pray and wait, expanding your belief system and acknowledging that the child belongs to the Lord. God is faithful; He would have none perish.

DAY 189
Living Outside The Circle

But He is unique and who can turn Him?
— JOB 23:13

God is unique! You are His unique creation! Do you accept your uniqueness? In the course of my life as a believer, I have met people who would be considered by most to be "odd." God creates man, man bands together, man determines his concept of what is normal using the criteria of the similarities shared by the majority, and some are left outside the circle of behaviors that constitute this notion of normalcy. Are you one of those out-of-the-ordinary people? Do you laugh at inappropriate times or talk when you should listen? Spill your deepest secrets to strangers? Did you have a ponytail when others did not or a shaved head when others had a ponytail? Are you loud in a crowd? Quiet at a party? When everyone is wearing suits, do you show up in a tee shirt? Do you laugh though no one understands your humor? Do you make people uncomfortable with the way you rearrange your silverware and organize your condiments in the restaurant? Do you invite people over and proceed to make them sit and listen to your latest recording of locomotive trains as loudly as the stereo will play? Do you feel like you have to play the people game every day? Are you the odd one out? Do you live outside the circle of what is typified as normal? If so,

I welcome you. There is plenty of room in the family of God for you. Please do not go away! We need you so much to bring color into our world. We need you to remind us that God creates outside the circle. We see God in you. Let Him shine through your uniqueness, and do not change!

I will tell you of one of God's favorites who lived outside the circle, an odd man. It was a time in Israel when the people needed a deliverer. The odd one, David, was overlooked as a potential candidate and directed to remain in the fields. The odd one was not to speak, though it was he for whom the prophet was looking. The odd one believed God, in Whom he had found favor. The odd one slew the giant, and yet later when he found his enemy in a cave, he refused to slay him but instead cut a piece of cloth from his enemy's garment. This odd man actually danced in the streets; his wife despised him the rest of his life for it. God sums up this "just too odd" man, David, by saying, "I HAVE FOUND DAVID, the son of Jesse, A MAN AFTER MY HEART, who will do all My will." There are so many odd people in the Bible, and I love to read about these people who lived outside man's circle but always within the circle of God's love and acceptance. The important thing is not whether or not you are odd, but that you allow the creative God to be Lord of your uniqueness. I thank God today for all of the odd people I have known who "do all His will."

DAY 190
Living to Man

The fear of man brings a snare,
But he who trusts in the LORD will be exalted.
Many seek the ruler's favor,
But justice for man comes from the LORD.

— PROVERBS 29:25, 26

Living to and for men is one of the worst kinds of bondage, for anyone living to man cannot live to God, the Giver of freedom. We have a saying, "I love you, but I do not live to you. I live to God." I will again preach of my own weakness: I determined some time ago that I would no longer meet with politicians. Why? I always compromise! I have met wicked men in places of authority and found myself compromising. The men should have been rebuked. If Jesus did not go to the "leaders" in His day, then what business do I have going? There is just something about being in the presence of image that shakes me. It is my weakness; I am sure some can withstand it, but I cannot; I end up living to man. There are several ways to live for man: giving glory, taking glory, giving judgment, receiving judgment, showing partiality because of worldly resources, groveling at the image or position of "greatness," discussing man's "secret" failings, refusing to ask a question, avoiding a confrontation, or reacting to criticism. I have done it all, and I tell you it is a miserable way to live. What makes it so miserable is the awareness that there is another way to live, free from man-pleasing; however, this freedom comes through faith. We must believe completely and unreservedly that we have a God who provides for us in every way, financially, physically, emotionally, and spiritually. We must believe that He opens doors, provides the way, and gives us wisdom. We must believe that He gives us everything needed, and that in Him we will find everything that we have looked for elsewhere in vain. For it is only in seeing that God meets all of our needs that frees us from the root of living for men, that root being the belief that man can provide something that we need. If assurance, significance, value, and worth come from God, what does man have to offer? If man has nothing to provide that we need—no praise, position, or possession—then we are free not to live to man. Again, living for the approval of man has at its root the belief that man can give us something that God will not. Therefore, we compromise our own eternal goal to get something perishable, even though what man offers always seems to come at a high price. When we live to men, we must ask ourselves what their favor will give us: our name on a piece of paper, a conversational piece of name-dropping that will elevate us when in a social setting, a job interview, or their approval over our work? Once we move in faith toward the Provider of all, we will be free, free indeed. It is great to trust God and not trust man, it is beautiful to acknowledge that God provides, and it is wonderful to let the heart become a graveyard for criticism because of the understanding that people's praise would not fill the void that only Christ can fill. Now, some will say, "Then we can be hermits; we do not need men!" Not at all! We need them in order to love them.

DAY 191
Lonely

For none of us lives to himself alone and none of us dies to himself alone. If we live, we live to the Lord, and if we die, we die to the Lord. So, whether we live or die, we belong to the Lord.

— ROMANS 14: 7, 8

I suppose that there are times in everyone's life when they feel all alone. Actually, this is an awareness of something that has always existed. A person may have always been alone but only recognize it at a time when there is not activity around him. One woman, when widowed for a short time, aptly said, "I know God is with me, but this morning I fell and there was no one there to pick me up." In the outer life loneliness is more readily recognized; however, in the spirit and soul we were all born lonely. There has never been (in spite of the insipid teaching of having a "soul mate") anyone who can touch our mind, heart, soul, emotions, will, and spirit. No one, that is, save One, and that One is Jesus. Psalm 25:16, "Turn to me and be gracious to me, for I am lonely and afflicted." Psalm 68:6, "God makes a home for the lonely." If you have invited the life of Jesus to live within, you have learned that He is the only One who fills loneliness and assures you that you never were alone. I like feeling lonely and turning to Him to discover His nearness. I like the fact that He alone can fill the emptiness that is deepest within me. I cannot imagine that He wants to be that near, but He does.

DAY 192
Lost Kingdoms

Again, the devil took Him to a very high mountain and showed Him all the kingdoms of the world and their glory; and he said to Him, "All these things I will give You, if You fall down and worship me." Then Jesus said to him, "Go, Satan! For it is written, 'YOU SHALL WORSHIP THE LORD YOUR GOD, AND SERVE HIM ONLY.'"
— MATTHEW 4:8-10

I went to the British Museum, possibly the best natural-history museum in the world. However, I think it should be called the British Museum of God's Judgment on Godless Kingdoms, for that is what it really reveals. From the Incas, the Greeks, the Romans, the Egyptians, the Africans, and many more, one readily sees the result of kingdoms that are anti-Jehovah. Evolutionists and anthropologists have perpetrated the notion that ancient societies were idyllic before the advent of Christianity, which spreads guilt and condemnation; that is preposterous. We forget one of the lessons of the Old Testament, and that is that God raises up kingdoms to punish the godless, non-God-fearing kingdoms. Where are these idyllic kingdoms, anyway? The Incas were performing so many ritual killings and bloodlettings that I believe God permitted the Spanish to be the instrument of judgment. All kingdoms passed away because of their wickedness. The respected Indian prophet, Sundar Singh, visited Europe in the 1920's. He prophesied about the coming punishment that would be WWII, and he did not see the looming war as a "natural disaster," but as God's judgment. Of course, his message was not received. Many in Europe say that they lost their faith because of the Great War. That is not true. The Great War revealed that they had already lost their faith. God's judgments are always true. I make many mistakes, but I fear making a false judgment, and therefore I am not a fan of condemnation teaching. However, this is not condemnation teaching, for I am merely pointing out what appears to be an absolute, that God raises up kingdoms to destroy corrupt kingdoms.

By the way, in the museum, the letters "A.D." preceding or "B.C." following dates are more commonly being replaced with the letters "c.e." (Common Era) or "b.c.e." (Before Common Era) as a means of being more sensitive to non-Christian religious traditions. The world would like us to forget that it is the "year of our Lord." But Jesus Christ is real, He will judge, and His return is near. In the course of the ministry travels I have been taken to so many museums, parks, attractions, and more. In the end I have this assessment, "All is vanity; we must abide in Jesus."

DAY 193
Love

We love, because He first loved us. If someone says, "I love God," and hates his brother, he is a liar; for the one who does not love his brother whom he has seen, cannot love God whom he has not seen. And this commandment we have from Him, that the one who loves God should love his brother also.

— I JOHN 4:19-21

The basic gist is that we are going to love and be loved. First we were loved, now we love. God loved us first. If anyone boasts, "I love God," and goes right on hating his brother or sister, thinking nothing of it, he is a liar. If he will not love the person he can see, how can he love the God he cannot see? The command we have from the Spirit of Christ is blunt: Loving God includes loving people; we must love both. This passage has such a bite! Again, the true test of our walk with Jesus is not found in the perfect situation but where we are our weakest. So often we say that we love Jesus, yet at home, at work, at church, or on the highway, the evidence weighs against it. We like to point to the places where we love. He points to the place where we do not. It is not that we should go down in a heap of condemnation, however. Remember, the purpose of life is to lose our own righteousness, kingdom, power, glory, and pride. We really are weak, and apart from Him we can do nothing. We just must not tell one another we are abiding if we do not love our wife, husband, or brother.

DAY 194
Loving the World?

If you were of the world, the world would love its own;
but because you are not of the world, but I chose you out of
the world, therefore the world hates you.

— JOHN 15:19

I have asked men and women alike who have fallen in lust with a perfect face and body, "How much are you willing to pay for sex?" Often they act surprised, but I know they are just in lust with a person, not in love. They overlook all the lacking qualities of character in favor of hoped for fulfillment of fleshly desire, which is too bad, since a fleshly person will beat the love right out of a mate. Of the men and women that I disciple, those who married just because of fleshly attraction have less sex than anyone else. It seems that after marriage the "beautiful" mate must prove that he has something more to offer than sex and withdraws. When the honeymoon is over, the true lack of character of the person is revealed, and in time, the love "felt" is beaten out of the mate. Why say all of this? Because I want to make an analogy about the world! It looks good, but marry it, and it will beat the love held for it right out of a person. I was once asked, "If drugs were legal and free, could I take all I wanted to and be happy?" The answer was, "No, you could not. The world does not work that way. Once it gets you, it will abuse you and will, in time, beat the desire you had for it right out of you." That is why drug users eventually become suicidal.

One fellow asked, "If it were legal, I would have several wives, or at least several affairs to fulfill my sex desire." Well, many have done just that and come to pieces. They did not come to pieces because the behavior was illegal, but because man is made in the image of God, and to act in a manner not supported by God is unnatural. The world is a vicious lover, but once it has you, it will not let go easily, and all the while it will continue to hammer the love you have for it out of you. In this way, God does not fight the world but uses it.

DAY 195
Lust

It is God's will that you should be sanctified: that you should avoid sexual immorality; that each of you should learn to control his own body in a way hat is holy and honorable, not in passionate lust like the heathen, who do not know God.
— I THESSALONIANS 4:3-5

It is impossible to lust over someone you love, and you are to love your neighbor as you love yourself. The real root of lust, then, is lack of love for mankind. When you lust, you see the person as an object, a thing, not as the possession of God, the creature for whom He died. Lust is taking an animate object and treating it as inanimate. When you see people on the street, at school, in the office, on television, or in advertisements, do you recognize their aliveness and potential for knowing Christ, or are they merely things? The first contact with someone is very important, for it is the sensation from which can spring a relationship. In the beginning, if someone is viewed as merely an attractive object, no matter how lofty the relationship becomes in your mind, the end will be rejection. The object, like a new set of golf clubs, will lose its glitter. True love never views another as an object but always values the person. Jesus has proven that we never lose our attraction, for we are bone of His bone; we belong to Him. We are vital!

Many have come to the place where they despise lust in their lives, so they focus on overcoming it, which is a basic error! To refer again to an analogy, think of a pink elephant with black polka dots. Once the image is firmly placed in the mind, try to forget it. A person cannot forget the thing on which he is focused; neither can lust be overcome by focusing on it. Jesus is a genius in His dealing with lust! We are not to suppress it, focus on it, or try to kill it; rather, He replaces it with another focus, LOVE! Jesus never destroys desire, but the sex drive is supplanted by a higher desire, the desire to love.

Love wants what is good for others. An affair, mindless sex, and premarital sex do not have roots in love but in self-centered, temporary pleasure. Love is wonderfully freeing and therapeutic as the great reconciler, bringing together a God-given desire—which under self's control would become animalistic—with a genuine expression of love (read Song of Solomon). If a man truly loves, he will not use the prostitute, for her good is his desire.

DAY 196
Man Is Like a Piece of Paper

But now he has reconciled you by Christ's physical body through death to present you holy in his sight, without blemish and free from accusation if you continue in your faith, established and firm, not moved from the hope held out in the gospel.
— COLOSSIANS 1:22, 23

I often think in terms of man's being like a piece of paper, born a blank sheet. Because of the pride of his forefathers, any blank sheet is cut off from God. Man begins to look to others to meet his needs, though only God, the Father, can provide what he seeks. Therefore, black dots begin to appear on the paper. An easy remedy is to fold the paper so that the dark spots are not seen. Next come other spots, another disappointment, another rejection, and the solution is the same. Fold the paper! On and on it goes until the paper is a teeny square, so small that no dot can fall on it. But how tightly folded it is! Did you know that houses are being made of cardboard? The secret was to find a way to compress the paper to the point that it could not take on moisture. So is man, compressed to the point that life-giving water cannot penetrate it. How many are walking around as little folded bundles, having forgotten the first spots? Only Jesus can unfold us. Some have been folded for so long that the paper nearly cracks as it is unfolded. But unfold He does; He will reveal and heal the very last spot. Our life is one in which we are constantly being unfolded. Nothing will remain hidden from His sight. "Come and do Your work, Spirit of Jesus."

DAY 197
Man's Deepest Needs

He who believes in Me, as the Scripture said, 'From his
innermost being shall flow rivers of living water.'

— JOHN 7:38

Jesus knew who He was, where He came from, where He was going, who His Father was, and that all of His friends were going to deny Him. What was His response? He picked up a towel and washed the disciples' feet! The behavior of others did not determine His actions. This is true freedom, the freedom from the actions of others. How many of us have our actions predetermined by others and, in effect, are not living life but merely responding to it?

Being physically born from below, our life initially centers on the things of the earth. We look to another to meet our spiritual desires, desires that only God can meet, such as the affirmation of worth, acceptance, security, love, and commitment. We then find that this other first wants us to meet his or her needs. We are—as one lady said at a conference—two ticks with no dog! We then become angry and bitter toward the mate, the friend, the pastor, or the child. However, the anger does not stop there. We begin to hate ourselves for needing others' love and acceptance before getting on with life. We hate having our mood controlled by the glance of another, the casual unkind word, the lack of interest in what we do, and the subtle hints at our inferiority. In short, we hate ourselves for not being free. We find ourselves under the control of others, slaves with hats in hand begging for our daily allotment of acceptance, security, and assurance. We hate what we have become: emotional leeches. We want to believe that others have created our feelings of inner ill will and misery; however, we know they have not; they have only revealed them.

Are you attempting to drink at a well that holds no water for your inner man? Do you look to your boss, your mate, or your parents, begging them to give what they do not possess? If so, then you have received the misery that you deserve. The end result is not only hatred toward those who fail at being God for you but also hatred toward yourself for being in such a pathetic situation. Anything that you make out to meet your deepest needs is a god, albeit a false god, that in the end must fail you.

We see today many who have made government god, demanding from it the things that God would give. As is normal for the carnality of man, they selfishly demand that god (government) intervene in everyone's life but their own, in order that others might be forced to meet their needs by not intruding on their comfort zone. However, nothing will meet the deepest longings of the heart except Jesus, who meets those needs and has structured life in such a way that no other can. Once disillusionment with all other sources of true love and acceptance has occurred, people can look only to God to meet the deep needs. He made each one of us for Himself, and in Him we all must find life. The answer, as always in the deep Christian life, is for the simple and the weak. Those who have lost the strength to pull the world toward them or drag themselves toward it may humbly say, "I have a God. His name is Jesus, and He meets all my needs."

We are not to desire to be lottery Christians, those who would buy spiritual lottery tickets to obtain in an instant what others have gained through a process. A lottery Christian wants to gain the fruit and maturity of spiritual men and women without going through the process of having doctrine, people, mates, teachers, vocations, or places fail them. God is not making mushroom believers but oaks. One is immediate; the other is a lifetime in the making. To discover that the world does not meet our needs is not a pleasant experience and normally takes some time.

One last point is that upon discovering, believing, and experiencing that Christ meets every need of man, we do not then withdraw from man. On the contrary, we are driven to man, but with a much different attitude. We do not run to others begging for life, but our desire is to impart to them some essence of the Life we receive.

DAY 198
Marriage Spiral

*For this reason a man will leave his father and mother
and be united to his wife, and they will become one flesh.*

— GENESIS 2:24

One of the sure signs of oneness in marriage is our ability to make our mates miserable. When we think about other couples, their misery is not ours. That is, their mates do not make us unhappy. How could they? We are not one with them! Oneness is an interesting term in the Bible used to explain the body of Christ, our relationship with Jesus, His relationship with the Father, and, of course, marriage. The best illustration for oneness is found in a mixing bowl. When we place flour and sugar in the bowl and turn on the mixer, the flour and sugar become one. At that point it is impossible to separate the two. If we try to add food coloring only to the flour, we will find it quite impossible, for it has also united with the sugar. When we marry, God turns on the divine mixer and blends the couple together. Marriage is not an attempt by two individuals to live together; on the contrary, it is the death of individuality. As the beaters turn, either one throwing dirt at the other will find himself dirty as well. Even Satan recognizes this oneness, for he appeared before God requesting to destroy Job. God allowed Satan to proceed with the one condition that he could not take him. Satan subsequently took Job's flocks, children, servants, crops, wealth, and even his health. There was one thing that Satan did not take: his wife! Why not? Because even Satan knows that a man's wife is his very life, and he had been commanded not to take the life of Job. The wife was safe.

Many believers have marriages that suffer from what I call marriage spirals that occur when the conduct of one creates in the mate an abhorred behavior. For example, a husband is made to feel that he is a failure at home. This causes him to spend longer hours at work where he is appreciated, which causes him to be a greater failure at home, which in turn drives him feverishly into his work. To come out of the spiral, both must begin to relate to their mate differently, not on the basis of unconstructive behavior but on the basis of heart's desire.

Do you know your mate's deepest heart desire? Ask him or her. You will be surprised. The believer's desire will be to be a blessing as a mate, to be a godly mate and parent, and even to make you happy.

The purpose of marriage is not to have someone to do for you; rather, it is so you have someone to do for. Happiness will only come as you love and do for others. Leave it to God to do for you. When asked to list the characteristics of a perfect spouse, most often people will list things only God can provide: love, listening, help, and patience. Notice that the feet needed to fill those shoes belong to Jesus. If you want a happy mate, then you must point your mate to Christ, who alone can meet those needs.

DAY 199
Maximize Your Joy; Walk In Faith

For we walk by faith, not by sight.
— II CORINTHIANS 5:7

I often say, "When you know the will of God, congratulations! You are an unbeliever! Abraham went and he knew not. Knowing not and going anyway is faith. Knowing everything and going takes no faith and is tantamount to unbelief." If we knew the will of God, what was around every corner, and if we always knew the outcome, how boring would life be? If we knew everything that was going to happen, our joy would not be full; in fact, our joy would be stolen. One example is Betty's and my need of paying bills. When the money is there, we pay and think nothing of it. However, when there is no foreseeable way of doing it and we open an envelope in which is the exact amount needed because the Lord put us on someone's heart, I cannot adequately describe the joy this brings. Had we known the check was coming, would we have had the same joy? If the Prodigal Son's father had always known the son would return, would his joy have been as great the day he saw him coming down the road? It is in not knowing, in walking by faith, that joy is made full.

DAY 200
Miracles Rooted in Unbelief

And behold, there arose a great storm in the sea, so that the boat was covered with the waves; but He Himself was asleep.
— MATTHEW 8:24

I have two thoughts on this passage. Jesus is asleep, the storm comes, the disciples are frightened, and they call on Him. Should we not always call on Him in a storm? Yet when they call on Him they are rebuked. Why? Jesus had permitted the storm for their perfection, a process interrupted by unbelief. Jesus stopped the storm, He did a miracle, and all that at their bidding, but it was not a positive. It was not a revelation of their importance but of their unbelief. Instead of crying out for the storm to stop, they should have crawled next to Him and gone to sleep, resting in the storm. The storm would not have harmed them either way; it was not the issue. What the storm could perfect in them or expose in them was the issue. In Christianity today, calling on Jesus and forcing a miracle is viewed as proof of spirituality, but the opposite is true. Imagine having a rebellious child; the parents have a choice in that storm: call on Jesus to stop it or lie down next to Him and rest. I know which one they will do! They will beg for the storm to stop!

My second thought is this: We have prayed to share in the power of the resurrection, the fellowship of His sufferings, and to be like Him in His death. What is the fellowship of His sufferings? It is many things. However, there is one thing that it must certainly be. If we are parents, we must have a child that refuses Him. That was His greatest suffering. All the created children of God, every one to the last man, refused Him. We must share in that pain to begin to see just how deeply He suffered. We begin to understand the gospel as we share in suffering, death, and the power. Suffering comes before the power. We do not like what is happening, but we can refuse to beg to be taken out of it, refuse to ask Him to quiet the storm before the storm has perfected us.

DAY 201
Malfunction

Flesh gives birth to flesh, but the Spirit gives birth to spirit.
You should not be surprised at my saying
you must be born again.

— JOHN 3:6, 7

There was something inherently wrong with man from the start. Man could not, as he was created, provide God with what He wanted, which was someone to love, someone with whom to fellowship, and someone that understood His heart. Man was created with a weak spirit that could either be drawn to heaven or attracted to things of the world. The lusts of the fleshly soul looked to everything outside the spirit for fulfillment; in short, it was fed by the world. Man lived in the fantasy that fulfillment and happiness could come through the world's events and offerings.

Upon receiving a new born-again spirit, the Spirit overcame the outer life's appeal, and man could now begin to be filled within and be freed from what the world offers. "Out of your innermost being will flow rivers of living water." At this point man had something much more significant in common with God than with the world, and the reality of the things of God could be sought by man. There was now fellowship on a much deeper level as what it meant to be made in the image of God became revealed. Life was no longer found in the fantasy but in the reality of giving, serving, loving, forgiving, and redeeming; for now he was content to die an unknown, die abused, die without money, die losing, and die totally free.

DAY 202
Marriage And Oneness

Stop depriving one another, except by agreement for a time that you may devote yourselves to prayer, and come together again lest Satan tempt you because of your lack of self-control.

— I CORINTHIANS 7:5

I was listening to a woman who had a rather spectacular testimony. She had been a gang member and into drugs and a lesbian lifestyle. Several other sisters in Christ were discussing sex and marriage when she blurted out, "There are a lot of times that I do not want to have sex with my husband, but I do! I do because I want to proclaim to Satan, 'You will not come between my husband and me!' I want to proclaim, 'We are one,' no matter what the enemy says, and I want God to know I believe Him, that what He has brought together no one will separate." My spirit leapt within. I leaned over and gave her a hug, announcing to the group, "I believe her." Sex in marriage is a proclamation that we are one no matter what. As I have mentioned before, there are several issues in marriage, but every issue is separate. We lock ourselves out from ever finding an answer to an issue when all issues are lumped together. There are many more issues in marriage than sex, but that is the issue this article addresses.

I like traveling, but I have had some horrific experiences. Some involved the tiny airplane seat. Some had to do with the need for luggage, for I despise having to carry so much from one country to the next. I remember traveling in the Amazon, being poisoned by the local water, and thinking I would die. In Northern India it was a bad chicken meal that I thought was killing me. If I am invited to speak elsewhere in the world, must I decline the invitation because I have discomfort on the plane, I loathe lifting luggage, and I sometimes get sick traveling? How much would I miss out on? I could take any one negative experience and just quit, but instead I have allowed the bad experiences to make me a better traveler. Each trip is an individual event linked to previous trips only by what I learned from past experiences that can enhance my present journey. After many years of travel I have learned things that work and things that do not. Some international trips were just barely tolerable, but I so loved the people I went to see; they ministered to me and I to them. Some international trips were just average; let us just say I got there. But I so enjoyed the brothers and sisters at the end of the trip and those with whom I traveled. Some trips have been spectacular. I have been bumped into first class, where seats recline and people call me "Sir." I totally relaxed, but still what I remember the most were those brothers and sisters waiting for me after the travel. Any journey is tolerable because for me, the goal is not the travel but arriving to be with those at the end of the trip.

Sex in marriage is like a journey in the following three areas. First, couples will find that sex is most enjoyable with a minimal amount of baggage. So much baggage from the past is taken into the bedroom by some couples that there is barely room for them. Second, each experience must build upon the last experience. Third, the person is more important that the journey.

First, entering in without a heavy load. Many bedrooms are crowded from sex-based hurts of the past. Sex, which is intended to be associated with pleasure, has become synonymous with the pain of an impressionable earlier experience, such as abuse, date rape, performance-based acceptance, innuendo, pornography, comparison, or just being made to feel unattractive. All of these emotions and experiences from the past can become a heavy load. It is unfortunate that these things happen, but tragic if they continue to control a person's life today. Any issue that has to do with the senses or natural desires takes special care, since it is impossible to walk away and never have to deal with it again. I remember a fellow who had an obsession with water. He had to go all day, even on the hottest days, without drinking water, or else he would drink too much and even possibly drown himself. Next question: Where could he go to escape the temptation to take a drink of water? As you can see, problems that deal with the natural pose unique problems. The sex desire is part of the natural; sexuality is built into mankind, so if one attempts to run from it, he runs from himself. To tell one to forget all bad experiences associated with sex and then tell him to go have sex will, more often than not, throw him right back into the emotions he is trying to avoid. The question is how to participate without dragging up all the past emotions. First, it must be realized that the world has done a good job of selling sex as the center of life. The sexual experience as described by the world is just as unreal as an airbrushed, enhanced photo of models. Second, the fear of poor performance will cause anxiety and poor performance. Fear is invited in and must be invited out. The fear of sex cannot be dealt with by obsessively thinking, "I must not think of sex," for by so doing, sex is exactly what is thought about. It must be handled with every thought of sex being taken captive to Christ. How? When the thought of fear comes, the direction of the mind must be changed completely by telling the mind, "I am not going there; I refuse to think that." By turning to the Lord for enabling with this, it really is possible to have life centered in something other than sex. It is possible to lower expectations of sex while maintaining expectations for the spouse. Third, recognize that the life that was hurt has been buried with Christ. It is impossible to change the past, but it can be buried by an act of faith. Throughout the day as the doubts about performance ability come, speak out loud, "I believe that I have been crucified with Christ."

This brings us to the second aspect of the sex journey. Each new experience builds on past learning experiences. The bad experiences are not to turn a couple away from intimacy, but rather they give the couple something to build from. There is no need for a couple to obsess on what went wrong at the beginning of the marriage. They are no longer at the beginning of the marriage; they are in the now. They can learn from what was unpleasant and not repeat the mistake. All of life is instructing the believer in what is the Way and what is not.

Finally, the most important goal of the sex journey is not physical stimulation; rather, it is the person. For the woman mentioned above who would have sex with her husband so that Satan would not come between them, sex was not the issue, but keeping her faith and her husband was the goal. Sex is meant for oneness and the acceptance that comes from that oneness in marriage. To make sex the goal is self-defeating and will correspondingly bring less satisfaction, because the mate senses he is less and less the goal and more and more the object, rejection sets in, and no one is satisfied. When the person is the goal, the times between sexual activities are much more fulfilling, much as when an obese man said to a very skinny man, "I enjoy my meals too much to live as you do." To which the skinny man replied, "But I enjoy the time in between meals much more than you!" He made a good point, for when food is the goal of life, how are we to enjoy the majority of our time we are not indulged in eating? The person who finds satisfaction in living in the between times is happy much more of the time. When the in between has the goal of affection, then not only is the sex life enjoyed, but also there is joy where we spend the majority of the time of our relationship. Sex cannot be the goal. The woman who wanted to proclaim to Satan that she was one with her husband had made oneness the goal, and if sex helps proclaim it, then so be it. For her the journey brought her to a wonderful place!

DAY 203
Ministering With And Ministering To

*But we request of you, brethren, that you appreciate those
who diligently labor among you, and have charge over you
in the Lord and give you instruction.*
— I THESSALONIANS 5:12

There are those to whom we minister and also those we
find ourselves ministering with. Regardless of the capacity,
we remember that service in the Body is not a pyramid
scheme wherein those who know the most and sound the
most Christian are at the top, while all others strive to
reach the top (anyway, only air is to be found at the top!).
Rather, we minister horizontally with the full knowledge
that we have nothing that every believer does not already
possess. However, in this horizontal relationship are those
to whom we are called to minister, and it is always our
desire that at some point in time we will labor with these
very same brothers and sisters in ministry to others. We
can tell those we minister to by their attitudes. If they are
judgmental, argumentative, overtly or covertly cutting us
to pieces, and pitting themselves against us, we know that
these are the ones we need to minister to. We do not use
their behavior as an excuse for having nothing to do with
them. (Matthew 5:46, "For if you love those who love you,
what reward have you? Do not even the tax-gatherers do
the same?") Rather, we simply recognize that we cannot
yet minister with them. We become so distressed when
we discover that someone we thought was a co-worker
is slandering us, when instead we could simply recognize
that this person is not one that we are ministering with,
but to. We need not be upset at the carnality of others, for
we can remember our own. A long-time friend and I were
watching a young man minister in what was obviously a

great exercise in the flesh, since we noticed more of him than of Jesus. My buddy turned to me and whispered, "Do you know what really bothers me about that fellow? He reminds me of us when we were his age." How true.

I have noticed that the only thing that can suspend an unfinished civil war is a common enemy to unite the previously warring factions. Often those who walk in the flesh pick a common enemy and draw up a truce to support one another in the fighting. Any of us might be picked as that common enemy, but again, this only reveals those to whom we are to minister.

DAY 204
Ministry That Wears Us Out

Therefore, since we have this ministry, as we received mercy, we do not lose heart.
— II CORINTHIANS 4:1

I remember talking to a pastor that told me that his great heart for the people had led him to fatigue and depletion. I responded, "'A great heart of compassion led me to exhaustion' sounds so much better than saying, 'Playing God has led to my exhaustion!'" But it was playing God that caused his malady. It is impossible to become exhausted if ministry is the flow of Jesus' life through us to others.

We are not the source of living water, life, or wisdom, but rather the channel; I cannot imagine a garden hose getting that worn out! However, when we play God we strive to become the source; we attempt to get in our child's skin and live his life, we convict our mate of carnality, we force on others the building program, and we make disciples in our own image. We must refuse to play God and rest while connected to the Source. Does this mean we just lie around like the garden hose? Yes! The Gardener will cause the flow! We are to be used as the avenue for the drink, but we are not the drink.

A friend told me of a time that his children asked him for an automobile. He replied, "Why are you asking me? Go ask the person that I have to ask when I need a car. Go ask your Father in heaven!" If we continue to play God for others there is always the risk that they will not find God for themselves. God does not have one single grandchild. Everyone must find Christ for himself. There is so much in the discipleship process that God must do, and without His activity, nothing of lasting value will happen.

I was in the north of Italy when, not being able to read Italian, I parked the car in a no-parking zone. I got out of the car and noticed an officer writing tickets. At that I put two and two together and immediately turned around, got in the car, and pulled out. Not content with that, the officer waved me over and attempted to explain that I was going to get a ticket, which I only surmised from his waving the ticket book and pen and his appearing to be detailing in Italian my offense! Really, for all I knew he was writing free passes to the circus! I, on the other hand, was pleading my defense in English. Neither of us really knew what the other was saying. In the end we both threw up our hands in frustration and walked away. If the Holy Spirit is not working in someone's life, he simply will not be able to hear anything of our translating and interpreting what God has given us to say. "HAVING EYES, DO YOU NOT SEE? AND HAVING EARS, DO YOU NOT HEAR?" (Mark 8:18) If we have been able to hear and see, it is because of the Holy Spirit. "But blessed are your eyes, because they see; and your ears, because they hear" (Matthew 13:16). Responding to what He allows us to hear and see is a different matter, but hearing and seeing comes from Him. Trying to make a person see and hear is wearing. Simply rest, allow the years to speak against the minutes, allow the person's life experiences to witness to Life, and stay connected to the Source. Ministry then can come through us to another.

DAY 205
Missed The Will Of God In One Area? Pick It Up In Another!

The mind of man plans his way,
But the LORD directs his steps.

— PROVERBS 16:9

Anyone who feels he has missed the will of God in one area of life can pick it up in another. Here is what I mean. Imagine that you married an unbeliever. Many will hint or blatantly tell you that because when you came to a Y in the road you went left instead of right, for the rest of your life you must pay for it. The decision will direct all of your days. There is no need trying, since you have already messed things up. That is a lie. Just because you married out of the will of God does not mean that you cannot pick up the will of God today. You can move into His will and love the unbeliever, just as He does, "for God so loved the world." You can share with your mate. Even in a worst-case scenario wherein your mate leaves you, you can still pick up the will of God today, which is to walk in the Spirit, gain the revelation of Christ, and come to know the One who knows you. There is so much in the will of God, but again, missing it in one area does not mean that you cannot pick it up in other areas for a life perfectly aligned in Him. I have seen many that married in the will of God but later did not pick the will of God. So what if ten years ago they chose the will of God? Is that helping them today when they are not? Remember, we are all in the process of growth. I am not going to hold the mistakes that my children made at age five against them, and God, whose plan is not thwarted by our decisions, continues to strive with us all of our days. We make the plan (an act of faith); He directs the steps (an act of foreknowledge).

DAY 206
Natural Emotions In An Unnatural Place

*For the sorrow that is according to {the will} {of} God
produces a repentance without regret, {leading} to salvation;
but the sorrow of the world produces death.*

— II CORINTHIANS 7:10

There are many Y's in the road of life. Many have gone right instead of left, heading down a path from which return is difficult. It is no secret that the Church today finds itself coping with a subculture in which extramarital affairs are commonly occurring. How does this happen? There are the simple, obvious root problems and solutions: "The lust of the eyes, the lust of the flesh, and the boastful pride of life." Many are looking for spiritual needs (love, acceptance, assurance, security, and significance) in the wrong places. Having experienced rejection from self and others, they look to another person to love or validate them. An easy solution is repentance and a turning to the One who does love them. Then there are those who are just plain stupid. I remember a traveling salesman telling me that he hated staying at a particular hotel. "There are many single women there, and I always end up having an affair!" The obvious solution, which apparently had escaped him, was not to go to that hotel! These are the easier problems concerning affairs, when at the root there is very little emotional attachment.

However, when there is emotional attachment, the problems escalate. It deserves repeating that there is a Way and a not the Way. Jesus is the Way, and every other way is not the Way. The world's way of premarital sex and cohabitation is not the Way, and it is a road from which it is difficult to return. In one survey (not that I trust surveys) 40% of all affairs took place with a previous boyfriend or girlfriend. Obviously there was an emotional attachment from the past that was never broken. I am vexed by every young woman who, having been convinced that she would marry a fellow, goes to bed with him, and months later she goes to school to find the boyfriend no longer talking to her and dating someone else. The girl has been living in an unnatural situation where emotions were expended at a level of marriage, but life did not make a return on the investment. For the girl it is the turmoil akin to divorce, but for the boy, a mere switch of dating partners. Some situations are better left avoided, but many have been told the perfect Way to live, and if they fall short they cannot see any other avenue.

Often I am asked, "Is it possible to fall in love with two people?" My answer is, "Of course it is. That is why I stopped dating once I got married!" It is not difficult to have emotions for someone other than the mate. Often I draw a circle and call it "natural situation." Within the circle I draw another circle and call it "natural emotions," wherein one would list feelings of love and affection for the spouse. Both the emotions and the situation are legitimate. Next I draw another circle called "unnatural situation," and within that circle I draw the same little circle called "natural emotion." Here is where I find many who are having an affair. They have all the natural emotions that come from dating and spending time with another, and yet they are in an unnatural situation with someone other than their spouse. Being in such a situation brings no peace and is exactly why I say that we are to stop dating once we are married. What is the solution to withdrawing from an unnatural situation? It is difficult, for even though many actually hate where they are at, they cannot deny the feelings that they have for another. To simply kill the emotions does not work and will only produce another unhealthy situation. This is because it is unnatural to attempt to eradicate natural emotion, which cannot be eliminated cafeteria-style, exterminating a little here and a little there. The person would be left with dead emotions in the natural situation of the marriage; he would no longer feel for anyone.

The reader may be asking, "What is Mike talking about? It is silly to speak of married people having feelings for someone other than their mate or married people returning to their mates and still struggling with emotions for another! If I were the mate in that situation, I would just say, 'Get a life, and when you decide you can love only me, then, and only then, return!'" I know what you are thinking and understand why you are saying it. However, these are real situations that I have had to deal with regularly in believers' lives. If the article does not apply to you, praise God and move on.

For those who find themselves wanting to follow God and yet being pulled by emotion, what are you to do? Confess the Way! Jesus is the Way, and every other way is not the Way. Invite Christ into the center of the situation.

Tell Him exactly where you are at and do not hide a thing, for "power is perfected in weakness."

Just as an aside, I visited with a believer who was settled on having an affair. After years of rejection this believer had found someone who "truly loved" him. I knew no matter what I said he would go ahead with his plan. Emotions were ruling. After making my case for the Way, I said, "I know you are going ahead with the affair. Would you do something for me? Every time you leave the house, invite Jesus to go along with you. Invite Him into the center of your affair!" The person looked quite shocked, but I pleaded, "Please, invite Jesus to go along with you. Just pray, 'Jesus, come and go with me.'" The person agreed. Nearly one year later I saw him again, and he said, "Mike, I did what you asked. I invited Jesus to go with me always. I have broken off the relationship I thought I could never end. I have broken it off not because I stopped loving the person, but because Jesus always went with me and allowed me to move against the emotions." See how Jesus brings everything into its natural place? I do not want to cheapen someone's emotions, which in themselves are not bad, but the place where they are being exercised can be very bad. If you find yourself in an emotional affair, confess it truly, hide nothing, hold nothing back, tell the Lord, and invite Him into the center of it. He is the only one Who can move you back to a place of peace (natural emotion in a natural place). Leave the place of the unnatural by beginning to invite Him in. We have a God, He is real, and He will make a difference.

One more thing about affairs is that they need not wreck and destroy the oneness of a couple any more so than does rape. Soulish love, mental oneness, emotional oneness, and even physical oneness do not compare with spiritual oneness. A husband and wife are one in Him, and nothing will change that. Forget what is behind, build on your spiritual oneness, and move on. Do not let a momentary event steal a lifetime of experienced oneness in the Spirit.

Many have gone down a road they should not have. Then comes the thinking that if only they could go back in time, they would do something different. Reality is that once they were back in time, they would be the same persons they were at that time, making the same mistakes. All this is true, but not the truth. We must end this article at truth, and truth is Jesus. Do you believe in Jesus? If so, you will answer the following in the affirmative. Do you believe that God causes all things to work together for good? Yes, all things, even the stupid mistakes that you have made. Do you believe it? I do, and I know we can all press on to the high call in Christ Jesus.

DAY 207
Need a Babysitter?

Trust in the Lord with all your heart and lean not on your own understanding; in all your ways acknowledge Him, and He will make your paths straight.

— PROVERBS 3:5, 6

I remember a couple with an out-of-control child. Every night cookies were put on every other step and down the hallway leading to the child's bedroom. This is how they got the child to go to his room at night. You can imagine the luxury of dropping the child off at a babysitter's for a night's rest. Aside from all the issues this situation brings up, it made me think how emotions can be a lot like uncontrollable children. They wear us out, and we would be happy to drop them off at a babysitter's just to get a break from them. We need a break from our emotions and obsessive thoughts, so we stop off at the babysitter of drugs, alcohol, TV, gambling, videos, romance, and more. We want something else to take charge of our emotions and thoughts to give us a break. There is another option, though. When they are such a hassle, we should just desert them. We cannot control them, so we need to abandon them at God's doorstep and admit that we are powerless and done in.

It has taken me some time to come to the place where I could say that sin is stupid, but it is! It is stupid because it does not fit our new nature, the life of Christ. If I were to ask a group of farmers to wear dresses, high heels, and pantyhose for one week, I imagine that they would be quite uncomfortable. Obviously, it is because the attire does not fit their nature! They are men; they want men's clothing. Likewise, we believers are uncomfortable when depressed, angry, unforgiving, full of criticism, or sinning simply because those do not fit our new nature, the life of Christ. If a believer goes to bed angry with his mate, he punishes himself. If a believer refuses to forgive, he punishes himself. If a believer returns to a past sin, he punishes himself. Someday in heaven it will be revealed that the commands of God were never a burden (I John 5:3). The proof will be in the fact that when they were neglected or disobeyed, His children were miserable. Whenever they were kept, we were happy! Dwell on this: Sin and punishment are one and the same. We need not punish a cancer for being a cancer; cancer is its own punishment. The woman caught in adultery was brought to Jesus. She never asked for forgiveness, and yet Jesus did not condemn her. Why? Her behavior had already condemned her; there was no need for Him to say anything. Sin is stupid! It has been said that the fruit of sin is either rotten or green, but never ripe, juicy, and satisfying. Sin simply does not fit a believer any more than the clothes and behaviors of the opposite sex.

DAY 208
New Radical Church's Advertising Program Offers Fuller Parking Lots Than Walmart

And I, if I be lifted up from the earth,
will draw all men to Myself.
— JOHN 12:32

In the Christian religion (running rampant in churches and different from the Christian faith) so many things are incorporated just because they are contagious, rather than received because they inspire belief. If one church is having great success at bringing in believers from the other churches, pastors and committees flock there to discover and imitate the program, which can be quite complex, with everything needing to be timed to the minute. Songs must be ordered in such a way as to "lead people to worship." The facility must be user friendly, and the latest pet social ill must be addressed with the utmost sensitivity. Well, amen! An older friend whose pastor was onto a new church growth plan stopped him by saying, "This plan costs too much and is too complex!" The pastor answered, "Do you not see that both parking lots are full?" The old man responded, "The parking lot at Walmart is full every Sunday, too. Now here is my plan for growth. It is simple and does not cost money. 'If I be lifted up, I will draw all men unto Me!'" The pastor shook his head and walked off, but what the old man said was true! We do so much work, when a focus on the crucified/resurrected Savior would ensure that He did the drawing. If God gets all the glory, then He does all the work. To hear many evangelists speak, you would think that they are doing the drawing. They have yet to learn the difference between a crowd and an audience. A fellow once said to me, "Wells, you know all the repetition of your message is not keeping people away; it is why we come. I like hearing that Jesus is everything." I know, then, that it is Jesus Who will draw the people. However, this simplicity takes faith; unbelief will always make things complex. The way to life is narrow and will take a narrow mind. Man will not enter in through the broad way with a broad mind. The narrow mind believes the simplest of things.

DAY 209
No Anchors

I will not speak with you much longer, for the prince of this world is coming. He has no hold on me, but the world must learn that I love the Father and that I do exactly what my Father has commanded me.

— JOHN 14:30, 31

As a ship will never leave port if the anchor is not hoisted, often our flesh has an anchor somewhere in the world holding our spirits, and we never seem to be able to sail on. As long as we have a fleshly anchor, the enemy will have something in us and we will not be cut free from his oppression. If we shrink back in inferiority when we have to talk to people, why is that? There is a fleshly anchor that is holding us in bondage. Is it pride, so we do not want to make mistakes and appear foolish? Is it unbelief, so that we do not believe our value to God and instead walk in insignificance? See how an anchor keeps us from sailing? When we can be controlled by another's look or negative word, why is that? How can someone calling us rotten names wreck our day? It cannot unless there is an anchor. When outer events, words, and behaviors can shut a believer down, it is because there is something in him to which these events are anchored. We must not be consumed with what we are doing but why, for in the why we will find our freedom. There is something He would show us that must go. When it goes, we will be free, and when the god of this age comes through others' words and behaviors, he will find that there is nothing in us . . . nothing except Christ!

DAY 210
No Contribution

Trust in the Lord with all your heart and lean not on your own understanding; in all your ways acknowledge Him, and He will make your paths straight. Do not be wise in your own eyes.

— PROVERBS 3:5-7

I am finding a new freedom in the little phrase "no contribution." We all hate to admit that we have no contribution to give the Lord. We make excuses and avoid that fact. "I did not pray enough before the meeting." "I did not study enough before the Bible study." "I should have been there." What you are really saying is, "Had I prayed, studied, and come, I could have contributed something." God is I AM, the God without contribution. Add anything to I AM and you will not have I AM. Since God gets all the glory, then God must do all the work. I have enjoyed saying to God before my meetings, "I am making no contribution. Nothing! I have nothing. And with what You give me, I will be happy." If the meetings go well and people are blessed, amen; I did not make a contribution. If they do not go well, amen, I still did not make a contribution. Since I have nothing, I did not make a contribution. Whatever He gives me is more than I had. I came into the whole thing empty. Whatever I get is also whatever I needed; it was the will of God.

DAY 211
No Fear in Love

There is no fear in love. But perfect love drives out fear, because fear has to do with punishment. The one who fears is not made perfect in love.

— I JOHN 4:18

Alex Mathew in India tells of a friend he had, Michael Francis, who had a career and a family when he contracted leprosy. Once his disease had been cured, he stood in front of the hospital filled with fear. Would his family come and pick him up? They did not. He said he had faced his worst fear, the fear that they would not come, and yet he stood. In Jesus, he still stood! From that day he was never afraid again. He sat homeless on a concrete slab in the streets and told Alex, "See this concrete that I sleep on? It is as soft as velvet. I have found it to be the Savior's lap."

What is your worst fear? Have you ever feared what you would do if you lost someone you love? Have you ever feared that the person you love might say to you, "I do not love you; I never loved you"? Have you feared that your inferiority, worthlessness, lack of acceptableness, and deficiency of love might be revealed? It is just fear. When it comes, do you know that if you have Jesus, fear will wash over you like a wave, and you, too, will still be standing? It is an amazing thing to be confronted at last with your worst fear and to find yourself still standing. You will find it a liberating experience, just as Michael Francis did, and you will be free in a new way, knowing there is nothing left to lose, and therefore, there is nothing to fear.

DAY 212
Not of This World

And do not be conformed to this world, but be transformed by the renewing of your mind, that you may prove what the will of God is, that which is good and acceptable and perfect.

— ROMANS 12:2

Here is a simple test. Please answer the following from the heart.

—Would you rather meet the President of the U.S. or a new believer in Christ?

— Do you believe that computer-chip dates determine your destiny?

—Imagine meeting a famous celebrity and a Christian on the same day; neither had you previously known. Arriving home, which one would you first tell your family you had met?

—You have the opportunity to speak to a small group in the inner city, and a famous politician calls you for a private meeting. Would you cancel the little group meeting?

— When reciting your family history, do you immediately tell of all the famous people to whom you are related?

—In a social gathering, do you drop the names of celebrities, sports figures, and politicians you have met?

—Do you discuss the ideas and statements of politicians as though they are important facts?

—Do you brag about the intellect, talent, and abilities of someone close to you?

—Do you believe that people are rich because of their great talent, ability, and effort?

—Would you lay down your life to maintain the glory of a man?

See how easy it is to be influenced by and conformed to the world? The world has done a good job convincing us of its ultimate importance. Since the glue, Jesus, that holds all men together witnesses constantly to something higher, the world must clamor for our attention by constantly bombarding us with messages of its importance, lest we stop for a moment and question.

DAY 213
Obsessions

Finally, brethren, whatever is true, whatever is honorable, whatever is right, whatever is pure, whatever is lovely, whatever is of good repute, if there is any excellence and if anything worthy of praise, let your mind dwell on these things.
— PHILIPPIANS 4:8

Imagine that the place you are presently sitting as you read this article represents your whole life. Everything in the room holds some aspect of your past, present, and future. Now pick up the most insignificant object that you see, such as a pencil, a coin, or a saltshaker, and slowly move it toward your eye. Keep moving it until this insignificant object blocks out half of your world. Something that is really of no great consequence to the rest of us has become of paramount importance to you. In fact, you will have great difficulty living the rest of the day with half of your vision blocked. This is exactly what the enemy does to believers. He picks something from our past, present, or future and has us obsessing on it until we believe that there is nothing we can do in life until this one thing is resolved. Some obsess so long that they eventually begin to listen to the voice of the enemy telling them that this one thing is so consuming that the only option is suicide! Obsession is wrong in two fundamental ways. First, Matthew 5:36: "You cannot make one hair white or black." That is, you cannot control the past, present, or future. Second, regret over the past is for unbelievers. It vexes me greatly when I see believers wallow over some stupid mistake in the past. We have a God, He takes our sins, and the proof that He cleanses us from them is the very fact that we are distressed when we think about the past. Therefore, He is to be our daily focus.

Imagine that your mind is divided in half. One half of your mental energy goes to your mate, job, church, family, and hobby; the other half of your thought-life goes to your obsession. If you give up your obsession, what will you do with the vacuum? Philippians gives the secret: focus on Him! One thing I found that makes life enjoyable is to give myself to something bigger than myself each day. So while an obsession is bigger than the person who gives himself to it, God is indescribably bigger than the obsession. Satan wanted Jesus to worship him; the word used for worship is indicative of "giving attention to." Jesus refused to give His attention to anything other than God. We will not worship an obsession.

DAY 214
One Praise Before An Event Is Worth 1,000 Afterward

"For I know the plans that I have for you," declares the LORD, "plans for welfare and not for calamity to give you a future and a hope. Then you will call upon Me and come and pray to Me, and I will listen to you. You will seek Me and find {Me} when you search for Me with all your heart. And I will be found by you," declares the LORD.

— JEREMIAH 29:11-14

I believe it! He has plans for me. Everything is working toward those plans; nothing is working against me, for He is for me. I believe that His plans include a future and a hope. I believe that He is listening to me. I believe that I have sought Him because He first sought me, and I believe that I have found Him. But today I cannot see it! It seems dark. It feels empty. It looks like a reversal. What am I to do? This is the testing of my faith, because I know He has never disappointed me. Therefore I will praise Him! It is in this darkness that my praise means the most to Him. In this time of darkness before the fulfillment, one praise offered to God is worth one thousand after the promise is received. Today if you have no job, praise God! If your marriage and family are not working out, praise God! If you have found yourself once again in defeat, praise God! If physical ailments have led to spiritual defeats, praise God! One praise before the trial ends is worth one thousand after it.

DAY 215
Only Trust What Jesus Has Done In a Person

I have been crucified with Christ; and it is no longer I who live, but Christ lives in me; and the life which I now live in the flesh I live by faith in the Son of God, who loved me and gave Himself up for me.

— GALATIANS 2:20

Let me tell you a secret about others. The only measure of dependence you place on them should be on the things God has done in them. Depend on them for anything else and they will let you down. When we see strong people, we have the tendency to want to trust them. However, if it is a fleshly strength that we are trusting, then one day they will let us down. At times I have told people of my strengths, my boldness, or my knowledge, and I have heard others do it, as well. Such talk is foolishness, for we are covertly asserting that we can be trusted, followed, or listened to because of our strengths. This is proof positive that we are not to be trusted. It is better to hear of someone's many weaknesses and work alongside that person, for in each place he is weak, he is reliant upon God's strength. If a man tells me he was very critical until God worked in his heart, revealed his own wickedness, and then lifted him up, I know that such a man is safe with my problems; I will not receive judgment from such a one, I will receive grace.

DAY 216
Oranges

And so, as those who have been chosen of God, holy and beloved, put on a heart of compassion, kindness, humility, gentleness, and patience; bearing with one another, and forgiving each other, whoever has a complaint against anyone; just as the Lord forgave you, so also should you. And beyond all these things put on love, which is the perfect bond of unity.

— COLOSSIANS 3:12-14

Once a fellow took an orange and asked his audience, "What is in this orange?" Everyone answered, "Orange juice." However, once he squeezed the orange, black goo gushed out instead of the expected sweet juice. We can think of our own life as the orange. Throughout our Christian life we find ourselves being squeezed, and that squeezing reveals what is within us, whether something sweet or the black goo of self-centeredness. When our flesh life is revealed through the squeezing of others, do we prefer to focus on the person or circumstances that squeezed us, the injustice involved, and the error of their way? Or do we concentrate on our own carnal response? It is far too easy to accumulate arguments condemning the behavior of others and justifying our own. However, a believer never has an excuse for self-centered behavior, for we live by a spiritual absolute that no matter what, we never have an excuse for not loving. When the believer finds himself squeezed and the black goo oozes out, he must admit his condition and not focus on the others who squeezed him.

In India a story is told of a Mogul king who, upon wanting to pick a successor and retire, assembled by invitation some five hundred young men from the kingdom. He presented a seed to each of the young men and asked that they plant it and tend it for one year, at which time the king would examine each of the young men's seeds and determine who would be king through what he saw. One of the young men took his seed home, planted it, fertilized, watered, and tended it day and night, and yet nothing grew. At the end of a year the young man told his father he was too embarrassed to present his empty pot to the king. His father persuaded him that since he had done his very best, he should not be embarrassed and must go present himself to the king truthfully, no better or worse; he had worked hard and must present himself honestly. Therefore, the young man went to the city on the day he was to present himself to the king. With his empty pot he took his place with the other young men, all of whom had pots that held banana plants already bearing fruit, mango trees, or a variety of beautiful flowers. The king began his inspection, examining all five hundred young men with their plants. As he walked past the only boy with an empty pot, the king hesitated briefly and then continued examining the others. Eventually, though, the king returned to the boy with the empty pot and announced, "You will be the next king!" "Why," asked the young man, "should I be king when I have nothing?" The king responded, "I boiled all the seeds before I handed them out so none could grow! You alone have presented yourself in honesty, and you will be the next king." Remember, there was a man who asked his son to be healed by Jesus, who responded, "If you believe." The man then presented Himself in truth by saying, "I do believe! Help me in my unbelief." The boy was healed. The King rewards honesty and exalts the humble. Many times the need of the believer is the simple one of presenting himself before God in honesty, no better and no worse than he is and without justification!

As couples we often initially attracted our mates through being loving, kind, self-sacrificing, complimentary, and forgiving. With the passing of time, once the discovery was made that the spouse could not meet our deepest needs, the behavior deteriorated to complaining, judging, self-serving, anger, bitterness, blaming, and carnality. At this point we can either present ourselves to God and confess our carnal behavior or with great zeal begin to look for excuses for our negative behavior, which are most easily found by holding a magnifying glass up to the mate to reveal all his or her glaring faults; these we can proclaim as having caused our carnal lifestyle. This is all done in the hope that we will be excused and our mate condemned. This reminds me of the Kansas tornado, the circumference of which is where all the damage takes place, for there is nothing within its center. It is a great whirl around emptiness. There are those of us who continue to destroy everything outside ourselves, and yet we remain empty, totally unfulfilled by such behavior. Stop destroying, stop excusing, admit our true condition, and we will find that "out of our innermost being will flow rivers of living water."

DAY 217
Our Reality is Jesus

For by Him all things were created, both in the heavens and on earth, visible and invisible, whether thrones or dominions or rulers or authorities—all things have been created through Him and for Him. He is before all things, and in Him all things hold together.
— COLOSSIANS 1:16, 17

I have often spoken of my trip to the interior of the Amazon with my brother when we met a man who was only a head. Yes, it is true, only a head. The rest of his body was no bigger than a book, with no arms, legs, or the appearance of a stomach. He was a head. Many see his photo and are as vexed as I was the day that I first laid eyes on him. We all wonder, "How would I cope with no legs or arms?" But for him it is not all that vexing, since it is his reality; it is how he was born, and he knows nothing different. It would be another matter had he been born fully formed until an accident turned him into that condition.

Today you, too, have a reality, a life that is all that you know, and one you believe to be very rich and full. If you had the opportunity to live just one moment in full abiding, you would find your life, your reality, to be terrible, nothing more than a shadow of what you could experience. You have only touched the hem of His garment, so to speak. To know Him in the power of His resurrection and to be like Him in His death, and then to accept how you live today would be intolerable.

There is surprisingly little written within the Christian community concerning the division Christ brings in families. In contrast, much is said about the need for forgiveness, understanding, varied personalities in relationships, coping with the controlling in-law, showing Christ's love, being long-suffering, and witnessing to the lost in the family. All of the aforementioned have their place and merit, but why neglect Jesus' statement that He came to bring a sword, that He would set parent against child, and child against parent (Matthew 10:34-37)? These words are neatly overlooked, and those who have found the sword operating in their own family have also found themselves being judged by other Christians as being less spiritual. When there are hiccups in the relationships of the spiritual person, the occasion is often used to look for something "deep" that is wrong with him. Because of such pressure from others who maintain that conflict-free relationships are proof of spirituality, many throw their own bodies in front of the sword that Christ would wield, remaining in miserable relationships and attempting to improve the flesh-life of others by pandering to it. In choosing to appear to be "conflict free," they are creating a lifetime of needless struggle with those who walk in the flesh.

It is my contention that Christ is more glorified through a believer's deliverance before an event than in the event. If the truth were told in all relationships, we would find ourselves delivered years earlier than when we compromise and concede in order to preserve a false peace.

"I have a mother who continues to attempt to control my family. What am I to do?" "I have a father-in-law who dominates all our family time; how are we to respond?" "My mother has a terrible marriage, so she gives all of her attention to my children. She smothers them and questions every decision I make concerning them. How does a Christian act in that setting?" "My parents will not work and insist on staying with us for prolonged periods. The stress is eating me up. What is your suggestion?" "My wife can never visit my parents' home without being criticized and maligned. What can I do to help?" What is our response to be to our relatives who are carnal, immature, and/or controlling? With the foundational principle at work of loving and praying for our enemies, we are first of all to tell the truth. The believer is not commanded to be silent concerning the carnal behavior of others, but only not to judge the persons engaging in that behavior. The epistles are written as an expression of the truth, and yet they do not judge the persons involved in the various wrong behaviors as worthless no-hopers. My wife has made many observations about my behavior that were helpful. She was not using those observations to say she was leaving me. I knew she loved me, was committed to me, and was staying. A brother once told me something about my behavior that he did not believe I would "swallow." He said, "Do with the information what you want; I will love you all the same." Taking up the cross and denying self will lead believers to tell the truth about another's behavior as the Spirit leads regardless of the conflict and rejection from which they might rather wish to escape. Have we told our mother, father, sister, brother, or child the truth about his or her behavior, or have we lied through our silence in order to avoid conflict? The sword will either cut away the flesh and bring freedom, as it did for me when my friend told me something that he did not think I would swallow; or it will cut away a carnal relationship when the truth is not received and the person disappears because he only tolerates relationships wherein self and performance reign, not truth. When we take the time and trouble to point out error in someone we love and we are rejected, the rejection is very revealing. For instance, if one of us waited five years to tell the truth, and we are rejected, it demonstrates that the previous five years of pandering to the flesh accomplished nothing. The truth could just as easily have been told the first day and the whole mess gotten out of the way. As the person to whom the truth was told continues to justify himself, tell others his story of being abused and unappreciated, label the truth-teller accusing and condemning, and even question the truth-teller's mental state and commitment to the Lord, we will know the right decision was made to tell the truth. The truth is cutting that one off from false brethren as only truth can, moving all things to their proper place.

I want to stop and make an important distinction in regard to those you, as a believer, consider to be family. Do you find it easier to tell those at work the truth about their behavior than family members? Is it easier for you to accept the rejection of a brother or sister in Christ than an earthly brother or sister? If you answered yes, then there is a fundamental problem of your having forgotten to which family you primarily belong, the family with whom you became one through your true birth. Jesus reminds us that we are His family many times, such as when He said, "If they have called the head of the house Beelzebub, how much more THE MEMBERS OF HIS HOUSEHOLD?" (Matthew 10:25). Your earthly family does not get special treatment simply so you can avoid rocking the boat! Because of the fear of rejection, it can take years to learn to love walking in truth, but it must be done! It is time to tell the truth about the controlling mother, the interrupting visits, the conflicting messages to the grandchildren, the alcoholism, and the divided home. Remember, I have already stated that we have no excuse not to love. Therefore, in one hand we carry love, and in the other, truth. Say the truth in love and let it divide, as it must. It is time!

A question might immediately come to mind: "What if I am wrong about my assessments?" Remember that if you pray before you speak, God is participating in your conversation. Also, if you are wrong, just as you have no excuse not to love, neither does the one to whom you are talking (even if he is an unbeliever).

It is valid to be vexed spiritually about the behavior of others. However, there is a deeper discomfort that comes from being silent about that behavior. Is it time to say something to your child that is involved in fornication? "I will be here for you, but not there for you. I disapprove of your behavior." Is it time to say to the controlling mother-in-law, "I will be judged for the success of this family; therefore, I will take the responsibility. Enough advice, manipulation, and control"? Is it time to say to the alcoholic father, "No more attending the Christmas party drunk and disruptive. I have decided to set a different example for my children"? Has the day arrived to tell the parent who calls to report all the marital and financial problems, "Why are you talking to me? Talk to the person I have to talk to when in turmoil; talk to Jesus. Good bye"? Christians are not called to a life of compromise.

When you confront your family member, you will in all likelihood be rejected. When a child is told for the first time he cannot have candy after throwing a fit, he throws a bigger fit. Expect your family member to throw a fit. However, you must stand fast or you will create a monster. The end result may be years of isolation from your family, with your only consolation being that you told the truth. Expect the enemy to whisper, "What kind of Christian are you? You are keeping that person from salvation, and you must honor your father and mother." Do not listen. There is no greater honor shown those who begot you than walking in truth, and no one can blame not having a walk with Christ on the behavior of another. You are a Christian who allowed Christ to wield His sword in your relationships.

To act on family matters is a faith act. Faith decisions are not made easier with time, for they are the same today, one year from now, or ten years from now. Time is never a variable. How long have you waited to tell the truth? Could it be that today is the fullness of time? When you do, things may not improve in the life of the carnal. However, you can get on making your family an example of Christ without interruption and turmoil. Do it! Decide what is right for your family, in Christ, and tell the truth. Let the division come if it must.

DAY 218
Peace of God

Let the peace of Christ rule in your hearts, to which indeed you were called in one body; and be thankful.
— COLOSSIANS 3:15

The peace of God is unique to Christianity, something no other religion offers. It is the gauge in the walk of a believer, for he may not know when it comes, but he will sure know when it leaves. If peace goes when others attempt to focus life on something other than Jesus, then that is not where God wants him. If he is approached with an emphasis other than Him and peace goes, he can just say, "Amen," and walk away. When Jesus is kept as the focus, the believer can forgive, know he is forgiven, and need not get involved in lesser true things, for he has and can cling to the Truth.

DAY 219
People are Dipsticks!

But the fruit of the Spirit is love, joy, peace, patience, kindness, goodness, faithfulness, gentleness, self-control; against such things there is no law.

— GALATIANS 5:22

A dipstick is used to check the level of oil in an engine. People are dipsticks! It is true, but not in the way we might think. The Holy Spirit is the lubricant of the believers' lives; when fully lubricated we run smoothly, without friction, quietly, and calmly. When we are running in the flesh, God sends someone along as a dipstick to check the level of lubricant; it may be the driver that cuts in front of us, the rebellious child, the gabby lady at church, or the self-centered husband, but what they will find in us is frustration, anger, impatience, and hostility. We can think in the back of our minds, "They are such dipsticks!" They have been sent by God, and if we will but stop and see Him in the situation, we can turn to Him, acknowledging that we are short of the oil of the awareness of the Holy Spirit, and pray, "Father, fill me up!" He does, and we can thank God for those who came along and warned us we were running low on oil before we blew up.

DAY 220
Persecution

Therefore I am well content with weaknesses, with insults, with distresses, with persecutions, with difficulties, for Christ's sake; for when I am weak, then I am strong.
— II CORINTHIANS 12:10

Not that I speak from want; for I have learned to be content in whatever circumstances I am.
— PHILIPPIANS 4:11

In general, people being persecuted are ushered off to a remote place, a factory, or a small cell of isolation where there is no need for them to have daily concerns about providing for a normal lifestyle. It does no good to concern themselves with food, clothing, family, friends, work, heat, or electricity. So in the case of Christians, what normally would take attention away from Christ flies to the background as in essence they are cut off from everything but Him. This accomplishes the exact opposite of the end desired by the persecutors, because far from being a punishment, persecution actually causes believers to experience Jesus in a far more unhindered nearness. This testimony is heard often from those who have experienced persecution.

Why bring up such a subject? Many believe that the end is near since there are many interesting signs taking place, one sign being the promise of persecution for our faith. I have noticed that the end result of this speculation for many is fear of the future, fear of the enemy, feelings of hopelessness, loss of control, and a clamoring to be prepared. There is no need to worry that the end of life is to be centered in fear, for the believer who has been able to stand against the anti-Christ movement in television, media, schools, music, politics, and morals need not perceive the standing against persecution "as though some strange thing were happening to" him (I Peter 4:12). I have often wondered which would be worse, to be ushered off to a prison camp or to have one's child tell him that he has listened to the teachers at school and decided that he is homosexual. Will it not be easier to suffer for the name of Christ than to watch a beloved child suffer in sin? Not only will God give grace needed at the time, but the believer will grow during the time of physical persecution, learning that when he is weak, then He is strong, and experiencing the freedom of self-denial while following Jesus down a road he had always thought too difficult. Do not be filled with fear, for God always gives the provision where needed.

DAY 221
Political Comedy

Because the foolishness of God is wiser than men, and the weakness of God is stronger than men.

— I CORINTHIANS 1:25

Sometimes it is comical to watch the world and its wisdom. Leaders sit in their meetings acting as though the weight of the earth is on their shoulders and it will be their wisdom and cooperation that will make for a better world. They actually, in their pride, believe themselves to be the sharpest knives in the drawer. They never really help people, and the facts have proven it, for the issues haunting man are not addressed. Nothing is said about relationships with God, with family, or with self. Since they have no insight into the important things of life, they try to convince us that what they do know are the real issues of life. It is folly, for the foolishness of God is much greater than the wisdom of man. Jesus has the answer for believers, and we must not allow ourselves to be brainwashed.

DAY 222
Practical Abiding

Abide in me and I in you.

— JOHN 15:4

"Abiding in Christ sounds good. However, sometime tomorrow a driver will pull in front of me, and I will find myself cursing him. It will all happen so fast that I will not have time to think about Jesus. What am I to do?" Good question, but it reveals that we are consequence-conscious and not cause-conscious. The real reason for the problem is not the driver but neglect and strength. Getting up in the morning, we do not expect anything negative, we are feeling strong, and therefore we do not invite Jesus to come go with us. If we had invited Jesus, we would be driving with a Jesus consciousness. When the driver pulled in front of us, our response would be natural and immediate. We would find ourselves blessing those that curse us. Jesus in the morning prepares us for trouble in the afternoon.

Often I see those who because of frustrations with their circumstances fall back to the idols of the past. Yes, committed believers going back again to slander, bitterness, anger, withdrawal, punishment, lust, immorality, drugs, alcohol, and the list goes on. They are angry and tired of trying to be something better, to live above circumstances, and to imitate Christ. They are tired, mad, and no longer care. Their thoughts go something like this, "I have tried and cannot change." "I am sick of Christians and their talk of happiness." "God does help a few, but I am not one of the lucky few, and I had better admit it." "For now sleep will deliver me from this miserable state, and in the future death will. I cannot wait." "I am a victim of people intent on making me miserable." Notice in all these statements happiness and joy are tied to circumstance. To the degree circumstance is good we feel good, and the converse is also true. But Jesus was victorious over circumstance; in Him we are more than conquerors. The solution is not to fix circumstance, but to draw near to Him in this moment and to share in His life as more than a conqueror. I am not writing this to be disagreeable; it is a fact. To the degree we look to circumstance to make us happy, to that same degree of misery we deservedly descend! Believers are created for God, and much is invested in us; therefore, happiness only comes when we are in the midst of God. This is an absolute that can be proven! Take the challenge! Next time you compare your miserable life with the success an unbeliever enjoys, next time you are angry over circumstances, next time you despise the power that the flesh, sin, and Satan have over you, just draw near to Christ! Spend a few minutes in fellowship and prayer; only crack open the Scriptures and see if there is not a change. Within fifteen minutes you will desire to press on, to lay aside old sin, and to share Him and the happiness He gives. Your life will truly make sense. There is nothing His presence will not cure! You will then clearly see that if God gave us the easy life, we would soon neglect Him, living our lives fulfilled in the flesh but unfulfilled in the Spirit.

Upon returning, finding your place before Him, and living out of His presence, the enemy will use guilt, the only weapon that is then available to him. Often a return to the Lord is accompanied by a flood of guilt, for in His presence all is clearly seen: the deeds of the flesh, the self-centeredness, the stupidity of doubting God, the wasted time, and the mistreatment of others. The blinders are removed and the enemy, knowing your enlightenment, wishes to make the most use of it. Using your renewed sensitivity from being with the Lord, the enemy will point out all the insensitivity of the past, hoping that the guilt of it will cause you to run from God and the perceived coming judgment. Do not listen! Stand fast! God has drawn you near not for discipline but for love. The discipline was self-inflicted from avoiding His presence, but discipline is over. It is now time for restoration, fellowship, forgiveness, and love.

DAY 223
Prejudice

But Jesus was saying, "Father, forgive them; for they do not know what they are doing." And they cast lots, dividing up His garments among themselves.

— LUKE 23:34

Prejudice! What an ugly social ill. America is accused of it justifiably, yet I have never been to a country that did not practice it. Every race has within it those who are prejudiced. Many of us were encouraged from youth by the government to dislike the Russians and the Japanese, and now that same government enforces laws against discrimination. Women hate men and men hate women. People are too tall, too fat, too skinny, too short, too stupid, too educated, too spiritual, too carnal, too legalistic, and too liberal. Do not trust parents, do not trust teenagers, do not believe husbands, know that employers are out to get us, and do not share a weakness with a spouse.

Upon recognizing and pointing out prejudice in a society, many attempt to fight it with more prejudice toward those who have it, discriminating against and avoiding them at all cost. It is vexing to become like one's enemy, with bigotry and distrust driving hate and dislike. How is prejudice destroyed? Like all other societal ills, it is incredibly simple to cure with love! Once love enters the equation, everything changes. Love is not selective but inclusive. Love does not sort out who is right or wrong but shows no partiality and makes us more than conquerors.

On one occasion I was talking to a friend of a different race; he had made a conscious determination that he and his children would learn all they could about their culture. My response was, "Has all the information you have learned concerning your race changed your marriage, given wisdom in raising your children, or taken away the feelings of inferiority, failure, or depression?" He admittedly said no. I then responded, "Neither has the study of my race." Jesus never commented on the outer life. He was racist toward the inner life, the life of Adam, the life that causes misery, and He wanted it dead and replaced with His life (Galatians 2:20). Once we receive His life, we receive love, which frees us from all of the above and gives the needed wisdom for daily living.

DAY 224
Pride

Pride {goes} before destruction, and a haughty spirit before stumbling.

— PROVERBS 16:18

Pride, like Satan himself, is the master of disguise. We see the overtly proud person whose acts are so obvious in his haughty attitude as he thinks himself better, looks down on the afflicted, and expects to reign. We see him and find him disturbing because he amplifies what is hidden in us, though we think, "What a jerk! If only he could get a good look at himself from the outside!" However, he is blind and proud of his nakedness. What I want to talk about is disguised pride, something much more insidious.

Did you know that depression is usually disguised pride that occurs as a person reacts to the blow of the realization that he cannot be perfect, control himself and others, or do any manner of a good job of imitating God? Self-hatred is pride, for how can one hate self unless he has fallen from the lofty image he had of his own flesh? Self-deprecation can be pride. "Oh, I cannot do that; I am too stupid and have never succeeded in anything. No one likes me. God could never use me." Just how much time does the self-deprecating person spend thinking about himself? Victimization is pride. "Oh, let me tell you what they said to me. How could anyone say that? How could anyone be so unkind?" "I got cheated; the family took my money. Do you think I deserve to be treated that way?" Being offended is pride. "How dare you say that to me!" Self-defense is pride. Does one really think that his flesh is so wonderful that it needs defending? Then there is inferiority, and that is definitely pride. The inferior have spent so much time looking for good in themselves that eventually they find the bad; if they know good, they will know evil. Jealousy, hating one's unrighteousness, obsession on failure and rejection, the feeling that one does not deserve anything, expecting the worst, being negative, all are pride. See how it is the master of disguise?

DAY 225
Problems

But as for me, my feet had almost slipped; I had nearly lost my foothold. For I envied the arrogant when I saw the prosperity of the wicked. They have no struggles; their bodies are healthy and strong. They are free from the burdens common to man; they are not plagued by human ills.

— PSALM 73:2-5

It is easy for the believer to become discouraged when comparing his life to the unbeliever's and only the outward is taken into consideration. Since the unbeliever receives today his good things and the believer waits for his good things, a disparity could well exist. However, many believers have made the mistake of thinking that being a child of God means financial wellbeing, good health, and respect from his fellow man. The real head-scratcher for the believer, then, can be to find himself lacking in these while the unbeliever appears to be fulfilled in every worldly desire. David made an objective observation that the wicked do better! Today, when the believer is bombarded by the media and by observation with all that he "should" possess, the temptation to examine what unbelievers possess is all the greater; and many will make the assessment that they are lacking, they possess less, they suffer more often with illness, and they do struggle more. However, there is a trade-off that should not be ignored, for in possessing a life void of material and physical struggle, something else is created in the soul of man, such as pride, violence, hardheartedness, iniquity, an evil mind that knows no limits, malice, arrogance, oppression, boasting, and a big mouth (Psalm 73:6-9)!

Let me ask a question: Would you like to be free from all sickness and monetary pressure to live a life of ease? What if I stood two people in front of you, one a prosperous unbeliever with a good job, a new house, an attractive mate, and children on their way to college driving new cars. The other is a believer who just lost his job, has a rebellious child, has told his children college is out of the question, has nicknamed his car the "Prayermobile" (never knowing if it will start), and has a mate with a terminal illness. Which person would you choose to be? Be honest! Which would you pick? I suspect on any given day you would pick the life of the unbeliever, or at least would attempt to negotiate a compromise! It is the tendency of man to want to accept Jesus as Savior and call on Him in the future but in the meantime live as the unbeliever. Even though the suffering of the believer delivers him from pride, violence, hardheartedness, iniquity, an evil mind, malice, arrogance, oppression, boasting, and a big mouth, the pull and appearance of the prosperous outer life of the unbeliever is too great, too attractive, too overpowering, and too appealing to turn down. We know we should be happy with Christ within, but we are not! What is the solution? What can make the life of a believer desirable? What can make suffering, a small home, lack of job security, uncertainty with the future, and even struggles in marriage appealing? Only one thing!

"When I tried to understand all this, it was oppressive to me till I entered the sanctuary of God; then I understood" (Psalm 73:16-17). There are many tasks in life that make no sense until they are begun. Often while in campus ministry I would have students tell me they were not going to date or get married. However, once they met that special person, they wondered why they had not dated sooner. I have observed those who, for fear of rejection, hate to look for a job. Instead they sit at home depressed, wishing for employment. Once they begin to look for opportunities, their countenances immediately change. Many, through fear of failure, never start higher education, but once they begin, the fear gives way to hope and wishing they had started sooner. Experience proves over and over again that once we are in the midst of something, it makes perfect sense. Often the problem is getting someone involved to the point that he can see the logic of what he is doing. Tell a drug addict his drugs are being taken away and watch his panic ensue. However, after being drug free, no longer controlled and free to choose, the wisdom in taking away the drugs becomes obvious to him. My point is that the things of God, the ways of God, the desires of God, the life of the believer, and those things given to the believer by God make no sense until we are in the midst of God. David was baffled until he entered the sanctuary! This Old Testament sanctuary is not the equivalent of the church building today; the sanctuary for the believer is the heart, the dwelling place of God. Once we turn within to Him to abide in His presence and bask in the life He has given on the path we are walking, the adverse circumstances make perfect sense. I will go one step further. All problems make us happy and give a feeling of being special. "I bear in my body the marks of Christ," said Paul with gladness.

When we compare the easy living of the unbeliever to ours, what are we to do when we apparently come up lacking? Should we strive for more? Should we bemoan our condition? Should we rebel against God in anger? Should we become depressed and withdraw? Should we question? No! We need only turn to Him for the life we are living to become special; we sense we are called out, we know we are not of this world, and we are happy.

Believer, do receive something today that will forever escape the unbeliever: inner peace, rest, and fellowship with our God. Turning to the presence of Christ within moment by moment will make your life in Him make sense! You will be happy, more than a conqueror, free from the power of sin, and sharing in all that He has.

DAY 226
Programs

*Woe to you lawyers as well! For you weigh men down
with burdens hard to bear, while you yourselves will not
even touch the burdens with one of your fingers.*

— LUKE 11:46

Often I go through quite busy times, where it seems that
I am getting less and less done. There is so much to do to
get ready for international trips, coupled with emergency
calls that come daily. I just do not get the time with the
Lord I need. I think how maybe when I get on the road I
will have a little time, but then the Lord speaks to me. "If
you avoided me eighteen hours of every day to do evil, it
would be quite obvious to you what the problem is. But
you have been taking eighteen hours away from Me to do
good, and it is not so obvious." Which is worse, to draw
away from the Lord to do evil or to do good? To do good
is more dangerous, for doing good never appears to be the
problem, and therefore the problem is able to hide. Good
is the enemy of the best. Jesus is the best, and so I instantly
put everything down and go for a walk to pray and let
everything begin to fall into place.

Not everything that is true is truth. A teaching may
come from Scripture and be true but not truth. How do
we tell the difference between the two? True teaching that
lands at my feet and tells what I must do is not truth. True
teaching that ends at the feet of Jesus and explains what He

does for me is Truth, for Jesus is the Way, the Truth, and the Life. If what we are hearing does not end at His feet, it is not truth. Few of the programs filling the churches are truth, and so they rival the work of Christ.

Do not be discouraged. God does not fight sin and evil, He uses them. Many need to go through all the programs and see how inherently incapable of bringing about true spiritual growth they are before becoming sick of them and willing to listen to a message of Christ as Life. I have had myriad programs and true things flung at me. People get so excited about a program and all that will happen as a result of all that I must do, they must do, and others must do. I just let them talk and then hand them my card. I know it is not Truth, and I will let the years speak against the minutes. Programs work for the Kingdom in that they contribute to the hard work of bringing a person to the end of himself and to ultimate emptiness. "If God is for us, who is against us?" (Romans 8:31)

DAY 227
Propping Up The Kingdom

They shall speak of the glory of Thy kingdom,
and talk of Thy power.
— PSALM 145:11

Do you know that you belong to Jesus? Of course you do! You do not belong to man, to an organization, or an institution. You belong to Jesus. You are His and He belongs to you. There is so much comfort in that fact. Do you know, also, that there was enough dynamite in one thing Jesus said to blow to pieces any institution? "Man was not made for the Sabbath but the Sabbath for man!" In short, we are not commanded to prop up the kingdom of man, period! Many will work on the good heart of a believer to pressure him to support or submit to the building of their kingdom. He should not, for he is not made for man but for God. In Buenos Aires, Argentina, at the end of the walking boulevard, Florida Street, is a large, beautiful tree with branches so big that sticks are placed vertically under the limbs to support them and keep them from breaking off. The weight of each limb is unbelievable, but the little stick is able to keep it supported. Many in the Kingdom of God are like little sticks supporting the kingdoms of men, and we must refuse this role of being concerned with extending man's image. We are created for but One, Jesus, and we do not—nor can we—support Him. He is the One who supports us.

DAY 228
Rachel and Leah, Law and Grace

> *So it came about in the morning that, behold, it was Leah! And he said to Laban, "What is this you have done to me? Was it not for Rachel that I served with you? Why then have you deceived me?" But Laban said, "It is not the practice in our place to marry off the younger before the firstborn. Complete the week of this one, and we will give you the other also for the service which you shall serve with me for another seven years."*
>
> — GENESIS 29:25-27

Grace gives what the Law promises. Hebrews 7 makes it clear that the law is set aside because of its "weakness and uselessness." However, the Law does serve a purpose in preparing us for grace. On occasion I am confronted by those who are in opposition to teaching about the grace of the Lord Jesus for fear that it will lead to passivity. (Of course, this is the stated but never the real fear of grace, which is generally rooted in the fleshly outworking of control, insecurity, competition, and kingdom building.) However, I am not as opposed to them as they are to me, because I know that teachers of the Law are needed. The flesh of man seems to have the need to be exhausted under the Law before it will listen to grace. Grace is the last resort for the flesh, for grace fixes hope squarely on Jesus. The Law will never give what it promises. Jacob worked for the bride of love (grace). However, he did not get her and instead got the bride of Law. Work will not give love and grace, for it can only give law. When at last the bride of love was given, Jacob still had to work, but now the work flowed from love. He was not working for something but from having the bride of love, and the work did not really seem toilsome. This is a type of what God does once Law exhausts us and He then gives what Law could not obtain. We will then work, but the work will be from a position of love and grace. Again, grace gives what the Law promises. Beautiful!

DAY 229
Raising Children Practically

Woe to those who are wise in their own eyes and clever in their own sight!

— ISAIAH 5:21

Often I am asked to share some basic principles that I have found in childrearing. Below I have mentioned a few.

1. The attitude of the parent must be always to approach the child with an empty bag. Even if a parent's I.Q. were 200, God's is infinite. When a parent comes to the child with his own knowledge of what to do, he will almost always get it wrong. Everything in life teaches us dependence on the Lord. The child has specific needs that only God knows. Therefore, the parent who does not know what to do is better off at the time of need to seek the One with the infinite I.Q. How does this work out practically? A parent need not react right away when he sees the child acting out; he can

just wait, pray, and see what the Lord would have him do. In every situation he can see God or himself; if he sees God, he can have a move in the Spirit. If he only sees himself, he only has a move in the flesh. God is working something in the parent as he works with the child. Waiting before he acts and listening to Him both work something in him. God is intensely personal with each one of us. Remember when Jesus brought the exact fish to the exact place to the exact man (Peter) to meet an exact need? When the child acts out, it is the exact thing needed for the exact parent to meet an exact need. In short, the child will drive a parent to his knees, and that is not bad.

2. The situation must be entered in faith and with the belief that God does not fight sin or failure but uses it. That is very important, because a person does not rule his belief system; it rules him. A parent must see that God will work in his child's life. God does not have any grandchildren; all must come to Him on their own and out of need. Therefore, the child needs some failure, turmoil, and pain. My prayer for my kids has always been, "Father, allow enough in their life so that they will see they need You, but not enough for them to be destroyed." Jesus is God's peace. He sees the believer today, and yet He sees the believer in Jesus in heaven. No matter where a Christian is today in his struggles, the Lord sees him complete in Christ, and He is at peace. The parent sees his child today and sees Christ today, and he also has peace.

3. You must be willing to fight with the child and be miserable. There are so many messages that this young

generation gets from the world that ours did not. For every one time you tell the child something is wrong, the world is telling him one hundred times that it is all right. I hate fighting with young people, but we must. Many women have told me how disappointed they were that their father did not exert any influence to keep them from dating a particular boy. In my house I decided that I would fight over drugs, sex, and alcohol, and nobody would be happy if those things were happening.

4. Let the peace of God rule in your heart. You may not know when it comes, but you do know when it leaves. Simply listen to it for guidance as to when the child needs confronting, hugging, or nothing at all to be said.

5. It sounds simplistic to tell people to rest in faith, listen to His peace, and go in emptiness, but only until it is tried! The greatness of faith is not determined by how much one receives but by how long he can wait though receiving nothing.

DAY 230
Reason For Pain

You will keep in perfect peace him whose mind is steadfast, because he trusts in You. Trust in the Lord forever.

— ISAIAH 26:3, 4

One predominant reason for pain is to bring us to the end of trusting ourselves, the source of much misery. Many call this brokenness, a state not necessarily achieved through becoming a drug addict, clinically depressed, or a gutter resident. It can arrive very quietly, in the deepest recesses of the heart, as a result of trials nowhere close to the magnitude of the aforementioned. It is "simply" giving up on our independence from God.

Once while staying in a mountain cabin I noticed a moth beating its wings against the window in a vain attempt to enjoy the freedom offered by the outdoors. I decided I would capture and release it, but the more I tried to help, the harder the moth tried to escape! Not until it became totally exhausted and unavoidably relaxed was I able to pick it up and let it go outside. Many believers are wound so tightly that they beat their inner man's wings against the invisible forces of life that bind and enslave them; the only solution they know to be possible is trying harder, but they must "let go and let God" in order to become relaxed souls the Father will take into His hands and give freedom.

Yes, believers suffer, and we can thank God for being in the midst of unpleasant occurrences, because these very things bring those He loves to perfection.

DAY 231
Rebuke Versus Condemnation

Therefore you have no excuse, everyone of you who passes judgment, for in that which you judge another, you condemn yourself; for you who judge practice the same things.

— ROMANS 2:1

Do you know the difference between rebuke and condemnation? Jesus may on occasion rebuke you; I have had it happen to me. On different occasions others have rebuked me, but in both instances, whether rebuked by Jesus or a brother or sister in Christ, I have noticed that the rebuke did not end with me, for they pointed me to The Way, Jesus. However, condemnation is different, delivering knowledge about what I do wrong, and the whole thing lands at my feet. That kind of knowledge has no power and should therefore be rejected. Be careful when pointing out what is wrong in another, for it takes no great spiritual insight but is merely a revelation of your own actions manifested in the person. We know this to be true from the Scriptural truth that you who judge practice the very same things. Do not point out something unless you are prepared to help with it. If all of the stupid people you know suddenly agreed with your assessments and asked for help, would you be ready to offer it?

DAY 232
Red-faced Monkey

Do not be conformed to this world, but be transformed by the renewing of your mind, that you may prove what the will of God is, that which is good and acceptable and perfect.

— ROMANS 12:2

When it comes to the topic of battling sin, one rule must never be broken, and that is that we are never to battle sin! It is a misplaced focus. No, we are never to fight sin if we desire to overcome it. Let me illustrate. There is a story of a fellow in India who was traveling from village to village selling a magic potion. The man would ask for a clean bucket, into which he would pour clear water and some of the magic potion. As he stirred the mixture, through sleight of hand he would drop in three or four nuggets of gold. When the water was drained off, there was the gold. In one community a moneychanger watching the demonstration asked if he could purchase the formula for 50,000 rupees. The fellow was more than happy to sell, and after receiving the payment, he turned to the moneychanger and said, "There is one thing you must never do while making the gold, or else the potion will not work. While stirring the water and adding the formula, you must never, never think of the red-faced monkey!" As you can well imagine, the moneychanger was never able to make gold! Wherever he went, from the Himalayas to the south of India, no matter how hard he worked to block it, the red-faced monkey would pop into his mind. So it is with sin; as long as it is made the focus, it will never be overcome. I have often commented that God has delivered me from many things, but not once was I freed from anything on which I was centered.

Many have focused on their sin ten, twenty, thirty, and even forty years; their sin has become so much a part of their life that they are not even sure what they would do were they to be miraculously delivered. If 25% of thought life were concentrated on something consuming and immediate deliverance occurred, exactly what would replace that portion of mental energy? What would fill the vacuum? The solution to warring against sin is to set our minds on something other than the sin. This cannot not be done by consciously avoiding the sin, but rather by making the Lord the focus of daily thought life. If our focus is not kept on the things above but is allowed to traffic in the things of the world, we as believers will be led to Christian fatalism, the belief that this life in these bodies will constantly be given over to defeat and misery. Thus we will accept continual suffering as the norm and wait for the day we will be caught up into heaven. The truth is that all suffering has a purpose and, in the end, produces abundant living today.

DAY 233
Relational Filter

Jesus answered, "I am the way and the truth and the life. No one comes to the Father except through me."

— JOHN 14:6

What is truth? This question that has survived millennia and been addressed by myriad philosophers is one that Jesus answered simply and quickly: "I am the Way, the Truth, and the Life." Truth is Jesus, not only the spoken words of Christ but also every action, attitude, and activity of His life. He is the definition of truth.

When attempting to discover truth concerning an individual's character, we must discern Jesus' view of the person rather than observing him through self-made glasses that distort him, glasses that are the product of our own failures, inferiorities, past experiences, perceived motives, misunderstandings, ignorance about personalities, biases from subculture, expectations, and self-serving notions. Jesus wore no such glasses when it came to interacting with others; He knew what was in all men and He laid down His life for man! What did He see that we are blind to? What is the truth about others that we are missing? What makes us judge rather than lay down our lives? The truth about mankind, family, and fellow believers is known as we examine not only what Jesus said about man but also His actions and attitudes toward man. If these are not used when establishing knowledge about a person's character, our thoughts and judgments will quickly spiral into chaos. This very same truth, the life of Christ, must then be released to all with whom we come in contact. We must cease responding to the words of man and begin addressing his condition.

DAY 234
Remember The Bell Ringer

Your attitude should be the same as that of Christ Jesus:
who, being in very nature God, did not consider equality with
God something to be grasped.
— PHILIPPIANS 2:5, 6

Imagine going into a grocery store where the clerk rings up the sale, puts your hard-earned money into the register, and then places your groceries under the counter and asks you to leave without them. How would you respond? I imagine that most of us would throw a fit, screaming at the injustice of paying but receiving nothing. There might even be an ensuing fight.

In contrast, imagine walking by the Salvation Army bell-ringer at Christmastime and putting $20 into the bucket. Would you be upset if the bell-ringer gave you nothing in return? Not at all, for you give to the bell-ringer a gift from the heart, expecting nothing in return.

Sad to say, very little giving within many Christian homes has its origin in the goodness of a heart turned toward Christ. When a good deed is done for another and anger occurs because of lack of response, the reaction proves only that the action was not done from the heart without strings attached. It reveals that whatever was paid was done so with the expectation of receiving something in return. This kind of giving is bondage that yields no joy. Giving is a delight if we desire nothing in return. I pray that God would give us bell-ringer marriages.

DAY 235
Returning To The Place We Never Left

Peace I leave with you; My peace I give you. I do not give to you as the world gives. Do not let your heart be troubled and do not be afraid.

— JOHN 14:27

There were two sisters. One left home and never wanted to return because she remembered it as a miserable place. The other left and always mourned for home; she could never return but always wanted to. She had never left home in her heart and therefore never really enjoyed her new family. What was the difference between these two sisters? One, in her heart, kept returning to the place she never left.

The prodigal son went to the pigpen, but actually he had never left it. There was a pigpen in his heart, and so he had only returned to the place that he had never left. We must leave the old place, the pigpen, allowing the Lord to destroy the place. Let me explain. For years I suffered with depression and suicidal thoughts. One day I prayed, "Lord, I am leaving this place of suicidal thoughts; You have destroyed it. I can no longer return there." Since that day, when the enemy brings the thoughts, I just say, "I cannot go there; that place is dead. Satan will have to tempt me with something else. That place I cannot return to." We have places of insecurity, depression, guilt, sin, addiction, and flesh that we must allow Him to destroy. How do we do that? It is simple! Just say, "Jesus, I give you that place. Please destroy it so I can never return there." Once we pray, from that day forward when we are tempted to go there we can remind ourselves that the place is gone; there is no place to go. The truth is that we too often—like the prodigal son for a time—have not truly grown sick of the place and do not yet want to give it up. Do not worry; life is not supporting that decision, and we will come to a place where we are sick of it and allow Him to destroy it.

DAY 236
Roosters

I can do everything through Him who gives me strength.
— PHILIPPIANS 4:13

It is interesting that often in Latvia a church will have no cross atop it but instead will have a cock crowing to represent the denials of Peter and remind us not to disavow the Lord! Believers can let it remind them of their own denials, their faithlessness and His faithfulness. From Peter's experience we can learn never to say, "Lord, I will not deny You," but instead, "Lord, when it comes to the time that I will need to stand, I cannot. I will need You to go with me and hold me up!" Close observation of every photo taken of a certain Russian politician will reveal four fingertips on each side of his ribcage. The man could not stand alone, and there was always someone hidden behind him holding him up. He was weak and pathetic, just like I am! However, instead of being propped up by an equally feeble human, it is Christ holding me up! I am happy if anyone were to look closely and see His fingertips.

DAY 237
Satan

And the seventy returned with joy, saying, "Lord, even the demons are subject to us in Your name." And He said to them, "I was watching Satan fall from heaven like lightning. Behold, I have given you authority to tread upon serpents and scorpions, and over all the power of the enemy, and nothing shall injure you. Nevertheless do not rejoice in this, that the spirits are subject to you, but rejoice that your names are recorded in heaven."
— LUKE 10:17-20

The Epistles mention Satan only fifteen times, the whole of the Bible forty-seven times, and of that, fourteen are in the book of Job. In contrast, Jesus is mentioned 880 times and Christ 493 times. Elementary math reveals that Jesus is leading, thirty to one. How, then, has Satan become the focus of so many believers? Why has he been given equal billing and considered by many to have power equal to Christ's?

"Again, the devil took Him to a very high mountain, and showed Him all the kingdoms of the world, and their glory; and he said to Him, 'All these things will I give You, if You fall down and worship me.' Then Jesus said to him, 'Begone, Satan! For it is written, "YOU SHALL WORSHIP THE LORD YOUR GOD, AND SERVE HIM ONLY"'" (Matthew 4:8-10). Some of what the word "worship" means is "to give attention to." The thing that we give attention to is actually the thing that we worship. It is frightening to find so many believers that worship Satan by giving him their undivided attention. When Satan is our focus, it is not unlike any other obsession: we will find him everywhere in everything.

In the early 1970's a brand new emphasis entered the church scene; I say "brand new," for aside from the fact that there are absolutely no Scriptures to back up the claim, Church history is also void of the emphasis. The new teaching was that Christians could be possessed by demons. In all of Paul's dealings with troubled believers, not once did he even hint that the solution to their freedom rested in having demons cast out of them. In fact, that would be a basic contradiction to Paul's making this point in I Corinthians 3:16: "Do you not know that you are a temple of God, and {that} the Spirit of God dwells in you?" "Temple" here refers to the Holy of Holies, where no evil can dwell. Faced with this theological problem, some Christians, still wanting to prove the point that we could have demons, restated "possession" to mean "oppression," with yet a need for the casting out of demons in the body, though not the spirit. The result of this mindset is that Satan gets everyone's attention and no one gets on with

Christ; naturally, Satan would prefer that we busy ourselves casting him out instead of inviting Christ in.

I questioned a brother concerning this particular kind of "ministry." If someone has a demon of lust that could be cast out, and then he finds himself lusting again, what is he to do? His response was, "Once the demon goes, he needs to abide; he is lusting again because he is not abiding in Christ." I thought that rather interesting, for if in the end abiding in Christ keeps a fellow from lusting, why did he not just begin with abiding? Again, lesser truth always gives way to the greater.

In a meeting I was once asked a loaded question by a person who knew that several in the room were casting demons out of believers; what did I think of the practice? All I would say is, "There are a lot of waves that take us from shore." He pressed me further, but I only repeated my answer, because indeed, this emphasis has been a wave that passes back and forth through congregations; if it were truth, it would become foundational, but it always seems to give way to the next wave, the next titillating catch phrase or notion to ripple through meetings. We are not disagreeing with the fact that there is activity from Satan; however, dealing judiciously with him merely involves lifting up Jesus! At the very same moment Christ is lifted up, Satan is renounced.

DAY 238
Satan Works on a Permit

And He said to them, "I was watching Satan fall from heaven like lightning. Behold, I have given you authority to tread on serpents and scorpions, and over all the power of the enemy, and nothing will injure you. Nevertheless do not rejoice in this, that the spirits are subject to you, but rejoice that your names are recorded in heaven."

— LUKE 10:18-20

When one king defeats another king, the subjects of the defeated kingdom become slaves. Satan conquered the man Adam and became the ruler of the world over which Adam had been given dominion. Through defeat, man yielded what was his to the enemy. However, when the second Adam, Jesus, conquered Satan, things above, below, and on the earth became the Son of God's. We are in His Kingdom, and therefore, what is His is ours. This simply means that we do not have to be controlled by spirits! The believer who does not like a spirit can remember that in Jesus' Kingdom he has authority over it. In Africa I met an old woman who would not call alcohol by that name, choosing instead to call it a spirit. If the spirit of alcohol is controlling some Christian, it is by his permission. I have known those that are controlled by the spirit of suicide, and there simply is no excuse for that when by drawing near to Christ a believer can simply tell the spirits to leave. Being in His kingdom, what is His, He has shared with believers. All spirits must now yield to Him. As I have said before, at the highest revelation of Jesus there will be no opposition.

I have been asked, "How much power does Satan give his followers?" None! How can a lesser creature give something to a greater creature? Man is greater, and therefore, all Satan can give is a lie, which is where he excels. None can argue with the fact of believers being oppressed, but that occurs when someone believes the enemy's lie. Being the father of lies, Satan can visit his children, and so a received lie actually opens the person up to the demonic world and all manner of attacks from without, including psychosomatic manifestations. Many have made the mistake of not recognizing the work of Satan, so as a heavenly disciple, do recognize his work, but more importantly recognize the work of Jesus that made Satan fall from heaven, and camp at the work of Christ.

DAY 239
Seeing The Lord in Everything!

And he threw stones at David and at all the servants of King David; and all the people and all the mighty men were at his right hand and at his left. And thus Shimei said when he cursed, "Get out, get out, you man of bloodshed, and worthless fellow! The LORD has returned upon you all the bloodshed of the house of Saul, in whose place you have reigned; and the LORD has given the kingdom into the hand of your son Absalom. And behold, you are {taken} in your own evil, for you are a man of bloodshed!" Then Abishai the son of Zeruiah said to the king, "Why should this dead dog curse my lord the king? Let me go over now, and cut off his head." But the king said, "What have I to do with you, O sons of Zeruiah? If he curses, and if the LORD has told him, 'Curse David,' then who shall say, 'Why have you done so?'" Then David said to Abishai and to all his servants, "Behold, my son who came out from me seeks my life; how much more now this Benjamite? Let him alone and let him curse, for the LORD has told him. Perhaps the LORD will look on my affliction and return good to me instead of his cursing this day." So David and his men went on the way; and Shimei went along on the hillside parallel with him and as he went he cursed, and cast stones and threw dust at him.

— II SAMUEL 16:6-13

Here was the greatest king in all of Israel allowing an ignorant man, a lesser man, to cast insults and stones upon him. David feared that the man might actually be a messenger of God. In short, David was able to see God in the situation. The true strength, greatness, and faith of David are revealed in this simple situation. Do we see God in every situation? If not, we can begin by taking a trip to the forest, for there we must read from a different book, the book of creation. Examine everything there in detail. Look at how everything is put together perfectly. In this place we may begin to see that our lives are put together perfectly . . . that God only allows, in His love, what is perfect for us. We believers are going to end well; however, in a circumstance today God will reveal the thing that needs dealt with lest it make our lives miserable in the future. David could see God at work in a man that was cursing him. What do the drivers cutting us off in traffic, the mate ignoring us, the impertinent office worker, or the rebellious child reveal in us? Is it God's not creating but using something in our lives? Can we take a step back and see God?

Let me give you an example. I rented a car and was overcharged $20. How unfair! However, God showed me something. The proof of my faith in His provision does not only come through willingly giving to a stranger, but in unwillingly having money stolen from me. It was God. Do I really believe that He provides my money? Do I believe that He is my security? Do I believe that it is up to me to keep my finances within my control? I stood there and could see that it was not the car rental employee I needed to deal with, it was God, and so rather than wanting to stop the situation, I wanted to yield to it. Another time I took a "romantic" dinner cruise with my wife off the coast of Hawaii. Everyone had assigned seats. We walked to the top deck for a view and returned to find someone sitting in my wife's seat. We had to sit apart on our romantic cruise. In my spirit I knew it was God. I just thought, "God bless you," and was able, yet not I, to lay it aside. Make no mistake; it was God. All of you chosen of God must know that nothing is happening in your lives that is an accident. We all want to be like Christ but shy away from the experiences that would reveal Christ in us. Let the people around us throw their stones and curses. We are much better off yielding to it than taking their heads on a platter.

DAY 240
Self-hatred

For from Him and through Him and to Him are all things. To Him be the glory forever! Amen.

— ROMANS 11:36

Is it really self-hatred? Do I really hate myself? No, self is still worshipped through self-hatred. I merely hate the hatred. Self is still the focus and remains alive and well. "I hate myself because I cannot be more Christian and overcome sin." Really? Actually, you love self and are upset that the king of your kingdom is not doing better. Who said self could do better? You are only discouraged in your pride in self. You thought that it could do so much and was going so well, but now it has failed you. You do not really hate self; you hate that self is not stronger. If you hated self, you would accept the death sentence on it, see the thing that you thought was taking you out as actually bringing you in, and boast in your weakness. Because of so great a sacrifice as what Jesus made on the cross, regret is a luxury that a believer does not have. When you sin, you can call on the marred Jesus for cleansing and forgiveness, for to continue to wallow in shame and self-loathing is simply pride. Admit where you are to leave where you are. Admit your love of self, that you want it to do better, and that you want glory. At that point you can have a move from God. As He lives Life through you, His peace will fill your days.

DAY 241
Separating Light From Dark

God set them in the expanse of the sky to give light on the earth, to govern the day and the night, and to separate the light from the darkness; and God saw that it was good.

— GENESIS 1:17 & 18

The day that you received Jesus you received everything. How could you not? He is, actually, everything. Colossians 1:16, "For by Him all things were created, {both} in the heavens and on earth, visible and invisible, whether thrones or dominions or rulers or authorities—all things have been created by Him and for Him." Each day, since that first day, it has been the mission of the Holy Spirit to convince you that you are lacking in nothing. In opposition, Satan has taken it upon himself to convince you that you are lacking in everything, to persuade you that your job, mate, kids, situation, physical appearance, and position in life are all substandard. He also has to convince you that holiness, mercy, fellowship, maturity, blessings, and forgiveness must all be worked for, his goal being to have you so consumed with what you think you do not have that you will never recognize what you do have.

Sometimes I feel as though my office, wherever I happen to have it set up, is a place where light and darkness meet, and it is God's gracious work to separate the two. My job is to witness to the work of the Spirit, the Jesus that is in believers. So many come to my office possessing so much, and yet they cannot see the blessings for obsessing on the negatives. They are men with beautiful families, children that are not rebellious, financial security, and a wife who puts up with and even loves them, despite their goofy behavior. Yet the devil has blinded them to the point that they cannot see positives in any of it; they sit there recounting the offenses they have had in life, the people who have let them down, and their failed attempts to be Christian. Every preacher must learn to be free from the fear of repetition. I am! What gets a person's attention gets him! We are to obsess on what is true, right, pure, and lovely. I guess everyone is just self-centered enough to think only about himself! We mingle light and darkness to the point where we do not know the difference and all of life is gray. Pray for a word from Him that would separate the two!

DAY 242
Sex and Bitterness

See to it that no one comes short of the grace of God; that no root of bitterness springing up causes trouble, and by it many be defiled.
— HEBREWS 12:15

"Why should I pretend when I simply do not enjoy sex with my mate?" "How can you have sex with a husband that you do not respect?" "How can I continue in a relationship with a wife that I no longer love?" These are questions often asked. When a husband says, "I do not love you," his message is really, "You are not lovable." This seemingly puts the responsibility for his failure to love squarely at the wife's feet; she is now accountable for becoming "lovable." The carnal man always excuses his failures by blaming another. His interpretation of "I cannot love you" is at odds with God's, for love defined is the desire to do what is best for and to another. The degree of how unlovable another may be has nothing to do with loving. The motivation to love originates in the person doing the loving; it is not to be engendered by the one being loved. To give the behavior of another as an excuse for not loving is merely to condemn oneself. It is not an acknowledgment of a flaw in the wife, but a proclamation of a shortcoming in the husband. His true assertion is this: "I am so self-centered that I will do no good for you unless I am getting something for myself. My attention is so precious that you must earn it. I am god sitting on the throne, and until you perform well enough, I cannot take notice of you. I must be worshipped." The husband can only hope that God does not view him in this same light.

"I do not respect him, and therefore, I cannot be expected to have sex with him." To placate the "women's liberation" movement that has come in the back door of the church, the teaching of mutual submission has gained popularity. It goes like this: "A woman can only respect if the man is loving; if the man is not loving, then the woman cannot be expected to respect." This teaching takes a person full circle and leaves her immaculately unchanged. In a sense I understand the emphasis, for submission has taken on the implication of inferiority. However, as I have mentioned before, submission does not indicate inferiority. We respect our bosses and submit to them even when it would be impossible to argue they are better than we are. It is the way of things, it is order, and it works better than if everyone were to go his own way. I remember a girl who could not swallow her medication because she had been told that to take medication was a sign of unbelief. There was a message attached to the medication; she really was not rebelling against the medication as much as the message attached to it. Submission and respect have nothing to do with superiority or inferiority. I remember talking to a young—sixteen years old—newly married couple. The husband was upset because his wife was not submitting to his wisdom! Frankly, he had no wisdom! He was looking to her respect and submission to change something within him; if only she would change, he would feel better. Respect and submission have nothing to do with the husband's being wiser or feeling better. A carnal wife rebels at the thought of respect and submission and excuses the behavior with, "How can I respect someone who does not love me?" "How can I respect someone that only wants sex?" "How can I submit to someone who is obviously inferior?" As one brother said, "Be careful about judging your husband's lousy discernment. He picked you, did he not?" However, once the justification for not respecting is laid, the wife will begin to isolate herself to avoid finding herself in a situation where she would have to "give" her body. This is primarily accomplished in two ways. First, she will become extremely critical, looking for every trait and occurrence that could justify her behavior and withdrawal. Second, she will be so domineering that her husband withdraws voluntarily; he begins to equate sex with rejection, becomes weary of the rejection, and automatically removes himself from the situation. I must say to the wife the same thing that I said about husbands. To say, "I cannot respect," is actually to say, "I am god, and you have not performed adequately to merit my favor." Making the statement, "I cannot respect," is more a revelation of the wife's spirituality than the husband's. Respect means to see the significance of another. For a wife to say she has no respect is to see herself as judge and jury determining who is significant and who is not. All things have significance, because God created all things and holds them together. The righteous said to Jesus, "When did we see You naked, hungry, thirsty, or in prison?" To which He responded, "If you did it to the least of them, you did it to Me." The heart of the Creator is found in the very least; there are no insignificant people, no people so low as to deserve anything less than respect.

Therefore, having defined love and respect and wherein responsibility lies, the next question to field is obvious. "Okay, I get the point, but how do I love and respect when I do not feel like it?" We have no excuse for not loving and respecting, so we must see the true purpose of love for the husband and respect for the wife. No command is given that is outside of us. Christ is not the Word become principle, but the Word become flesh dwelling within our hearts. Jesus created us, He lives in us, and He holds us together. Therefore, what we read of Jesus is not just text but our texture, the very fiber of our being. The command to love a wife is not written outside the husband on paper but written into his very DNA. The command to respect a husband is not written in black and white outside the wife;

it is written in her very nerves, heart, and physical mind. These commands are not imposed on couples; they are written within them, and therefore, exposed. I can prove it. I have never found, and never will find, a woman engaged in not respecting her husband who has a lift in her spirit, a glowing countenance, or an exuding joy. The same is true for a husband that refuses to love. In contrast, I have found delightful believers who radiate the love and glory of God in horrific marriages. These have learned the secret that love/respect is for their own good and happiness. They do not like the turmoil that is brought about by personal rejection of God's command that is written within. Their way is not the Way. Moving in their way invites chaos into their being and a civil war they cannot win. Once the husband sees this, his wife's respect and submission are no longer the issue. He will love regardless for his own peace and happiness. Her respect is not his issue with her, but her issue with God. The husband is free and out of the loop. His every waking moment is not spent trying to prove something. He is free! The same is true for the wife.

Would you be happy? Lay aside self-merit and justification in order to love and respect. You will find yourself displaying a countenance that others desire.

DAY 243
She Is My Sister, He Is My Brother!

> *And Abraham said of Sarah his wife, "She is my sister."*
> — GENESIS 20:2

For those of you who are married, what are some of the words and concepts that stir in your mind when you hear the words "wife" or "husband"? When I say that I have a wife or call Betty "my wife," many things come to mind, for there are myriad issues associated with the term "wife." I think of the children, finances, the home, the emotional, physical, and mental aspects of our relationship, future and past events both good and bad, commitment, oneness, pains and joys, holidays, babies, ultimate goals, and more. After all, she is my wife.

There is much written on the relationship of husband and wife. However, I want to investigate an overlooked aspect of marriage, a greater relationship than marriage, that of brother and sister in Christ. In heaven there will be no marriage, for the earthly relationship of marriage will end on earth. "For when they rise from the dead, they neither marry, nor are given in marriage, but are like angels in heaven" (Mark 12:25). When I look at my wife and call her "Sister," everything changes. Just as the word "wife" brings with it a multitude of feelings, situations, and actions, so does the word "sister." She is my sister in Christ; I am her brother in Christ. Those two words, "sister and brother," move us to a different realm with completely different issues and goals. Once I call her "Sister," I acknowledge that she is not my own; she has a Father and is a member of a family. As my sister she has a goal that goes above and beyond that of being half of a married couple. God is the goal and the desire of our hearts; we must encourage each other in Him. Who did what and said what is not of ultimate importance; He is. All of the little annoyances of the day do not matter. Earthly mistakes are not the issue. Security is not in finances or who was wisest with the money. Together, He is our goal. When offended, we recognize that we deserve to be offended until we cannot be offended, for of what use will we be in the kingdom if we still get offended? I cannot judge my sister, for, "Who are you to judge the servant of another? To his own master he stands or falls; and stand he will, for the Lord is able to make him stand" (Romans 14:4). There is something higher than marriage for a couple, another dimension, and there is a better place from which to relate. Sometime today, turn to your wife and call her, "Sister," or to your husband and say, "Brother." For too long we have only seen our mates as wife or husband, and there is more.

DAY 244
Should I Know Good?

"Why do you call Me good?" Jesus answered, "No one is good—except God alone."
— LUKE 18:19

Eating from the tree of the knowledge of good and evil was prohibited, and that prohibition is still in effect. We are not to eat from it, for to the extent that we know good, we will also know evil. We eat from the tree for the appeal that we will be like God. However, our problem is that when we set out to know and practice good, we know evil, and we do not do the good that we wish; instead we do the evil. In short, we cannot handle the knowledge that comes from this tree. However, if we are intent on knowing good without the pitfalls of evil, then we can set our hearts to know God. God is good. God is love. The knowledge and experience of Him is freeing.

DAY 245
Silence in Arguments

And they were saying this, testing Him, in order that they might have grounds for accusing Him. But Jesus stooped down, and with His finger wrote on the ground.

— JOHN 8:6

Arguments have their roots in pride and are calculated to prove intellectual superiority, but they lack power. I have personally won arguments against those enslaved to drugs and alcohol, but they went away still slaves. I have won many arguments concerning marriage, but those couples, too, went away to visit the lawyer. I have won countless arguments with philosophers, psychologists, evolutionists, atheists, and cult leaders. They all went away to worship the image they were seeing in the mirror.

Jesus divided His dialogue with men into two categories: argument and ministry. Argument He usually avoided. Some came requesting food or power, not ministry, and from those He withdrew. Some sought to draw Him into a melee, and we find Him quietly drawing in the sand rather than heatedly presenting His point. Why? His response would have only fueled more debate with those who had a vested interest in not moving at all from their position. Jesus came to minister. If by His own Holy Spirit He was made aware that ministry was not possible, Jesus simply withdrew or refused to speak. As an Indian friend says, "The refusals of Jesus define Him!" For we do, in fact, know more about Him from His refusals than from His accomplishments. He refused the best seats, refused to make a loud noise proclaiming Himself, He refused to hurt the one who was hurting, He refused to minister spiritual truth in the power of the flesh, He refused to defend Himself, and He refused to condemn the woman caught in adultery.

Like Jesus, we must have a goal of ministry, not dialogue. When we begin to talk to our child, friend, co-worker, or pastor and realize we are standing there alone, without the power and witness of the Spirit, it is time to be quiet and draw in the dirt. If He is not ministering, then neither should we. Remember, the issue is not who listens to us, but whether we are listening to Him.

DAY 246
Simplicity Takes Faith

You are from God, little children, and have overcome them; because greater is He who is in you than he who is in the world.

— I JOHN 4:4

At that very time He rejoiced greatly in the Holy Spirit, and said, "I praise Thee, O Father, Lord of heaven and earth, that Thou didst hide these things from {the} wise and intelligent and didst reveal them to babes. Yes, Father, for thus it was well-pleasing in Thy sight."

— LUKE 10:21

Often I hear this type of comment: "That is a simplification." "The answer is too simple." "You are taking a simplistic approach to a complex problem!" I hope that I am! I want to be simple, for all that Jesus taught concerning life was simple. In fact, He took the complex and made it simple, and yet believers are the first to shout foul, shallow, and unlearned when the Christian life is made out to be simple. Why? Simplicity takes faith, while an unbelieving, fleshly approach to life demands understanding. If man can maintain the idol of understanding, he can maintain unbelief, since there will always be the need for one more indisputable fact before action is taken. This is why there is no end to the pursuit of knowledge for the unbelieving believer, who never intends to act. If knowledge were obtained, action would be demanded.

When we minister to discouraged believers, the answer needed is simple. However, a simple answer requires faith, which is just what the defeated are missing. Therefore, it is important to make understanding a starting point, not the end of discipling, to bring believers to faith. No matter how eloquently the information is presented, the whole issue will rest on faith. If the element of faith is removed from what is being taught, then Christ Himself is removed. We believe and we act. The secret is that when we are unbelieving, we can ask Jesus to help us in our unbelief, and at that point all the forces of heaven and earth will back us and push us forward in a believing life.

DAY 247
Sin Will Not Send You To Hell

For while we were still helpless, at the right time Christ died for the ungodly.

— ROMANS 5:6

But God demonstrates His own love toward us, in that while we were yet sinners, Christ died for us.

— ROMANS 5:8

And He Himself is the propitiation for our sins; and not for ours only, but also for those of the whole world.

— I JOHN 2:2

I cannot walk up to an unbeliever and proclaim that because he sins he will go to hell. No one is going to hell because of sin. The sin issue concerning the human race has already been dealt with at the cross. Jesus died for the ungodly! Man is not doomed because of sin; rather, man is doomed because of pride; it is pride that sends man to hell. It was pride that caused the initial fall in response to temptation. God prioritizes what is considered bad by listing pride first, unbelief second, and sin third. Somehow we have reversed the order.

When the resurrected Christ appeared to the disciples, they did not recognize Him. To prove Who He was, He showed them the marks of crucifixion, the same marks that kept the disciples from recognizing Him. Before a crucifixion the Romans would take a whip made of twelve strands of leather (glass embedded on each side with a hook on the end) and strike the victim 39 times across the back and once across the face, completely disfiguring him. Jesus was marred beyond recognition, and for all of eternity He will bear those marks. At the right hand of the Father sits the marred Jesus. We will never fully understand the price that the Word of God paid to become a man; however, we know that it was great, for He is still a man in heaven. Is it any wonder that we will see Him in heaven as the Lamb that was slain and fall down in worship?

Because the sin issue has been dealt with, all that God requires is our belief in and receiving of the marred Jesus that sits at His right hand. Unbelievers will not perish because of sin but because of the pride they hold dear that denies the Son of God who made the supreme sacrifice.

DAY 248
Someone Greater Than The Book

*All things were created by Him and for Him. He is before
all things, and in Him all things hold together . . . so that in
everything He might have the supremacy.*
— COLOSSIANS 1:16, 17, 18

Imagine that it is the year 700 A.D. Evangelists have
passed through town, and you and a few others have
accepted Christ as your Savior. They then leave town.
There is no possibility of receiving a Bible, you have no
further instruction, nor do you know when someone more
learned might be arriving. What would you do? Would
your situation be hopeless, with the prospect of growth
in Christ an impossibility? How important would it be to
"mine the riches of the Scriptures"? What would you do
during your quiet times? How would you hide the Word
of God in your heart?

Many today leave the impression that Jesus died
sometime between 29 to 33 A.D. and yet man was never
really saved until the printing press. Is He greater than the
Book? History reveals that myriad believers have been in
touch with the Book but out of touch with the Savior. This
is a constant danger! Time has rendered its verdict! Perfect
theology has not produced Christ-like believers.

Once in my office a pastor stated that he would like
to see New Testament miracles, but those would never
happen until we became immersed in the "word of God."

The miracles he wanted to see were the raising of the dead and the walking on water. However, when we are in touch with the Son of God, the miracles that we see may be as simple as walking across the room and kissing a grumpy mate. These small miracles come only from fellowship with the living Christ and the release of His life within us.

I lean on Scripture continually for my teaching, and it is Scripture that teaches, "You search the Scriptures because you think that in them you have eternal life, but it is these that bear witness of me" (John 5:39). He is greater than the Book! When He comes first, the Book holds life. When He comes second, the Book is lifeless.

DAY 249
Something Much Worse Than Racism

"For I hate divorce," says the LORD, the God of Israel, "and him who covers his garment with wrong," says the LORD of hosts. "So take heed to your spirit, that you do not deal treacherously."

— MALACHI 2:16

The governments are always emphasizing what they think they can fix and glossing over what they cannot. Often governments bandy around the topic of racism as

one of the worst sins in the world. I have spent much time in places where I was the brunt of racism, and I can live with it. I will tell of something that is much worse than racism. I know of many families, of many different races, wherein the husband and wife hate one another. This I cannot live with, and governments do not address this problem, even though it is known that if we have peace and love at home, the struggles outside the home are minimized. I was so blessed one time in Brazil when I was there to speak at the gathering of a family ministry; listening to the believers in the trenches of this ministry, I learned that they regarded themselves as warriors in the battle to bring Christ into the very center of divorce. As a direct result of this ministry, I was even told of a judge that had decided that no couple could be married or divorced in his court without first going through Christian counseling. Hatred between husband and wife is the worst form of "racism." If only governments would attack it with fervency. Of course, we know why it will not happen, for to attack it, Jesus must be brought into the equation. He and His disciples are the only ones among all religions teaching that a husband must love (without excuse) his wife and a wife must respect (without excuse) her husband. Without conversion, both are impossible.

DAY 250
Soulless

> *For our struggle is not against flesh and blood, but against the rulers, against the powers of this dark world and against the spiritual forces of evil in the heavenly realms.*
>
> — EPHESIANS 6:12

My father once asked me, while visiting the former Soviet Union, "What is the deal with the art?" I explained, "Years of refinement went into making a picture, statue, or painting that could communicate nothing. The art is about nothing. It was dangerous to communicate something." Communism was about nothing, it inspired nothing, it is the spirit of nothing, and it lingers. There is a difference between soulish people—those who live without the influence of Christ's Holy Spirit on mind, will, and emotions—and those who live in a soulless state. Much of what I have observed in Africa, the former Soviet Union, and other places is soullessness, and to me that is much sadder. The spirit of indifference is growing in its power in such places, where man fought over the flower until it was pulled apart. I am not surprised at some of the demonic attacks I have experienced in these areas, with their histories of having one group oppressing the other until neither has anything, and then both wondering what it was all about. I know what it was all about: Satan. Our battle is not against flesh and blood but spirits and principalities.

I have mentioned before that if we understood why Satan would destroy a marriage, we would be much more afraid of him. He will destroy it for nothing! No reason! He is indifferent. After all is lost, people often just look around, wondering what happened. At the time it made so much sense to be angry, to protect self, and to pay back insult for insult. Having depleted everything, they stand back and wonder what it was all about. A boy gets a girl pregnant, and upon that discovery, he does not want to hear from her again. Why? His involvement was all for nothing, in complete indifference. The thumbprint of the enemy is always indifference. We must pray to see the spiritual principalities move.

DAY 251
Sowing and Reaping

Sow for yourselves righteousness, reap the fruit of unfailing love, and break up your unplowed ground; for it is time to seek the Lord.

— HOSEA 10:12

Coming from a farming community, I have sat on a tractor more than once and thought how nice it would be if we did not have to do that every year. Every farmer knows the truth that he cannot sow once and then keep reaping for the next seventy years. The effects of sowing and reaping last for one season. Therefore, if we were to apply this principle to consequences, we could readily see that they, too, are for a season. Sow to the flesh and reap to the flesh; sow to the spirit and reap to the spirit. Galatians 6:8, "For the one who sows to his own flesh shall from the flesh reap corruption, but the one who sows to the

Spirit shall from the Spirit reap eternal life." However, a person cannot sow to the Spirit once and expect to reap the consequences of that act for the rest of his life. The same is true for the flesh. If one sows to the flesh, for that season he will reap flesh. The answer is to start sowing to the Spirit in this season and the next, so in that way each new season will bring something new, beautiful, fresh, and living to reap, rather than by sowing to the flesh and reaping death.

It makes no sense that a Christian would commit a stupid act of the flesh and God would keep him under bondage, placing him for the rest of his life in a new category entitled "Second-class Believer"! Again, if it were possible to commit one sin that would cause suffering the rest of his life, then it would also be possible to commit one act of righteousness that would carry a person through his whole life. But abiding is for the moment, the season. God is not interested in punishing us for the rest of our lives. Often believers think everything that goes wrong is a consequence of a past mistake, like marrying the "wrong" person, succumbing to temptation and sin, or betraying a loved one. Very likely it is not the past that is causing misery but today's walking in the flesh.

DAY 252
Standing Alone

*If you were of the world, the world would love its own;
but because you are not of the world, but I chose you out of
the world, therefore, the world hates you.*

— JOHN 15:19

There will be several times throughout life that you will find yourself standing alone. It can be in times of deep inner need when no one comes to your aid. You might find yourself standing alone for truth in your workplace, home, or church. You may be rejected after sharing your faith or falsely accused with no one defending your character. Standing alone is not a unique experience.

There are several approaches that can be taken when you find yourself standing alone. First, you can act like Job. "I waste away; I will not live forever. Leave me alone, for my days are {but} a breath" (Job 7:16). He adjusted to his misery and became comfortable with it. Expectation and hope take effort. Pessimism holds out its hand and offers its own peculiar brand of friendship. Pessimism comforts by telling you what a clever person you are to recognize hopelessness.

Second, you can take the approach of Paul. II Timothy 4:14, "Alexander the coppersmith did me much harm; the Lord will repay him according to his deeds." That is, others have caused your misery; if it were not for others, you could be in bliss. Therefore, comfort yourself with thoughts of others suffering for the pain they caused you. Your pain is a ten; theirs will be a hundred. This approach definitely will not leave your pain at a ten, though; it will increase it.

Third, you can approach standing alone as did Jesus. Luke 23:46, "And Jesus, crying out with a loud voice, said, 'Father, INTO THY HANDS I COMMIT MY SPIRIT.' And having said this, He breathed His last." Though you are standing alone in your situation, you recognize you are never left alone. God will never leave or forsake you! Standing alone, there is no hindrance between you and the Father, not any other voice or opinion but His. Into His hands you commit your spirit! His hands! Can you imagine? He created man with His hands. He did miracles with His hands. He upheld His people with His hands. He keeps us from evil by His hands. In these hands you lay your spirit when you are standing alone. What happens next? The self-centered you breathes its last, for you cannot be in His hands and cling to selfishness.

DAY 253
Take the Blame!

Then let me bear the blame before my father forever.
— GENESIS 44:32

There is much said today about the person who is a blame-taker. We are told that blame is something that we are not to wear, and indeed, so few believers are willing to take the blame for their condition, yet there is a measure of integrity that comes from being willing to take blame.

Often when I have been discipling a person God has revealed something about him He was not yet revealing to the person. Therefore, I did not mention it but stored it in the back of my mind. I know that I have no right to bring out a shortcoming that He is not revealing, for with His revelation will always come the power to overcome it. When He reveals a failure, it is not a burden, for His power accompanies it, and with the power comes hope. My point is that oftentimes others have annoying, carnal, self-centered behavior that we see and they cannot. Why? Obviously, it is to work something in us. However, instead of looking to the Lord and within, we make the mistake of looking to them and wondering at their condition.

Have you ever thought that you are to blame for your response to carnal persons? That their behavior is revealing your heart and carnality? Has their behavior revealed bitterness, lack of love, and your own carnality? You are to blame for your response! Do not fret about seeing others' behavior; your behavior is the issue. When you are tempted to reject others who offend you, remember there is probably a bigger fish to fry, and that fish is you!

There is another aspect of blame-taking that is legitimate. II Samuel 12:4-7, "'Now a traveler came to the rich man, and he was unwilling to take from his own flock or his own herd, to prepare for the wayfarer who had come to him; rather he took the poor man's ewe lamb and prepared it for the man who had come to him.' Then David's anger burned greatly against the man, and he said to Nathan, 'As the LORD lives, surely the man who has done this deserves to die. And he must make restitution for the lamb fourfold, because he did this thing and had no compassion.' Nathan then said to David, 'You are the man! Thus says the LORD God of Israel, "It is I who anointed you king over Israel and it is I who delivered you from the hand of Saul."'"

Would David have judged another man's failure had he known he was going to hear, "You are the man"?

Unfortunately, I have spent a good part of my life judging others. I once had the opportunity to question an elderly saint, "Why do believers not finish well?"

He took a pen in his hand and asked, "Who holds the pen, who keeps it from falling, and who moves it from place to place?"

"You do," I responded.

He then "walked" the pen over to "look" at another pen that was lying down and had the upright pen say, "You pathetic pen! Look at you lying there; what a failure you must be!" Then the elderly gentleman dropped the pen he was holding and said that the pen is like a man who is touched by the glory of God, held by the glory of God, and moved by the glory of God, but then who takes the credit himself. All God need do is let go, and the man is as flat as those he judges. Man lives in pride, becoming a god unto himself and a god to others! A chill ran down my spine, for I could hear the voice of the prophet saying, "You are the man." The only reason I have not left my family or have ever ministered to others or had a revelation of grace is that the glory of God was holding me. When I see hypocritical believers, those caught up in adultery, those with rebellious children, or those steeped in carnality, I just want to shut up! If I stand, it is not because of my own great strength and wisdom, but only because of the glory of God.

We can have no pride except in His goodness and glory. As abiding believers, we do not want only to preach that there is nothing the nearness of Jesus will not cure; we want to demonstrate it, showing that we believe in the glory of God. "Lord, I take the blame for judging! But I have come to a place where I am extremely frightened and want nothing to do with judging."

DAY 254
Tend My Sheep

So when they had finished breakfast, Jesus said to Simon Peter, "Simon, {son} of John, do you love Me more than these?" He said to Him, "Yes, Lord; You know that I love You." He said to him, "Tend My lambs."

— JOHN 21:15

It is interesting that Peter was to tend the sheep in response to loving Jesus. I loved having sheep as a child; it was great fun feeding and watching them. They definitely do need tending. Jesus did not tell Peter to fatten the sheep; that is the job of the butcher. He did not say stimulate and excite the sheep; that is the job of the wolf. He gave the job of shepherding to Peter. So many wipe out because of lack of encouragement and food. What feeds the sheep is the true Word, Jesus. Just talking about Jesus will allow the disciple-maker to feed and tend the sheep. Often I meet people who are so down, so depressed, but simply bringing up the name of Jesus or something He taught or said will bring a lift to their spirits. This is tending. Much of what we see called worship today is only of man; it is not feeding, shepherding, or tending.

My grandfather hated feedlots. It was his feeling that cattle and sheep were something to be nurtured; they needed space and quality conditions. I was surprised once to discover that the feedlots were giving the cattle plastic pellets to eat, for after all, they took the place of grain and could be recycled. Despite the fact that there was no nutritional value in the pellets, they were formulated to trick the normal digestive system of the cow. Church today is full of plastic pellets. Oh, we sing, we jump, we worship (sing ourselves happy), and yet we leave so dissatisfied with nothing to keep us in the coming hours when spiritual strength is needed at work or at home. Tend the sheep! Simply speak of Jesus to one another. This is the food that will keep us beyond the conversation, the sermon, and the meeting. Colossians 3:16 & 17, "Let the word of Christ richly dwell within you, with all wisdom, teaching and admonishing one another with psalms and hymns and spiritual songs, singing with thankfulness in your hearts to God. And whatever you do in word or deed, do all in the name of the Lord Jesus, giving thanks through Him to God the Father."

DAY 255
The American Passport

For our citizenship is in heaven, from which also we eagerly wait for a Savior, the Lord Jesus Christ.
— PHILIPPIANS 3:20

The American passport is the most unique travel document in the world. Every other passport is the possession of the holder, but the U.S. passport always remains the property of the United States government. The holder does not own it, but rather it owns him and proclaims that the traveler is the property of the United States government. If other countries fully understood the position the U.S. government has taken concerning its citizens, they might allow no Americans to come in, because in a sense, America comes in with all of those individuals considered to be her property, and wherever that citizen stands is now possessed, in a sense, by the United States. Therefore, when an American traveler is detained or held hostage, the government has a moral and legal right to come and get its property, and it does come! This is why the Americans were among the first released from the Japanese embassy takeover in Peru years ago; the terrorists did not want the hassle. The American is by definition, then, an embassy, for wherever he is standing, that soil immediately under his feet is considered American. Because of this position, the American is always in a safe place, supported by a force much greater than him.

Christianity has rightly been described as a "much more" gospel, for what it gives is always much more! Our citizenship, our passport, our protection, and our representation are much more than the world can conceive of or offer. Wherever we go, we stand in Christ. In Him, we are more than conquerors. In Him everything is given to us. We are His possession. To let the Christian into a business or home is to let in Christ. I enjoy the concept of American citizenship, but I love the power and reality of a heavenly citizenship. Wherever the believer stands is a safe place, with a force much greater than himself behind him.

DAY 256
The Autistic God

Remember that you molded me like clay. Will you now turn me to dust again? Did you not pour me out like milk and curdle me like cheese, clothe me with skin and flesh, and knit me together with bones and sinews? You gave me life and showed me kindness, and in your providence watched over my spirit.

— JOB 10:9-12

I enjoy spending some time with acquaintances who are autistic; typically those with autism are very unique and, in my opinion, way beyond the norm for compulsive thinkers. They lock into something and their minds do not have the ability to shift to anything else. One friend had locked into turtles; everything was about turtles: must find a turtle, must hold the turtle, and must examine the turtle. After catching a turtle, he scanned every section of the turtle, his eyes moving like a computer scanner. In the end, he put it down and drew a perfect picture of a turtle. He knew every line and dimple. Now, man is made in the image of God. Look at any man and you learn a secret or two about God. After watching the man with a turtle, I had an insight into God. God is Autistic! I could just imagine God making the turtle, thinking of every detail, locking into it, thinking of everything, how it would breathe, how it would move, what it would eat, and creating all that it needed. I could just see God locked in. It was then that I understood a bit more about the exactness of creation, that every hair of my head was numbered, and that so much detail had gone into my life. Everything has been perfect. All of creation is perfect. He has given me exactly—yes, exactly—what I have needed: in sickness, in health, in poverty, in struggle, and in stress, everything perfectly!

This brings me to another point. We see the perfection and how it must work. We cannot change it. I am often asked, "How can you believe in a God who allows suffering?" My response is, "How can you believe in man who causes the suffering?" AIDS is not the judgment of God; it is the judgment of man. By playing God and refusing to recognize Him and His perfection, man has done it all, killing many people. God has made us perfectly, and sin is a foreign resident in the body. All of the glue (Jesus) holding man together will attempt to repel it. It is in this condition that man complains about God, and yet everything that has been permitted into our lives has been the perfect thing, exactly what we need.

DAY 257
The Battle of Romans 7

For we maintain that a man is justified by faith apart from the works of the Law.
— ROMANS 3:28

What does this passage mean to you? Many are beating themselves up over their sin, so much so that I assume they live under the Law. It is obvious that they believe they are justified by behavior. Abraham understood the secret: without faith, the Law cannot be birthed. Without first believing in God, Abraham would never have received the commands of God. I would not listen to any of the commands of the Hindu gods simply because I do not believe they exist. Law without faith gives birth to sin. For example, if I believe in the love of God, knowing full well that all He tells me is for my good, I will easily and readily keep the command to bless those who curse me. It is simple. However, if I do not believe in the love of God, I will read the command to bless those who curse, realize that I do not do that, never believe that it is for my good, and find a way around the command, saying, "I do not have to love them! Why should I? They have gone too far." The Law that was to bless me (if birthed in faith, in the love of God) now becomes the thing by which I am condemned; the Law, without faith, will always give birth to sin. It is easy to see how Abraham was walking in the greater way of faith; even without the Law he was justified. Abraham believed God, and it was counted to him as righteousness. Sweeter words were never spoken.

I determined long ago to spend my time in the love of God and not in the Law. As I have discovered the love of God, the command has been found to be easy. In fact, I refuse to listen to the Law unless it is in the context of faith in Him and His love. The Law is good if birthed in faith, and moving deeply into the faith of Jesus brings a higher life than living in the Law, for faith in Jesus will lead to an expression of exactly Jesus. Amazing! Without the Law, sin is dead (Romans 7:8). Sin counts on man's boastful pride that leads to attempting to keep the Law without faith. This accounts for why there is so much immorality in legalistic churches, where the emphasis is on performance, and little or nothing is said of faith.

A dating couple comes to the office stating they have been sleeping together and are under great condemnation. Is the solution to have them stop? If they stop because of the command without believing in the Love of God that gave the command, they will continue to struggle and "slip up." If they see the Love of God in the command and believe in Him who gives the command, the struggle will cease. If a child is told that by working he will obtain a bicycle, and the child believes the parent, the work will be a great joy. But what if the child does not believe the parent?

Will the work be done grudgingly or with joy? If the child were never given the promise, he would not be working grudgingly, which is sin. In the end, that child would be better off had he never heard the promise.

The problem is simple: the Law was given to men of faith, and men of unbelief have attempted to keep it—which they cannot do, for Law is birthed in faith—and the result is sin and condemnation. In this light Romans 7 becomes quite clear; the battle described is not the battle of the old man against the new man, or a battle that exists before conversion or after conversion. It is describing an absolute battle between faith and Law, a battle that includes the unbeliever (going to hell) and the unbelieving believer (going to heaven). At any time, either the unbeliever or the unbelieving believer can perceive in his mind the Law of God and want to keep it, for he knows that it is good. Yet because of lack of belief in God, the person is divided, his entire being cannot keep the Law, and the end result is sin and condemnation. Do not think that the way out is recommitment, harder work, rededication, vows, knowledge, or strength; the way out is faith in Jesus. "So then it does not depend on the man who wills or the man who runs, but on God who has mercy" (Romans 9:16). The Gentiles have pursued the promise by faith and gotten it, but the Jews sought by Law and lost it. "For with the heart man believes, resulting in righteousness, and with the mouth he confesses, resulting in salvation" (Romans 10:10).

Where do you begin in your struggle? Stop fighting the Law and start confessing Jesus with your mouth each day. Before you go to sleep, do not let your thoughts end at the Law you have not kept. Instead, let your thoughts end at Jesus, in whom you believe. This brings us to the final hiccup! Security only comes in faith, regardless of whether you are a Calvinist or an Armenian. These two camps become one under the Law, because to attempt to find security in works will only bring about insecurity. Read Romans 7 and think of it differently; Paul is talking about living in the Law and how impossible it is to live so. The Law reveals what you did not know was sin, and then it does not give you the power to obey. After the knowledge, you find yourself doing the very thing you do not want to do. This passage applies to all that live by the Law.

DAY 258
The Birth of Simplicity

I tell you the truth: Anyone who will not receive the kingdom of God like a little child will never enter it.
— MARK 10:15

Once when we had a small Christmas party, it was my privilege to bring the devotion. I asked God to give me a deeper insight into the birth of His Son. A still, small voice whispered, "It is the birth of Simplicity." It is said that every great discovery is a simplification. The greatest discovery ever would also be the greatest simplification. Jesus is God simplified! Jesus is God comprehensible!

I find it interesting that evil is difficult as it entangles man; for instance, it takes effort and a good memory to be a liar. In contrast, good is always life reduced to its simplest form. Truth is straightforward; one can have a bad memory if living in truth, for a story will always be the same. Most countries where I travel use the bargaining system; the buyer offers half the asking price and then offers and counter-offers until he works his way up to one-third off. This drawn-out procedure consumes many hours of valuable time and often creates bad tempers. However, in the U.S. and Europe, there is a one-price system introduced by the Quakers in response to the simple command of Jesus to let our yes be yes and our no be no. He simplifies life.

Jesus reduced life to two rules: love God and love man. This is part of the genius of Jesus. True beauty is revealed in the absence of additions and pretense. Jesus must have been the most beautiful Man ever to live, for His presence was stripped of everything useless. He spoke the word to men (Mark 2:3). What was the Word? It was one Word among thousands. It simplified life! It was significant! He was asked thousands of questions, answered only the significant, and answered them quickly.

"Are You the Son of God?"

"Yes."

"Are you the King of the Jews?"

"Yes." Jesus is the simple Word, the simple answer. He teaches simplicity in all. "Truly I say to you, whoever does not receive the kingdom of God like a child shall not enter it at all" (Mark 10:15). Only as we live in simplicity will we really live.

DAY 259
The Body

So we, who are many, are one body in Christ, and individually members one of another.

— ROMANS 12:5

One man said that the proof of God was the wondrous working of the thumb. Look at where it is and how it operates. God put us together physically. The more we understand the body, the more revelation we can have into THE Body.

There is the unseemly member, thus named because of the prevailing attitude from our awareness after the fall of man, though God ordained its function. We cannot talk about this unpresentable member in the physical body, but we know which one it is. Did God do right in locking up and assigning to this member the perpetuation of His ongoing creation? Are we right when we decide what is seemly and unseemly? God puts more abundant honor on the members that lacked it. One day I discover that I am the less honorable member of the Body, when I had judged that it was you!

When a young man falls in love and produces a photo, what does he show? The face, of course, not an x-ray of the kidneys. "These are the lovely kidneys of my girlfriend." However, if the kidneys are not working, the young lady will not be presentable. What is the point? More and more I view what I do as an end result of the Lord's work through the organs, the unseen others. Many things have to come together for me to speak at any one church or meeting. Somewhere along the line I had to meet the host, or he at least needed to hear of me. He had to love the message. He had to know the people who could help him organize and set up the seminar, and all of them had some particular gift and other acquaintances that helped facilitate it all. All had to have jobs and finances that allowed us to be together at the exact time, all of us excited about our God. Someone invented the airplane, cars, e-mail, and more to get us here. I must stop for I am going mad! Do you see why I believe I am the less honorable member? The Scripture says to "grieve not the Holy Spirit." Falling out with those on whom I am so dependent is just wrong. When we fall out with another member of the Body, for whom Jesus shed his blood, it grieves the Spirit. There is no forgiveness for unforgiveness, and every time we judge a person, we are guilty of unforgiveness. When judgment begins, where will God start? May the Church not go blindly on its way of not recognizing the Body.

DAY 260
The Call Followed By a Roadblock

For this reason I have often been hindered from coming to you.

— ROMANS 15:22

To this end also we pray for you always, that our God will count you worthy of your calling, and fulfill every desire for goodness and the work of faith with power.

— II THESSALONIANS 1:11

God will often give the believer a call to accomplish something and then close every door to make the fulfillment impossible. Why? Because with the call comes a provision. The same One who gives the call must also accomplish it. However, the flesh of man will take the call and not the provision, choosing to look for fulfillment in self-power, and if completion is possible, sink into glory, kingdoms, pride, strength, and righteousness. The call and the provision are one; the problem is that we do not see them as one. Therefore, immediately after the call, all attempts to fulfill it must fail. We need not look far for an example. Joseph, after the call to be the leader of his family, actually thought it a turn of bad luck to end up in a pit. Then it was good luck to be taken out of the pit, followed by bad luck to fall in with men who sold him into slavery. Then more good luck came and made him head of a house before another turn of bad luck arose when he ended up in prison. In the end, though, he saw it was God who brought Him out. It was all God. The call and the provision were one. He completed the call with the provision and took no glory. This is to be the end result of a perfect call of God.

When you get a call, do not think that is all of it. Listen and wait for the provision. Do not try to do the thing on your own. You will only end up in a pit.

DAY 261
The Christian and The Supernatural

As the crowds were increasing, He began to say, "This generation is a wicked generation; it seeks for a sign, and yet no sign will be given to it but the sign of Jonah."

— LUKE 11:29

The fact that believers often clamor for the supernatural is understandable, since many have been covertly taught that God's stamp of approval is His supernatural response in our daily activities. Having God continually act in supernatural ways for us personally is viewed as proof that we are special, not mere dots on the planet. Those who have accepted and identified with the above theory make the following types of statements. "God noticed me! I have worth, value, an identity." "God sought me out. I had no intentions of getting married, of becoming a minister, of moving to another place. I said, 'God, if You want me, You will have to come and get me!' Then God spoke to me, He visited me, He turned my car around." In other words, "I am special, He wants me, He comes after me supernaturally." This emphasis also leads the "less fortunate" to make the following statements: "God let me down, He does not notice, care, or work in my life." "I guess I do not measure up or will ever be good enough," or, "I will no longer trust God! He allowed my wife to die of cancer, a child to rebel, my unwed daughter to get pregnant, financial bankruptcy, my marriage to be a failure, or my ministry to dissolve." In short, so this belief system goes, those God loves He blesses, and those He wants to get even with find evil! What seems good reflects His pleasure, and what we perceive as bad indicates His displeasure. The measure of God's concern for us, then, is seen as His supernatural activity in life to the degree that it makes us comfortable and leaves us feeling good.

Maintaining this kind of thinking is, first of all, anti-God; second, it is Taoism; and third, it is eating from the tree of the knowledge of good and evil. This rationale places incredible pressure on believers to act and speak in such a way as to solicit the supernatural activity of God. We are strained, hating ourselves for not doing enough to reap God's pleasure and angry with Him for not noticing us. We dislike the partiality that He shows, then hate ourselves for disparaging God, and feel we must protect God's image as well as our own.

Now for a moment let us lay aside all thoughts of the supernatural and move in a different direction to ponder God's working in the natural.

Often when discipling a discouraged believer I will ask the question, "Did you sometime in the past five years, five weeks, or maybe five days, while reading your Bible, listening to a sermon, or reading a good book, happen to say to God, 'You can have my life. I want all that is possible for a human who knows You. I want the deep spiritual life; I want a marriage that works'?" Invariably the believer will say yes! I then respond, "Well, that explains it. If you wanted to remain unchanged and comfortable, God would not be using the natural in your life to perfect the answering of your expressed desires."

What is God's goal for the believer? We can read it in Matthew 5 - 7, the Beatitudes, the Sermon on the Mount, Christ's life, now the Christian's life. Everything that we read there is supernatural. Any believer who has attempted to love an enemy knows just how supernatural it is. It takes more Spirit activity to walk across the living room and kiss a mate who offends us than it does to walk on water. In order to reveal the supernatural, the Lord created and dropped man into the natural world, wherein all that comes to him by way of mind, emotion, and body is intended to produce what is unnatural as the natural gives way to the supernatural. The supernatural does not give birth to the supernatural; angels are angels. However, men made of dust, dwelling on the natural earth, can become the sons of God! Supernatural? I think so! Explaining the process of allowing the natural to make us supernatural is somewhat like describing childbirth; it is never really understood until it is one's own experience.

Let me give some examples. We go through the natural experience of having no money, no job, and no hope in sight. All of this drives us to look to Him whose presence makes us sense the true wealth in which we participate. Next we can find ourselves relaxed with a lightness of heart concerning finances in the midst of a clamoring world. Supernatural!

We develop out-of-control feelings that come from watching a government make decisions that we cannot live with. First we attempt to change the flesh in the power of the flesh, then we eloquently describe the inconsistencies we see, at length we become disheartened, and in the end we pray. His presence gives comfort, His power fills us with assurance, and His love brings us hope. We know the whole lot in life passes through His hands, and so we rest, we trust, we get on with the real mission, and we live supernaturally in a world falling apart.

The media reports each night how someone, somewhere, is being abused, and we are left feeling hopeless and negative, a state that may suit the world, but it drags down the spirit of the believer. We were made to love God, love life, love our fellow man, and love our work. We draw near to Him to be a positive in a negative world. The sense of wrongness with our lot gives way to the relationship as we experience the greatest positive, Jesus, and become light in the world.

DAY 262
The Command Never Resented

But from the tree of the knowledge of good and evil
you shall not eat.
— GENESIS 2:17

The command not to eat from the tree of good and evil has never been resented. We are not to eat from the tree. If we do, we will split in two and be bound to circumstances. If it is good to win a million dollars, it must also be true that it is bad not to win the million. Once I make a judgment about what is good or bad, I hang myself with consequences. Jesus said, "There is none good but God." If we refuse to recognize what is good and evil and only see God, we will not be bound to circumstances. Do we really know what is good or evil? We say, "Have a good morning!" Do we know what a good morning would be? We assume that we do, and after all, we do not like saying, "Have an evil morning." But if this is the morning that someone gets so depressed that he cannot stand it any longer, cries out to God, and gives his life to Jesus, is that a bad morning? We must just see God.

In India the story is told of a man whose only son broke his leg and could not help in the fields. Everyone said, "That is bad." The father responded, "It may be good or it may be bad; only God knows." The next day the army took all of the young men in the village to fight a battle in which they were all killed, but the man's son was left behind because of the broken leg. The people responded, "That was good that your son broke his leg." The man again responded, "It may be good or it may be bad; only God knows." The story continues on for some time through various twists and turns, but it makes the clear point that we know nothing of the purpose of a natural occurrence at its beginning. The end of the natural is often the supernatural action of God.

The "good" or the "bad" happens not in order to signal God's pleasure or displeasure; rather, all that takes place in the natural is God's working the supernatural into believers. We must be silent until we see the end. We do not immediately jump to conclusions when we see failure in a family, a relationship, health, or finances. It may be God's working in the natural. This is not a contradiction to what is taught in Psalms and Deuteronomy, for we do know that obedience brings a blessing and disobedience a curse. When we are abiding, we often have that sense of how the forces in the world are actually nudging us along, and, as I have stated in the past, I feel certain that, generally speaking, believers have fewer flat tires. However, the Book of Job clears up any misconception that horrific occurrences in the life of a good man indicate that the man is evil. Nor do the failures of others close to us point toward life's judging them. It can mean that God is working through the evil for all of our good. Job's friends made a wrong assumption. The greater includes the lesser: If one submits to God, he will automatically resist the devil. God created the being that eventually became Satan and therefore is the greater, and He will use the lesser for all of His purposes. In faith we can stop making judgments and just see Him. The wonder of our God is that He "causes all things to work together for good to those who love God, to those who are called according to His purposes" (Romans 8:28), and that means "good" according to His definition

DAY 263
The Consuming Fire

Know therefore today that it is the LORD your God who is crossing over before you as a consuming fire. He will destroy them and He will subdue them before you, so that you may drive them out and destroy them quickly, just as the LORD has spoken to you.

— DEUTERONOMY 9:3

A fire is so interesting; it sucks the life out of the object that it consumes, so it is only possible where there is some level of life. Fire is life exiting. Simply burn a log and watch energy and life departing from the wood. All that will be left after life exits is ash, a lifeless, dead thing. One day the earth will be destroyed by fire. It makes sense. Jesus, the Life that holds it together, will be withdrawn, fire will be the result, and the life will be returned to the Father. When Jesus exits, there is nothing left. He is the Divine Glue that holds all things together, but by fire the glue leaves. II Peter 3:7, "But the present heavens and earth by His word are being reserved for fire, kept for the day of judgment and destruction of ungodly men." A great fire is coming to the earth, to things above the earth and those below. When Jesus, who is eternal, exits, a fire that is eternal will remain. There is a fire for those who have not believed. It is only extinguished by faith in Him. Belief is the only thing that can quench it. In the end, the unbelievers will get their wish. He will depart completely from them, and all that will be left is fire.

DAY 264
The Divine Escalator

Yet I am always with you; You hold me by my right hand;
You guide me with Your counsel;
and afterward You will take me into glory.

— PSALM 73:23, 24

I have said it once and imagine that it will be said a thousand times more: There is nothing that the presence of Jesus will not cure. I can prove it! Once a brother told me he was divorcing his wife and did not want to talk to me about it for fear I would talk him out of it. I stated that I did not want to talk him out of it; I only wanted him to spend some extra time with Jesus to prepare himself for all the turmoil that comes with divorce. He agreed to spend the weekend seeking the Lord for strength to go through with the divorce, but at the end of the weekend he reconciled with his wife. I knew, of course, that once he was with Jesus the seemingly insurmountable problems of the marriage would fade away. Every believer has known God's presence, not in emotion or intellect, but rather in the calm peace that He gives that makes us know (really know) that we are more than conquerors! Why do we leave that peace, His presence?

I imagine it this way. We are standing on the mountain with Him, and all is well. Then an event knocks us down a little, then a person sets us back a little more, then a sin, then a behavior, then finances, then the children, and then hopelessness. When the slide from the top finally ceases, we find ourselves lying on our backs in a pit with the beloved Savior no longer in sight. In fact, all we can see are the obstacles that will have to be overcome to return to the top. It would be too much effort to overcome sin, a failed marriage, loneliness, financial problems, or feelings of hopelessness. "I am a failure." "I am too weak." So we lie there.

Here is the secret! We can roll over on our stomachs, crawl only about five feet, and there hidden in the bushes will be an escalator! We need only crawl to it and lie there; it will take us all the way back to the top of the mountain, all the way back to His presence. It takes no effort of our own, nor must we overcome anything, for the escalator is powered by the blood of Jesus, and He always willingly takes us back to the top.

DAY 265
The Flesh Is Fixed In Stone! It Can Be Added To But Not Subtracted From

And those who are in the flesh cannot please God.
— ROMANS 8:8

To me, acknowledging the flesh is a cornerstone in understanding how the Christian life is lived in a practical way. The old man, the Adam life, the old nature is dead. Something was crucified with Christ, and that "something" is the old man, or the Adam life, or the old nature. A Christian does not have two natures; that teaching merely reflects a type of Christian "Buddhism." Dual-nature teaching is nothing more than the teaching of yin and yang. There is no battle between good and evil, which come from the same tree. If you know that which is good, you will know evil. Christ's life in me (good) is not battling the old nature (bad). The old nature has no power; it is dead. It does cause frustration as we trust in or try to improve something that is dead, but be assured it is dead. Victory does not come from our helping the Jesus inside us win over the old nature. If this were true, then when we introduce someone to the option of Christ's coming in them by faith, we are introducing them to a nightmarish lifetime of struggle, something the Bible does not teach. A believer's old nature, Adam life, old man is dead, and he has only one life within, the life of Christ. So how does that explain the struggle? As Scripture reveals, we do have flesh. Man comprises spirit, soul, and body. When the spirit is disconnected from the body and soul (mind, will, emotions), whether through the death Adam introduced (in an unbeliever) or by the choice of a believer, that person (believer or unbeliever) will live in the flesh. Flesh, then, is being under the direction or influence of something other than the Holy Spirit from God. An animal has a mind, will, emotions, a body, and a world environment; his life's expression is determined by how he moves in those without any influence from the spirit. Hence man, without the control of the spirit (an unbeliever dead in the spirit or a believer blocking the spirit), is called carnal or animal. Flesh is unique in every animal and in every individual. By nature we are born cut off from God. Through nurture the flesh is shaped into something unique. This is accomplished by the events that come to mind, will, emotions, and body through both the inner circumstances (a mind, will, and emotions not controlled) and outer circumstances (a world and the body, mind, will, and emotions of others out of control). Once the flesh is shaped, it is fixed in concrete, and this is the most important point. Once developed, the flesh will not change.

The flesh can, however, receive additions. An example might be a boy who looks to his father for security, and the father abandons the boy. The boy's flesh is now developed into something insecure. Then one day the boy receives a new life that replaces the old nature, the Adam life, or the old life; he receives the life of Jesus and is attached to the Vine. Christ's life is secure, and the boy recognizes a security that is in Him, Christ's security. It is a mistake to think that this newfound security is the boy's; it is Christ's security flowing in him, and he is a partaker. However, his insecure flesh has not changed. Any moment, as a branch on the Vine, the boy can simply, in a prayer of recognition, say, "Jesus, Your security is welcome here. Thank You that I can partake of it." If he will do this, he need never experience the insecurity of his flesh. However, if the boy takes his eyes off of Jesus, stops abiding in the moment, and blocks the Holy Spirit of Jesus by choice, he will discover that the flesh, the developing of his being when he did not have Jesus, has not changed one bit. He will feel insecure, because the flesh is flesh. At this point, he can even add to his flesh by letting the chaos that is without and within rule over him. Many, after accepting Christ and walking moment by moment with Him, have, through choice, closed the door to Him and added to their flesh. Twenty years ago I never talked to a Christian who was struggling with Internet pornography.

Now it is common. It is a new addition, but the root is the same; the flesh was blocking the Spirit and looking to something else to feed the mind, emotions, and body. The remedy is easy. "Put your eyes back on Jesus." The life of the Vine that is free from pornography will flow into the branch, and the believer will experience a freedom that is not his but is now his. However, close the door to the Vine (it closes when pride says, "I can"; it opens in humility by saying, "I cannot"), and the Christian will discover that not only is the flesh feeling insecure, but it is also craving pornography.

The flesh can be added to but never subtracted from. This is so important that I cannot emphasize it enough. It is deception to believe that the flesh will change. The enemy uses this deception in many ways. First, he has believers following one program after the other to change the flesh, when they could simply abide. Second, the enemy uses carnal believers with strong flesh to make comparisons between themselves and others and put the sincere believers' minds on the flesh. I call those who constantly tell what is good and what is bad and who make comparisons "Christian Buddhists." They make people worse. Always. Third, the enemy has the believers trying to undo what they see as bad flesh by doing good. This is an incredible deception because of the insidious nature of the flesh. If someone people-pleases all day long, he will hate people at night. If a person jams his head with positive thoughts all day, he will be overwhelmed with negative thoughts at night. An individual who controls his appetite all day will gorge at night. Good feeds evil. I had a white horse; I also had a black horse that never wanted to be ridden and stayed far from the gate; the white one liked me and always came close to the gate. However, whenever I opened the gate for the white horse, the black one would race like mad, seizing the opportunity to escape past the white horse and me. The black horse used the white one. But the point is that if a person lets his "good" flesh out for a romp, bad flesh will come out, as well. Walking in the flesh is never the answer. Fourth, the enemy tells us that as Christians there is no room for failure, but the truth is that we must accept that our flesh never changes. In becoming Christians, our flesh never did improve. It can be a depressing revelation (for the self-righteous) or the most freeing thing in the world if we will abide, if Jesus is our focus. The most famous Christian ever written about had ugly flesh until the day he died. If it were not so, how could the Apostle Paul say with such conviction, "In my flesh dwells nothing good"? That is something he would have said until the day he died. In some ways I would like to ban books about the "great" Christians that subtly draw comparisons between them and us on the grounds of their strong, well adjusted, demanding, and risk-taking flesh. That is just wrong. There are no great men of God; there are weak men with a big God. Remember, when we are listening or looking to a Christian and being ministered to, it is Jesus that we are seeing. That person, when not abiding, is not any better than a drunk or the worst person we know. He has not brought himself to a place of improvement through years of "Christian" discipline.

Now, this revelation is one of the most beautiful that I have ever had. It is the awareness of weakness that keeps me near, keeps me handcuffed moment by moment to Jesus. Some would complain and call it a thorn in the flesh, but if the awareness that apart from Him I can do nothing keeps me near to perfect love and participation in perfect victory, why complain? Do not get discouraged if you find yourself exactly as you were, or worse than you were, before becoming a believer. It is the flesh, and it has not changed; it is not going to change. God gave it to you so you would be miserable without Him in the moment.

He knew you had flesh, and He is not fighting it but using it. Give yourself and those around you some grace. Do not be so shocked when the pastor is seen cursing, the evangelist is angry, the Christian co-worker got drunk, or a friend was caught viewing Internet pornography. It is the flesh, and because the old man is dead, they, just like you, can choose to move back into the abiding relationship of the Vine. Do it, and in that moment, His victory is yours. But remember, self will be subdued with your flesh. It is God's stronghold to keep you near.

A brother asked me an honest, heartfelt question: "Michael, if you fell, how would it affect all those who pray for you?" Immediately I responded, "It would not affect them, except that they would be concerned for me. Brother, if you wanted to walk away from Christ, my behavior would not keep you near Him or drive you away from Him. You have already been tested, and if you were going to leave Christ, you would have gone by now. There are cynical Christians, Christians who press on, and Christians in carnality. After the fall of any pastor or evangelist, the cynical remain so, those wanting to move on keep moving on, and carnal believers continue in carnality." I went on to explain that my motive for serving God could not be to prevent others from stumbling. I serve God for His fellowship, not for ulterior motives.

DAY 266
The Flesh Of Man, Nothing To Boast About!

Immediately the word concerning Nebuchadnezzar was fulfilled; and he was driven away from mankind and began eating grass like cattle, and his body was drenched with the dew of heaven until his hair had grown like eagles' feathers and his nails like birds' claws.

— DANIEL 4:33

Man is flesh, flesh is animal, so what do you expect from yourself when you are in the flesh? What do you believe that God expects out of you? Do you really think that the depths to which you have sunk have surprised Him? He knows you! The problem is that you do not know yourself, and until you do know yourself, you will trust in, cling to, and rely on yourself. Let God lift His hand even for a moment, let Him subdue the Holy Spirit within, and you will see what, without Him, you really are.

It is amazing the things in which we boast. In an attempt to be like God we are constantly looking for that one thing that makes us a standout. Intellect is one of the most comical. There really is not much of a spread between the IQ of the learning disabled and a "genius," but so much is made of it. Then there is wealth; around the world the man with money is about as close to being considered a god as one can come. We are fed the positives about mankind by manipulators to make us believe we are something other than flesh. Then there is great shock at what man can inhumanely do to others.

"The flesh is hostile to God." This is an absolute. In the grace of God He may, as I mentioned, lift His hand and allow you this revelation. Being shocked at what you become is a revelation of just how blind you were to your true condition without Him. So many say to me, "I cannot believe I did that!" I can believe that they did whatever, and I know they are capable of doing far worse. Once we see what we are, we can see what He is and then come to our senses as we turn to, trust in, cling to, and rely on Him.

"But at the end of that period, I, Nebuchadnezzar, raised my eyes toward heaven and my reason returned to me, and I blessed the Most High and praised and honored Him who lives forever;
For His dominion is an everlasting dominion,
And His kingdom endures from generation to generation.
All the inhabitants of the earth are accounted as nothing,
But He does according to His will in the host of heaven
And among the inhabitants of earth;
And no one can ward off His hand
Or say to Him, 'What have You done?'
"At that time my reason returned to me. And my majesty and splendor were restored to me for the glory of my kingdom, and my counselors and my nobles began seeking me out; so I was reestablished in my sovereignty, and surpassing greatness was added to me. Now I, Nebuchadnezzar, praise, exalt and honor the King of heaven, for all His works are true and His ways just, and He is able to humble those who walk in pride." – Daniel 4:34-37

DAY 267
The Flesh, The Great Equalizer

. . . and those who are in the flesh cannot please God.
— ROMANS 8:8

I used to hate my flesh; I could only see it as the enemy. If only I did not have it. I was looking forward to the day when I could slough it off, being free at last. Much has changed. I no longer hate my flesh; I accept the need for it and the wisdom of God in putting me in the flesh, for it keeps me near to Him. For that reason alone I would be grateful for it. If I move but a bit from Him, my flesh returns, I get miserable, and I go running back. Who could really hate such a thing? The flesh is also the great equalizer. A "great" man can be preaching, move into the flesh, and instantly he is no better than the bum he may be looking down on. I have watched a "great man" in a restaurant when the meal is not as he ordered it. There is an explosion and unkind words. Instantly he must reckon with his roots; he, too, is flesh. There are no "great men," but little men with a great God. See how the flesh equalizes, keeps us humble, and therefore, keeps us safe?

DAY 268
The Forgotten Man!

Now Jabez called on the God of Israel, saying, "Oh that Thou wouldst bless me indeed, and enlarge my border, and that Thy hand might be with me, and that Thou wouldst keep {me} from harm, that {it} may not pain me!" And God granted him what he requested.

— I CHRONICLES 4:10

One fellow in the Bible prayed, his request was granted, and we never hear from Jabez again! Why? This is an awesome example of choice. Every creature other than man lives under compulsion. The caterpillar must become a butterfly; the tadpole must become a frog. Man can choose what he will become. He can choose earthly comfort or he can choose maturity. Jabez chose comfort. His choice is in stark contrast to the choices made by men we continually read about in the Bible. Listen to Solomon's choice (II Chronicles 1:10), "Give me now wisdom and knowledge, that I may go out and come in before this people; for who can rule this great people of Thine?" The result followed in verses 11 and 12, "And God said to Solomon, 'Because you had this in mind, and did not ask for riches, wealth, or honor, or the life of those who hate you, nor have you even asked for long life, but you have asked for yourself wisdom and knowledge, that you may rule My people, over whom I have made you king, wisdom and knowledge have been granted to you. And I will give you riches and wealth and honor, such as none of the kings who were before you has possessed, nor those who will come after you.'" What would you be, a Jabez or a Solomon? Both were God-worshippers, both lived upright lives, but they made different choices. Look to Jesus, the Author and Perfecter of our faith, who never sought an earthly kingdom, freedom from pain, or to be delivered from trouble. Because of this, His kingdom will endure forever, by His stripes we are healed, and Life (capital L) came out of death. Again, what do we want? The frightening thing is that we can have what we want.

DAY 269
The Gift Of Trials

In this you greatly rejoice, even though now for a little while, if necessary, you have been distressed by various trials, so that the proof of your faith, being more precious than gold which is perishable, even though tested by fire, may be found to result in praise and glory and honor at the revelation of Jesus Christ.

— I PETER 1:6 & 7

In a need-related Gospel there can seem to be the promise that if we come to Christ, our whole life will become so wonderful; we will have a perfect marriage, a better job, and a new-model car. Also, faith, like some magic formula, will zap away all of our problems, trials, and difficulties. If people come to Christ expecting those emphases to accompany the Gospel, as soon as the anticipations do not materialize and persecution and trouble come, young faith has no roots and withers away. Sometimes people in this instant age get locked into the "Immediate Success

Syndrome" and expect faith to propel them to some type of utopia wherein Christians are immune from the pressure, problems, and hardships of life that are common to all. Some proponents of this style of "faith" teaching would instruct Paul to wash his mouth out because he gives such graphic detail of what life was like for him. In the paraphrased version of II Corinthians, Chapters 11 & 12, read what he says:

> "I have been jailed more often than anyone
> Beaten up more times than I can count
> Flogged five times with the Jews' thirty-nine lashes
> Beaten by Roman rods
> Pummeled by rocks
> Shipwrecked three times
> Endangered in the city, the country
> Betrayed by those who were my friends
> I went without, hungry and cold

"Then he receives wonderful revelation from God like no other, saying he was given a gift of handicap to keep from getting a big head. Following all of these happenings in his life, he goes on to say that Satan did his best to get him down, but what the enemy did, in fact, was to push him to his knees, further into Christ. He revealed that at first he did not recognize it as a gift and asked God three times to get rid of it, but God said, 'My grace is all you need; My strength comes into its own in your weakness.' Once Paul heard that, he was glad for what happened, quit focusing on the handicap, and began appreciating the gift. It was a case of Christ's strength moving in on Paul's weakness; the weaker Paul became, the stronger became Christ."

Can any of us honestly say that we would call our trials, problems, or circumstances "gifts" that we appreciate? Perhaps it has been easier to see the hand of God in them in retrospect, but like Paul, we know that they sure did not seem like gifts at the time. We must learn that one "Hallelujah" before and during the event is better than ten afterwards. Life is not what we make it, as we often hear said, because if it were, we would make it a whole lot different, especially when it comes to putting comfort in our center. Life comes to us without our acting or even asking; it just meets us every morning when we awaken. Life's storms come, and no one is exempt or necessarily to blame, but when they do, we should interpret the trials in God's light and cause them to serve us as they did Paul. We try to get rid of what we see as negatives in our life; we complain, we whine, and we blame others, none of which, of course, change a thing. Perhaps we do what Paul did and pray for God to remove them, or we go out in a special prayer line to try to find a magic formula to be free.

Paul said Satan tried to get him down but only succeeded in getting him on his knees. Even those things that Satan has designed for our destruction will, in the hand of God, work together for good. We all have these trials; as John says, they are common to the brotherhood all over the world. We have difficulties, disappointments, friends who betray us, and all the other difficulties associated with life, but once we have the revelation of God's methods, we quit focusing on the problem or handicap and begin appreciating the gift. The wrapping on the gift may seem very unattractive and unacceptable, but as it squeezes us, we find the treasure of the life of Christ within. If we can see that the negatives in life are actually gifts, then we can embrace and appreciate them with the knowledge of God's grace; that is, the desire and power God gives to help us respond to every life situation according to His will. It is not what happens to us in life that matters, but what we do with what happens. Rather than asking God to change our circumstances; we can recognize that He sent those circumstances to change us. Real ministry is birthed out of our negatives. David said, "I was enlarged in my distress." Remember, our weakness is not our problem but our qualification; the weaker we get, the stronger He becomes. Like Paul, we must see the revelation that weakness is a gift and then not only stop focusing on the weakness but appreciate it and allow it to turn us to Christ. So instead of asking God to help us with our problems, our problems are helping us with God. They can actually turn us around 180 degrees to where Jesus once again becomes our focus.

DAY 270
The God of the Whole Earth

Do we not all have one Father? Has not one God created us? Why do we deal treacherously, each against his brother, so as to profane the covenant of our fathers?

— MALACHI 2:10

It is interesting that in other religions we are told about THEIR god. Many are threatened with death if they do not accept THEIR god. I remember seeing the "great" god Kali;

he is a rock with a robe on him, covered with the blood of goats. I had never heard of THEIR god. I was whisked away to a back room to have him explained to me and to be given the opportunity to follow him. If we do not follow some of THEIR gods, we can be threatened with death. On a layover in Mecca I was not allowed to leave the plane for fear that I might touch the ground and defile the place. THEIR god did not want me. Herein lies the difference with the Christian message. We are not going to others to talk to them about OUR god; we are talking about the only true and living God; how can there be another? "Or is God the God of Jews only? Is He not the God of Gentiles also? Yes, of Gentiles also" (Romans 3:29). We are not to be telling them of another God; we are telling them that they have our God. Our God is their God and Creator whether they believe it or not. They cannot choose to make Him God, as in other religions. He is God. They can acknowledge it, but the acknowledgment will not make it so. They are not our enemies; they just need to be brought back into the family. For many hundreds of years they have opted out, led by the men of pride. The Man of humility would bring them back. There is only one God.

DAY 271
The Green Lady

And {let} the rich man {glory} in his humiliation, because like flowering grass he will pass away.

— JAMES 1:10

I was talking to a friend about the United States. He, like many others, is frustrated with the lack of common sense, lack of righteousness, and prevalence of greed that exists at so many levels of government. I reminded him that in our lives there have been many people we have loved. They have now passed away, and yet we remember them with fondness. Because they are deceased there is no need talking about them as though they are alive. The America that he and his father before him remember is no more; it has ceased to exist; it is over. She is just as dead as the green Statue of Liberty. What we see today is only a shadow of what it once was. We can speak of what it was when alive with great fondness. Reading the stories of Washington and Lincoln, the forming of the Constitution, and the many selfless acts of countless people who helped develop a country based in Christianity, one cannot help but be inspired. However, there is no need to be bitter about the death, and we are living in exciting times! Jesus' return is near, and nowhere in the Bible does it say that in the end times one country will stand with Jesus. All of that must end as anti-Christ men fill their cups with their own judgment. Deterioration in society does not create evil men and wicked hearts; it simply reveals them. Those who hate believers are coming to the surface. We will know them, and we must learn not to entrust ourselves to them. "If the world hates you, you know that it has hated Me before it hated you" (John 15:18). Do not be discouraged; His coming is near, and a kingdom far greater than the one formed with the Constitution will be ours forever!

DAY 272
The History of Satan

But when He, the Spirit of truth, comes, He will guide you into all the truth; for He will not speak on His own initiative, but whatever He hears, He will speak; and He will disclose to you what is to come.

— JOHN 16:13

Traveling as a missionary to remote places I hear explanations of Scripture from those that many in the West would call ignorant people. I do not agree with that assessment, since the disciples themselves were uneducated men except for the education they received personally by Jesus. There are still men like that all over the world. Their views are often "outside the box" of Western Christian thinking; however, I like the different perspectives. One fellow detailed the existence of demons; his explanation went something like this: God had created the angels, and some, because of their love for God's glory, were constantly in His presence. The names of two of those angels were Michael and Lucifer. Lucifer began to lust for the throne of God; seeing this wickedness in Lucifer's heart, God demoted him. At that Lucifer decided to build his own kingdom in heaven and set about recruiting other like-minded angels. A great battle arose and Lucifer (now the devil and Satan) and his followers were cast out of heaven. He then took his hoard to earth to set up his kingdom there. However, there was a problem. Earth is physical and therefore cannot be touched by a spiritual being. All the beauty of the earth is like a hologram. He reaches out to touch it and his hand passes completely through it. Spiritual Heaven could be touched by a spiritual being but physical earth cannot be. Man was created to be a spirit and physical. Man can both enjoy the things of the spirit and the beauty of the physical earth around him. Satan, being spirit, came to a logical conclusion. As a spirit he would inhabit the flesh of man, thus allowing himself the luxury of enjoying the physical earth and continuing his mission of setting up a kingdom. Then again, there were two more problems. First, the human recipient had to be willing, and with a spirit alive to God, no man would be willing. Therefore, Satan set out to deceive Adam and Eve. His temptation reveals his own heart's desire, "Wouldn't you like to be like God?" Adam and Eve gave in, became dead to God in the spirit, thus opening the way for demon possession. The second problem is equally significant: The flesh of man was created for a human spirit that is breathed from God to dwell in it. When a demon spirit enters, the body becomes sick, insane, unpredictable, and distorted; Christ is holding the body together, and to put something anti-Christ in it makes it come apart. Also, demons are not comfortable in human flesh; it is confining and, they believe, beneath them. If they do destroy a person, their attitude is "So what? At least Christ cannot come and dwell here now." They can also enter animal flesh, which to them is repulsive but better than nothing. Imagine what once was an angel being demoted to living in pig flesh. Man is made in the image of God, so indwelling him makes the demons feel somewhat victorious. Remember, they wanted God's place in heaven. Therefore, it appears that dwelling in human flesh is the only way for the physical world to stop being little more than a vague haze and for the demon to have what little satisfaction is possible away from the presence of God in heaven. It is also the only way for Satan to have the appearance of a kingdom. He is so full of pride that an unseen kingdom simply does not suit him. He wants masses of men under his control in order that his kingdom will be visible. Hitler relayed the visible kingdom of Satan. The flesh is made for a human spirit, so eventually demon-possessed men fall to pieces and their inhabitants move on, so the recruitment—also called oppression—continues, when a demon whispers doubt after doubt about the Love of God into a man's heart with the hopes of the man's rejecting God and becoming a willing recipient. What happened next was not expected: God became a man! He had conquered Satan in heaven, so then He moved to earth in a man's body to do the same thing. Jesus, the conqueror, now offers His Spirit to all who are willing. God became a man through birth and not possession; therefore, the human flesh is perfectly comfortable with His Holy Spirit; it fits. Once Christ dwells in a man, that man no longer has recruitment potential for the enemy. In every person that believes in Jesus, the demons are expelled and the kingdom of darkness shrinks. Satan does have one other option: retreat to another spiritual place, hell, where a spiritual being is able to touch spiritual things. The problem is that everything spiritual in hell is dead, black, painful, and miserable, plus there is a constant devouring taking place. Also, Jesus has plundered the place, killing the allies of death and sin, taking captivity captive, and even breaking open the gates of hell to take whoever believed in Him. Jesus had extended the Kingdom of God from heaven to earth and even encroached a bit on hell! In his angry, prideful mind

Satan has little choice but to continue moving about the earth. Satan is now more anger-driven than pride-driven. Like the child who destroys every toy when he does not get his own way, Satan in his blind anger destroys everything around him, with the one major difference that he never feels regret. God permits his existence for the purpose of using him in the process of perfecting the saints. The day will come when Jesus returns; the devil and his followers will have brought full judgment on themselves and will be cast into eternal darkness.

I like the explanation and could not find any Scripture to go against it. What struck me was the cycle presented of demons' wanting to be God, attempting to build a kingdom, and then being forgotten. Is that not the way of prideful man?

DAY 273
The Holy Spirit

When the Helper comes, whom I will send to you from the Father, {that is} the Spirit of truth, who proceeds from the Father, He will bear witness of Me.

— JOHN 15:26

What is the Holy Spirit? It is the Spirit that represents God, who is holy. There are many different types of salesmen in the world, each representing something different. Car salesmen are different from appliance salesmen, because they are representatives for two different products. In the same way, there are many spirits in the world, all representing something different. The Holy Spirit represents Jesus and will not be doing things contrary to what Jesus did. It is unfortunate that so many spirits proclaim a witness to Jesus but actually are like that man who says he is merely doing a survey when he really wants to sell windows. These false spirits are not representing Jesus. There was a Hindu, considered a god, who was just plain weird; he jerked as he talked and walked, and he made no sense. He was god, so he said, but he made god out to be strange. Another Hindu god thirsts for blood. Is this really god? We see many spirits in the Christian world that portray something much different from Jesus but proclaim they are from Jesus. Was Jesus weird, spectacular, entertaining, or exhibiting uncontrolled emotion? Was He educated or consumed with taking up offerings? Did He offer visions, promise wealth, or sing until the miraculous appeared? The Spirit of Jesus will represent Jesus; He will never be something strange and weird.

DAY 274
The Ice Climber

Because the mind set on the flesh is hostile toward God;
for it does not subject itself to the law of God, for it is not

> *even able to do so, and those who*
> *are in the flesh cannot please God.*
> — ROMANS 8:7-8

The flesh is that condition of being under the influence of something other than Jesus. Made from the dust of earth, it is always dragging the soul (mind, will, and emotions) into the things of the earth, wanting a kingdom in the dust from which it came. The flesh, when exercising power over the soul, silences the Spirit of Christ within. Flesh is an amazing thing and brings us face to face with the fact that apart from Him, there is little that separates us from animals.

I like to think of the flesh as an ice climber. Where I live there is a sport made of climbing up frozen waterfalls. This is dodgy business, and the climber must be careful to find a place for the pick and spiked shoe. A tough spot is at the top, where the water last flowed. At this point the climber must actually go up at a grade that slopes away from the surface. Sometimes I pray, "Jesus, make me like that ice that is at an angle and so difficult to cling to. The flesh is looking everywhere for a foothold." The flesh will have me thinking of being offended or of those I have offended, of self-righteous acts and unrighteous acts, and of guilt or justification. Positive or negative, it does not matter to the flesh, just so long as it stays in control. It insidiously uses anything to gain ground, and I am still amazed at what will keep the flesh ascending. However, it has trained me and worked for me, for now as I feel its climb to control, I know that I have moved away from the Lord. I move back, let Him tilt me a little in His arms, and the flesh goes tumbling.

DAY 275
The Invisible King

Jesus said to him, "Because you have seen Me, have you believed? Blessed {are} they who did not see, and {yet} believed."

— JOHN 20:29

I really love the fact that Jesus is invisible to us! I want Him to remain invisible. Of course, without faith, it is impossible to please Him. We know that. But for me, there is more. I love the fact that He is invisible. Often I enter a country wherein Christianity is illegal, especially in the Muslim countries. However, because He is invisible, I enter the country with His hand on my shoulder and no one notices. I bring with me the whole Kingdom and its King. If He were visible, it would not be allowed; because He cannot be seen, no one says a word. We enter, and with us comes all that is true about Him. Beautiful. Thank You, Jesus, that You are invisible. I also like the invisible currency of His kingdom. Often I have taken a few dollars to a place and given them to a Christian cloth-maker. The cloth is given to a Christian seamstress, and the clothes given to children at a Christian school. Everyone reaps the benefit, and every penny is multiplied. Amazing.

DAY 276
The Joy of Following

Fixing our eyes on Jesus, the author and perfecter of faith,
who for the joy set before Him endured the cross, despising
the shame, and has sat down at the right hand
of the throne of God.

— HEBREWS 12:2

Buddhism, with its yin and yang, comes from the tree of the knowledge of good and evil, teaching that no matter how much good is done, evil is always making its appeal at a person's heels. It also teaches that in choosing the life of good, one would be forgoing the pleasures that come from evil. This causes a tension within the follower. Evil offers so much in the temporal, the Buddhist admits to that. However, the good person must deny himself of these temporary pleasures. The Buddhist would have us believe that he has given up his will. However, it is his will to do only what he perceives as good. The will of a Buddhist is quite alive and is the center of his life. He is not living in faith but living in what he perceives will make him the happiest; the reason that doing good looks better than succumbing to evil is simply because evil is not perceived as making him as happy in the end. A good person is the positive piece of film that was created by the negative, the evil person. Both have so much in common. Both want to do what will make them the happiest. Both want the freedom to choose what will work the best for them. Both want their own will. Both are creating an image. Both want to be equal to God. Both want to create in their image. Both want to persecute those who will not agree with them. I bring this up because this cursed tree and its teaching, reasoning, and thinking is thrust upon the believer from almost every quarter from the time that he first accepts Christ.

Our will is not the issue. Our concept of good and evil is not the issue. Our highest goal is not image, equality, being right, comfort, or discomfort. His will is the issue and is so much higher than anything that comes from the tree of good and evil. "Thy will be done" is our prayer. In losing our will, our determination of what is good or bad for us, we have not given up anything. In following Him we are not losing something, denying ourselves something, or missing out on what the world has to offer. Our will for His will is one of the greatest favorable exchanges that there is. Our will, good or bad, is temporal; it is of the earth. It has no power. His will is of heaven and has an eternal power.

I question that we know what it is to possess the will of God when we speak in terms of what has been lost to follow Him. What is lost is often spoken of with a fondness. "I had and could still have money, women, houses, respect, and security. I gave it all up for Jesus." Was it something that was liked but that had to be renounced for Jesus' sake in order for the person to be a Christian? Or was it something that Jesus, through grace, revelation, love, and mercy, allowed the individual at last to throw off? "Oh, I cannot go to that place, move to another place, take a different job. You see, I have given up my will to do only what is His will." When I hear people say that it sounds so much like they really would like to move and take a different job, but they have chosen something higher than the rest of us, having decided to forgo selfish indulgences to simply walk with Jesus. As long as following His will is communicated as a sacrifice, we have not yet known what His will is. Doing His will is not denying oneself the things he would really like to do. His will is not competing with the world. His will is not a good force fighting a bad force. Christians are deceived into believing that by doing His will, they are missing out on some of life's pleasures, such as the respect of men (good) or the indulgence of the flesh (evil). The will of God is not the opposite of the will of man, not good fighting evil. God's will is the revelation of the heart and mind of God; it is very personal to Him. To be allowed into His will, to do His will, is something to which nothing on the earth can be compared. The will of God is not something that we enter into because of the fear of punishment or the promise of reward. Just being in the will of God is reward enough, bringing joy and filling us.

I remember traveling on the back roads of India in the famous Indian Ambassador (an Indian-built car that's style has not changed since the early 1940's). My Indian teacher unexpectedly pulled me close to his side and began to whisper, telling me his family's most intimate details and concerns. I paused to take it all in. My teacher was telling me, the student! This is not done in India. I was being invited into the most secret place of his heart. I knew the significance of the moment was that I was being included as the culmination of years of travel and fellowship. Though a weak analogy, it illustrates the privilege of being allowed into someone's heart. To know the will of God is to be privy to His heart and participate in it, a very special privilege. Jesus was not burdened by the will of God but genuinely delighted in it; it was His food. Being included in God is not giving up anything. It always brings joy, even when the will of God is a cross.

The prayer "Thy will be done" does not reflect thinking in terms of giving up my will to do His will. My will is rubbish; I have learned that I do not want it in any way, shape or form. I want to be in His will, in His heart, to do His will, to let His will be done. Think of it! To know that He can put me down to bring me up, take me out to put me in, let me come apart to remake me, and all of this is His perfect working. His will is nothing that I ever thought it to be. My weakness is a magnet for His strength, His perfection loving my imperfection.

To think He invites us to participate with Him in His will! We gladly participate. In His will nothing is going wrong, but it all is working toward the revelation of His glory. "Father, let Your will be done in my life."

DAY 277
The Kingdom of God

But you are a chosen race, a royal priesthood, a holy nation, a people for God's own possession, so that you may proclaim the excellencies of Him who has called you out of darkness into His marvelous light.

— I PETER 2:9

One of the most difficult things to explain is the Abiding Life Ministries International organization. I think I know why. While most are attempting to build an organization, we are busy reminding His people to recognize the organization that already exists. The church is not built by human endeavor but is something that is recognized. I hear people say, "We are building the Kingdom." That is not true; actually, they are tearing down the real Kingdom of God by their unbelief in its existence, as shown through their attempts to build it. There already is an organization, and our job at ALMI is to persuade people of the fact that they already belong to it. The organization is called the Vine and they are branches, not branches attached to branches but branches attached to the Vine, I do not want people to join me; I want them to join Christ. Not only is it a great blessing to every branch to have the revelation of being in the Vine, it is an equal blessing to me. I do not have to make rules to try to create what the Holy Spirit will do naturally in His attached branches; I will leave that for the kingdom builders who wield their authority and try to do just that.

DAY 278
The Life Of a Demon

and he had his dwelling among the tombs. And no one was able to bind him anymore, even with a chain; because

he had often been bound with shackles and chains, and the
chains had been torn apart by him, and the shackles broken
in pieces, and no one was strong enough to subdue him.
And constantly night and day, among the tombs and in the
mountains, he was crying out and
gashing himself with stones.

— MARK 5:3-5

Have you ever wondered what the day-to-day life of a demon is like? When we read the story of the demoniac in Mark 5, we most likely think of the demons recognizing Jesus, the miraculous deliverance, or the hardhearted people who would rather unlawfully have pigs than Jesus. However, there is something else to be gleaned from the story, and that is insight into the life of demons. They were many and therefore "strong," yet they confined the man to living in tombs, among the dead, as though they do not desire a dwelling place among the living. Their life cannot be termed as glamorous. Also, we learn that day and night they cry and gash their host. Could it be that the torment they displayed toward the man reflected their own miserable state? I think they are somewhat like fish out of water; they were made for heaven but chose a pit that they hate, and yet that is all they are now suited for. Therefore, they surface into an environment (earth) that is held together by Jesus. That makes the whole world hostile to them. Earth is not comfortable for demons. This is why we find them among the rocks with less of creation, less of Jesus to witness to them. Why would they choose to be here at all? Suffering on earth with their sworn enemy, Jesus, is better than being with their leader. If Jesus cast them out, they would have to return to Satan. They beg not to return, and herein lies insight into life with their master. It would be better to be in pigs than return home, the exact opposite sentiment of that seen in the Prodigal Son. This confirms what I suspect of Satan: He regards all things with indifference, even his "companions." Statistically speaking, a majority of children who abuse animals will grow up and abuse people. When Satan treats man as he does, how well do you think those in his own household fare? All the evil that he has gotten men to do he does even to those of his own house. He has no glory and therefore extracts anything available from those around him. He is a parasite that will suck what little is left out of a dead thing. No wonder even a demon would beg not to be sent back to such a one, when a better outcome is over the cliff in a pig! Is it not hard to believe that people actually want to follow Satan? It could only be pride; after all, pride is what took Satan and his hoard out of heaven to begin with. Often I have had someone say something along this line to me: "I do not fear hell. I will deal with it when I get there." Well, amen, no one has to wait for hell to get a taste of it when he can go outside, douse himself with gasoline, set himself on fire, and beat his head against a rock while he is burning. That will give anyone a little picture of what it is like.

DAY 279
The Life Of Grace Is a Stricter Life, a Higher Life

Therefore do not be ashamed of the testimony of our Lord or of me His prisoner, but join with me in suffering for the gospel according to the power of God, who has saved us and called us with a holy calling, not according to our works, but according to His own purpose and grace which was granted us in Christ Jesus from all eternity.

— II TIMOTHY 1:8-10

It is not possible to minister to those who cannot hear, such as legalists who know nothing of grace. For example, a legalist can be in the middle of the overt sin of an affair and still preach the next Sunday on purity. Why? How? It is simple! Legalism feeds the flesh. Sin and legalism are one and the same. There is no pressure of contrast between legalism and sin in a person's being. Unrighteousness and self-righteousness both satisfy the flesh.

However, a grace man cannot go on sinning, for the grace of God will rip him in two. When preaching grace, God will always come for that man's words in order to make him really understand grace and realize he does not have an excuse. Factor in the work of the cross! He has been crucified and is dead to sin. How, then, can he continue to sin? If he does, with this understanding, he will come apart. The standard is so much higher in grace. It is the legalist who can actually practice sin without conviction. Embrace the message of grace, practice sin, and be ripped in two!

DAY 280
The Lord Rebuke You!

*But Michael the archangel, when he disputed with the
devil and argued about the body of Moses, did not dare
pronounce against him a railing judgment, but said, "The
Lord rebuke you."*

— JUDE 9

In my life, I have had the Lord rebuke me. I will never
forget it, nor do I ever want it to happen again. Nahum
1:6, "Who can stand before His indignation? Who can
endure the burning of His anger? His wrath is poured
out like fire, and the rocks are broken up by Him." I was
rebuked for slander, judgment, and image building. After
the rebuke, if He had not picked me up, set me on my feet,
and whispered, "I love you," I would not have ever gotten
up again. I would have quit and hidden. That would have
been it for me. Others would never have heard from me
again. Hebrews 10:31, "It is a terrifying thing to fall into
the hands of the living God." I have been there, but I share
this to make a greater point. The worst possible thing that
we can do to Satan is to say to him, "The Lord rebuke
you!" It wipes him out, sends him away, reminds him of
the fact he has no glory, and it frees us from oppression.
I am a living witness to what can happen under a rebuke.
However, because of unbelief, many fight Satan instead of
just passing on to him a rebuke of the Lord. There has been
a spiritual warfare movement afoot for years to sidetrack
believers into worshipping Satan, in the sense of giving

attention to him. These well-meaning believers give Satan more notice and attribute to him more glory (the ability to act, control, and bring all things to a desired end) than do overt devil worshippers. Many churches have dedicated themselves to being "warrior" churches. Imagine being dedicated to fighting a battle that has already been won! It is unbelief. Satan is already defeated. "Satan, the Lord rebuke you! You have no power!"

DAY 281
The Love Of God!

For while we were still helpless, at the right time Christ died for the ungodly.

— ROMANS 5:6

Two boys in a village began to fight, and one boy killed the other; upon seeing what happened, the villagers began to chase the boy to put him to death. The boy ran to the house of the chief and fell at the doorway, crying out to the chief for his protection. The chief came and, seeing the crowd, asked for an explanation of what was happening. The crowd yelled, "The boy killed another boy in a fight, and we have come to take him and kill him." The chief said, "I cannot allow you to take him, for he has fallen at my doorstep," and at that he lifted up the boy and put him in his house. Then the crowd yelled, "The boy that he killed was your son! Give him to us." The chief's face became despondent. The crowd continued to yell, but the chief went silent until, after a long time, he spoke again, saying, "Then I will adopt him." In wonder the crowd departed.

Do you believe in the love of God? Do you believe He would do the same for you? He has, and no matter what has happened in your life, the love of God is up to something.

DAY 282
The Love of God In Missions

May the Lord direct your hearts into the love of God and into the steadfastness of Christ.
— II THESSALONIANS 3:5

A friend has made an interesting observation, saying he had been listening to several mission reports and support appeals in an attempt to discover what was missing. He could not put his finger on it, he said, but there was something different from when he was a child. As he searched through the statistics and the financial and physical needs of missionaries and missions, the stories of conversion and the hardships, he finally noticed what was different. In none of the reports did he hear that the missionaries were compelled by the love of God or that they were madly in love with the people, and it was vexing to him. I listened and thought to myself how true it is that the task can so easily become more important than the individuals. How easy it is to forget the greatest thing, love! That simple observation has driven me to my knees, not to generate love, but to bask in the presence of Love, for it is an appreciation of His love that drives me to love. The root of missions must be love.

DAY 283
The Most Wonderful Revelation!

Let all who seek Thee rejoice and be glad in Thee; And let those who love Thy salvation say continually, "Let God be magnified."

— PSALM 70:4

In the course of our lives many revelations will come. There are, of course, revelations that those in a variety of ministries would bring to us. For example, some would say that we need the revelation of our flesh, our sin, our failure to be good parents, our attitudes, and our lies. However, there is a revelation greater than these. Have we had the revelation of how much we really care for Jesus, of how much we really love Him? It is the most important revelation. What is the cause of our misery when we are dabbling in the flesh, walking in sin, being offended, pursuing material gain, and having friendship with the world? It is because we love Him! In the deepest part of our being we are in love with Jesus.

Sin, Satan, the world, and the flesh attempt to keep us from this revelation, and though we find no satisfaction in them, they constantly whisper, "More." Once we can admit that we love Him, really love Him, and can go nowhere else and want nothing else, then all those things of the flesh must flee. I want to be clear. We do not lay aside the flesh so we can love Him; we lay it aside because we do love Him. Our misery with the flesh is the proof that we love Him alone, but this takes revelation. He may permit the flesh to take us to the bottom to prove it to us. Once we have had enough, we can shout it: "I love Him! I love nothing else, nothing else will satisfy, and all of life has been proving it to me!" Amen!

DAY 284
The Multi-Faceted God

May it never be! Rather, let God be found true, though every man {be found} a liar, as it is written, THAT THOU MIGHTEST BE JUSTIFIED IN THY WORDS, AND MIGHTEST PREVAIL WHEN THOU ART JUDGED.

— ROMANS 3:4

Matthew 6:26, "Look at the birds of the air, that they do not sow, neither do they reap, nor gather into barns, and {yet} your heavenly Father feeds them. Are you not worth much more than they?"

Yet I have watched birds starve to death in the winter months.

Matthew 6:28, 29, "And why are you anxious about clothing? Observe how the lilies of the field grow; they do not toil nor do they spin; yet I say to you that even Solomon in all his glory did not clothe himself like one of these."

In the interior of Liberia the locals were afraid to return to church, for they did not have clothes. They had lost them in the war.

Proverbs 22:6, "Train up a child in the way he should go, even when he is old he will not depart from it."

Many, many parents have done all that they knew to do, and yet their children departed from the Lord.

Psalm 121:7, "The LORD will protect you from all evil; He will keep your soul."

History is replete with the stories of millions of martyrs that died at the hands of evil men.

I could continue with the illustrations, but I am sure you get the point. Let God be true, but what do the facts say? The simple answer is that you must believe God when bad happens. The emphasis is on belief, and yet believing is exactly what the believer was doing, believing God for food, clothing, protection, and a child that would be blessed. Is the Christian to believe God's words or believe that God causes all things to work together for good? Which is it?

We live in a world of dimensions. I have seen Mount Everest! I have, and I will argue the point; I saw it with my own eyes in Nepal. However, the mountaineer would beg to differ, saying that I only saw one side of Mount Everest, and therefore I did not really see it. To see it, I would have to walk around it, climb it, and possibly look under it. I am, to them, less than a novice. I bumped into former President Ford one day. As I was leaving the restroom he was entering. "I know President Ford! President Ford has met me." Do I? Has he? Is it not interesting that as dimensional creatures we insist on being non-dimensional or one-sided in our views? If someone is employed to paint and it is discovered that he is not a good painter, he is dismissed with the words, "You are worthless!" Is he worthless? Later that same person attends university, becomes a physicist, then a Nobel Prize recipient. Yes, but he could not paint; he was labeled worthless. My point is that Church history is replete with examples of teachers, scholars, and preachers that are non-dimensional when it comes to God. They have never walked around God, so to speak. They only see one side of Him, and if something comes at them from another side, they manipulate it until it fits their single-minded view of Him. Ecclesiastes 11:5, "Just as you do not know the path of the wind and how bones {are formed} in the womb of the pregnant woman, so you do not know the activity of God who makes all things." Some evangelists, teachers, and others only see the provision side of God. They preach Him as the great general store in the sky. Whatever someone may want is his if he has the faith. Their airplanes, diamonds, and wealth prove it. If that is their single-sided view of God—God created man to give to him, and that is all God does—then this single-sided view will eventually drive them into deception, manipulation of Scripture, self-image protection, and shipwreck. Of course they will be presented with Scriptures that are "outside the box" of what they see God as being. If a person sees God non-dimensionally as the Great Physician only, a variety of blame will be heaped on the sick, illness in his own family will have to be spiritualized away, and again more Scripture distorted and twisted.

What glasses do we wear when looking at God? Can we take time to walk around the mountain, climb on top, and mine underneath? If our awareness of God embraces the fact that He is multi-faceted, we will see each Bible passage as part of a giant jigsaw puzzle that reflects God. We will see that all things work together because God is in all things. We will see that only God can do what God does.

I like kit cars. They come in hundreds of pieces in a huge container with three-dimensional diagrams; a one-dimensional diagram would be useless. The job is to use a variety of tools to put together the automobile, using the exact tool for each exact job. It is impossible to find the one tool that will do everything. Oh, people claim to make all-purpose tools! However, at some point the user throws it to the ground in disgust.

The day Jesus received me I was in pieces. No one would have imagined that I was made in His image! Who would think I was a Son of God, holy, righteous, acceptable, and equipped for every good work? He set about to put me together. The tool that He used would be the perfect tool for that day and purpose. It would have been the wrong tool for the next day, but He does everything in order. My multi-dimensional God has such a vast array of tools, every one true and every tool absolute. In His tool chest are sickness and health, wealth and poverty, good and bad, mercy and judgment, love and hate, wounding and healing, broken relationships and mended ones, adornment and nakedness, excluded and included, decreasing and increasing, pruning and reaping, giving and taking, drought and rain, sanity and insanity, rebelliousness and compliance, death and life, and I could go on. If someone does not believe that these are His tools, I can show a Scripture for each one that proves they are. Job is a good example in that God used good and bad to perfect him. Hebrews 1:3, "And He is the radiance of His glory and the exact representation of His nature, and upholds all things by the word of His power." Jesus was never one-sided. He was putting every man back together. See Him use a unique tool on a unique person. He was love but not the one-dimensional love that man has and perceives.

Stop seeing so one-dimensionally! Stop protecting your limited view of God! Start trusting that God is putting you together. To begin your journey out of a flat world, start by taking a walk around Jesus. If a passage does not make sense to you, if it has not been your experience or you do not see how it fits into the whole, do not just stand there! Walk around Jesus and look at Him from a different angle; it all fits perfectly. The passages mentioned at the beginning of the article are for a particular time, to accomplish a particular task in our lives. If a passage applied all the time we would be thwarted and never grow into the revelation of Christ. I am not copping out! Look at your own life! In times of darkness and need you grew up in Christ. Generally Christians define love one way, but for Jesus every act—from cleansing the temple to healing the leper—was one of love. James 1:17 reminds us that "every good thing bestowed and every perfect gift is from above, coming down from the Father of lights, with whom there is no variation, or shifting shadow."

DAY 285
The Opposite of Glory

*The heavens are telling of the glory of God; and their
expanse is declaring the work of His hands.*

— PSALM 19:1

God is glory, and He will not give His glory to another.
It is not right to say, "God, if you complete the plan I have
for my family, the church, and myself, I will give You the
glory." I did not know that He had lost His glory for you
to give it back to Him. The glory is His, and apart from
Him there is no glory.

Glory is God, and He is written into the very fiber of our
makeup and being; we, along with all the earth, proclaim
His glory. The heavens declare His glory, which is in all
things He creates. So what is the opposite of glory? If all
things have His glory in them, then the opposite of glory
would be nothing attempting to be something. Who fits
that description? Satan! He is a nothing attempting to be
something! He is not a created being but a resultant being,
the result of walking away from what he was created to be:
an angel glorifying God. He wants more than anything to
be a something. Glory is revealed in accomplishments, not
destruction, and the enemy has no glory except that which
is given him through those who fear him! Apart from that
he has none of his own. That is why Satan so loves to hear
the believers talk of his power, abilities, intelligence, and
his capacity to strike fear in all those who would oppose
him. God is the glory, and apart from Him there is no

glory. Satan was not the last enemy to be defeated, but the first. Luke 10:18, "And He said to them, 'I was watching Satan fall from heaven like lightning.'" Like fallen man, Satan does not acknowledge the Creator and has become a nothing. God is glory!

DAY 286
The Parallel Universe

And we know that God causes all things to work together for good to those who love God, to those who are called according to {His} purpose.

— ROMANS 8:28

Sometimes I think that God must have a parallel universe, because it is so beyond the comprehension of man to think that in everything taking place He is working, and not only working, but working things for good! Talk about a willpower of steel. He will not stop until all things have worked together for good for those who love Him. We can begin to see the world that way, and no matter what happens ask, "How will this be for good? How can this be for good? Can God do something good with this?" When we see God in all things, all things change.

I see so many little ministries; they are the ministries of the "lesser man" in this great time and have come into being because God is causing all things for good. We praise Him, we thank Him, and we rejoice in our God. "Thank You for a will that will not bend until everything around me is for good!"

DAY 287
The Perfect Day

This is the day which the LORD has made;
let us rejoice and be glad in it.

— PSALM 118:24

A fellow came to see me who was suicidal. He had long exerted his resolve against homosexuality and had recently lost the struggle and stumbled. He is not a homosexual or there would not be the conviction of God after such an act. Still, he felt he was less than a conqueror and was done trying; he was ready to check out; he definitely wanted the most recent failure to be the last. I looked at him and said, "Today, Brother, is the best day of your life. There is no way that today could be better. If you had perfect victory in the past, today would not be better. In fact everything, and I mean everything, that has happened in the past is making this the perfect day. For today God is going to deal with your . . ." I paused. He thought for certain that I was going to say homosexuality. However, homosexuality was merely the cobweb, not the spider. He stopped me to say, "There is no way that you can say today is a perfect day." I replied, "You will not say that in a minute. For what God is going to deal with today is your unbelief and self-righteousness!" It cut him like a knife, for he knew this was the real problem. As we sat talking and sharing, God dealt with the real problem: the man's unbelief and self-righteousness. When finally he left, as he walked out the door he was so happy and had such a lift in his spirit that he turned and said, "This is the best day of my life!" Often we think we know the problem, when it is just the consequence, not the cause.

DAY 288
The Pine Tree

So every good tree bears good fruit, but the bad tree bears bad fruit.
— MATTHEW 7:17

So, my brothers, you also died to the law through the body of Christ, that you might belong to another, to him who was raised from the dead, in order that we might bear fruit to God.
— ROMANS 7:4

In the spring the tips of the needles on a pine tree are nearly blue and are young and tender. Did you know that you could actually eat those tips? They are quite nice. The giant pine is so strong, so majestic; it can withstand the greatest storm. Yet when it is growing, it is tender enough to offer nourishment to man from a source not normally thought of as nutritious. So is the believer: strong in Christ, but in a place of growth very tender. I have seen others, as well as myself, so gentle in times of growth; in these times we offer others the most nourishment, and from a condition wherein we did not think nourishment could come. Did you ever imagine that our loss, our suffering, and our stress could actually feed the family of God? It does!

DAY 289
The Problem Fixer

"For I know the plan that I have for you," declares the Lord God, "plans for welfare and not for calamity to give you a future and a hope."
— JEREMIAH 29:11

What is the plan that God has for us? Many believe that God's plan is a specific area of service, a place to live, or the right job. The aforementioned are merely the vehicles that help complete the plan, but of themselves they are not the plan. His plan is the expression of Christ's life through us as described in chapters five through seven of Matthew. Therefore, it really is not of ultimate importance where we move or what vocation we take up, for God is able to use every event of life to complete His plan. Our only responsibility before moving out in any direction is to say, "If the Lord wills I will go to such and such a place."

How often do we find ourselves struggling, stumped by a problem, and then once the answer is discovered, we have a sense of elation. We are made in the image of God; He, too, enjoys fixing a problem. As our loving Father, He fixes every problem that man creates. The first problem that Adam and Eve created was the most severe: They cut themselves off from God. He fixed the problem in a way that we far lesser beings would never have imagined by becoming a man Himself. In our free will we move where we want, work where we want, have as many children as we want, and God does an amazing thing, in that every problem resulting from our decisions is guided by Him to move us deeper into His plan, the expression of His life within us. Is it not amazing that He causes all things to work together for good for those who love Him?

DAY 290
Your True Nature

Until we all attain to the unity of the faith, and of the knowledge of the Son of God, to a mature man, to the measure of the stature which belongs to the fullness of Christ.

— EPHESIANS 4:13

In a village next to the Niger River I noticed a cage holding one lone, odd-looking eagle. All of the basic features were there, and it was white on the body, neck, and two-thirds of the wings, but the end of the wings and the head were black. I was told, "That is a white eagle." That seemed confusing, with the black coloring on the wings and the whole head. Then it was further explained, "It is a young white eagle; as the bird grows, the white will push its way to the tip of the wings and beak. The mature bird will be completely white in the end." Again, all things created are preaching Jesus. The DNA of the bird dictates that it will be a white bird. As the bird grows, it expands into what it really is in fact: a white eagle. It does not become a white eagle; it is a white eagle, even when the black is on it. Growth and maturity will force out what does not belong to the very nature of the bird.

The head is where thoughts of the flesh hide in hopes of manifesting themselves. The black on the wings represent our unbelief, the only thing associating us with earthly living. Would it in any way be possible to stop the growth of this bird? No, but if it remains caged, the expression and exercise of its growth and maturity would not be seen. This white eagle gives me hope. First, it will grow, and what it is will be revealed; it has no choice in the matter. Second, God will not keep it captive. There will be a mounting up in the fullness of time.

Imagine giving birth to a child if its actual growth was in your hands and it was up to you to make it grow. Would you not be a nervous wreck? You cannot make a child grow, for that is God's work. Likewise, you do not make yourself grow spiritually! That is God's work, a work that He has ordained by writing into your very DNA that you are a child of God; Christ's life is written into your very nature. In the end, you cannot make one hair [one feather] black or white. Your "color" is the outgrowth of the new nature that He has given you.

By the way, eagles devour the serpent and are feared by all the other little creatures that sneak about.

DAY 291
The Revelation of Quietness

How long, O LORD? Will You hide Yourself forever?
— PSALM 89:46

People with certain temperaments see general communication as a waste of time, hating to play what they see as the people game. On the other extreme is the person uncomfortable with quietness, though anyone quiet enough to let another person keep talking would soon find out many things revealed about that person. This is why I believe that God is often quiet; He waits to see what comes out of my heart when He is quiet. His quietness will not create something in my heart, but it will reveal something. Often I see believers experiencing the quietness of God and beginning to complain, move into unbelief, and almost immediately look for another option.

These things have always been within them, but quietness revealed them. When the Lord is quiet it is better to be quiet also until we see what comes out of Him. We would be amazed.

DAY 292
The Revelation Of Self and Then The Revelation Of Him

But seek first His kingdom and His righteousness, and all these things will be added to you.

— MATTHEW 6:33

The way of the flesh for the believer is to do what he likes and then hate what he is doing; this cycle can cause depression, which often (not always) has its roots in the desires the flesh is either exercising or wanting to exercise. Depression, then, can have its root in desire when we seek God for what we want (our will), and if we do not get it, we get depressed. If we do get it and then discover that it was not really what we imagined it to be, there also is depression. Could we take time to understand that if we have ever prayed earnestly for, "Thy will," then "Thy will" is exactly what we are getting? If we are confused, perhaps we thought that "Thy will" would be something spectacular, comfortable, and blessed as defined by the world, including harmony in marriage, obedient children, and more. Let me explain. He is bringing to each of us the revelation of Christ that we NEED, and to prepare us for that revelation—so we will not be exalted and destroyed—He is giving us what we are getting today. The revelation of Christ can completely destroy us if we are not prepared in advance by His will. Paul says so. He explains that a thorn was given him so that in the abundance of revelations, he would not be destroyed. What we are getting today in "average" life is everything we need to precede His revelation. Remember, the purpose of prayer is not to change the will of God, but to give us peace as we come in line with His will. This is the greater time, wherein He is going to use us as lesser (in the view of worldly churches) believers, and this is how we are prepared. We must stand fast and not be discouraged, for today's hiccups, rejections, conflicts, abuses, and concerns are what are needed to prepare us.

DAY 293
The Revelation Of The Heart

But because of your stubbornness and unrepentant heart you are storing up wrath for yourself in the day of wrath and revelation of the righteous judgment of God.

— ROMANS 2:5

In these times we are not creating hearts as much as watching them be revealed. It is the time for the revelation of hearts all around us. When someone says, "I cannot believe in a God that allows suffering," that person's heart is being revealed. He knows that God did not cause the suffering, but he is taking the occasion to blame Him. If He did take away suffering, do we honestly think that such a person would immediately repent and turn to Jesus? No, the statement or the event is simply a revelation of the heart. We will be surprised in heaven to discover all that God has done for suffering people. Just as the heart of His own Son was revealed in hardship, so have many others' hearts been. In a place where there has been persecution, that type of suffering accelerates the revelation of the heart and allows us to see men for what they really are. "I see men, for I see them like trees walking around," said the man being healed from his blindness. Do you know the hearts of those around you? They are not revealed in comfort. One day you might see that those you thought were enemies are friends and those believed to be friends were enemies. It is the time for the revelation of hearts.

DAY 294
The Sharecropper Christian

Even so consider yourselves to be dead to sin,
but alive to God in Christ Jesus.

— ROMANS 6:11

The story is old and well known of slaves who were set free, but because of the previous owners' manipulation and the slaves' fear, the slaves remained. These slaves came to be known as sharecroppers. In the end, they worked harder than a slave and were often cheated out of their share.

A sharecropper believer could be defined as one who was set free, no longer is a slave to sin, was purchased with precious blood, and yet he stays in bondage to sin. The problem is not the Master's voice, it is not fear, not the power of sin, Satan's oppression, not a stifling past, or anything on earth. The problem is unbelief. Step out and say no to sin, and see if it is not true, see if the state of being set free is not a reality. Make a choice. Today say no to negative living. Say no to self and hug the mate. Say no to bad habits and watch it stick. The person in Christ has been set free, not for someday but for freedom now. Stop being a sharecropper believer.

DAY 295
The Sin of Withdrawal

Whoever loves his brother lives in the light, and there is nothing in him to make him stumble. But whoever hates his brother is in the darkness;
he does not know where he is going.
— I JOHN 2:10,11

Some forms of idolatry are rarely discussed as sin, and because of that they can bring more destruction than the "major" sins. One such idol is that of withdrawal, wherein people under pressure, sensing rejection or conflict, merely hide. They give up on others to meet their deepest needs, although their frustration, of course, proves that they have been looking in the wrong place for acceptance all along. They isolate themselves, block their emotions, and determine not to get close to another person (or other persons) again. By way of analogy, their life goes something like this: Each time someone hurts them, they get busy and lay up a row of emotional concrete blocks to encompass themselves. With the next hurt comes another row of blocks; then with the pain of a relationship, another row. With injury from a child, friend, or spouse, one more row is laid, and so on. Eventually a top is placed on the invisible structure, and at this point they are completely isolated, resolving not to let anyone in again and determining never to be hurt again. They are now prepared to receive every condemning thought about others that the enemy may whisper, along with his taunts that since others have caused their misery, others should never be allowed close enough to do harm again. Is that really what the Lord would have for His people? Is not the differentiation between the Christ within and the self-centeredness within revealed through interaction with His people? If we would grow in Christ, we should never withdraw from others, but rather allow both the revelation of self-centeredness and the work of the cross of Christ to replace such behavior with the expression of His Life.

DAY 296
The Stressed Vine

After they had preached the gospel to that city and had made many disciples, they returned . . . strengthening the souls of the disciples, encouraging them to continue in the faith, and saying, "Through many tribulations we must enter the kingdom of God."

— ACTS 14: 21, 22

In California are several fruit-tree farmers I am honored to call friends and brothers in Christ. In the midst of the tree farms are the great vineyards of Gallo wines. The grapevines are flooded at the right time; fertilizer and bug spray are added, and generally these plants are quite pampered to produce great clumps of grapes that are used to make $7.00 bottles of wine. In one section of the vineyards are found areas of very special vines that were frozen nearly to the point of death before being planted, and then their water and fertilizer are withheld; they are watched carefully to see that they constantly remain on the verge of death. The end results are very petite grapes, which, because they have been stressed, are packed with flavor and fragrance and are used to produce $200 bottles of wine.

I like to parallel the condition of the stressed grapes with the existence of many believers who submit gladly to God when He is producing stressed fruit in their lives. Job looked at others who believed in God and wondered at the ease of their life. They had become "the big vines" with less problems, no experience of loss nearly like his, and with much fruit. However, it was not $200 fruit. A stressed grape takes more care, and in that the stressed believer can rejoice, remembering that God is watching over him with special attention!

DAY 297
The Ugliest Religion in the World

I am the vine, you are the branches; he who abides in Me, and I in him, he bears much fruit; for apart from Me you can do nothing.

— JOHN 15:5

What, exactly, is the most ugly religion in the world? I have come in contact with countless religions, and I believe that I have found the absolute worst one. Christianity! That is right, Christianity! Why? Every other religion is created to be a religion, centering in laws, sites, chants, and ceremonies, things that signify the very nature of a religion. However, Christianity centers on and in Jesus. Christianity centers on a relationship with the Founder, who is not a teacher of new rules but is the Son of God, who was raised from the dead, actually living in and through the followers. When reduced to a list of behaviors to be imitated, Christianity is just too high of an ideal to attain. Since no one can imitate Jesus, the religious have to come up with a set of laws that they can imitate to exalt themselves over others. Take Jesus out of it and Christianity becomes ugly, if not out-and-out goofy. The religious cannot emphasize Jesus, else in so doing they hold up a model they are not able to imitate. Therefore, they hold up everything else that appears spiritual. Things I have heard during my travels are nearly unbelievable. "Wear a white shirt when you preach. White allows the Holy Spirit to get out of you easier!" "Jesus said to love your neighbor. That is why I am right to have an affair with my neighbor." "The color red is never to be worn by a Christian; it is evil." "A woman is never to enter the sanctuary in anything other than a dress." "Command God to give you wealth and health in the name of Jesus. He has to obey you." I could go on and on, but to what end? Christianity as a religion is undeniably ugly. By bringing Jesus back to the center where He belongs, letting Him live through us and lifting Him up without fear, no religion on earth can comparably measure up to Christianity. The world would be so uncomfortable by the contrast that they would have to rid themselves of us, just as they did Jesus.

DAY 298
The Wolf In Sheep's Clothing

Beware of the false prophets, who come to you in sheep's clothing, but inwardly are ravenous wolves.

— MATTHEW 7:15

While traveling in the jungle I noticed something quite remarkable; I had never seen anything like it. A vine had embedded itself in the bark of a tree. It was so well hidden and blended so perfectly with the bark that it could hardly be noticed and did not stand out at all. It had worked its way up the tree and even had leaves that looked like those of the giant tree. It appeared to be the tree but was not.

There are many carnal programs that have embedded themselves in the churches to the point that they are actually considered spiritual. They have been around so long that no one questions them; they have been baptized as far as our consciences are concerned, and yet these things are exactly like the world. Why is it that the world can come up with something to entertain its minions and the Church then tries to compete? If something were really of God, why would we not think of it first? The modern form of education was born of a Christian notion; the schools were Christian and the world followed with its schools after seeing the value in what was being done. I really delight in the fact that we believers can gather together in a small room where Christianity is illegal, have no stimulus or expression of the spectacular, and yet if the Holy Spirit shows up, in the quiet places of the heart we hear Him and are never the same.

DAY 299
The World

When He, the Spirit of truth comes, He will guide you
into all truth.

— JOHN 16:13

I was asked, "If vegetarians eat vegetables, what do humanists eat?" Humanism, which through such vehicles as the U.N. and EU (European Union) has taken hold of so many developing countries, is an attempt to wrestle moral authority away from the Church. It is nonsense on several levels. First of all, humanists present their objecting messages to people who would not act a certain way anyway. They show pictures of dolphins swimming in industrial waste, which enrages the people who would not be irresponsible with the waste anyway and leaves those who are fouling the water unaffected. Such activities throw words at a problem and accomplish nothing. Second, humanists define a problem that does not exist, set out to fix it, and by so doing create a real problem that is greater than the imaginary one. Third, there is no basis for certain moral statements made. Humanism has a moral foundation vaguely familiar to what is seen in Christianity, and yet it denies Christ and His power. Fourth, it is filled with compromise. One compromises to someone who is already compromised. It is compromise compromised, so loose in the end that it is ridiculous. Yet the humanists push away through the U.N. and other groups in nearly every developing country in which I work to spread their merely man-centered wisdom of the world. If Christ had not opened my eyes, I would probably be on the front row listening; I do not have any illusions about finding substance in my own flesh. One persecuted Christian was telling me about other believers who had compromised with the cruel government. I said, "That would be me!" He said, "You would not!" I said, "I would. There is nothing good in my flesh. I own it and now look to the Lord to keep me."

DAY 300
There Is No God In the Past

He again fixes a certain day, "Today," saying through David after so long a time just as has been said before, "TODAY IF YOU HEAR HIS VOICE, DO NOT HARDEN YOUR HEARTS."

— HEBREWS 4:7

Man for sure possesses the present and, in a certain measure, the future. Man does not possess the past, ever! If we choose to live in the past, we choose darkness and we exclude God, for He will not move to the past with us. Therefore, every time we venture into the past with our mind and emotions, we venture there alone. In fact, God calls us, always, to move from the past, for to dwell there is to find ourselves in a place where there is no hope. The Jews were in the world without a hope. That is, they were trusting in the things of the past—the law and the security of ritual and formula—and neglecting what God was bestowing on them in the present, which is Jesus.

Does it not make sense that God wants to be the God of the NOW? We speak of a personal relationship with Him. How can a relationship be personal if it is not a current relationship? To move into the past is to move away from God, and it is sin. Many today are counseled to relive the past in order to mourn over it and work through it; they are even warned that if they do not, their life will remain in constant turmoil. If the past created my problems, why would I want to return and spend time there? In my office I spend up to one hour looking at the past of an individual. The only reason is to bring understanding of its impact so that the person need never go back to it. Living in the past will always thwart growth, not something enjoyable to anyone.

In the past we all had wonderful successes and terrible failures, times of great joy and unbelievable depression. Fine, but now what? Today hear His voice! God says do something today and do not live out of the past, where it is true we provoked Him, but I refuse to discuss that. I want to discuss today. Yesterday is no excuse for today! Many use it as such. "I cannot love today because of emotional hurt yesterday." "I cannot give today because of all my rejection yesterday. I need to take." Experience what it means to be a person walking with God daily, a present activity. Not only do we walk with Him, but He walks among us, all in the present. Leviticus 26:12, "I will also walk among you and be your God, and you shall be My people." We need never allow the enemy to steal the present by moving us to the past, and the past is anything that happened before you read this article.

DAY 301
Three Kingdoms

Jesus said to them, "Truly I say to you that the tax-gatherers and harlots will get into the kingdom of God before you."
— MATTHEW 21:31

There are three kingdoms to which one can belong, the kingdom of good, the kingdom of evil, and the kingdom of God. The kingdoms of good and evil have much in common. Both are fortresses with folks inside attempting to get out and others outside attempting to get in. Inhabitants are kept inside through threats, punishment, intimidation, and the fear of death. Wars are mounted and men enlisted to expand both. The comparisons are endless, for they come from the same tree. Interestingly, a good kingdom delivered Europe from an evil kingdom, and when it was all over, Europe became post-Christian. Conversely, think of all the pockets of the Kingdom of God that can be found in countries long ruled by evil kingdoms, where no good kingdom stepped in to deliver the people. Both the kingdom of good and the kingdom of evil are enemies of the Kingdom of God. Good is the enemy of the best, and though moralism is an enemy of Christianity, many persist in seeing Christianity merely as the kingdom of good as they exert effort toward changing the world system to agree with it. We are all suffering fatigue from the world's presentation of what it portrays as compassion. Pictures are shown of some injustice somewhere in the world from dolphins in tuna nets to stolen aid for the hungry. Unfortunately, such images only stir up those who would never do such things to begin with; they do nothing to change the behavior of the people who participate in the atrocities. It could be concluded that "good" people only point out the behavior of bad people to make themselves look and feel better. "Good" people feel they have done something by throwing words at a problem; they want to project to others an image of doing something valuable to resolve the world's problems, to raise money for the organization that discovered the bad thing, or to blindly assist in the way they think is right.

Is it not interesting that Jesus, in the midst of the Roman system, said nothing about it? In the midst of slavery, abortion, taxation, the annihilation of cultures, and unjust government, He said nothing. Instead, He emphasized the Kingdom of God. He was not fighting evil with good. In fact, He equally resisted evil and good (Pharaseeism) with the Kingdom of God. We must decide how we will live, and that, in turn, will determine that to which we will respond and make our life's goal. We can live in the evil kingdom and return good with evil. We can live in the good kingdom and make sure evil is punished with evil, or we can live in the Kingdom of God, returning evil with good.

Jesus could see clearly the Invisible Kingdom, and He has given us the capacity to see the same. When we see what He sees, our priorities change. We cannot be bothered by (if it is true) the depleting ozone layer to the extent that it would take us from our mission that has eternal significance. It can be annoying to turn on the television and be told by the unbelieving world what needs to be of utmost significance to us, when their whole outlook revolves around such things as gun control, freedom of speech, freedom from religion, equality, expressions of discrimination, whales, and more. Then there are the methods that are guaranteed to fix all the problems: education, understanding, ribbons, walks, and money. Well, amen. It is said that earth is as close to hell as a believer will ever come and as close to heaven as an unbeliever will ever come. This has caused me to change my attitude and lower my frustration, for this world is all the unbelievers have. If they want to keep it nice, improve it to suit themselves, and throw their lives into working for what is ineffective, they should. I was told of a South American politician who stole one billion dollars. I responded, "Is that all? Since he is going to hell anyway, he really should have taken more!" Jesus is the issue, and everything else is a non-issue, for it will cease to exist on the day that every knee bows. Nothing else will matter. However, we are not to be frustrated with the world when it loves the world; the world loves itself and its own, and that is all the world has, for the world has nothing in Him nor He in it.

DAY 302
To Prevail

Thus David prevailed over the Philistine with a sling and a stone, and he struck the Philistine and killed him; but there was no sword in David's hand.

— I SAMUEL 17:50

It is a wonderful story of David's prevailing over Goliath without a sword. The power of God was revealed in David's weakness; David was weak in himself, yet strong in the Lord. "Then David said to the Philistine, 'You come to me with a sword, a spear, and a javelin, but I come to you in the name of the LORD of hosts, the God of the armies of Israel, whom you have taunted,'" I Samuel 17:45. David's confidence in the Lord gave strength to the others, for after watching him they defeated the enemy. Weakness is never to be feared but embraced, first for our benefit and second for the encouragement of all those around us. If a believer will only acknowledge his weakness, God will act. "I am too weak to witness." Praise the Lord! I now know that when that person does witness, it will be Christ speaking through him. "I am too weak to love." Happy to hear that! Now it will be Christ loving through him. "I am too weak to overcome my temptation." Great news! When we say, "I cannot," we are only stating why we qualify for God to move in and around us. Our weakness will cause us to prevail and inspire others. I love the way God works!

DAY 303
Too Easy on Sin!

Do not regard lightly the discipline of the Lord, nor faint when you are reproved by Him.

— HEBREWS 12:5

But when we are judged, we are disciplined by the Lord in order that we may not be condemned along with the world.

— I CORINTHIANS 11:32

Often after finishing the first few lectures in the Abiding Life seminar I will be questioned as to whether I am not being too easy on sin. There is an interesting fear among many that unbelievers and other believers may think that they are in some way going to get away with sin. These people would like to hear me stress that God is going to judge them. However, there are inherent, biblical problems with emphasizing judgment. First, our sin judges us on the spot. Because we are held together by Christ, to invite something that is anti-Christ into our being is to invite immediate judgment; it is too late to warn people after they have sinned, for sin brings its own judgment with it.

Second, if any believe that the Abiding Life message is easy on sin, we ask them to look to the cross. God is not easy on sin; He always made it clear that sin required a blood sacrifice, and His Son died because of sin. The popular term "cheap grace" must never be uttered. Grace is not cheap; it cost the Son. God is not easy on sin or man's inner life that sins, for He crucified it. The cross proclaims to all that God is concerned with sin. To say that we need His life is an acknowledgment of our concern. I will not listen to that accusation.

Third, when I hear, "People must know that God will judge their sin," I know it is a statement of unbelief. God has already judged all men in Christ. To wait around for judgment is to wait for something that has already happened. "But God demonstrates His own love toward us, in that while we were yet sinners, Christ died for us. Much more then, having now been justified by His blood, we shall be saved from the wrath of God through Him" (Romans 5:8 & 9). "That God was in Christ reconciling the world to Himself, not counting their trespasses against them" (II Corinthians 5:19).

Fourth, the person who worries about sin's not being preached has forgotten that he came to Christ through the preaching of the good news. All men have sinned and have recognition of that fact. The idea that Christians are sinning because they are ignorant is not plausible. The Holy Spirit is faithful to shed light on our sin. Again, God did judge sin in the form of Jesus Christ, and because of this judgment we have received grace and mercy. Therefore, grace and mercy is our message.

DAY 304
Trees

I am the true vine, and My Father is the vinedresser.

— JOHN 15:1

A certain tree farmer has taken the time to show me all the procedures involved in harvesting almonds. I have decided that the strenuous effort involved in bearing fruit does indeed rest on the shoulders of the gardener, whose job it is to prune, level the land, water, fertilize, mow, and out-and-out baby the trees in the hope that all conditions will be perfect for the trees to accomplish what they do naturally in God's order, bear fruit! It is interesting to note that when the trees are laden with almonds, a steel arm grasps the trunk of the tree, an umbrella-type contraption is inverted under the tree, and the arm shakes the tree until it provides the gardener with his hard-earned fruit.

God does it all. We need only attain to what believers do naturally as we are tended to, and sometimes God must shake us to get the fruit that is His.

DAY 305
Twenty-Something, Bored and Scared

Then the men became extremely frightened and they said to him, "How could you do this?" For the men knew that he

was fleeing from the presence of the LORD,
because he had told them.

— JONAH 1:10

A large segment of the twenty-something crowd feels both bored and scared about the future, with fear of working a dead-end job, doing the eight-to-five routine, preparing for retirement, and finally ending up sipping liquefied Jello from a straw in a nursing home. They shrink from commitment. Many have come from broken homes and from the time of their youth experienced the fear that comes from believing that a family breakup is imminent. The knot in the stomach from hearing the fighting, seeing the drinking, and hearing the accusations made them miserable. We cannot blame them; they have witnessed firsthand marriage as something to be avoided. Fear has created an unbelievably aloof and boring generation with their attempt to live life and yet avoid life by engaging in the same old safe things: reliable relationships, secure jobs, lack of risk, and avoidance of pain. Yet all the while they feel more and more bored and self-centered.

There is hope for those in this generation, for there is nothing that the nearness of Jesus will not cure, no, not one thing. The normal progression of life cannot be avoided without a person's imploding. Man is meant to grow up, leave home, become self-sufficient, work a job, get married, have kids, become too old to work, and yes, one day die. It is the normal way of things. It is not boring, but it is only truly exciting if a normal life is lived with Jesus. Do not think that Jesus, God Himself, was bored helping to raise his brothers and sisters, taking care of his mother, living in a small village, and making furniture. We see in Him that the normal progression of life coupled with the progression of walking with the Father blended perfectly together, making it all exciting. My own life has been anything but boring, and I really thank God for everything that comes with, and everything He accomplished in me through, "normal life." I have never been bored. In every situation it is exciting to see what the Lord is going to do. Jumping into the middle of normal life with Jesus grants the discovery of a great adventure!

Again, why does the twenty-something crowd feel lost? They are avoiding the normal progression of things out of fear. They have seen the worst end result of marriage and children and are avoiding it. Therefore, they are moved to act like adolescents well into their late twenties.

DAY 306
Two Tracks

Do not think that I came to bring peace on the earth; I did not come to bring peace, but a sword.

— MATTHEW 10:34

There are times in life when we would like everything to run on one track, and, as with every issue, there can be both the legitimate and the illegitimate side. For example, because of a vocational change a man is asked to move, which will make him miss his friends immensely. He would like God either to take away his yearning for his friends or allow him to stay put. He wants life on one track. Mourning for the loss of relationships speaks well of the man; however, to be undone and refuse the move does not.

Running on one track and forcing everything to fit within the one theme can be destructive. A woman visiting me proclaimed, "I am a terrible Christian. The Bible says, 'In everything give thanks,' but my husband recently died and I cannot stop crying." True, the Bible does say that. It also gives accounts of many men of God as they tore their clothes in anguish at the news of the death of a loved one. It is legitimate to weep but may be illegitimate to weep for years. We need to accept that in our Christian life there are more tracks than one that run parallel concurrently.

Unbelieving man wants to systematize God so that everything is on one track. This order would alleviate the unknown and relieve us of the necessity to exercise our faith. God has never been, nor can He be, systematized. We are not Muslims who base their lives in teaching and creed. Rather, our lives center around a person, a relationship. This leads to situations such as being urged to honor father and mother, and yet at the same time being warned to reject father and mother if they get in the way of following Christ. In a relationship with Christ both truths are possible, for in Him we can love and honor the parents, but He comes before them, and so if parents want to come before Christ they are not covered by Matthew 15:4 but are under the command of Matthew 10:37.

I am not saying that the Christian life is one of balance; that would be Taoism. We are not attempting to find the middle ground. Instead, every issue in life is a coin with two sides, and it takes both sides, though they can be opposing, to make up the coin. Whether one side is legitimate and the other is illegitimate depends upon the Lord's leading in the situation.

DAY 307
Uncovering Your Brother's Sins

Now the sons of Noah who came out of the ark were Shem and Ham and Japheth, and Ham was the father of Canaan. These three were the sons of Noah; and from these the whole earth was populated. Then Noah began farming and planted a vineyard. And he drank of the wine and became drunk, and uncovered himself inside his tent. And Ham, the father of Canaan, saw the nakedness of his father, and told his two brothers outside. But Shem and Japheth took a garment and laid it upon both their shoulders and walked backward and covered the nakedness of their father; and their faces were turned away, so that they did not see their father's nakedness. When Noah awoke from his wine, he knew what his youngest son had done to him. So he said, "Cursed be Canaan; a servant of servants he shall be to his brothers."

— GENESIS 9:18-25

There is a lesson for us. Are we to uncover the nakedness of our brother? Many believe it is their job to find the sins of others and then expose them to everyone. Not only is this contrary to Matthew 18, but it will bring a curse upon the fault-finder insofar as he is complicit with the enemy, who accuses the brethren before our God day and night (Revelation 12:10). Let God deal with a man's nakedness. I know a pastor who discovered a hidden sin that another pastor committed some thirty years ago, and out of spiritual jealousy he made sure that everyone found out about it. Is this how we treat the people of God? Yes, if we want to be like Ham. Should we not rather prefer to be like the other two brothers, backing up with the Blood that covers and not publicizing the failures?

DAY 308
Understanding the Deeds of the Flesh

The acts of the sinful nature are obvious: sexual immorality, impurity and debauchery.

— GALATIANS 5:19

The flesh is a condition well defined as being under the influence of something other than the Spirit of God, a condition into which every person is born. All humans have lived life in the flesh, uniquely expressing it with differing levels of intensity. Flesh is flesh and is hostile toward God. The condition of flesh is man doing what he wants and, if he is a believer in Jesus, hating what he does. The fleshly person is ingrown, wrongly sensitive, and angry, believing that the reason flesh does not satisfy flesh is simply that others have erected various obstacles. The root of fleshly living is pride that says, "I know what I need." The lengthy process of coming out of the flesh could not be accomplished by any man, no matter how great his intellect, powerful will, or passion. Rather, the process is built into the very nature of things. All creation works at freeing man up from the flesh. Even the world does not keep man in the flesh, but rather makes man sick to death of the flesh.

Man is spirit living in a body; the spirit has needs only God can meet. Looking to the flesh to fulfill the desire of the spirit leads to frustration as man becomes undone with the awareness of his condition. He is empty! He sees he needs something different from what his senses perceive. A revelation may come from the spirit that indicates, "I need the Lord." The spirit of man has been crying this out since its abandonment in the Garden of Eden. The experiences in the world testify to that truth, the Bible witnesses to it, others explain it, and in the fullness of time, when it becomes revelation clearly seen, a person is prepared to accept Jesus, who so fills the spirit with joy and gladness that the believer is more easily able to lay aside the empty deeds of the flesh, happy to say goodbye to them. No longer thinking in those terms, the deeds of the flesh are laid aside naturally! The Christian may shake his head in bewilderment at those who still struggle. Why even look to those things, when Jesus meets the need? After all, or so the analogy goes, "My bicycle has been stolen, but I don't care! Someone gave me a car!" It is important to note that at this point in the believer's life, he has laid aside the deeds of the flesh not because he wanted to or chose to, but because they were replaced by a divine act of the Holy Spirit.

DAY 309
Up and Out Versus the Down and Out

Jesus said to them, "Truly I say to you that the tax collectors and prostitutes will get into the kingdom of God before you. For John came to you in the way of righteousness and you did not believe him; but the tax collectors and prostitutes did believe him; and you, seeing this, did not even feel remorse afterward so as to believe him."

— MATTHEW 21:31 & 32

When Adam and Eve ate from the tree of the knowledge of good and evil, mankind became divided into two classes. Those who chose to emphasize the good are classed as self-righteous, or as I like to call it, the Up and Out. Those whose focus became evil became the unrighteous, or rather, the Down and Out. Jesus also divided fallen humanity into these two categories. Luke 18: 9-14, "To some who were confident of their own righteousness and looked down on everybody else, Jesus told this parable: 'Two men went up to the temple to pray, one a Pharisee and the other a tax collector. The Pharisee stood up and prayed about himself: "God, I thank you that I am not like other men—robbers, evildoers, adulterers—or even like this tax collector. I fast twice a week and give a tenth of all I get." But the tax collector stood at a distance. He would not even look up to heaven, but beat his breast and said, "God, have mercy on me, a sinner." I tell you that this man, rather than the other, went home justified before God. For everyone who exalts himself will be humbled, and he who humbles himself will be exalted.'"

Some in their own estimation elevate themselves above God; they look down on others, and they effectively remove themselves from the Kingdom of God. Then there are those who see themselves as worms, not daring to look up or move ahead; they, too, miss the Kingdom of God. In the Christian life both types might as well still be meeting in the temple. I have found it interesting during several hundred hours of discipleship with couples to find so often in the conflicts both an Up and Outer and a Down and Outer. The Down and Outers much more readily admit their failures but are slow to make improvements because of an overall pessimistic and inferior view of themselves.

I would like to describe the characteristics of each before we move on to the resolution of the problem. I have purposely exaggerated in some ways the attributes of Down and Out and Up and Out in the hope that we can recognize the seed before it becomes a deep-rooted tree in our lives. I also want to warn readers from the outset that the purpose of the following descriptions is not so this article can be pointed out to either the Up-and-Out or the Down-and-Out person. Anyone doing that will have become the very thing that he or she despises! I am not in the habit of eloquently delineating a problem and then not describing a way out, for the way out is the issue, not only for the Up and Outer and the Down and Outer, but also for the mate that must live with one.

The Down and Out are consumed with themselves and their failures; they spend prolonged hours dissecting their miserable plight and the role of others in their condition. They use all surrounding circumstances, rejections, perceived rebuffs, and personal failures to commit emotional suicide, for through dying emotionally they relieve themselves of all responsibility to move ahead, look honestly at complaints, or work at improving their plight. The Down and Out allow life to live them. They are victims for whom life is barely worth living, since the whole world is the adversary. Comfort comes from accepting their miserable predicament of not being suited for living as well as from the belief that others are simply born with the blessing of God. Confront this type of person and be prepared for pouting and vengeance that come in the form of withdrawal, avoidance, refusal to speak, fits of depression, inactivity, and self-punishment. If the Down and Out are not really down and out, they will make sure that their behavior is, as through passivity, drugs, alcohol, television, laziness, or a variety of idols they make their outer life fit with their inner life. They are procrastinators; because of all the feelings of inadequacy and failure, responsibilities and jobs are postponed. The Down and Out cannot live with themselves and therefore cannot live with anyone else. They give up on relationships, for no amount of effort and self-sacrifice will work, so why try? They are very difficult to live with. As their negative behavior intensifies, first they want others to tell them that they are not really as bad as they feel or as their behavior indicates (although no positive affirmation will be believed). Second, they reject others before they can be rejected. Third, they begin an affair with suicidal thoughts. Fourth, they then begin to obsess on all the wrong that anyone has done to them, thus casting blame and once again avoiding personal responsibility. Fifth, they begin to justify their rebellion. No matter what form it takes, they are right in participating. After all, there is no hope, no one who really cares, and there is no need to fight, for they are already defeated. All of the above excuse their lack of obedience concerning the fifth chapter of Matthew. In fact, communicating with God always increases self-perception, but the Down and Out have an excuse not to talk, for they surmise that God is not interested in them. If He were, life would consistently be wonderful, with God pandering to their every emotional up and down.

The Down and Out are the worst of pessimists; lack of hope has produced a cynicism, and why not? All hope is in themselves; they have not looked outside to God and therefore find the discouragement that exists within all men who try to live independently from their Creator. They do not look up before they act, but rather look around. This assures that they are inconsistent, because decisions are made depending upon the response of others to them. If the Down and Out happen to be parents, they even look to the approval of children before they act. Their motto is,

"People-pleasing at any cost," although others' happiness is not the goal except insofar as it is useful in raising their own self-esteem. Disgusting? I think so, and deep inside they know so. Is it any wonder that the Down and Out are susceptible to the enemy's attacks of suicide?

The Up and Outers are self-righteous, self-reliant, self-centered, all knowing, and consumed with looking at the failures of others. When a suggestion is made to them that might lead to improvement, an explosion ensues. The Up and Out cannot take any criticism, are not teachable, and believe that they possess more wisdom than others and make better financial, family, personal, and spiritual decisions. If only their plans were fully followed, they know that all would go well. Though criticism is not tolerated, it is liberally and generously meted out, and why not? They fully believe they are the standard for all that is right! The Up and Outers lack patience with others, and their approach to problem resolution is for the other people to change. During a dialogue with Up and Outers the topic at hand rarely gets talked through to its conclusion. Instead, most of the time is spent on their examining what is said, making sure that nothing could in any way be construed as shedding negative light on them, for their lofty position over others must be maintained. Do not expect an apology from the Up and Outers or ready forgiveness if they have been offended, for in that case they will sit on their throne awaiting penance until the wrongdoer is once again deemed worthy. When a wife is an Up and Outer, myriad covert messages are left for the husband, all intended to leave no shadow of doubt in his mind that he is unacceptable, unspiritual, a failure as a father, and the major annoyance in the family. When the Up-and-Out wife finally succeeds in driving her husband away, this merely proves what was always said, and now she is a victim who often expresses shock and surprise at the loss. Up and Outers produce the mates that they have described, often under their breath, for years. Those who give their best for years to their Up-and-Out mates and still come up short give up like adolescents and rebel. There is no longer an incentive to try. Often while doing marriage discipleship I will ask each mate to describe five things that he or she has personally done to bring the marriage to a place of misery. The Up and Outers, even after as much as forty years of marriage, can think of nothing. If I continue to press the issue long enough, eventually a failure is mentioned, but immediately there is a justification, such as, "I should not have listened to my mate," or "If he had not been so carnal I would not have been driven to my behavior." No shortcoming is claimed as theirs. UNBELIEVABLE! On a spiritual scale of one to ten, Up and Outers view their mates as ones. Therefore, no matter how well a failing mate does, it will never be enough, and it certainly does not merit respect, physical affection, or support, even before the children. Ask the Up and Outers about their righteousness and hear their superior tone as they enumerate their positives, believing that they always walk in truth, act exactly as a Spirit-filled believer should, and cannot think of a thing for which they should be embarrassed. They struggle with the no-hopers to whom they are married and therefore conclude that only Jesus can meet their needs, so they are free from the expression of Matthew 5 in the marriage. They privately "marry" Jesus and wait for heaven when they will be rid of the ball-and-chain and can get on with heavenly living. They actually believe that on Judgment Day Jesus will look at them and say, "You poor thing! How did you ever manage with such a thorn in the flesh? Step aside while I chastise your mate." Disgusting? I think so!

What misery is produced when any combination of the above finds its way into the dynamics within a marital relationship. Both soon feel hopeless, that they have done their best, that the other has made their life less than abundant and more frustrating, annoying, hopeless, and unfulfilling, while they feel abused, misunderstood, condemned, trapped, mistaken, tired, weak, pointless, undone, disillusioned, stupid, unappreciated, and cheated. All this despite what Jesus said, "I came that you might have life, and have it abundantly." How? When? Impossible? "Forget it! Keep it to Yourself! I am tired, and there is nothing left within me, so leave me alone. Paul had more faith than I do, but I have adjusted to that fact. Just let me coast out of life; I no longer want to fix the problem. I will pour myself into my kids, the job, the hobby, or the ministry; at least there is some satisfaction there if I cannot have fulfillment." Can you imagine this type of person handing out tracts, attending church, and witnessing to others? Well, the Church is full of them.

That cursed tree! Who would have considered the long-reaching results of eating from it? Our lives have become a living hell, the source of which can be centered in another person's actions, attitudes, words, affection, and verbal and non-verbal communication. Man determines our destiny, our outlook on life, daily happiness, and even our desire to live. Amazing. We do not look to God; He is forgotten, He is distant, His behavior inconsequential, His love neglected, His voice forgotten, and His power lost; the Tree of Life eludes us.

What options remain? Suicide, a new mate, seminars, long discussions on rejection, marriage encounters, merely existing, counseling, convincing the others to change, confessing our denial, positive thinking, the agreement of others, misery support groups, Scripture memory, medication, hostility, obsessive analyzing, separate bedrooms, or the constant overt punishing of a mate.

What is the way out? The first step is critical, the foundation on which all others will be built. We recognize that if the self-perception of the Up and Out were correct, Jesus would not have had to come to earth. In fact, God could have waited two thousand years and sent the Up and Outers to set things straight. The same is true of the Down and Outers; if they were as miserable and hopeless as they say, why would Jesus even come to die to redeem them? The misery that we deal out to others and to ourselves has its roots in a false self-perception.

Colossians 2:12: "Having been buried with Him in baptism, in which you were also raised up with Him through faith in the working of God, who raised Him from the dead." Jesus died for the Up and Out and the Down and Out. We have been buried with Christ, and in Him we are something different, we have received a new identity. We are now neither of the above, for our righteousness is in Him, and Christ's righteousness appeals to all! As believers we are to repent of both self-righteousness and unrighteousness, and then those are to be avoided at all costs. We now possess Him and therefore possess all. Our eyes no longer adjust to the false light of self, but only to Him. Self-centeredness, no matter what the form, has no value.

Here are some steps out of self-obsession.

1. Repent of self and of judgment toward self and others.

2. Spend a minimum of sixteen hours refusing all thoughts concerning self.

3. After a prolonged examination of those others that make you miserable, or after examining your personal failure, go to a mirror, stare at the bitter, angry, and frustrated person in the mirror, and then break out laughing. Admit your stupidity.

4. Go back to the foundation of your life, which is not a teaching but the person of Jesus. All that the Sermon on the Mount describes is actually the Life you now possess.

5. Repent of the self-righteousness, the unrighteousness, or both in your life. Give yourself no occasion for the flesh, no excuse for your lack of self- or other-love! Take up the cross, deny self today, and release the new Life that stands fast in the truth whether dealing with the Up and Out or the Down and Out.

6. Put one foot in front of the other. Move toward Christ, remembering He has loved you when you were an enemy of the truth. Now love those who are your enemies.

When Jesus was forsaken and denied, He did not go Up and Out, saying, "I will get a new group of men to work with." Nor did He go Down and Out by giving up. He died for the people to see them redeemed. Move past self and flesh toward Christ. It is not a difficult journey once the first step is taken.

DAY 310
Vengeance

Never take your own revenge, beloved, but leave room for
the wrath of God, for it is written, "Vengeance is Mine,
I will repay, says the Lord."

— ROMANS 12:19

Vengeance is an interesting thing in that it promises satisfaction, and yet it brings emptiness and a depletion of spirit that punishes. No vengeful people have a lift in their spirit, a twinkle in their eye, or a bounce in their walk. No! Time and experience have rendered their verdict: Walking in the flesh does not work, nor is it an option, because to participate will increase misery; quite simply, man is not suited for it. Why do we have thoughts of vengeance? Why do we want to get even? What satisfaction could come from seeing the downfall of another?

Vengeance seems to offer us the morbid satisfaction of relieving our anger, revealing our superiority, punishing those who have wronged us, making others share in the misery they have caused, returning pain to those who offend, and making life unbearable for those we hate. In short, vengeance makes others pay. However, vengeance is a liar with empty promises! It is a leech that sucks out all we are in Christ insofar as compassion, love, and forgiveness are concerned. Vengeance depletes, starves, and in the end poisons us. The world created and held together in Christ does not support the success of vengeance. Our souls and spirits rebel and are repulsed at its slightest introduction. To walk in vengeance is to walk in self-punishment. We are not suited for it! Vengeance is not the way to life.

DAY 311
Voice of God

My sheep hear My voice, and I know them,
and they follow Me.

— JOHN 10:27

I have found that there are two primary reasons that believers are not hearing God. First, imagine a mother looking out the front window of a house watching her children play in the yard, where she has told them to stay. As long as the children are in the yard, do they hear from the mother? No! They do hear her voice if they move to the sidewalk, and they feel the mother's force as they move into the street. When the children hear nothing, it is proof that they are in the will of the mother. Often the silence believers experience is due merely to being in the will of the Father.

Second, if we are not hearing from God it is important to ask whether we did the last thing that He told us. God often speaks concerning our hearts, the direction of our lives, matters of forgiveness, or anything relating to Matthew 5-7. If we neglected the last thing that we heard from Him, that may be the reason we are not hearing anything new. We simply need to ask the Good Shepherd if we acted on the last bit of instruction; He is more than happy to point it out once again. Be aware, though, to discern whether later the enemy picks up the banner and begins badgering us over our disregard of God's communication. The enemy's voice is harsh, critical, condemning, judgmental, and he will often try to bring up past failures of which we have already repented.

DAY 312
Walk In The Truth

As you therefore have received Christ Jesus the Lord,
{so} walk in Him.
— COLOSSIANS 2:6

"Abiding in Christ really sounds great; however, it just does not work for me." I have heard that assessment countless times. My response is, "You mean that making Christ your focus has not helped at all?" Reply, "No, it helped for a few days, maybe a few weeks. It just did not go on working." Herein lies a problem with such rationale: If truth can set anyone free for five minutes, then it can set him free for a lifetime. Truth is absolute and therefore cannot go off and on like a light switch. Unfortunately, many think of truth as a pill that when taken once allows them to sit back and enjoy its benefits for a lifetime. This is a faulty concept, because truth does not envelop the believers and then move them along. Truth is something to be walked in as faith works alongside to bring experience. Faith allows us to receive the truth and walk in it. Those who tell me that focusing on Christ does not work are never focusing on Christ while they make the statement. To know the power of truth one must walk in it, and I have never had anyone that was abiding in Christ tell me that it did not work.

When we decide not to walk in truth we rebel, and the one thing that will most facilitate rebellion and render us the least uncomfortable during the process is anger. The progression is 1) rebel, 2) develop anger, and 3) justify the anger. Therefore, we begin to make a list of why we should be angry with the kids, the mate, the lack of a mate, the job, the depression, our past, relationships, finances, and on and on. The unfortunate person on the list to justify another's anger is left feeling that if he had not done or said certain things, the other one would not have had to rebel. Consequently, that person gets busy changing things in order to bring relief to the rebellious. It becomes his responsibility—rather than the rebel's own—to bring the rebel out of the flesh. However, we cannot rebel and blame anyone but ourselves; it was our choice not to walk in the Spirit; no one pushed us out, NO ONE! We use others' behavior as excuses not to walk in truth, and then we even blame the weakness of the truth for not being able to carry us along.

Believer, YOU CHOOSE! Your will is not broken. Today walk in the truth of loving an enemy, a mate, a friend, refuse all self-centered thoughts, and you will find the truth in power. John 15 is truth; it works; walk in it and it will once again prove its power to you to the point that you will shout, "It works!" Do not try to fix your present state with a complicated list of all that must change before you can walk in the truth. Truth is absolute; it does not need anything to be different to display its power.

DAY 313
Was It Me or Was It God?

For it is God who is at work in you, both to will and to
work for {His} good pleasure.

— PHILIPPIANS 2:13

How does a person become godly? How does a believer pass the test? How does a Christian reach the place where he says with confidence, "I have fought the good fight, I have finished the course, I have kept the faith" (II Timothy 4:7)? I regularly meet young men and women with attitudes of faith and trust beyond their years. Did they make themselves that way? Was it their choice? One fellow from Costa Rica at age five told his mother to stop going to the government's housing application office, saying, "If the Lord wants you to have a house, you will." A few months later, her employer bought her a home! From where did this five-year-old's faith and confidence come? How had he developed it? What discipleship courses had he taken? Which seminar was it that instilled such faith? Did he come to this place of faith through choice? If so, then he would have something in which to boast, but I do not believe it was choice. "For through the grace given to me I say to every man among you not to think more highly of himself than he ought to think; but to think so as to have sound judgment, as God has allotted to each a measure of faith" (Romans 12:3). I believe that there are no great men of faith; if the lives of those so named were examined with a magnifying glass, they would be found to be average persons possessed by great faith. "For consider your calling, brethren, that there were not many wise according to the flesh, not many mighty, not many noble; but God has chosen the foolish things of the world to shame the wise, and God has chosen the weak things of the world to shame the things which are strong, and the base things of the world and the despised. God has chosen, the things that are not, that He might nullify the things that are, that no man should boast before God" (I Corinthians 1:26-29). Ultimately, it is important to understand that it is God who is at work in any one of us.

DAY 314
We Are All Doing Better Than Jesus!

He was despised and forsaken of men,
A man of sorrows and acquainted with grief;
And like one from whom men hide their face
He was despised, and we did not esteem Him.
Surely our griefs He Himself bore,
And our sorrows He carried;
Yet we ourselves esteemed Him stricken,
Smitten of God, and afflicted.

But He was pierced through for our transgressions,
He was crushed for our iniquities;
The chastening for our wellbeing fell upon Him,
And by His scourging we are healed.

— ISAIAH 53:3-5,

I suppose that after all the years of traveling in what was once referred to as the Third World and having observed and participated in the affliction—and, let me add, attempted to relieve some of that destitution—I have come to two conclusions. First, none of us in and of ourselves have the resources needed to cure all of the world's ills or to bring equality of ownership. Second, God is using poverty and suffering in the world to drive men to Himself. Third, we all, even the poorest, are doing better in this life than Jesus ever did. Hundreds of stories about what people need have been told to me, often by those who have used pretense to gain access to me only to ask for money. However, I can see they still have more earthly possessions than did Jesus. He has not let them starve to this point, and, more importantly, they have not yet learned to live out of their own faith; they trust in man's provision more than God's. A person can get by on very little and be happy with that. Sometimes I think that we cheat people by giving too much. "In everything give thanks, for this is the will of God." They are doing better than Jesus did on earth.

DAY 315
We Must All Die; How We Die Is Not the Issue

Thou dost hide Thy face, they are dismayed; Thou dost take away their spirit, they expire, and return to their dust.

— PSALM 104:29

In today's interaction among Christians, so much is said about faith, health, and God's provision, and so little is said about death. If what we hear were true, which is that we possess assurance of health when faith is present, then man would not die. Man must die, just as every creature must die (Ecclesiastes 3:20), and all go to the same place, for they came from the dust and return to the dust. Earth, though, is not the final destination. As it fits the purposes of God in bringing the revelation of Christ in us, He does heal, provide, give materially, and even bring on emotional experiences. However, since at some point we must die, those are not one-sided absolutes, for if we are dying, does it not make sense that the scriptures relied upon by those proclaiming "health and wealth" would no longer be applicable in an absolute way? In Job 1:21 we read, "And he said, 'Naked, I came from my mother's womb, and naked I shall return there. The LORD gave and the LORD has taken away. Blessed be the name of the LORD.'" At the point of death, what good is a great wardrobe? All of us will exit the earth with nothing, so why have heaps of goods the day of death? If we must die, and God knows the exact number of our days, is it really an issue how death comes? For example, look at the thousands who die in persecution; God did not cause the deaths, wicked men did, and wicked men will be judged. However, He works things together for the good. Could it be that the day set for the death of a saint was absolute, yet God permitted the wicked man to be the instrument for the saint to exit, and the wicked man's judgment to be full? This is merely food for thought, but I believe we make too much of the means of death. We must all exit. Amen! Some live their whole lives in bitterness because a drunk driver killed a loved one, and they perceive this as a life cut short. Was it? Or was God ready to receive the saint, His work in that one's life complete, and the drunk was the permitted instrument? Our view of death does make a difference. Again, was it a life cut short or can we see that God, in Sovereignty, was using the evil of man as the tool for the death that must come to all men? I believe that there is provision in the years allotted to a man, and that God knows the day of his death. One man said this: "You are invincible until God is finished with you."

DAY 316
We Need Righteousness, His Righteousness

And may be found in Him, not having a righteousness of
my own derived from the Law, but that which is through
faith in Christ, the righteousness which
comes from God on the basis of faith.

— PHILIPPIANS 3:9

First man was given the Ten Commandments. Some kept them. Next came the Law; some, in their own estimation, kept it and became self-righteous. They did not understand that we need a life, not a list. Jesus, on purpose, set a standard that we could never achieve. His challenge to us was not that we try hard but a challenge to give up; He wanted us to see that a righteousness that would please God is unattainable for man. With His life on earth He raised the bar so high that all men would give up trying to jump over it. Therefore, Jesus said, "Whoever is angry shall be guilty" and "Whoever looks with lust has committed adultery" (Matthew 5:22 & 28). At that, many began to drop out of the righteousness contest. Some stayed. Then came the final blow, "If your hand offends you cut it off, if your eye, pluck it out." At that, no one was left to play the self-righteousness game. Jesus did not want us cutting off our hand or going about blind; He wanted us to see that we could not be righteous. We, however, want to find righteousness in ourselves and are surprised when we find none. We even expectantly look for it in others. Telling the people about all of the evil they are doing and how badly they are missing the mark is what many modern-day "prophets" enjoy doing, but that information should surprise no one. It is all summed up in one verse: "There are none righteous, no not one!" The righteousness that we need can only come through Jesus, the only One that is pure righteousness. Once we admit that we cannot be righteous, we will accept His. Righteousness is a gift no less than are faith and salvation. In Him we find everything that we have looked for elsewhere in vain.

DAY 317
We Need the Revelation of God

For I neither received it from man, nor was I taught it,
but {I received it} through a revelation of Jesus Christ.
— GALATIANS 1:12

At times I read the biographies of godly men who were famous in their differing denominations and experiences. Their stories are quite remarkable. Some have seen Jesus, others conversed with angels and spirits, and others reached a level of devotion not thought obtainable by man. I have noticed one common thread through all of the experiences. The understanding of Christ, the experience of His presence, and the understanding of His work was not the result of study, prayer, devotion or even holiness. The unique understanding and experience of Christ came before the devotion, experience, holiness, or knowledge. Devotion was not the cause of the experience but rather the result of it. In short, the experience, understanding, and growth came as a result of the revelation. Revelation was the beginning point; the initiator was not the work of the man. Revelation is Truth. Revelation is Jesus. Revelation is not merely understanding in the mind but understanding in the spirit. Simply put, knowledge is in the soul, the mind. Revelation comes first into the spirit before it works its way through the mind, will, and emotions and manifests itself in behavior. Revelation is not rooted in study. It comes directly from God. Revelation will carry man much further than will knowledge. We have come to understand, in a measure, the work of Christ, His work in us, and how things ought to be for the believer. However, this knowledge has also proven itself weak when we find ourselves at our lowest. We know the right thing but cannot seem to do it. This is where revelation is so important. Revelation is not birthed in lofty thoughts or the condition of the body but birthed in God. Therefore, its power is outside us, apart from circumstance, and away from the realm of the world's events. Revelation can carry us when knowledge cannot. So how do we get it? We have not because we ask not! We may ask for the revelation of God's Son, of His life living through us as believers, of His purposes and plans, and of the very character of God.

DAY 318
Weak Principles

You search the Scriptures, because you think that in them you have eternal life; and it is these that bear witness of Me.

— JOHN 5:39

I have to get something off my chest that has been bothering me for many years. In an attempt to be unique, and for legitimate reasons, many ministries have arisen over the years, each one saying it has a particular and supposedly new concept that is permanently life changing. Such claims are not true. All we hear are the victory stories; we are not getting the facts. I can be guilty of it myself, but I will tell you a secret: Exchanged life does not work. The cross does not work. Grace does not work. Evangelism does not work. Memorizing Scripture does not work. None of it works. I see what goes on in the inner circles, the things to which not all believers are privy. Among these organizations there have been divorces, affairs, homosexuality, and even worse, glory seeking, material protection (when supposedly the message within the material was given by God), bickering, competition, and more. I have seen it all, and here is why. The best teaching in the world can become a principle that eventually is viewed as needing to be protected. Therefore, only the stories that prop it up are told. I can honestly say that I have a nearly 100% cure rate in my office. Just about everyone will say they were helped that day. What about a year later, though? It is all really simple. It is not the principle of the cross that is effective; it is the Jesus who died on the cross. It is not the principle of grace that will keep a believer, but the grace of Jesus that will. It is not the principle of exchanging one's life for His; it is the reality of the living Jesus. It is not the Scriptures that keep a person in time of trouble; it is the Jesus to whom they point. It is a struggle to keep things focused on Jesus when principles can be packaged, names added, statistics given, and income produced. With Jesus, any who want and seek Him can have Him. He is much higher than any principle.

Walk with a principle for a year and a believer will find himself right where he began. Walk with Jesus for a year and he will be a year beyond where he began.

DAY 319
Weakness, My Friend

My grace is sufficient for you, for My power is made perfect in weakness.

— II CORINTHIANS 12:9

Often when I mention weakness, the Lord keeps asking me one question, "What is My strength hidden in your weakness?" It is known that every negative has a positive. I may be all too familiar with the negative, but the positive is not clear, though it seems to be coming into focus. Things I have struggled with are moving out of the shadows and coming forward into the light. The surprise is that they are not hideous monsters but appear to be tools in the hand of God. I sense there is something great there. I am convinced of something that I have taught for years: There is no one-time fix.

It is deception to believe that "the great Christian someday" will appear when we come to our senses, gain a nearly magical degree of power, never struggle again, and forever move forward without stumbling. In waiting for the great "someday," the working out of everyday faith is excluded. The wish for "someday" is a nonissue that sidetracks us from embracing today's path and the way it reveals our weaknesses. The ways of the flesh are such that a one-time deliverance, if given, would allow us to walk away from the One we love and the healthy dependence we must have on Him. Through struggle we continue to run to Him, initially to find victory, but because we find Him we approach for His presence alone. "Everyday" is the friend of the moment and abundance; its experience with weakness ushers us to fellowship with Him, where we hear His voice and strength is given as needed.

I have noticed one other thing. Believers are happiest giving to others of their time, prayers, finances, and attention. When I travel, something happens to me that took some time to figure out. When I am home, I have time to focus on me, on my general state. While on the road, I just do not have the time. Every waking minute is spent preparing for or actually ministering to others. Exciting things happen, there is a lift in my spirit, others have a lift, and I am enthusiastic and free. I simply do not have the natural abilities to minister in my own strength, but that weakness works for me. I must come out of myself, seek Him, and move out in faith. The solution is not to travel more, but to take more of the "traveling attitude" home with me.

DAY 320
Weird Meetings?

Now may the God who gives perseverance and encouragement grant you to be of the same mind with one another according to Christ Jesus, so that with one accord you may with one voice glorify the God and Father of our Lord Jesus Christ.

— ROMANS 15:5 & 6

But I am afraid that, as the serpent deceived Eve by his craftiness, your minds will be led astray from the simplicity and purity of devotion to Christ.

— II CORINTHIANS 11:3

Over the course of the years I have attended, witnessed, and been told of a variety of meetings and experiences that simply cannot be validated in the Scriptures. Attempts are made to authenticate and legitimize them through the Scriptures; however, most often this ends in a distortion of the Bible. So what about such meetings and experiences? Those that have such experiences will vehemently fight for them as justifiable experiences of the Spirit. Though many expressions are not consistent around the world, "other" types of experiences are. Some witness to having teeth turn gold, others to a cross turning to gold, uncontrolled laughter, pictures of saints that exude a fragrant and healing aroma, falling down and passing out, prophecies, people turning into pigs through prayer, and much, much more. I have heard many accounts, all told with sincerity and conviction. Again, what about such meetings and experiences?

First, I must keep it all in perspective and in the end really not care. Why? It is not because of lack of care for the people, but because even if the experience and meeting were legitimate, it was not my meeting or my experience, so why would I argue a standpoint? It is too easy for all of us to move into pride and trench in over a position. While Jesus was with the disciples, they were one. Take Jesus out of the center of any conversation and there will be division. I would not sacrifice my relationship with Christians over an experience that someone else had. It is far better to approach such experiences without an agenda of trying to prove or disprove. In comparison with my fellowship with a believer, I do not care. Therefore, I will often go quiet if I see that my observations would cause a division. This approach will not satisfy those that want to fight for the truth. However, the truth is not any experience but is Jesus.

This brings me to the second point: a meeting or an experience does not create a heart for Jesus, but it does reveal one. Camping on this point has helped me, for I see both types of people attending such meetings. One person goes for the spectacular, for the seeking of the experience, all in the hope of creating a heart for God or obtaining a shred of proof that he is acceptable to God. This person is most open to deception. Some with this attitude are even leading the meetings! Perhaps we could liken it to "Christian pornography" in the sense that the purpose of pornography is to stimulate the fleshly body, albeit unnaturally. The body is to be stimulated by one's mate, not by another through the means of a picture. In the same way, the mind, will, and emotions belong to God and are to be stimulated by His Spirit. However, "Christian pornography" would be allowing something other than God to stimulate the soul. Many in seminaries are addicted to "intellectual pornography," for they are always looking for the thing that will stimulate the mind. Many organizations are driven by men who have their wills stimulated through fantasizing about great works, or "pornography for the will power." Others are into "emotional pornography" through the stirring of the emotions in a meeting or an experience. It is unnatural to go to a meeting seeking something to stir the soul other than Jesus. When those with such a heart are describing the experience and are questioned, they will immediately shift course and say that it is all about Jesus, even though His name was never mentioned in the course of the description. Instead there was a forceful presentation of the experience and the meeting. This is a revelation of the heart. Remember that Jesus did miracles and generally told the people to be quiet about them. He did not want to draw people who were attracted by miracles. Actually, I believe that a false teacher is used of God to reveal false hearts; I do not mind when people go running to such a one, for they are obviously seeking something other than Jesus. Those things that stir the soul are, like the pornographic picture, substitutes for the real Person. In talking to a Pentecostal pastor and a Baptist pastor, I asked the same question. "Go back twenty years and think of the people in your church. Where are they today? How many are still moving forward?" Both pastors gave the same percentage; both have the same "results." One can only conclude that it is not doctrine that allows for forward movement but the grace of God and the choice of man. The doctrine of a meeting can be completely wrong, but we must not neglect those who attend such meetings, for there is a revelation of the motives of their hearts. Faith is an amazing thing. There are those who believe that God will meet them at the Baptist church. Will He? There also are those who believe that God will meet them at the Pentecostal church. Again, will He? Many believe they will meet Him in the mountains; will they? He is everywhere. He can be found in any place at any time. Therefore, good-hearted people go to strange meetings and meet Jesus. Their hearts are revealed. The proof is in the fruit of their lives. I have known those that have had very abnormal experiences, and yet it is obvious they are moving up in Jesus, talking more about Jesus, promoting Jesus, and not pushing the experience. What do we say to such things? Well, amen! I do not have to understand it to witness to it. I know people personally that were outwardly going nowhere until the experience came and something changed to make them Christ-centered.

In conclusion, meetings do not create hearts but they reveal them. Go to any meeting with the right heart and that heart will be revealed. Go to the weird meeting wanting to create some kind of heart and any manner of thing can happen. That is why people with a right heart come away from really strange things blessed, and those with a wrong heart are led further astray.

DAY 321
What A Ride!

To whom God willed to make known the riches of the glory of this mystery among the Gentiles, which is Christ in you, the hope of glory.

— COLOSSIANS 1:27

I do not like thrilling rides. Many do. Unfortunately, if I am with a group, I will be pressured to ride. One of the most horrific rides is a Ferris Wheel that instead of the normal chairs has capsules designed to spin wildly as the large wheel turns. I find myself all alone, buckled in, door shut, everything seeming all right, and then the ride begins. What a wicked, awful thing to do to a person! No one deserves that! It finally stops and I want out.

One day I asked Jesus to come and dwell within me. What a ride I have taken Him on, up and down, upside down, fast forward and immediate reverse, falling and flying. I would think that after a prolonged ride He would be ready to get out, but He does not. He stays and brings calm to my innermost being. When I allow it, that calm works its way out, the ride stops, and I rest.

DAY 322
What About False Teaching?

If anyone teaches false doctrines and does not agree to the sound instruction of our Lord Jesus Christ and to godly teaching, he is conceited and understands nothing.

— I TIMOTHY 6:3 & 4

Do we let people be deceived? There are a few issues here. First, we are to confront those things that are false and warn others. Second, we can follow a false teacher in two ways, by being fans and agreeing or by monitoring his words and actions to rebuke him; either way the attention is given to him and not Jesus. Third, often false teachers are not creating wrong hearts but revealing wrong hearts, such as when they get a following of people by teaching that Jesus wants us rich. This is appealing to what kind of people? What are their hearts for the Lord if they perceive that the goal of Christ's suffering is our wealth? Fourth, everyone works for us. Let people who follow what life will not support eventually come to the end of themselves and the end of their trust in others; we will still be there to offer Jesus.

DAY 323
What Counts

*The world and its desires pass away, but the man who
does the will of God lives forever.*

— I JOHN 2:17

Travel can be enlightening when encountering a lifestyle so different from the one accustomed to at home, such as having to become consumed with searching for the basics of water, food, shelter, transportation, and someplace to exchange money.

My brother and I had a vexing—no, haunting—experience when traveling in the Amazon region. At one point along the way we both stopped in amazement, as though we were looking at an optical illusion, for there on the sidewalk was a head, a human head with a body smaller than a box of cereal and bereft of arms, legs, stomach, and clothing, but the mouth held a pencil used to draw flowers on a small piece of paper. We left some money in a small bowl placed alongside and walked away wondering. Wondering at how much of what consumed our daily lives would apply to this person. Wondering at how we complain over such comparatively insignificant things; wondering at what this person's response would be were we to approach and relate how someone had offended us or how our Christmas celebration might be a bit slim this year. The head was disturbing and mysterious; his image would not leave us. This person with nothing had found life tolerable; he expressed a beauty within through simple art. In contrast, many with a multitude of worldly attributes, accomplishments, and possessions cannot stand life. The head was a good example of how life is not found outside man but within. I began to ask myself how much of what is taught in Christendom would apply to this person. I was left with the conclusion that if what we teach cannot be accomplished by this person, it is not simple enough to apply to anyone else. The deep life comes through faith and the activity of the soul and spirit, not the activity of the body. All doing is to be the result of faith.

DAY 324
What Do You Really Want From Me? Obedience?

He has told you, O man, what is good;
And what does the LORD require of you
But to do justice, to love kindness,
And to walk humbly with your God?

— MICAH 6:8

We always seem to make obedience the object of the Christian life, but obedience, as we think of it, is not the goal. Actually, God is certainly able to make us obedient if that is what He wants! He made Jonah obey, He made Paul obedient, and He made Pharaoh comply. He knows how to make us bow the knee, but that cannot be His preferred manner of receiving obedience. Paul says to imitate him because he imitated Jesus. Just what did he imitate? It was the fruit and root of Christ's life that Paul was imitating. The fruit came naturally when the root was tended to, that root being dependence on Christ, just as Christ was dependent on the Father. So first we must define what we are to imitate, for attempting to keep the commandments of Christ without dependence on Him will lead to legalism, frustration, condemnation, and death. In the order of things God has told us what He wants from us: "To do justice, to love kindness, and to walk humbly with your God!" I would like to focus on one thing, how to love kindness. It is an absolute that we are to love kindness. That means we must love the kindness that He has shown us, for if we cannot see that, how will we love it and show it to others? Basking in the mercy He has shown us will enable us to become intimately acquainted with it. Do you love or hate mercy and kindness? Many self-righteous believers actually hate it; in their flesh they want to be stronger so as never to be in need of mercy and kindness, and since they have avoided it, they cannot give it to others. Only in failure does the Lord reveal it to us. I can rightly say to the Christian whose failure has led to depression, "You do not love mercy and kindness, and you have never met them."

We are to glorify the Lord. The word glorify means "to show forth what is true about," and we are to show what is true about the Lord. What is true about Him? He is love, mercy, grace, kindness, and more. We show that this is true by believing and receiving it. In our failures people will see that one thing true about God is that we only rely on His righteousness and His extension of mercy to us. I know a pastor who begged for mercy from his congregation, they showed him none, and subsequently every man in that group encountered an untimely demise or unwieldy suffering. We take too lightly not our failures but our showing forth what is true about God. An old preacher started a meeting by telling something of his moral failures and then saying, "We are taking a break. You now know what kind of man I am in the flesh. If you want to leave, no one would blame you." I wanted to stay! I could see that he had received something that I wanted, the mercy to be forgiven and the grace to carry on! Well, amen, who is like our God?

DAY 325
What Does a Normal Cross-Section of Christians Look Like?

*For consider your calling, brethren, that there were not
many wise according to the flesh,
not many mighty, not many noble.*
— I CORINTHIANS 1:26

I would add to the list in that scripture verse. There are those that have had divorces, affairs, rebellious children, depression, anxiety, failed careers, dissatisfaction, anger, disappointments, brushes with suicide, and more. This list reflects a cross-section of believers that is only vexing if our goal is to display perfect flesh. However, when our goal is the preparation and perfection of the spirit, we see that many of these things are necessary, for because of them there will occur the loss of self-glory, pride, righteousness, strength, and kingdoms. All of these things are hindrances that need removal before we can manifest the fruit of the Spirit and His life, which is the true goal of the faith. Well-adjusted flesh may make us comfortable and look quite nice to us, but it carries with it a self-satisfied stench to the Lord that proves it is not the proper goal of our lives in Christ.

DAY 326
What Does It Mean To Live For Jesus?

And they shall not teach everyone his fellow citizen, and everyone his brother, saying, "Know the Lord," for all will know Me, from the least to the greatest of them. For I will be merciful to their iniquities, and I will remember their sins no more.

— HEBREWS 8:11 & 12

What does it mean to live for Jesus? That is a good question. I do not presume to know all the answers, but in my own experience I find that to live for Him is simply to enjoy Him. It is not about what I do or do not do. He loves and enjoys me and allows me to enjoy Him. When God revealed to me that He was not interested in changing me, but all He wanted to do was love me, the response this generated from me was amazing. I have come to see that His love for me has absolutely NO agenda. I John 4:8 indicates that God is Love; because I know that God is Love, then I can look to I Corinthians 13 to find what that Love is. God equals love, so God is patient, God is kind, God is not envious, God is not self-seeking. As I read through that list of what God is, I have to ask myself, "Is this the God that I know?" My answer too often is, "No!" At that point I have a choice. I can stick with my false idea of who God is, or I can take God at His word and believe what He says about Himself. For me to enjoy Him, I first must know Him. The more I know Him, the more I love Him, and the more I love Him, the more I want to know Him.

DAY 327
What If Christians Did Not Fight Evil?

Brethren, I do not regard myself as having laid hold of it yet; but one thing I do: forgetting what lies behind and reaching forward to what lies ahead, I press on toward the goal for the prize of the upward call of God in Christ Jesus.

— PHILIPPIANS 3:13, 14

When in a country that was formerly a part of the USSR, several questions can come to the forefront of any conversation. At the center of the debate is what Christians should have done. We know what many did do, but what should have been done? First, I do not want to condemn anyone for what they did do. Liberians in Africa have told me of their own city's bombing. Everyone in the market, upon seeing the bombs coming, began to run. Old people and babies that had been dropped in the melee were trampled to death. How do you suppose the babies' mothers felt the next day? Fear causes many instinctive reactions. However, once the crush of fear is past, it is possible to think more rationally about what a believer should do. I always like to build a foundation before attempting to discuss such questions. 1) God is love. 2) He permits what He could prevent. 3) He does not cause all things, but He causes all things to work together for good. 4) He could send evil to hell as easily today as tomorrow.

There are several ways of looking at things from this foundation. What would happen if every believer followed the command of Christ to love an enemy without reservation? What if tonight every Christian were killed by evil? What would the world be like if evil men helped the rapture of believers by killing them? If every believer were killed, earth would instantly become hell, because God's Holy Spirit would be dwelling in no person, a case of men on their way to hell when hell actually came up to them. Would the killing of every believer hasten or hinder the coming of Christ? If evil is present in the form of a physical force, army, or government, and if Christians are tricked into fighting it in the power of the flesh, would we actually be hindering the coming of Christ?

I talk to so many who came to a personal relationship with Jesus in a concentration camp in Siberia. What do we have to say about those things? Would the people have come to Him without Siberia? Some were persecuted and died immediately, and some lived years in a prison before eventually regaining their freedom. Did those who died miss out on something? I believe that we must see God, believe all things are in His hands, and rest. If we do not see Him, we will try to make sense—in a carnal, intellectual way—of all that happens. I think I can answer all questions with one word—God—because of the knowledge that we rest in Him!

DAY 328
What If We Lost the Big War?

All the trees of the field will know that I am the LORD; I bring down the high tree, exalt the low tree, dry up the green tree, and make the dry tree flourish. I am the LORD; I have spoken, and I will perform it.
— EZEKIEL 17:24

I have found that I can learn a lot from listening. One day I was sitting in a Latvian sauna. Knowing that the Latvians had suffered greatly under the Soviet occupation, what one man said was shocking to me. "I was in a remote area in Russia where the people had nothing, and I noticed that though in physical want, they were not in spiritual want. As I watched them, I began to wonder if we Latvians were not better off spiritually during the occupation than at present. I suppose that it depends on what one wants out of life." To me that was an amazing statement; I had never heard a Latvian—or anyone from the former countries of Soviet occupation, for that matter—say such a thing. However, it is something I have wondered. Does history bear out that great revivals take place in the midst of comfort or in the throes of want? This fellow may be right in remarking that comfort is not the best human state when Christ can so easily be neglected and substituted. The Chinese Church grew from fifty thousand to fifty million under persecution. Considering facts like that, what would happen if we took a position that what Jesus was talking about when He said that we are to love our enemies actually meant, without qualification, to love our enemies? I have come up against arguments, so I know that loving an enemy is open for interpretation and that boundaries for such a directive are quickly sought by "rational" human beings. However, what if Stalin would have taken over the whole world? What if he had been allowed to kill every Christian, and, as in the early Church under Roman persecution, Christians went to the lions? How long could evil reign without good to support it? How long would it have been before Jesus would have come? What if every Christian loved his enemies and did not use force against them in keeping with Scriptures such as, "Father, forgive them," and (Matthew 26:53 & 54), "Or do you think that I cannot appeal to My Father, and He will at once put at My disposal more than twelve legions of angels? How then will the Scriptures be fulfilled, which say that it must happen this way?" Would

Jesus already have returned? I understand that there are those committed to fighting evil, drawing the line against injustice, and seeing a Scriptural delineation between war and loving an enemy. I also understand the limited impact of my comments since, as was pointed out, I have not witnessed my family being taken off by evil forces. We feel that it is unthinkable to sit back and see our families murdered, and yet that is exactly what happened to the people in this place. The unthinkable has been done. It is not just a theory.

This discussion led to another. Americans seem to hit the panic button when they see people in physical need, so they come to the rescue with "things." An interesting observation was made that every country that America rebuilds becomes consumed with materialism (Japan, Germany, Korea, and Great Britain were given as examples). I could see the validity in the point. Pictures of people without food are given more weight in the American churches than pictures of thousands bowing to Mecca. I have been guilty myself of telling stories of the incredible physical want in lieu of the horrific fact that hundreds of millions in India do not know Jesus. Well, amen, it was interesting sauna talk with interesting perspectives.

DAY 329
What Is a Government?

> *Every person is to be in subjection to the governing*
> *authorities. For there is no authority except from God,*
> *and those which exist are established by God. Therefore*
> *whoever resists authority has opposed the ordinance of God;*
> *and they who have opposed will receive condemnation*
> *upon themselves. For rulers are not a cause of fear for good*
> *behavior, but for evil. Do you want to have no fear of*
> *authority? Do what is good and you*
> *will have praise from the same.*
> — ROMANS 13:1-3

A just government has the moral authority from God to punish an unjust government. However, the passage can be confusing. As I write this I am in Nepal, where it is illegal to become a Christian, illegal to baptize, and illegal to preach. The Scriptural passage above was used by the Communists for years to manipulate Christians to come under their absolute authority via subjection. Rebellion against communism was said to be rebellion against God. As I have mentioned before, we Christians stand or fall by our definitions. What exactly is a "governing authority" that gets its authority from God? I have been in numerous countries where the "government" is nothing more than an organized crime mob imposing its wicked will upon the people. In some distorted way these crooks seek to decriminalize their behavior by seizing power and naming themselves "elected" officials. "Laws" that are passed are merely excuses to steal from the poor. "Taxes" are imposed to take even more; every angle is worked to take and take and take. The role of government in the Bible is to protect the people through laws that are of benefit to all, not to support a band of immoral thieves. Solomon is the greatest example of a governing authority that was established by God; he sought wisdom to help and guide the people. Punishment was meted out in the light of this wisdom. I do not think a criminal can demand subjection on the basis of having biblical authority to do so, when he does not fit the definition of a governing authority. Well, amen, I know many have had to suffer under such criminals. Though they are not true government and we are not bound as Christians to be in subjection to them, we are bound to love, pray for, and bless our enemies, as well as bless the criminal, give to them that ask, and go the second mile. However, the action taken is not out of compulsion from the belief that they are a government, but rather out of something much higher, the life of Christ within.

DAY 330
What Is It That We Must Do and What Is It That God Will Do For Us?

"Do not work for the food which perishes, but for the food which endures to eternal life, which the Son of Man will give to you, for on Him the Father, God, has set His seal." Therefore they said to Him, "What shall we do, so that we may work the works of God?" Jesus answered and said to

them, "This is the work of God, that you
believe in Him whom He has sent."
— JOHN 6:27-29

"Are we just to sit around?" This is a typical question from believers just realizing the length to which their self-effort has been involved in their Christian walk. An airplane will not come to my house and get me. I have to purchase the tickets, fight traffic as I drive to the airport, and stand in a long line to get on the plane. However, once I am on, the plane does for me what I cannot do for myself. It is clear in the Bible what is man's responsibility and what is God's. Often the two meet. "If a man does not work, let him not eat," yet, "Why do you worry about what you will eat? Look at the sparrow!" Man is to work, but not for the reason that he thinks. Work is not to secure food but is in obedience to the commandment of God. Work makes us healthy, happy, and content, as well as less anxious and depressed. If man is fed when he does not work, he will be discontented. Man works for different reasons, all good, but it is still God that provides the food. The Bible is replete with teaching that tells us what God does for us. He is the author of salvation. We cannot make someone a Christian. He is the One Who causes all things to work together for the good. Making things "happen" is not our job. He gives us His righteousness, His love, His victory, and His peace. We cannot obtain those things through work. He changes lives; we must rest as we look at others. I could go on. In fact, I find that 95% of what people are working for is already given by Him. Unbelief is what keeps people working for what God has already supplied.

However, there are things that we must do that God will not do for us. We must call on the Lord, humble ourselves, rest, be content, take the blame, be offended, forgive, cast our fears upon Him, refuse to let our minds dwell on Satan's lies and accusations, and pray without ceasing.

Then there are things we do and He does at the same time. It looks confusing, but in experience it is not. Imagine you are offended by your mate; you must own your weakness, acknowledge that you have run out of fleshly love, and invite in His love. After that you must walk across the room and initiate restoration. What happens next has nothing to do with you; it is His love flowing freely through you. It is Christ in you living through you as though it were you, but you know that it is not you. It may appear to be you to those outside looking on, but you know that it is entirely the Lord!

DAY 331
What Is Not The Will Of God

And out of the ground the Lord God caused to grow every tree that is pleasing to the sight and good for food; the tree of life also in the midst of the garden.

— GENESIS 2:9

How often we meet believers who are looking for red lights that will stop them, because they do not know whether they are doing God's will. Did Adam and Eve spend their days in paradise looking for red lights? Obviously not! God told them from the start that there was a red light in front of the tree of the knowledge of good and evil that prohibited their partaking of the fruit. From every other tree they were free to eat, and those trees fed not only the physical hunger of man but also the desires of mind, will, and emotions, for they were pleasing to the sight. The tree of life (Jesus) was there, also, the One that would feed the spirit of man. Man was free to eat from all. God clearly told of the tree that was not allowed so that man would not have to walk through the garden examining each tree and wondering if it were allowed, living a life of exhaustion and worry rather than getting on with the enjoyment of life, the dwelling place, and God Himself. Man was to be free! It takes far too much energy to know all that is allowed; it is much simpler to understand the few things that are not allowed. God has the habit of telling us what the red lights are so that we can get on with abundant living and not be sidetracked by the constant examination of the permissible while missing Him. By knowing ahead of time what the red lights are, we can get on with living in the Kingdom of God and enjoying what we are doing.

If you are confused in knowing the will of God, discern in Scripture what you are not to do and avoid those things; all else is permissible. We are to love our neighbor as our self, and when we are not doing this one thing, little else matters. Do you see how simple it is? If we avoid self-centeredness, we will find that 90% of what we do is allowable. It is permissible to move where we want, take the job we want, go on the vacation that we desire, and choose a place of fellowship and service; but it is not permissible to be bitter, judgmental, to participate in the deeds of the flesh, or to lack love and compassion, for all of these feed self-centeredness. Many strain over knowing the right car to buy when the real issue is whether they are loving their mates, not provoking others to anger, or not being competitive.

DAY 332
What Is The Flesh?

All flesh would perish together, and man would return to dust.

— JOB 34:15

who were born, not of blood nor of the will of the flesh nor of the will of man, but of God,

— JOHN 1:13

No one can be born again by the will of the flesh, insidious in its ability to take the eyes off of Jesus. It is impossible, for in the flesh are the senses of man that constantly need feeding. One may think of them as instinct gone amok. The flesh constantly screeches for attention and has a thousand methods at its disposal to get it. Senses in the body and soul (mind, will, and emotions) are given attention whether with pain or reward, feeding or starving, or conscious avoidance or obsession. Any consideration given them keeps them alive and in charge. The greater truth is that the senses want to be activated; the lesser truth is how they are stimulated, which is by eating from the tree of good and evil. The desire for food (wish fulfillment or fantasy) will keep senses alive just as much as condemnation from eating too much. Look at the anorexic or observe the obese, and both scream "flesh in control." Either an overwhelming desire for sex or the self-condemnation from looking at porno will loudly proclaim that the flesh has regained control. The senses in the soul lead to pride, whether in thinking of oneself as intelligent or stupid; both are still flesh, just as is thinking of what one can do or not do or of being caring or not caring. Again, flesh is simply the senses of body or soul being in control. People in the East have a tendency toward denying the flesh in an attempt to appease it, while those in the West feed it in an attempt to appease it. Of course, the Westerners do not come out ahead, in that nothing is enough to satisfy it; like a tick, flesh will feed until it explodes and destroys itself. Nor do those in the East really have an advantage, since there is ultimately no way to withhold from the flesh.

Nevertheless, the flesh is flesh and is hostile to God, which explains why flesh desires to be in control so that man is flesh-centered. If man becomes Christ-centered, the senses of flesh would not be fed but would be subdued before Christ. The flesh can never be more than a slave, and a rebellious one at that, for by the works of the flesh will no flesh be justified. Believers and non-believers alike have flesh. The saddest thing is to witness someone who has abandoned his will to flesh. I meet many Christians that struggle with the sin of homosexuality but are not homosexual, and someone meeting them would never guess their particular deed of the flesh. However, meet someone who has by choice yielded to that area of the flesh, and it is evident in his or her body. Just a few minutes with that person reveals the object of their fleshly leanings.

Now, why would God put us in flesh? I am not talking about a physical body but the accompanying anti-God desires of the senses that reside in the physical body and in the soul. Well, it has been said that the greatness of a man is not determined by what he does but rather by what he refuses to do. The man who feeds his flesh through adventure and the procession of praise for victory or the mockery for defeat is not as great a man as he who says, "Not my will but Thy will be done." Having flesh and its senses allows man the unique opportunity of choice, of living on the earth but not being of the earth, of living to God and not to senses, and the discovery of something higher in this life, spiritual fulfillment. Flesh, or rather the call of the senses to stay alive, is a constant reminder that we must move our eyes to Jesus. It is another stronghold allowing us to stay focused. If God is for us, then who can be against us? Again, the flesh is never a friend; we may buffet it and make it a slave, but it will never be a friend. The flesh is a strange thing in that it cannot live on its own but must thrive on something that is living. It adapts to resemble the thing on which it lives, but it is not really a living thing. When man dies, his fleshly condition dies.

DAY 333
What Made Me Weep Made Me Rejoice!

The son said to him, "Father, I have sinned against heaven and against you. I am no longer worthy to be called your son."

— LUKE 15:21

The situation that makes us weep can, with a change in our attitude, make us rejoice. We say with the Prodigal Son that we are "no longer worthy." Those three little words can be the source of pain or joy. It is the source of pain if we are trying to create worthiness. However, it can be the source of joy when we see that Jesus came to be our worth. It is interesting that so many sought to take the life of Elijah. He would not let any take it. Yet he wanted God to take his life upon this one discovery: "It is enough, take away my life, I am not better than my fathers!" He had discovered that he had no worthiness and wanted to die. We do the same thing when we fail, but God wants us to see that we lack worthiness so that we can recognize that Jesus has become our worthiness. When we see this, we will wonder why we ever sought to have worth of our own. We must see that Jesus is everything we need. Greater things than He did we will do. Can we believe it? If not, it is because we are looking to ourselves— our flesh and our efforts—for its fulfillment. We have no worthiness, but we can give up on ourselves, for Christ is in us. He is our worthiness, our strength, our holiness, our righteousness, and when we see it, He will flow through us. Seeing that which we are not must always be followed by

seeing just what He is in us. What initially caused us to weep will make us rejoice.

DAY 334
What Qualifies God To Be God?

The one who does not love does not know God, for God is love.

— I JOHN 4:8

What qualifies God to be God? Why is God eligible to receive worship and to have all glory, honor, and authority? What makes Him a father or gives Him the right to make judgments, to tell others what to do, or to have a kingdom? The answer is really quite simple: God is love! He is perfect, complete, defining, and all-encompassing Love. This means that God is patient, kind, is not jealous, does not brag, is not arrogant, never acts unbecomingly, does not seek His own, is not provoked, does not take into account any wrong suffered, hates unrighteousness, rejoices in truth, bears all things, believes all things, hopes all things, endures all things, and never fails. Is there anyone more qualified than God to be in charge?

Well, of course! We already knew God is love! That is exactly the problem: we knew. It is something in the past that we remember being told, but we have moved on to consider loftier aspects of God. The revelation of His love is the foundation for everything we will ever learn and every experience that we have (good or bad); it is the source of our devotion and obedience.

One time as I walked through the forest, I noticed that what should have been the fresh green sprouts on the tips of a pine tree had turned yellow, and the year's growth was wasted. The tree would begin next year at the same place it had this year. It reminded me of how new growth within us, no matter how glorious, will be killed without the continued revelation of His love.

We easily mouth the words, "God is love," but do we have the revelation of it? To have God at the backs of our minds throughout the day is to confine love in the background. As stated many times, we stand or fall by our definitions. We need definitions, but words cannot describe love; the grandest, most complex vocabulary will not get the job done of enabling us to know what love is. Is it possible with words to describe the great I AM? Then it is equally impossible to describe Love, for God is Love. God did not even try to describe love with words, because they were not good enough! So the Word became flesh and dwelt among us. To know Love we must know Jesus.

DAY 335
We Love With His Love

*By this all men will know that you are My disciples, if you
have love for one another.*

— JOHN 13:35

As I mature, I relate to Peter in deeper and deeper ways, ways in which I wish I did not. Christ's question to me, "Michael, do you love Me?" can elicit the response, "Lord, You know that I like You." No need lying to Him! He knows my deepest attitudes. What amazes me is His response back, "Well, I do really love you." How can He say that? Because He is the epitome of Love that is always being acted out. He tells us to love an enemy. Does He not do what He commands? If I am His enemy, will He not love me? He tells us to forgive when offended. Will He not then forgive when He is offended? We see the Sermon on the Mount as a teaching to follow and forget that it describes His actions, attitudes, and behaviors toward us. Love qualifies Him to be God!

Do you have the revelation? He loves you! He loves your few hairs left on your head, the way your eyes squint, your height, your looks, the shape of your hands, that odd-looking toe, the wrinkles, the way you speak, and every other aspect of your uniqueness. You do not believe me. I will let eternity speak against the years. I can wait; I will be proven right. When you get to heaven, you will see yourself as He sees you. When you do, you will not ask to have anything changed. You will even keep your so-called deformity. Many of you have gone your whole lives believing yourselves to be unlovable. Unlovable simply does not exist for perfect Love.

Do you have the revelation? He loves you! He has an intense yearning for you. Some of you are grandparents who know the excitement that wells up within when your grandchild is coming, the abundance of photos you take, the writing down of the child's sayings, and the attention you direct to his every little act. Multiply that times one billion and you might get an inkling of God's love for you. If you can see it in the deepest part of your being, then anything that He asks of you, you quickly do without question, knowing the request is based in love. The obedience of Jesus toward the Father was not a task, something that must be performed implicitly; rather, His obedience was always a joy because He had the revelation of God's love. If God, who loved Him so much, asked for something, that something must be firmly rooted in perfect love. Jesus was so convinced of God's perfect love that when He was asked to go to the cross, He went with joy. I do not mean He was laughing, but He knew perfect Love was up to something, such as that the cross meant a crown! God is Love! Hebrews 12:2, "Fixing our eyes on Jesus, the author and perfecter of faith, who for the joy set before Him endured the cross, despising the shame, and has sat down at the right hand of the throne of God." You see commands as coming from an authoritative father figure, one who is keeping you from having fun, and you fight obedience. God is not your earthly father! The missing dynamic in perfect obedience is the revelation of perfect love. How can you believe God and act if you are not first convinced of His love? II Thessalonians 3:5, "And may the Lord direct your hearts into the love of God and into the steadfastness of Christ."

DAY 336
We Need a Revelation of Love

We have come to know and have believed the love which
God has for us. God is love, and the one who abides in love
abides in God, and God abides in him.

— I JOHN 4:16

Do you have the revelation? He loves you! When you judge God as having traits like your earthly father—critical, explosive, angry, controlling, passive, silent, and disconnected—then you find ways to avoid Him. Avoiding Love! As you avoid Him, you fail, for apart from Him you can do nothing. Failure ushers in fear. You need to go to Him; however, you have been away for so long the fear of what will happen if you approach is greater than the fear of staying away. He loves you! I John 4:18, "There is no fear in love; but perfect love casts out fear, because fear involves punishment, and the one who fears is not perfected in love."

Are you getting the revelation? It is the foundation for all new growth. God is Love. There is far too little genuine repentance evident among believers today. What passes for repentance is an adolescent "I am sorry" that actually means, "I am sorry I got caught." "Jesus, I am sorry that I failed" can be translated, "I am sorry that I messed up my image!" This mere appearance of repentance never works change into our lives. We take sin lightly because we have taken His love lightly. Once we understand His love, then when we see our sin we can enter into true repentance. If you have ever had a child rebel, you will have a glimpse into what I am saying. You nursed the child, held the child in your arms, dreamt of the future, wanted for him, sacrificed for him, believed in him, and even turned a blind eye to defects. Then one day all of that came crashing in when you found drugs, birth control, or worse in his room. You had heard of its happening to one of the neighborhood mothers, but it did not bother you nearly so much; it was not your child. The weight, the pain, the turmoil, and the tears hit you as love crushed you. You remembered the article in the paper, the x-ray image of a brain with dead cells, and tales of self-mutilation. It was a sickening feeling. Something had to be done. Next you confronted the child, who had any of a variety of responses. "Everyone does it." "I was keeping it for a friend," which because of so much pain the parent actually wants to believe. Or perhaps, "You had no business going through my things." The child basically says whatever it takes to get you out of the room so he can get back to his own reality. It is quite obvious who is suffering for the sin: the one who loves him. Mother and/or father are bearing the sins of the child in their own bodies on crosses that love built. If there were any way to take the burden off of the parent and place it on the child, the child would see things differently and understand that he was destroying love. The simple, "Everyone does it," would be replaced by, "I will never do it again." This is one reason that all of us need the fresh revelation of Christ's love: We have too easily let Him bear the weight. Though Love will bear it, why be like that adolescent in the sense of being accustomed to love, familiar with it, expecting it, and therefore giving little value to it? I Peter 2:24, "And He Himself bore our sins in His body on the cross, that we might die to sin and live to righteousness; for by His wounds you were healed." Oh, to know His Love. Ephesians 3:19, "And to know the love of Christ which surpasses knowledge, that you may be filled up to all the fullness of God." If you had the revelation of how much He loves you, when there was sickness, death, tragedy, struggle, defeat, or any suffering, you would stop and think, "Perfect Love is up to something." And for the joy that you know Love had set before you, you would endure it. Well, amen, only He can reveal Himself, for to reveal Love is to reveal Himself.

How would you feel if you were to tell me the problems in your life, and after each one I responded, "God loves you"? What would you think? Would you be glad that you talked to me? I am guessing that if you are like the majority of people, you would walk off feeling slighted, but if so, that response reveals a greater problem than a rebellious child, an unfaithful husband, or the rude relative. For when the answer, "Jesus loves you," means nothing—and in reality it is the only answer that means anything—the root issue is revealed that the Church has gotten away from Jesus. How do I know the Church does not have the revelation of Love? Love is not regarded as the greatest of things. The word love is used and its definition touted, but it is not practiced. There is a reason. Words have no power, and that is why the Word had to become flesh. There is no way to know Love if Jesus is not known. If the Church had the revelation that Jesus is the definition of love, the words "Jesus loves you" would be enough for any situation. I cannot be emphatic enough that reading about Jesus will not bring the revelation needed, just as it is good to read a friend's letters but better to be with the friend. Why should I be abused for saying what I am about to say? "Fellowship with Jesus is better than reading the Bible." Reading the Bible is good; the Bible says it is good, and I am saying that it is good. II Timothy 3:16, "All Scripture is inspired by God and profitable for teaching, for reproof, for correction, for training in righteousness," but personalized teaching by Jesus is better! The complaint that "I was taught that Jesus teaches me through the Bible" need not be refuted here; I am not arguing the validity of the Scriptures. I am talking about a completely different topic. Do the Church, the Para-Church organizations, the Bible translators, the seminaries, the Christian counselors, and the majority of Christians believe that Jesus is alive? I do not think so! I rarely hear it mentioned, as though it is one of Christianity's best-kept secrets that the Founder is not dead! He overcame death, and He is alive! Oh, we sing it, shout it, and proclaim every Easter that He is risen. Of course, that afternoon we are working through a problem with our pastor, reading a book, or talking to a friend when we could be talking to Jesus! It is in talking with Him, listening to Him, fellowshipping with Him, and working things out with Him that we slowly come to the revelation of Love. The Word became flesh so that we could know the Love of God, and His Love is the foundation for what has and ever will happen.

DAY 337
God's Definition of Love

Though you have not seen Him, you love Him, and
though you do not see Him now, but believe in Him, you
greatly rejoice with joy inexpressible and full of glory.
— I PETER 1:8

We must stop trying to define love in human terms. It is too narrow and incorrect. We are human, so our definitions will be lacking. Therefore, it is only God who can define Himself. As humans we are so far off on our definition of God that when He came, no one recognized Him! "See how great a love the Father has bestowed upon us, that we should be called children of God; and {such} we are. For this reason the world does not know us, because it did not know Him" (I John 3:1).

Again, we stand or fall by our definitions. The world's definition of love is the fulfillment of the lust of the eyes, the lust of the flesh, and the boastful pride of life. When a different person, position, or thing seems to further feed all three aspects of the flesh, the carnal person might well "fall out of love" with whom or what he had and say he "loves" that other person, job, or material possession. For someone in the world to say, "I love you," is to say, "You are meeting all three aspects of my carnal nature," and that is why the world's love is so fragile. Remember the breakups in high school? Some had the honesty to say, "I found someone better!" Better at what? Better at meeting the lust of their eyes, lust of their flesh, and the boastful pride of their life.

How hard it is to hang on to someone with such stiff fleshly competition from others! The world's love is definitely performance-based. When we do not meet a child's carnal needs we may well hear him mutter, "I do not love you!" Is it any wonder that some people become hermits? For in an unenlightened sense the effort involved to win the love of another is exhausting, never ending, and ultimately disappointing. In the world when someone says, "I love you," the object of that love had better keep performing. Another problem is that the flesh is like the fire that never says enough. A child of ten years eats more than a child of one month. Therefore, by the very nature of carnality, what satisfied yesterday does not today, and the looming phrase of "You are not meeting my needs!" seems always just a day or two away. Feeding the flesh of another by meeting carnal needs is a Catch-22, for it paves the way for a greater fleshly need that cannot be met, and that finally leads to rejection. This is the baggage and definition many of us were carrying with us the day we met Jesus and heard Him whisper to us, "I love you!" "He loves me! Oh no, now I must perform. I must meet all of His needs. He has a need for me to be perfect, holy, righteous, blameless, forgiving, giving, consistent, pure, free of all lusts, and more." If we open the Bible and start reading when we believe the above definition of love, we will be overwhelmed by all that must be done to keep the relationship with Him alive. Slowly the flesh begins to wane in its ability to keep the relationship working. We fall short and we await the breakup. When He whispers again, "I love you," we do not believe it. We still remember high school when the boy or girl said, "I love you," just to placate us; the next day we discovered he or she was off with someone else. Suffice it to say that in and of ourselves we just do not know what love is.

For the one who has the revelation of His love, everything changes. It is best experienced, but I will try to describe it. His love is an absolute. His love is a standalone love. His love never needs feeding. His love is not dependent on another. Just as a tree is a tree, a man is a man, and the sun is the sun, love is love. Nothing that happens on earth will affect the sun; the sun is the sun. It stands alone. It does not shine on condition. Someone can hate a rock all he wants, curse at it, throw it, and tell it to stop being a rock, but the fact is, his actions do not change the fact that the rock is a rock. God is Love; Love is His character. If someone's actions could change His love, then man's behavior could change God. But God cannot be changed. "Jesus Christ {is} the same yesterday and today, {yes} and forever" (Hebrews 13:8).

DAY 338
What Love Is Not

Do not love the world nor the things in the world. If anyone loves the world, the love of the Father is not in him.

— I JOHN 2:15

Who of you thinks that you are greater than God? Do you think your actions can change the very nature of God? Being stupid and falling into sin and failure is a different topic; the topic here is love and whether you think those things can change the very DNA, so to speak, of God. He is and forever will be patient, kind, never arrogant, never abusive, working for your good, not provoked, not keeping a list, hating the bad that happens to you, rejoicing with the truth, bearing with you, believing in you, hoping for you, enduring to the end, and never failing. It blows your mind! You perform your whole life to be loved because love is conditional, and then along comes Jesus, loving without condition. In a sense, He just cannot help Himself! He is love. As I said, this revelation will change everything!

In our quest for love we have exhausted ourselves performing, competing, and blaming. The standouts in the race to be loved are (not all, but many of) the entertainers, politicians, the title holders, and the "successful." In the end they die after having relived their few moments of glory and experienced loneliness, bitterness, and reclusion. In brief, if we do not know that God loves us, we will continue to work for man's love. Some feel so rejected and worthless that they are working for the whole world's love to overcome the feelings. This is why many live to man and not to God. Avoiding man is another form of living to man. Once we have the revelation of God's love, nothing else will matter. Some think I live in the clouds, but I am quite serious about God's love. When a carnal husband tells his wife that she does not meet his needs and he is leaving for another woman, it hurts not only because of the rejection but the fact that the relationship was never deeper than flesh. Her response, "God loves me!" is not mere words but fact that must come by revelation. The realization that God Himself loves a person is an acceptance that dusts earthly rejection.

Perhaps in your opinion (because the world brainwashed you) your life, your job, and your ministry have never really gone anywhere (the same could have been said of Jesus working at the carpenter bench in a small village with narrow-minded people). But through revelation to say, "God loves me," makes none of that matter. Does He love the pastor with a big church more and the one serving a small congregation less? Does He love the believer more that has straight A's on his spiritual report card and less when he earns D's and F's? Does He love the one with a doctor's degree more than the eighth-grade dropout? Tell me, what do you think? God's love is not and cannot be worked for; God's love can only be enjoyed. No matter what you have been up to today and what you will be doing tomorrow, you can say, "God loves me!" We allow men in the pulpit to tell us covertly that they are more loved because of what they have done. I tell you, they are boasting in their unbelief! To know that He loves you softens every blow that life can hand out. You were left out? He loves you! You had to quit university? He loves you! You were going to seminary but decided on business school instead? He loves you! If you had gone home a day earlier you could have seen your grandmother before she passed away? He loves you! One bumper sticker made to be cheeky says, "Jesus loves you, but everyone else thinks you are a jerk." It does not offend me; I like the truth that is in it. If everybody thinks I am a jerk, but He loves me, that truly does make all the difference. To hear that He loves us means very little to most, for their ears and head hear the words but their emotions say, "He loves me if . . .!" This causes them to discount His love and go on working for what they already have.

God has been trying to teach you what His pure love is for years. He has never forsaken you, when you were faithless He remained faithful, and He is not making you pay consequences. Still you might lack the revelation of His love. Simply pray and ask that you might see it. It will set you free! God loves you! The revelation must come through Him, and Love will make life make sense. Love reveals that your relationship is not man-generated but God-generated, not man-maintained but God-maintained. Often we hear, "Do not give up! Keep trying! Hang in there! You can make it! You are further along than when you began! If you will just lead one person to Christ it will be worth it! Keep studying, then you will understand." What is the source of all such piffle? Its source is ignorance that gets spewed from the foundation of a man-based relationship incognizant of the Love that makes the relationship completely God-planted, God-germinated, and God-harvested. Through Jesus God continued to shout that the relationship was Love-based, and yet every question directed toward Jesus proved that man understood the relationship to be completely performance-centered. I like hiking and pointing out the wildlife, for just as a painting reveals the painter, so does creation reveal the Creator. I find it very frustrating when someone cannot see the deer in the middle of the field; worse yet is the person that cannot hear me telling him where the deer is. Eyes that cannot see and ears that cannot hear are vexing. We hear that our relationship is God-based, we see that it is, and yet we go on working for what we already have. Christianity without the Love of God as the foundation produces religion, and the Christian religion is the ugliest of all, because every other religion was created as such—with man instigating and executing what is believed to establish a relationship with "deity"—but in Christ God initiated the relationship with man and finished the work to allow it. If Christianity is approached with a religious spirit, it gets, as some would say, real goofy! A religious man may imitate Buddha, Mohammed, or a New-Age teacher; it is just man imitating man. But can a religious man imitate God? Impossible! Jesus was not imitating God; Jesus was God. Christ's life is God's life.

Again, Christianity is God-generated. Let me ask you a question. Imagine you have known your husband, wife, or friend for many years and know of his many foibles. Over the past month you have been acutely frustrated with the person's lack of spirituality, when he comes to you and tells you that Jesus appeared and spoke to him. How would you take it? Would you doubt that it happened? Why? You do not see the person as being holy enough? Or if you did believe it, would you be jealous, because in your heart you believe you are just a better person? These attitudes reveal that you do not adequately know the Love of God.

DAY 339
What The Deeper Life Is Not

From the fullness of His grace we have all received one blessing after another.

— JOHN 1:16

I was talking with a very caring, loving, and spiritual brother in the Lord when he made the comment that he could not understand much of Christian counseling and theology, so he concluded that it was unintelligible because he was a simple man and the information in the books he was reading was just too deep for him. It so vexes me to hear such things, for the books he mentioned were not unintelligible to him because they were too deep, but rather because they were too unbelieving. It is unbelieving man who makes the Christian life deep, difficult, and hard to understand, because he has no intention of following the simple commands of Christ. The unbelieving believer has a vested interest in saying such things as, "It cannot be that simple; we need to know more," and, "We must find the balance." The statements of Jesus to love God and your neighbor would not be classified as profound by the elitist "deep" thinkers, but for the believing they represent the river of life that never goes dry. One who has Christ is deep, among the wisest of the wise! His mind is being renewed and he leads the world! One who has Christ possesses the Way of life, and so his world is coming together!

DAY 340
What To Do When Accused Of Being False

Who is the liar but the one who denies
that Jesus is the Christ?
— I JOHN 2:22

. . . regarded as deceivers and yet true.
— II CORINTHIANS 6:8

Every believer must be prepared for the day when he is accused of being a false teacher or a cult leader. It has happened to me, and so I have begun opening nearly every conference with the admonition that not everything I say is true; I am a man in process and make mistakes. However, the one thing I always will say in a conference that is truth is that Jesus is the Way, the Truth, and the Life. Sometimes I say the wrong thing, sometimes I am wrong, and other times I am misunderstood when a person hears what I am not saying. However, there are those with an agenda to disregard the message of abiding in Christ moment by moment by discrediting me; my words, written or uttered, are examined to confirm a pre-established bias. These believers are something like pre-conversion Saul, wanting to stir up the crowd to lay their robes at the feet and stone any who do not agree with their positions 100%. They throw around words such as cult, false teacher, and heretic, harsh assessments for one who teaches that nothing but Jesus matters. I have often told those who are looking for ways in which they can discredit me that if they would simply sit down with me, I would give them a list of my harmful attributes. I have been negative, I have not always abided in Christ, I have walked in the flesh, I have judged, I have been bitter, I have not walked in love or loved without hypocrisy, and the list goes on. But then again, knowing my own frailty is why there is no record of my ever trying to get anyone to follow me. My emphasis consistently runs toward following Jesus. Well, amen, false judgments must come, and some with a vengeance.

What am I to do? First, I must see God in it. David looked at the man on the hill cursing and spitting and refused to allow his soldiers to harm the man, because he wondered whether God had allowed it for His own purposes. There is a purpose in being judged falsely and loving enemies. I may not want any enemies, but I cannot learn to bless those that curse me without ever having been cursed. I want to rise above distractions and follow Jesus, but I never want the distractions. Just as Judas delivered up Jesus, and from that treacherous act Life was given to man, so God sends us our own Judas, who in ignorance delivers us up in order that we might discover that the Jesus within is greater than the slander without. If I am not preaching Christ crucified, then in all honesty I want God to remove me from the lives of others. But if I am preaching Christ, I will let God deal with the detractor on the hill.

Second, I cannot allow the judgments of the carnal to become my focus. This is the most demonic side of accusations, that a hitherto unknown person might actually steal a believer's focus away from Jesus. In a worst-case scenario in which what is being said is true, health would come from a glance back to Jesus, not a prolonged look at and dialogue with the detractor. Therefore, when I am attacked, I am best off to go silent and start talking all the more about Jesus, not wasting time defending myself. To win the alliance of an accuser is not a victory! By attacking me and making me his focus, the accuser proves that he does not agree with the message of keeping our focus on Jesus.

Third, I can freely tell other believers that they can help by not defending me to anyone. I am God's servant, so those who accuse should be sent to the Master of the servant. The servant is not greater than the Master; the Master is all that matters. We defend the preaching of Jesus always; we defend the messenger never. When we start defending someone we love, our flesh is stirred, our focus moves from Jesus, our peace departs, and our accuser has accomplished the goal of the "accuser of the brethren." This is the most difficult thing for me; I can stand to be slandered, but I cannot bear seeing those I love slandered. It is important that we do not defend men, for it is always a trap the enemy has set. When someone we love is falsely accused, we should respond by talking about Jesus. Our goal is Jesus. Remember, the detractor's job is to detract us from Jesus to a lesser issue.

Fourth and finally, I want to have compassion for those who make false judgments, for I have done it myself. I have gotten everything wrong. Having this in my past, I can say with complete confidence that I would rather be the one being judged than the one doing the judging. The one being judged can come away sweet, but the one involved with judging will always go away depleted and under the judgment of God.

DAY 341
What Will He Do In Our Weakness?

Every good and perfect gift is from above, coming down from the Father of the heavenly lights, who does not change like shifting shadows.
— JAMES 1:17

I was on an international trip when I was asked to have tea with an evangelist before a church service. The purpose of our time together, as it turned out, was so that he could reveal that I do not read my Bible the proper way, that Westerners cannot really minister in this country, my messages are a bit too complex, and the altar call was done entirely in the wrong manner. I received it; I can see it is difficult to have me around and I am a real labor for this person. Therefore, here is how I began the meeting that followed. "I am aware of my weaknesses when I travel in another country. I do not speak your language, I wear the wrong clothing, I do not preach, pray, or have an altar call as you would, and I am going to mess up many things. I want to acknowledge this and ask for your prayers. If anything comes out of the meeting, it will have to be God, and it will be obvious to all. I am happy to stand here and say, 'I can't,' because that confession stirs something else in me: the assurance that He can." Well, the people really prayed for me, and God gave a wonderful message on the Lord's Prayer. The weakest believer who goes to Jesus is better off than those with great understanding and little time spent with the Lord. I told them of the leper, Michael Francis, a believer and a law student in India that developed leprosy. His wife took the kids and abandoned him. He died a homeless beggar. Before he died, Alex Mathew asked him, "Michael, what is abiding?" As he sat on the concrete platform, ears, fingers, and toes eaten away, Michael moved his palm across the sidewalk and said, "See this cement that I sleep on? It is as soft as velvet to me, for it is the very lap of Jesus. Every night He holds me here. That is abiding." He did not know much, but he knew Jesus.

DAY 342
What Will You Learn When You Are Cheated?

Let each one do just as he has purposed in his heart; not grudgingly or under compulsion; for God loves a cheerful giver. And God is able to make all grace abound to you, that always having all sufficiency in everything, you may have an abundance for every good deed; as it is written, "He scattered abroad, He gave to the poor, His righteousness abides forever."

— II CORINTHIANS 9:7-9

I actually believe that the Lord, on occasion, has allowed me to be cheated, stolen from, to misplace money, and even to have it fly out a window or drop down a sewer. Why? We can say that our security is in Him, that we believe in His provision, and that we are living under His control. However, our reaction to money lost is an indication of where we really stand in relation to those things. When I give, and give liberally, I am in faith. I have control over the giving. However, theft is uncontrolled giving without the consent of my will, giving I had not planned on, giving of what I had laid aside for a predetermined use. If I react negatively when it disappears, what does that reveal about my heart? It is a fact that I am living under His provision, and as the Scriptures say, "The Lord gives and the Lord takes away; blessed be the name of the Lord."

DAY 343
Whatever Makes You Happy!

Fixing our eyes on Jesus, the author and perfecter of faith,
who for the joy set before Him endured the cross,
despising the shame, and has sat down at the
right hand of the throne of God.

— HEBREWS 12:2

The Spirit is always whispering to me, "Do whatever makes you happy!" The enemy has invested a good bit of time getting believers to buy into the lie that walking after the flesh is satisfying and that righteousness is somehow less than exciting, if not downright boring. One time in a foreign country I sensed that the Lord wanted me to take a walk and listen, but I was not going to go. I started to leave, then came back, thinking that the man who had organized my meetings would want to talk to me. However, he walked right by and never saw me. I decided on the walk. Here is what happened next. As I walked, the Lord spoke, "Why do you hang onto your self life?" I thought long and hard to answer, "Because I think I can find some enjoyment." Just then an old woman with a cane appeared, dragging a bag and her purse. I passed her and then was quickened to stop and turn back; she was fearful at seeing my suit and being on a lonely road. I reached in my pocket, opened her hand, and inserted some money. She immediately broke down weeping and explained something in her native tongue. She sounded hopeless, something about having to go and having nothing. She cried so much that I reached forward to hold her as she wept. I only said, "Jesus." I walked away, crying myself, and the Lord spoke, "Do the things you hold onto give you that much joy?" I turned to look once more at the old woman, and she was gone. All night I could smell on my clothes the distinct odor of a homeless person, but the aroma had a sweet memory attached to it. Nothing compares to God's little surprises. The Lord did not bless her so much as He had blessed me through this encounter. And the Spirit continues whispering to me, "Do whatever makes you happy!"

DAY 344
What Is Your Address?

Beloved, now we are children of God, and it has not appeared as yet what we shall be. We know that, when He appears, we shall be like Him, because we shall see Him just as He is.

— I JOHN 3:2

Our bodies reside at a physical address that generally gives us great comfort. There are many advantages to having this place of abiding, such as the enjoyment of coming back after a long trip. There really is no place quite like home.

Just as we have a physical address for our bodies, we also have an emotional and spiritual address, a place we most often go to receive, ideally, comfort and refuge from the world. Unfortunately, many have an address on Abused Street, Racism Street, Alcoholic Street, Co-dependency Street, Women's Rights Street, Denial Street, Thankless Husband Street, Anti-nuclear Power Street, Political Party Street, and more. Just as we would be at a loss to know what to do if our physical homes burned down, many would not know what to do in the absence of their emotional address if the hurt from the past, co-dependency, ten steps, or abuse were taken away. These are people who are not comfortable until something is said about the abuse of women in the church, the rejection of people because of race, those who misunderstand divorce, Christians that are too judgmental, or the failures of a mate. Isolating themselves from information that does not support their address, they wrap themselves around issues, wrap the issues around themselves, and desire to entice and wrap up others. They are not wrapped around the person of Christ. They have for so long felt at home at their assumed address that their minds and hearts effortlessly end up there. I am not saying that there is no truth in their particular emphases; I am saying that Truth is not found at those addresses.

Because the believer has been crucified with Christ, was buried, and received a new life, the believer has also received a new address on "Child of God Street"! In each home on that street dwells a wonderful, loving Father, our Leader, Guide, Lord, and Savior, Jesus, and the great Comforter. All are invited to come on any day for a great meal. To be satisfied in life, each of us must give ourselves to something greater than ourselves. We cannot obsess on self. Obsession does more damage than any actual event. If life is reduced to what has happened to us, what we look like, the actions of others, or even our own sin, we will end the day depleted. We must go home to the proper address, where something bigger than ourselves awaits to greet and nurture us: the Father, Son, and Holy Spirit.

DAY 345
When Life Is Not Working

And after you have suffered for a little, the God of all grace, who called you to His eternal glory in Christ, will Himself perfect, confirm, strengthen, and establish you.
— I PETER 5:10

I often hear someone say, "Nothing is working out!" That is never true for Christians, so they are only suffering from the lack of a doctrine that properly explains defeat, suffering, reversals, broken relationships, sickness, and disappointments. While it is obvious that many of the above are the result of sin, God is so big that He can use what we have done. I am not teaching that we sin so grace will abound, but neither am I saying that grace does not abound. When we bemoan how things are not working out, we have something we are judging those things against. Often we have judged them against what we believe would be "good things," the opposite of which we call bad and "things not working out." Let me illustrate. One thing we label "bad" and "things not working out" is seeing a child rebelling. It was bad that the Prodigal Son rebelled, took his inheritance money, and went away to squander it; however, the fact that he came to the end of himself and returned home, never to leave again, was actually "things working out." We have a definition of the state comprising "things working out" and judge everyday life against it, but is our definition correct? Is it true that "things working out" never includes suffering, getting sick, having a conflict, being in want, or depression? If so, "things" certainly never "worked out" for Jesus! For me, "things" have worked out if at the end of the day I have lost my pride, my glory, my strength, my righteousness, and my kingdom, for those things hinder the free flow of the greatest treasure that is inside me: Christ in me, the hope of glory. I have found that as I have given the proper definition to "things working out," nothing has gone wrong. When I judge what took place today against this model, things are working out perfectly. Can we yield to it? The proof that we have chosen God's glory is that we shed ourselves of our own.

DAY 346
When Will My Child Arrive?

And he was longing to fill his stomach with the pods that the swine were eating, and no one was giving {anything} to him.

— LUKE 15:16

Many a parent wants and waits for his child to arrive at the right place. The parent experiences anxiety at the reversals. When will the child arrive so that the parent will be able to rest and stop worrying? At this point the parent must define what arriving is, and the parent's definition must fit with God's. Most often a parent is playing God and merely giving the concept of arrival his own definition, one that bolsters his identity and image in his own eyes. Is God asleep, or is He working out, in order, what needs to happen in the child's life to secure a spiritual future? In the pigpen the Prodigal Son had arrived; he was exactly where his father did not want him but exactly where the Father in heaven wanted him, for it was in the pigpen that the boy's future would be secured. The pigpen was a turning point that brought with it the finality that the boy would never again be tempted to go there. What if there had been no pigpen? What if he had arrived home with just a little money left? Would he have arrived? No! He would have been home without the commitment to really be there. The place where we lose glory, pride, righteousness, strength, and kingdom is the place that must come first. A parent's child may be exactly where he needs to be. He may be only in the process of arriving.

DAY 347
Where Is Jesus?

Jesus said, "But I, when I am lifted up from the earth, will draw all men to myself."

— JOHN 12:32

Once I read a church newsletter while pretending that I was an unbeliever considering going to church. Would I be interested in finding out more about what this particular church emphasized? Most of what was written could have been left unsaid. There were a few articles that contained the popular Christian psycho-babble. Some activities were listed with the encouragement that if I, or someone I sent, attended, it would be life changing. I knew better than that! The newsletter was well planned and laid out, it had a certain appeal, but every attempt to interest the reader only prompted my conviction that these words had no power. Noticeably absent in the several pages was any mention of Jesus.

As I read, I wanted to be able to say something that would communicate the discovery of life. All the phrases that came to mind were worn out, holding very little meaning because of overuse. What could I say that was new? Then the Spirit whispered, "Speak of Jesus in My power. In My power the same old word is always new!" I was reminded of visiting in another country the most successful missionary that I personally know. When I asked the secret of success, he responded, "I only speak of Jesus. I have not spent years understanding the culture or the language; I have only spoken of Jesus."

To stand back and objectively listen as a believer witnesses to someone certainly does not sound that dynamic. In fact, the words may have often been said before by others. Freedom from self, sin, the world, the rejection and hurt of others, money for which the world clamors, worry, or fear, all such talk from those who abide in His power is different, not in content so much as in power. Then it is not merely said to another that God loves him; the listener can sense God's loving him through the speaker. Each day in Christ is new, exciting, and appealing.

DAY 348
Who Among Us Is Like Jesus?

If you abide in Me, and My words abide in you, ask
whatever you wish, and it shall be done for you.

— JOHN 15:7

I have a challenge for those who have been believers for many years. Read through the commands of Jesus and see, after all these years, how well you are doing. How much progress has been made? Has there been a ten, twenty, thirty, or forty percent improvement? How do you act at your worst now? This is not turning into a guilt-based article; I just want to make the point that you still fall way short. Why? I believe there are two things that we must always keep in mind when reading the commandments of Jesus. First, He was setting a standard that unregenerate man could never keep. The bar was being set so high that no one would be able to reach His level of righteousness. Peter listened every day and knew well the teaching to love an enemy. The end result was cutting off a man's ear! Often overlooked is one aspect of Christ's teaching: that it reveals not only what man should do but what man cannot do. Second, Jesus did it all; He did what He taught, and He did it freely, naturally, consistently, and without struggle. Therefore, He proved it could be done. Here is the secret to dealing with commands we cannot keep, commands that must be kept, and commands that He kept easily. The solution is simple: We admit we cannot; He moves and keeps them through us. It will be Christ in us living through us as though it is us, but it is not us. We do not aspire to live like Jesus; we gave that up. It is really Jesus living through us. Beautiful!

DAY 349
Who Is The Legalist?

For the whole Law is fulfilled in one word, in the statement, "You shall love your neighbor as yourself." But if you bite and devour one another, take care lest you be consumed by one another. But I say, walk by the Spirit, and you will not carry out the desire of the flesh. For the flesh sets its desire against the Spirit, and the Spirit against the flesh; for these are in opposition to one another, so that you may not do the things that you please.

— GALATIANS 5:14-17

Anyone who does not get up immediately after a failure is a legalist! Do we want to compound our sin by adding legalism to it? Okay, so we dabble in the flesh. No, I do not mean that we were drunk or involved in acts of adultery; those things do indeed cause tremendous damage, but I am referring to the insidious things that cause lifelong harm, like dabbling in pride, self-righteousness, unbelief, and independence. We could not see that the Lord would act on our behalf, and so we went our own way. We could not wait for God to move, so we took matters into our own hands. We obsessed on our condition, cast the blame on others, and now we are mad at all those around us. We could not find that missing object on which to explode, so we accused the first passerby. We verbally abused those around us. We were too busy to listen to the child or the mate and pushed past him. All day we have thought about the selfish and stupid people with whom we are surrounded. Past events, proving our assumption, whirl around with tornado-like force in our minds, and to make matters worse, we justify our condition. Someone might find himself reading this article in just such a condition.

Then comes the gentle whispering of the Holy Spirit, "It was I. I permitted it all! I am going to show you another hidden corner of your being where I can be your life." With the revelation that it was He comes the revelation of just what terrible Christians we are. Remember, with every revelation of Jesus must come an equal revelation of our flesh, for if not, we will spiral into an even deeper self-righteousness. Now what? How do we clean up the mess? First, what we do not do: We never allow a revelation of our flesh to drive us further from Jesus. This is the exact opposite of what the revelation was intended to accomplish. It is to show us what we are not and what He is. Do not compound it by running from Jesus. What could that accomplish? Only Jesus can heal us. Second, do not fall into self-hatred, which is another form of self-worship. Self-hatred leads to condemnation, another form of legalism. How can we be disappointed with self if we had not foolishly trusted in it? Third, get up and go again. We fall, but we fall forward if we are ready to move out of old behaviors and into Jesus. Always be ready to get up and go again. As a rock is a rock regardless of outside forces, so God is Love independently of man. Would we be persons of faith? Then get up and move toward Him. We will faintly begin to see that He is not fighting but using our failure.

DAY 350
Who Owns It?

But when Jesus saw this, He was indignant and said to them, "Permit the children to come to Me; do not hinder them; for the kingdom of God belongs to such as these."

— MARK 10:14

I admit it: I am on a mission to reclaim the Kingdom of God for those to whom it really belongs and from whom it has been taken away. The Philistines took the ark of God; it was not theirs, and no blessing came from it, only personal destruction. The Kingdom of God does not belong to the talented, the attractive, the manipulators, the magicians, the showmen, the popular, the intellectuals, the wealthy, or the educated. It belongs to the humble, childlike person, the weak, the trusting, the pure in heart, and the poor. I Corinthians 1:27, "But God has chosen the foolish things of the world to shame the wise, and God has chosen the weak things of the world to shame the things which are strong." The strong have only been cursed when attempting to take it and keep it. Their image is itself a curse. Yet these thieves have the ears of many. Recently, a pastor said, "It is so hard to feel success in the ministry when there are the mega churches with mega music and mega donations!" See how he was brainwashed? The epitome of success in the popular culture is not representative of the Kingdom of God, but the thieves make so much noise that it is hard not to get caught up in it. A skinny fellow who constantly hangs around body builders will feel he is lacking, if not inferior.

A believer who continues to hang around those who work in soul power will also feel less special, less blessed, and inferior. However, we are not of the flesh but of the Spirit; we do not compete in the arena of flesh. Thieves will make sure that we judge our condition by fleshly comparisons to themselves, but we are to stay away from them. We have Christ in us, so what do we lack? A spiritual man will continue to tell us of the riches that were ours the day we believed. He will never tell us something he possesses that we do not. We are complete in Christ.

The Kingdom of God belongs to you. Yes, you! You who work a boring job, you who are exhausted after a day of nurturing kids, you who are lonely, you who are broke, and you who are weak. It is yours! Never let a thief steal any part of it.

DAY 351
Why All The Planning?

Commit your way to the LORD, Trust also in Him,
and He will do it.
— PSALM 37:5

My son was traveling with me when he asked, "What is the plan? This is your first time in Nepal to minister, and so how will you go about it?" I said that we would begin each day by holding hands and praying, "Jesus, like a shepherd, lead us!" At the end of the prayer we would take off and see where Jesus did, in fact, guide us. I promised him that every night he would lie on the bed and think, "This was the most amazing day!" It was just as I said. Every morning we would pray and afterward meet someone that knew someone who would take us to someone. It was amazing. Once in an airport in northeast India we were lost and did not know what to do next. My son struck up a conversation with a fellow who soon was traveling with us to our next destination, got us a room, took care of every detail, and has been e-mailing us since. At the end of the day, we again said, "This was a most amazing day!" I am not saying that we should not plan, but we all plan too much. We waste time planning when we could spend time in fellowship with Jesus. We have a history with Jesus, and certainly our lives have not been carried out to the place they are today because of our tiresome and overbearing designs; our lives have unfolded. Jesus really has been leading us all along. In fact, the majority of our plans have not come to pass at all. I really believe that we can stop planning so much. Once when Betty met me after I had been ministering out of the country for several weeks, I told her I did not have a plan for the holiday. We would just get up, get on the train, get off where it looked interesting, and let Him lead us. At the end of the day we would sit and talk about the perfect museum, hotel room, restaurant, and trip. See how He leads? He leads believers all along. We are commanded over and over again not to worry. The time we spend worrying is better spent listening to and talking to Him. There are two cities that I know of in the world that are described in a particular way, and both are in the southern hemisphere: Canberra, Australia, and Brasilia, Brazil. Each one is called by many of its own inhabitants "the city without a soul." Neither was naturally founded and allowed to grow; both from the ground up were planned perfectly by officials to be the seats of government. A perfect plan lacks soul! It is dead and without character because it is controlled in conception and execution. When we plan things perfectly, we remove spontaneity and the unexpected; we take out our reliance on God and the anticipation we feel when we know He is moving. Remember, too, that when we know exactly what the future holds, congratulations! We are now unbelievers without the need to walk by faith.

DAY 352
Why Am I Carnal?

To whom God willed to make known what is the riches of the glory of this mystery among the Gentiles, which is Christ in you, the hope of glory.
— COLOSSIANS 1:27

While traveling I hear many stories that some choose not to believe. Well, I do not believe all of them, either, but I am just reporting the stories, not asking any to believe them. Here is one such report.

I know a man who says that he was caught up into heaven. While standing before the Father's throne, he was asked if he had a question. The man said, "What is it in me that makes me carnal?" At that the Father leaned over, held the man's head between his hands, and kissed him on the forehead; next, though, the Father began to gently shake him. As this occurred, it was as though the shaking was making what appeared to be little drawers all over his body open and spill their contents. All that came out was junk, useless little things. The man thought how these must be all the useless little things he kept and held dear that made him carnal. The Father stopped when all the drawers were empty and once again closed. Next the Father reached toward the man's heart and opened a secret drawer and took from it a little box. The man said that he became frightened, just knowing that little box held the thing that made him carnal. He watched as the Father took out of the box a grand, most beautiful jewel! The Father did not put it back in the box but put the grand jewel back into the drawer and closed it. The man was quite confused as to the significance of all of this when the Father spoke to him. "Yes, there are little things that make all men carnal. That is known. I am not interested in what makes you carnal; I am interested in the Grand Jewel that has remained hidden in you. My Son is in you. You must not look for the carnal any longer but examine and discover the Son who is in you." At that the man was sent away.

Believe it or not, I like the story. I believe that too much time is spent in self-absorption and not enough time examining the Grand Jewel that is in every child of God.

DAY 353
Why Am I So Fat?

And my God will meet all your needs according to his glorious riches in Christ Jesus.

— PHILIPPIANS 4:19

"Why am I so fat?" It is a question asked often in many places, so people can relate to it. A person who needs to lose twenty pounds will be able to sympathize with the person that needs to lose two hundred pounds, because after all, if a person has not been able to lose the twenty, what chance would he have of losing two hundred? The world's approach to a problem always starts from the outside in, so the idea would be to start with the body, look in the mirror to get disgusted, and determine with the will to do something about it, to follow some program. What if we recognized a different approach that started with the Spirit? After all, man was made out of the dust of the earth (body), and God breathed in His spirit to make man a living soul, capable of being alive in body, soul, and spirit. First, a believer must be comfortable with who he is as a child of God, whether fat or skinny. Some are only kings when on a throne, while others know they are kings even if placed in a dungeon. Is our identity fixed in Jesus or in the world? Are we more comfortable in a crowd when we are good-looking? If so, we are on the wrong track and there is a deeper root issue with which to deal. I believe more and more that obese people are often those with the greatest craving for God. I have talked before about our soul's being like a baby that needs pure milk. Our mind wants the wisdom of God, not the world's knowledge. Our emotions want the peace of God, not happiness. The Spirit drove Jesus into the wilderness, where for forty days His soul fed on God. When Satan came with the temptation to turn rocks into bread, He said, "No!" His soul was full. I have had more than one person (and my own experiences have taught me the same) say they lose their appetite when they are in fellowship with Jesus. For myself, I lose nearly twenty pounds each trip because I am not hungry when I am ministering. I get home and eat from boredom. How could I be bored if I am in fellowship with Him? The answer is obvious! I am not in fellowship with Him on the same level. When ministering I am so mindful of my need for Him in my weakness. However, I feel stronger at home and do not draw near in complete dependence. I must be weak at home, also. Hungry people are craving something, but what? Perhaps an inner hunger they attempt to satisfy with outer feeding? As we begin to eat the very thing that we should not, we should stop and ask why. Eating is one place in life where we need that precious ten seconds to say no. As our spirit is full, the temptation to overeat is not nearly so great. The peace of God should always be ruling. I know when I am eating and should not be. Therefore, it is becoming an obedience issue with the peace of God.

DAY 354
Why Are Christians In So Much Defeat?

Wretched man that I am! Who will set me free from the body of this death? Thanks be to God through Jesus Christ our Lord! So then, on the one hand I myself with my mind am serving the law of God, but on the other, with my flesh the law of sin.

— ROMANS 7:24, 25

Why are Christians in so much defeat? Do not think I am a heretic; just let me say this thought through to the end. Christianity as a religion has failed. Christianity as a moral system has failed. The Bible as a source of power has failed. Truth is not only preached but also demonstrated. Christian seminaries have failed and could be sued for false advertising; they have not created leaders or spiritual men. Christianity as a teaching is the best option; it has a better book and higher standards. But what does that lead to? Visit churches at the level at which I see them and you will find that covert, self-righteous deeds of the flesh and covert, unrighteous deeds of the flesh abound. Very little can be found of loving an enemy, allowing another to wound, or blessing those that curse. Some of the rudest people I have met are Bible professors who know so very much. We must admit Christianity has failed. We have the same rate of divorce as the unbelieving world. Why? Because Christianity has schools but is not a school, it has a book but is not a book, it has a philosophy of living but is not a philosophy, and it has doctrines but is not a doctrine. Christianity is Christ, period; it was never meant to be another religion but was always about a relationship with the living Christ. The legalists—those who have attained their own form of righteousness—would like to rip two passages from the Bible: "You search the Scriptures, because you think that in them you have eternal life, and it is these that bear witness of Me" (John 5:39), and "The Sabbath was made for man, and not man for the Sabbath" (Mark 2:27). Man is created to be connected to the Vine, Jesus, not to imitate Him, but to participate in His life. I am not a heretic, but I cannot believe how much trouble I get into by saying that Jesus is all we need.

DAY 355
Why Are Unbelievers Happy?

But I say to you, love your enemies and pray for those who persecute you, so that you may be sons of your Father who is in heaven; for He causes His sun to rise on the evil and the good, and sends rain on the righteous and the unrighteous.

— MATTHEW 5:44, 45

First, take a brief look at three definitions.

The Divine Glue:

Jesus is the invisible Divine Glue that holds all things together. "Yet for us there is {but} one God, the Father, from whom are all things, and we {exist} for Him; and one Lord, Jesus Christ, by whom are all things, and we {exist} through Him" (I Corinthians 8:6). This does not mean that every person is born again or that creation is to be worshipped. It does mean that Christ is in every created thing holding it together. "For in Him we live and move and exist, as even some of your own poets have said, 'For we also are His offspring'" (Acts 17:28). When I refer to the Divine Glue, I am referring to the person of Jesus Christ.

Sin:

The natural is holy. Why? It is because the Holy One holds it together. "For the anxious longing of the creation waits eagerly for the revealing of the sons of God" (Romans 8:19). Why? Because the sons of God will see that the God who holds them together holds the world together and will therefore treat it with more respect. One unavoidable aspect of sin is that it invites something anti-Christ into one's natural being that is held together by Christ. It is to invite a solvent into one's being, causing him to come apart. On this level, then, sin and punishment are one and the same. The punishment for sin is immediate! Every sinner punishes himself. Sin is like that, as though through it man has a go at his own body with a hammer and chisel! "They exchanged the natural function for that which is unnatural . . . and receiving in their own persons the due penalty of their error" (Romans 1:26, 27).

The Glory of God and Worship:

"And every created thing which is in heaven and on the earth and under the earth and on the sea, and all things in them, I heard saying, 'To Him who sits on the throne, and to the Lamb, {be} blessing and honor and glory and dominion forever and ever'" (Revelation 5:13). I was in Tonga with my brother when we decided to go to the only movie theatre in the nation. My brother disappeared and returned to invite me to go upstairs and look at the projector. I was fascinated with what I saw. The projector had two carbon rods that fed from ninety-degree angles, and there was a blinding spark where the two met, creating enough light to project the image onto a large screen. Every created thing has in it the one rod, the Divine Glue, that, when it meets with the rod, or Divine Glue, in another created thing, gives a spark of recognition, a light. One day everyone who has Jesus dwelling within (born again) will stand before the Jesus on the throne. There will be such a spark of life and light that all will fall down and worship. Even now, if it were not for the fact that God has stayed them for our faith's sake, the trees would shout to us, "Glory to God!" For now they are only allowed to whisper! "Let the field exult, and all that is in it. Then all the trees of the forest will sing for joy" (Psalm 96:12).

Those are the definitions; now to answer the question of why unbelievers are happy, for some are, though they do not have joy, which is the fruit of the Spirit. I would like to offer only one opinion; you may have another, and to that I say amen! Have you ever been walking in the mountains, turned a corner, saw a beautiful sight, and just sat there saying, "Praise God"? Though not born again, the unbeliever has the Divine Glue holding him together, this same Divine Glue that is also holding all other created things together. When the glory of God in one comes in contact with the glory of God in the other, there is a small spark called happiness. Christ is not abiding in the unbeliever but is holding him together. If the unbeliever limits contact with the rest of the created world, he will have less happiness. Hence the unbeliever under self-confinement to his house will appear to be a recluse with no happiness. The unbeliever who has more interaction with creation via nature, humanism, social activities, and human compassion will naturally have a greater experience of the Divine Glue as it holds him together witnessing to the Divine Glue without, and therefore will have proportionately more happiness.

The above brings some insight into what hell is. "They shall be cast out into the outer darkness; in that place there shall be weeping and gnashing of teeth" (Matthew 8:12). Why is hell such a place of torment? During the days of the unbeliever's life, the glory of the Divine Glue holding him together has witnessed to the Divine Glue holding all creation together. This has produced a measure of wonder and happiness. The unbeliever might have thought it was his perception that caused the happiness, but it was not. Even on the darkest night, in the loneliest place, in the worst of situations, there was like calling to like. There was hope! For where Christ meets Christ, there will always be hope. This is God's secret work in every person. God is witnessing to Himself through the natural to get the unbeliever's attention until his death. The frightening thing about hell is that it gives the unbeliever what he always said he wanted! Hell is remarkably full of God's absence; He leaves those within alone. After death there is no more witness! The Divine spark is seen no more! There is nothing to stir the unbeliever to hope or happiness. There can be no excitement or sensations, and it is a bleak new experience. For the first time God has truly left alone the unbeliever, who has entered a void. On earth darkness is held together by the Divine Glue, but hell is not darkness, it is an abyss. Hell is the granting of an unbeliever's wish, an empty separation from God.

DAY 356
Why Death? Why Life?

But if the Spirit of Him who raised Jesus from the dead dwells in you, He who raised Christ Jesus from the dead will also give life to your mortal bodies through His Spirit who dwells in you.

— ROMANS 8:11

Often, and particularly when we are at a funeral, we ask the question, "Why death?" However, I have found that the more pressing question is, "Why life?" Why are we alive? If we can grasp the deeper issue of what the purpose of life is, then death immediately loses its sting.

It is important to understand that LIFE is JESUS. God had to become a man in order to reveal how His creation worked. The inventor became the invention. He was LIFE on earth, and He conquered everything that works against

LIFE and returned to heaven as the Son of Man. God will never forget us, for at His right hand is a constant reminder of His commitment to us. Jesus is God, but also a victorious Man seated next to the Father. To forget man, God would need to forget His Son. Impossible!

There are two primary revelations that existence on earth brings to mankind. First, as the world squeezes us, we eventually come to the realization that we cannot live life on earth. At this point, Jesus makes His offer. "I lived on earth and overcame. Invite Me to live in you, and I will live life on earth through you." This is not to say we are robots; it is merely a recognition that the LIFE that lived successfully on earth is now in heaven with the ability to enter all men, making them sons of God. Second, once Christ enters our lives, the pressure of the earth continues in order that the new LIFE we have within might be revealed. Having enemies reveals that we have a LIFE within that can love an enemy. Being offended reveals the LIFE that dwells within that can return a blessing. There is a saying among believers that actually is Buddhist in origin and says, "Life stinks, but God is good." No! If stinking life reveals the true LIFE in me, then even stinking life is good. I want all that the world throws at me, for each time I am assaulted, three things happen. First, I try to fix it all, then I give up, and the Lord fixes me! Each so-called rotten event releases HIS LIFE, and my God keeps getting bigger and bigger than events or circumstances.

Why life? To receive and display HIS LIFE! Death is a continuation of that and is not frightening.

DAY 357
Why Did God Create Alcohol?

Now may God give you of the dew of heaven, and of the
fatness of the earth, and an abundance of
grain and new wine.

— GENESIS 27:28

Solomon, with all his wisdom, took a long hard look at the topic of alcohol and experimented with its use. Ecclesiastes 2:3, "I explored with my mind how to stimulate my body with wine while my mind was guiding me wisely, and how to take hold of folly, until I could see what good there is for the sons of men to do under heaven the few years of their lives." He drank wine in an attempt to discover its benefits. As the topic of alcohol is examined, the first thing to establish is the fact that God did create it. Often the argument is made that fallen man, attempting to feed the flesh, created alcohol, and indeed, there is specific testimony throughout the Bible as to the misuse of wine. Proverbs 23:20 sums it up, "Do not be with heavy drinkers of wine." Proverbs 20:1, "Wine is a mocker, strong drink a brawler, and whoever is intoxicated by it is not wise." The New Testament gives injunctions concerning those that are addicted to wine. Within the context of this argument against God's involvement in the creation of alcohol, the point is made that God created grape juice, or new wine, but never created alcohol. However, Scriptures do not support such a distinction. Judges 9:13, "But the vine said to them, 'Shall I leave my new wine, which cheers God and men, and go to wave over the trees?'" I cannot see how grape juice cheers the heart. Also, Isaiah 25:6, "The LORD of hosts will prepare a lavish banquet for all peoples on this mountain; a banquet of aged wine, choice pieces with marrow." The Lord is preparing a feast that includes aged wine! Then in Acts 2:13, "But others were mocking and saying, 'They are full of sweet wine.'" Sweet wine, new wine, aged wine; all wine contains some alcoholic content. The fact that something is misused does not discount either its Creator or its original purpose. If this were true, what could be said of the sex drive, medications, and computers? God has created wine. In fact, God required the sacrifice of wine, a libation, along with the other things that He created.

Exodus 29:40, "and there shall be one-tenth of an ephah of fine flour mixed with one-fourth of a hin of beaten oil, and one-fourth of a hin of wine for a drink offering with one lamb." There are other interesting or perplexing passages. Remember, Scripture must be used to interpret and limit the meaning of other Scriptures, so a validation of wine is not an endorsement of drunkenness any more than the rightful institution of sex in marriage is an endorsement of wanton promiscuity.

Psalm 104:15, "And wine which makes man's heart glad, so that he may make his face glisten with oil, and food which sustains man's heart."

Proverbs 31:6, 7, "Give strong drink to him who is perishing, and wine to him whose life is bitter. Let him drink and forget his poverty and remember his trouble no more."

Ecclesiastes 9:7, "Go then, eat your bread in happiness and drink your wine with a cheerful heart, for God has already approved your works!"

Finally, we have Jesus turning water into wine. John 2:7, 8, "Jesus said to them, 'Fill the waterpots with water.' So they filled them up to the brim. And He said to them, 'Draw some out now and take it to the headwaiter.' So they took it to him."

DAY 358
Why Does a God Of Love Kill So Many?

Then the Lord said to Job, "Will the faultfinder contend with the Almighty? Let him who reproves God answer it."

— JOB 40:1 & 2

Why did the God of love kill so many in the Old Testament? The answer is hard to believe, because we have been so indoctrinated by humanism, but the answer is quite simple: He did it for love. How could God's actions not be consistent with His love? Everything He does is an expression of His character. If there were an option better than the loving act of killing, God would have taken it. I personally have seen people so given over to sin that they were at the point at which death would have been a welcomed relief as an escape from the bondage. Once the heart is revealed and there is no desire for repentance, each day remaining in sin on earth only adds to the judgment to come. Would it not be gracious of a heavenly Father to take this life and stop the sin? Sin is unnatural and makes man miserable. God can stop our misery by having us turn to Him, and He can also stop our misery by taking our earthly life. We must ask ourselves an important question: What is the purpose of life if it is lived in sin? Is a life lived in sin really life? Love, love, love, God is truly love.

DAY 359
Why Does God Love Man?

Then God said, "Let Us make man in Our image, according to Our likeness; and let them rule over the fish of the sea and over the birds of the sky and over the cattle and over all the earth, and over every creeping thing that creeps on the earth."

— GENESIS 1:26

I grew up working with older men, and one in particular, my grandfather. I spent countless hours with my grandfather; we had a very close bond. It has been a few years since his passing. However, once in awhile I will meet an older man who reminds me of him, and I cannot help but be attracted to the fellow. I see my grandfather in a different "earth suit" through another person's attitudes, hard work, and fiery temper, and I always know where I stand with him. There is just such a fellow on the islands in the jungles, and I always try to stop and spend a day with him. I love the man in his own right, but I also love him for the characteristics that I loved in my grandfather.

Now to the question at hand: Why does God love man? How could He not? We are made in His image. "Let Us make man in Our image." My personal belief is that Jesus started the dialogue. I believe He is the one who made the suggestion, for He is the lover of my soul, the One who would become a man, and the One who would conquer and suffer for me. There was agreement and man was created "in Our image." When the Father looks at man He sees, however faintly, His Son. We are not the Son, but He sees the Son in us. How can He not love us? John 5:20, "For the Father loves the Son, and shows Him all things that He Himself is doing." When the Son looks at man, He sees dimly the Father. We are not the Father, but He sees something of the Father in us! How could He not love us? We remind Him of the Father He loves so much. Oh, yes, be assured that we are loved by the Father and the Son not only because of what we now are but of Whom we remind them. It is the glory of God that with each passing day Jesus lives through us, the faint image of Him will become a brighter one. Once again, it all comes down to Jesus. I John 3:2, "Beloved, now we are children of God, and it has not appeared as yet what we shall be. We know that, when He appears, we shall be like Him, because we shall see Him just as He is."

DAY 360
Why Does God Play in the Dust?

*On the contrary, it is much truer that the members of
the body which seem to be weaker are necessary; and those
members of the body, which we deem less honorable, on these
we bestow more abundant honor, and our unseemly members
come to have more abundant seemliness, whereas our seemly
members have no need of it. But God has so composed the
body, giving more abundant honor to that member which
lacked, that there should be no division in the body, but that
the members should have the same care for one another.*

— I CORINTHIANS 12:22-25

The weakest creature is the one that needs the most support.
The river can live without man, but man cannot live without
the river. In fact, the whole earth can exist without man, but
man cannot live without the earth. Everything on the earth,
in this sense, is greater than man. Man is made of dust, not
dirt or soil that have nutrients in them; dust has nothing to
offer. From the beginning God made everything to support
the weakest and most precious thing to Him: man!

When I use this example at the end of a conference, I
follow with the question, "Who is the weakest person here?"
I answer my own question, "The person who needed the
most support to be here! Who is that person? Mike! I needed
people to donate money to buy my plane ticket, others to
organize, several interpreters, electricity, artists, editors,
drivers, an audience, food, and more." It takes so much to
support this little bit of dust that I am left with nothing to

boast in save Christ. I then ask the people to pray that night, not for the speaker who is dust, but for all those who support the dust. It is a great revelation for all of us.

DAY 361
Why Sacrifice Jesus?

For in Him all things were created, both in the heavens and on earth, visible and invisible, whether thrones or dominions or rulers or authorities—all things have been created through Him and for Him. And He is before all things, and in Him all things hold together.

— COLOSSIANS 1:16, 17

Jesus is the glue that holds all created things together. "For from Him and through Him and to Him are all things. To Him be the glory forever. Amen" (Romans 11:36). Whether we are believers or unbelievers, when we invite sin into our being, Jesus (the glue) is made to bear the sin. Sin is imposed on Life, Life withdraws, and death begins to fill the vacuum; sin and death are dwelling where Life should have been. "But if I am doing the very thing I do not want, I am no longer the one doing it, but sin which dwells in me" (Romans 7:20). This result of inviting in sin—Life's withdrawal, sin and death's filling the vacuum—demands a sacrifice. Why? First, so we will understand that sin is not doing wrong, it is losing life. This explains the variety of sacrifices that we find in the Old Testament. Why would we be called to sacrifice two innocent doves? A dove's life represents many things: the evening song, loyalty in lifelong oneness, peace, the freedom to fly, and more. All of this is lost when sin is invited in. Second, innocent blood is shed. Darkness moves in where light withdraws. Death moves in where Life has withdrawn. We have the tendency to think only of how we suffer the penalty of our sin; the Divine Glue has suffered it all along. Third, innocent bloodshed and Life slain returns us to the place of origin, God. Receiving back Life stays the hand of God. He gave Life to all things created and jealously guards it, for it is precious to Him. Life is the Word; it is Jesus. He is angry when it is abused. He wants it all back, and when He gets some back it satisfies Him. "Then Noah built an altar to the Lord and, taking some of all the clean animals and clean birds, sacrificed burnt offerings on it. The Lord smelled the pleasing aroma and said in his heart: 'Never again will I curse the ground because of man, even though every inclination of his heart is evil from childhood, and never again will I destroy all living creatures, as I have done. As long as the earth endures, seedtime and harvest, cold and heat, summer and winter, day and night will never cease'" (Genesis 8:20-22). These sacrifices did not take away sin or its damage; at best, in a sense, they just covered the whole mess up. Continued abuse of the Life in man brought God to a point where He was not even interested in such sacrifices. Isaiah 1:11, "I have more than enough of burnt offerings, of rams and the fat of fattened animals; I have no pleasure in the blood of bulls and lambs and goats!" In the Old Testament there never was a demand for a human sacrifice, but sin and death had reached such a level of offense that no animal sacrifice could cover it up; a human sacrifice would seem to be the next logical step, but there was a problem. An innocent dove for a minor sin or a lamb for a moderate sin could easily be found, but where would be found an innocent man? "There are none righteous! No not one!" "You were dead in your transgressions and sins!" (Romans 3:10 and Ephesians 2:1) For a major sin there was no sacrifice; there was only a judgment. Death! Death did not appease God, it did not cover up the sin, and it really did not help man. Death through the Law was an attempt to keep the whole mess from spreading. It was the best to do in a bad situation. Jesus appears! He is perfect innocence. He is perfect LIFE! He is the Man! Remember that in the Old Testament when a man made a sacrifice, it represented how much of the image of TRUE LIFE he had really lost. Man's loss of God's glory is equal to the sacrifice. How far had mankind sunk when Jesus was sacrificed? What had they lost by the time He was put on the cross? On the cross hung pure LIFE. "He made Him who knew no sin to be sin on our behalf, that we might become the righteousness of God in Him," II Corinthians 5:21. The true Lamb of God came in the fullness of time. Man had lost everything pertaining to true LIFE. There were so many sins in the Old Testament for which there was no sacrifice but only judgment. This sacrifice was so great that it not only covered every sin, but it could also take AWAY sins of the whole world! When the blood and Life left this Son of Man, it was a pleasing aroma to God of pure, innocent LIFE! LIFE returned to God not in measure but in fullness. "For it was the Father's good pleasure for all the fullness to dwell in Him, and through Him to reconcile all things to Himself, having made peace through the blood of His cross; through Him, I say, whether things on earth or things in heaven," Colossians 1:19, 20. This gives God peace, for Jesus is God's peace and proof that one man was able to live on the earth without ever making LIFE withdraw, and He did it through weakness and complete dependence on God. The man who did everything proclaims that He did nothing, for it was the Father doing it through Him. His reward was to go and dwell in as many as He liked, making more sons like Him!

DAY 362
Will Your Preaching Disqualify You?

But I keep charge of my body, and bring it into subjection: lest that by any means, when I have preached to others, I myself should be a castaway.

— I CORINTHIANS 9:27

This is a beautiful, love-filled, strong warning by Paul, whose concern is legitimate. The fear is simple, that we will preach one thing and then do another, and thus discredit our message. The common interpretation of that passage would lead one to believe that Paul was preaching law and judging his lack of hypocrisy by his ability to keep the law. He already mentioned in verse 20 that he was not himself under the Law. I would be willing to assert that most who preach on this passage use it to set a standard that they do not even reach, then draw the contrast between what the listeners do and what Paul did, leaving the audience bleeding on the ground as hopeless hypocrites. Just what was Paul mentioning that he did not want to go against? We do not want our standard to be different from his. Paul was preaching grace, love, mercy, hope, and, more than anything, a devotion to Jesus. I believe it is these things, being preached regularly, that he was afraid not to do and disqualify himself. Many preach grace, but then when they fail, they move farther away from Jesus. They have just disqualified themselves from the message they preach. When a Christian fails he must get up and move forward in the love of God. If he cannot, there is a big problem. In short, Christianity is different, much different, than religious legalism.

DAY 363
Wings

Yet those who wait for the LORD will gain new strength; they will mount up {with} wings like eagles, they will run and not get tired, they will walk and not become weary

—ISAIAH 40:31

It has been believed for some time that the South American condor, when old, commits suicide. Many have thought that the great bird would gain enough altitude to ensure its death, fold its wings, and fall to the earth. I was talking to a friend from Argentina whose uncle, a famous gaucho, often observed the odd behavior of the condor and began his own investigation. He discovered that the condor was not committing suicide at all. Actually, increasingly with age the great bird lost its eyesight, so instead of catching the wind and riding high on his magnificent wings, the vulture would flap unnaturally with all its strength to avoid what it thought was imminent danger. The bird would continue fleeing what did not exist until it gained so much altitude that it would run out of oxygen, have a heart attack, and fall to its death.

I was recently told that many believers never receive answers to their prayers, so they need to learn to deal with disappointment. However, as believers we always receive answers to prayers, and the problem lies in so often praying wanting resolution; we want to know what to do or we want to direct the activity of God. We seek and do not find because we have wrongly defined what finding is. What we find when we pray, ask, and seek is faith, a simple thing that is much more enjoyable than immediate answers. Faith takes the whole situation out of our hands and places it in God's hands, removing us from the throne and stopping the frenetic beating of our little wings, giving us our birthright: the gliding, soaring wings of eagles. If through unbelief we begin to beat our wings and lose sight of Jesus, gaining what we think to be altitude, we are only giving ourselves heart attacks. I told Betty the story of the condor and asked, "Where do you think I will go with this story?" She responded, "For you, it can only go to one place: rest." We laughed, but I acknowledged the fact. Rest in God will not make us tired or weary. Rest is not passivity but trusting in God's activity.

DAY 364
With Him Or In Him

For in Him we live and move and exist. As even some of
your own poets have said, "For we also are His offspring."
— ACTS 17:28

A friend of mine was asked where he was with the Lord.
He responded, "I am in Denver." We laughed when we
talked of it, but what he said was really quite true. I have
often been asked, "How much time do you spend with the
Lord each day?" It is a false concept to think that we are
"spending time with the Lord," and therefore confining His
presence to a time and a place. It is much more accurate
to say that we are spending time in the Lord. This is a
great secret. The presence of God is not something that
we must search after. Psalm 139:7, "Where can I go from
Thy Spirit? Or where can I flee from Thy presence?" The
presence of God is simply something that we acknowledge
by faith. We live in His presence, we enjoy His presence,
and He is forever near, as near as the words in our mouths.
Today, all day, we are in Him!

DAY 365
Wives, Submit

Wives, be subject to your husbands, as is fitting in the Lord. Husbands, love your wives and do not be embittered against them.

— COLOSSIANS 3:18, 19

Let us get started on the right foot, for there is no need going for the cobweb when we can go for the spider. Both the women who cannot submit and the men who demand it are unbelieving control freaks. Let me explain, because this is not a popular topic. I suppose that the only other admonition that has been given such scrutiny and as many overhauls is "Husbands, love your wives." The goal of many for both verses seems to be to add so many qualifiers that both commands lose their sting. Evangelicals are somewhat comical in that they will fight to the death over someone's wanting to change the Bible, but they alter its intended meaning regularly with their commentaries. But if we believe "let God be true and every man the liar," women are to submit to their husbands. The obvious question that will be asked is, "Why?" Does the Bible teach equality? Yes, definitely, as when Paul tells us there is neither male nor female. Why would God take a woman, who is equal to a man, and tell her to submit? There are some obvious reasons, such as that a house divided cannot stand, the man is the head of the woman, and the family is not a democracy. However, for me this still misses the point.

God's school of discipleship has some very elaborate and tailor-made courses to bring about the great revelation that Christ is in us; seminaries have a laughable curriculum when measured against His. He is discipling us, hands on, all of the time. There are things that can be learned in submission that cannot be learned in any other place. There are lessons in submitting to a person perceived to be inferior that cannot be learned any other way. There are secrets about Jesus learned only in submission to an equal. There are aspects of a woman's flesh life that can only be revealed in submission, such as a faith that remains dormant in the unsubmissive.

I noticed some time ago that the ministry I am in has saved my life. I always was thinking it was for others, but finally I saw that it was for me. My flesh is so strong that were I not constantly in this course He has created for me, I would not have moved forward in faith. I see Jesus in it all. My point is this: Who really believes that the God who began a good work in us and intends to complete it would give us a command to make us miserable? The way some try to work their way around the submission passages reveals their flesh. "Am I to submit to an idiot?" Well, why not? First, are they suggesting they are better than Jesus, who, knowing He was God, washed others' feet? Second, what faith does it take to submit to someone who is better in everything? The lesson He is teaching in submission is an amazing one: that God is above the husband and that a wife's life does not rest in the hands of another. To see past man to God will affect every area of a wife's life. I no longer see governments as being in charge of my destiny; I see God behind them. There are several such lessons in Scripture where God is teaching each of us, right in our particular environment, that we can see Him. Slaves submit to masters, citizens to governments, members to their leaders, one to another, and more, all to increase our faith by seeing God behind them. Flesh is flesh, and no one is void of it. No intellectually discerning person sees one man above another, and yet we are all, in our various environments, to submit to someone. There is great peace when we see God and not the man. A woman's flesh needs this or He would not command it. There are no qualifiers. In the same way, a man's flesh needs to love when there is no reason to love; he needs the breaking of the flesh life and pride that only loving a person who has rejected him can bring. Every bit of it is for our good. One who does not want to submit wants to remain in unbelief, wants to continue to think man is in charge of his or her life, and wants the last word! Well, amen! But there is a better Way. The glory of God is revealed in choice. Each individual has the final word in choice. In the end, the struggle with submission is a struggle over the question of who is ultimately in control. Is it God or someone else? Do we have to be in control, or can we see God behind the person we will not follow? Just say, "Amen," and get on in Him.

There is, in my opinion, the mistaken idea that the leadership of a man is proven by those who follow. This appears to be a faulty definition when applied to Jesus, for He was the greatest leader that ever lived, and yet His followers nearly completely deserted Him at the end of His life. Leadership is showing the way, not forcing people into the way. Some carnal-minded men force subjugation onto women. Those men wear the penalty of their motives, for sin and punishment are one and the same. Men stand and fall in their "why," not their "what," and the "why" of these men is wrong. So we disregard them. However, there are women that will never be led because of their own control issues, and many who covertly will never be led but will not come right out and say it because they do see that as disobedience. Hence, they question everything. Others simply are not, from pride, going to let a man tell them anything. Finally, there are those whose husbands have proven over and over again to be stupid.

So what are men to do? Again, recognize that leadership is NOT determined by who follows. As a man and leader he should let his opinion be known. To the best of his ability, by seeking God for the direction in which he believes the couple or family should go, he must let his assessment be known. At that point he is a leader! Who follows is a matter of personal choice. If no one follows, the husband should not surrender his peace to the situation; he should surrender to God and let the others "do what is wise in their own eyes." This may sound like passivity, but in reality, what are his options? Stew in anger, or worse yet, force the mate to yield to him? Flesh will beget flesh. Everyone must stand on his own before his Maker. Just rest and get on in Him. After all, if a wife does not want to come under a husband's leadership, let her take it up with God. A husband has a big enough task of loving! Of course, there is another option, to fall into the minutiae of life. "I wanted to turn right, and my wife kept yelling, 'Go left!'" Now there is a conversation that we all want to be involved in. Then there are the follow-up statements of this drivel: "Well, I was correct, was I not? We should have gone right!" Everyone at the dinner table really enjoys these times of "fellowship." Is it really worth the hassle of triple answering and questioning over something that simply does not matter? It is better to say, "Right looks good, I believe it is correct (the issue of leadership is complete at this point); however, if you do not want to go right, amen, we are turning left." When there are no followers, then comes the issue of taking up the cross and loving; this deeper work in a man may not yet be complete. He can say it with a smile, for though he is not going to be followed, his leadership is not on the line; that has been settled. So what? If he is wrong, he saved some time listening; if he was right, he lost a little time and he needs to move out of pride and get on with talking about Jesus, the bigger thing we want to move on to.